The Epistolary Renaissance

Buchreihe der ANGLIA/
ANGLIA Book Series

Edited by
Lucia Kornexl, Ursula Lenker, Martin Middeke,
Gabriele Rippl, Hubert Zapf

Advisory Board
Laurel Brinton, Philip Durkin, Olga Fischer, Susan Irvine,
Andrew James Johnston, Christopher A. Jones, Terttu Nevalainen,
Derek Attridge, Elisabeth Bronfen, Ursula K. Heise, Verena Lobsien,
Laura Marcus, J. Hillis Miller, Martin Puchner

Volume 62

The Epistolary Renaissance

A Critical Approach to Contemporary Letter Narratives in Anglophone Fiction

Edited by
Maria Löschnigg and Rebekka Schuh

DE GRUYTER

For an overview of all books published in this series, please see
http://www.degruyter.com/view/serial/36292

ISBN 978-3-11-070967-4
e-ISBN (PDF) 978-3-11-058481-3
e-ISBN (EPUB) 978-3-11-058217-8
ISSN 0340-5435

Library of Congress Control Number: 2018951861

Bibliographic information published by the Deutsche Nationalbibliothek
The Deutsche Nationalbibliothek lists this publication in the Deutsche Nationalbibliografie;
detailed bibliographic data are available on the Internet at http://dnb.dnb.de.

© 2020 Walter de Gruyter GmbH, Berlin/Boston
This volume is text- and page-identical with the hardback published in 2018.
Printing: CPI books GmbH, Leck

www.degruyter.com

Table of Contents

Maria Löschnigg, Rebekka Schuh
Introduction to this Volume —— 1

Part I: Contemporary Epistolary Fiction: New Approaches

Maria Löschnigg, Rebekka Schuh
Epistolarity
   Theoretical and Generic Preliminaries —— 15

Part II: The Epistolary Short Story

Maria Löschnigg
The Epistolary Short Story and the Representation of History —— 47

Rebekka Schuh
Enveloped in Epistolary Illusion
   The Aesthetics of Reading and Writing Letters in Selected Short Stories by Alice Munro —— 73

Maximilian Feldner
Epistolarity in Twenty-First Century Nigerian Short Fiction —— 91

Kym Brindle
Wish I Was There
   Economies of Communication in Annie Proulx's *Postcards* and "Brokeback Mountain" —— 107

Part III: The Contemporary Epistolary Novel

Wolfgang Hallet
Epistolary Forms as Semiotic and Generic Modes in the Multimodal Novel —— 125

Lisa Kazianka
Isolation, Participation and Communication in Young Adult Unidirectional Epistolary Fiction —— 143

Ingrid Pfandl-Buchegger
From Ireland with Love
  The Use of Epistolary Writing in Cecelia Ahern's Fiction —— **159**

Ames Hawkins
An Open Letter to Nick Bantock OR Letters and/as Ephemera(l)
  Desire, Transposition and Transpoetic Possibility with/in Epistolary Form —— **181**

Toni Bowers
The Epistolary Revenant
  Teaching Against Linearity —— **193**

Part IV: Literature and Electronic Correspondence

Thomas O. Beebee
E-Mail Epistlemologies —— 211

Silvia Schultermandl
Stuplimity and Quick Media Epistolarity in Lauren Myracle's *Internet Girls* Series —— 227

Silke Jandl
In the Age of Vlogging
  Functions of the Letter in YouTubers' Fiction and Non-Fiction —— **243**

Elizabeth Kovach
E-pistolary Novels and Networks
  Registering Formal Shifts between Henry Fielding's *Shamela* (1741) and Gary Shteyngart's *Super Sad True Love Story* (2010) —— **261**

Gerd Bayer
The Right Sort of Form for "The Right Sort"
    David Mitchell's Tweet-Story —— 277

Contributors —— 289

Index —— 293

Maria Löschnigg, Rebekka Schuh
Introduction to this Volume

1 The Renaissance of the Epistolary Form

Without any doubt, epistolary forms have seen a renaissance in contemporary fiction. This is not least because, according to Toni Bowers (2009: n. pag.), 'epistolary fiction' now also comprises "fiction that unfolds through multiple forms of communication that have descended from the letter: e-mails, text messages, telegrams, postcards, tweets, transcribed tapes, greeting cards, answering machine messages, and so on". Interestingly, however, the digitalization of modern culture has not only led to a proliferation of medialized epistolary fiction,[1] but has also prompted a new interest in conventional epistolary forms. This may be explained, on the one hand, by the great meta-discursive potential inherent in a combination of staged digital forms and actual letters. On the other hand, it may be expressive of an urge to counterbalance cultural practices which largely exclude the material and sensual aspects of writing and reading. A third factor that could explain the renewed interest in the letter is its potential for defamiliarization. Paradoxically, an old form has been adopted and adapted to render new forms of narrative expression for a generation of readers who are largely unfamiliar with or no longer practice this form of communication.

Since "today's society is pervaded through and through, and even constituted, by electronic and digital mass media" (Nünning & Rupp 2013: 210), it is not surprising that the printed book, and narrative fiction in particular, have also been affected by this trend. The catalyzing effect of medialization on genre has, without doubt, brought forth an astounding variety of new epistolary forms and has, in general, contributed to the upsurge of a genre which has repeatedly been seen as "a technical dead end" (Bray 2003: 1; Showalter 1972: 121), despite the success and prestige of the letter novel in the eighteenth century. There are numerous examples of novels which experiment with Internet formats and which confirm the narrative potential of medialization. In Nick Hornby's *Juliet, Naked*, for example, a wide range of public and private digital modes are integrated into a third-person narrative featuring three different focalizers. The inclusion of e-mails and websites in Hornby's novel allows for thought-provoking juxtapositions of 'appearance' and 'reality' and offers critical reflections

---

[1] The term 'medialized epistolary fiction' is used to denote narrative literature which integrates (staged) epistolary modes from the Internet (cf. Löschnigg 2018).

on the quality and truth-value of precisely these new forms of communication. The critical meta-discursive impact is even more visible in T. R. Richmond's *What She Left*, which combines digital forms of information presentation with conventional letters. Other British examples of such fictions of the Internet are David Llewellyn's *Eleven* (2006), Matt Beaumont's *e* (2000) and *e Squared* (*e2*) (2009), and Lucy Kellaway's *Who Moved My BlackBerry* (2005), the latter staging 'Special Projects Director' Martin Lukes as the real author of the book. The young adult novel *PS. He's Mine!* (2000) is a collaboration between British writer Rosie Rushton and German writer Nina Schindler that embeds e-mails within the frame of a third-person narrative. Another noteworthy novel in this context is *Where Rainbows End* (2004) by Irish author Cecelia Ahern. Like *What She Left*, her novel mixes digital and conventional formats, marking the different modes by icons. A bestselling US-American example would be Maria Semple's *Where'd You Go, Bernadette* (2012), where the main character's daughter collects correspondence such as e-mails, memos, transcripts, and conventional letters in order to find her mother. Douglas Coupland's *The Gum Thief* (2007) and Lynn Coady's *The Antagonist* (2013) may be listed as Canadian representatives of this medialized novelistic form. Through their high degree of meta-fictional self-reflexivity, such medialized epistolary novels have a strong critical impact with regard to contemporary culture. As Nünning and Rupp (2013: 215) point out, they "more often than not parody or satirize the media formats they incorporate [...] and not only disclose literary fictionality but also direct attention to the border crossings which turn up every time one tries to translate real events into verbal or medial narratives – or into medial formats of any kind".

While it is hardly surprising that the Internet has brought forth a catalytic change (cf. Nünning & Rupp 2013: 202) in narrative fiction, it may seem astonishing that alongside the great amount of medialized epistolary fiction that has appeared over the past two decades the conventional letter has not only refused to disappear but has, in fact, made a comeback. Thus, one may claim that the epistolary renaissance that can be observed from the last decades of the twentieth century onwards is defined not only by the integration of staged digital modes, but also by a new interest in conventional epistolary forms such as letters, postcards and (handwritten) notes. This trend is visible, in particular, in the genre of the short story, but can also be discerned in the novel. Novels which solely use conventional epistolary forms include, for example, Irish author Cecelia Ahern's *PS, I Love You*, which features enveloped notes, American Jessica Brockmole's *Letters from Skye*, which is mediated exclusively via letters, and Canadian author Richard B. Wright's novel *Clara Callan* (2001), which tells the story through letters and diary entries.

Various factors may be responsible for this remarkable revival of conventional epistolarity. First, as is the case for example with *Clara Callan*, which is set in the interwar years, and with a number of epistolary short stories (see chapter one/Part II of this volume, "The Epistolary Short Story and the Representation of History"), the letter is an ideal means to transmit the aspect of historicity in stories set in a pre-digital time. Second, the epistolary mode has been taken up and successfully appropriated for feminist and postcolonial forms of expression, where the act of 'writing back' finds its congenial format in the you-related make-up of the letter. Third, in an age defined by digital communication, the conventional letter, as mentioned above, is a powerful tool of defamiliarization. It seems, in fact, that by including the 'archaic' form of the letter, contemporary fiction acquires the function of a counter-cultural discourse by setting itself off from the 'noise of our time', thus rechanneling 'reflected' emotionality into the fact-lived discursive practices of the late twentieth and the early twenty-first century.

The counter-cultural impact of conventional epistolarity also results from specific features of the letter that go beyond the textual level and may be subsumed under the category of the materiality of the letter. The material and sensual quality of the letter, which on the one hand caters to nostalgic trends, derives, on the other hand, from a need to reintegrate sensual aspects of communication and thus to redress the alienation from the physical and sensual which defines modern forms of communication. This longing for material evidence, for example, leads Annie, the main female character of Nick Hornby's novel *Juliet, Naked* (2009), to print out an e-mail from former rock-star Tucker Crowe, with whom she is about to start a romance, and to put it in an envelope in order to feel the magic of a real letter (cf. 121 f.). A letter, in short, is a concrete entity with a multitude of significations that go beyond its textual content and linguistic style. From the crackling of the paper, its texture and colour, the idiosyncrasy of handwriting, the choice of pen or pencil[2] and the smell of the letter to traces of coffee, wine, tears or even blood, the letter offers a wide range of (verbalized) non-verbal codes which the reader – alongside the intratextual addressee – is encouraged to decipher. However, physical and sensual qualities are essential meaning-carrying elements not only for the recipient of the letter, but the material dimension of producing an 'actual letter' also affects the writer. Again, *Juliet, Naked* may serve as an example which illustrates the lack of the physical

---

[2] In Julian Barnes' short story "Evermore" (1996), for example, the main character wonders whether the fact that the forbidden message on the field postcard was not written in pencil but in ink is really a "code for something" (346).

in digital modes of communication and the frustration that, in the case of Annie, goes with it:

> She stopped typing. If she'd been using pen and paper, she would have screwed the paper up in disgust, but there wasn't a satisfying equivalent with email, seeing as everything was designed to stop you making a mistake. She'd needed a fuck-it key, something that made a satisfying ka-boom noise when you thumped it. (70 f.)

As this passage shows, contemporary epistolary fiction is infused with practices of the digital age, thus reflecting cultural practices and appropriating them for new and powerful forms of narrative expression. At the same time, contemporary epistolary fiction – be it medialized or not – provides an important medium for a critical meta-discourse on exactly these modes of communication which define the culture of the late twentieth and the early twenty-first century.

Considering the undeniable resurgence of epistolary forms in contemporary fiction and its innovative re-appropriation (cf. Altman 1982: 195), it is astonishing, as Altman (1982: 196) notes, that "almost no one has investigated the reappearance of the letter in mixed forms in twentieth-century narrative". Whereas Altman's seminal book *Epistolarity* (1982) can still be seen as the most substantial contribution to the narratological and generic questions raised by modern epistolary fiction, the development of this form of narrative has subsequently gone in many new directions and incorporated a multitude of new (medialized) forms of epistolarity. It is therefore the aim of this volume to reconsider the genre of epistolary fiction and suggest new theoretical approaches which do justice to the forms that have evolved over the past few decades.

2 Epistolary Criticism and the Call for New Approaches

By considering digital as well as conventional forms of epistolarity in contemporary fiction, including novels *and* short stories, and by focusing specifically on narratological questions, this volume enters new territory in literary criticism. While a number of scholars have contributed to a critical elucidation of this narrative form, their publications have mostly focused on the eighteenth century and have only peripherally referred to newer forms of epistolary fiction. Many publications tend to be literary histories rather than narratological considerations of this genre, or concentrate on thematic concerns without paying much attention to the impact of narrative transmission. Thus, it can be claimed that the upsurge in scholarly criticism of epistolary texts, which according to Altman

(1982: 3), Beebee (1999: 199) and Harris (2001: 158) has run parallel to the renaissance of epistolary fiction, is definitely lagging behind. While it might be true that the recent publications of epistolary fiction have sparked a renewed scholarly interest in the epistolary form, this interest has not been primarily directed towards the newer examples of epistolary literature. Rather, as Altman (1982: 195) highlights, "very few critics have pushed beyond the eighteenth century". The great majority of recent studies of the epistolary form have a historical interest and attempt to trace the origins and development of epistolary forms in literature across different periods. Unfortunately, however, they tend to stop their survey in the mid-twentieth century, thus leaving out the intriguing examples of epistolary fiction from the late twentieth and the early twenty-first century. This is the case, for example, in Thomas Beebee's *Epistolary Fiction in Europe 1800–1850* (1999) and Amanda Gilroy and W. M. Verhoeven's edited volume *Epistolary Histories: Letter, Fiction, Culture* (2000). Among the few works of criticism devoted exclusively to epistolary fiction of the twentieth and/or twenty-first centuries is Anne Bower's *Epistolary Responses: The Letter in 20th-Century American Fiction and Criticism* (1997). Her study takes into account a promising selection of epistolary texts from the twentieth century and explores the use of letter writing as a strategy for female self-empowerment. With this focus, Bower is part of a larger interest in the connection between the epistolary novel and women (see Elizabeth Goldsmith's edited volume *Writing the Female Voice* [1989], Mary Favret's *Romantic Correspondence: Women Politics and the Fiction of Letters* [1994] and Elizabeth Heckendorn Cook's *Epistolary Bodies: Gender and Genre in the Eighteenth-Century Republic of Letters* [1996]). As far as form is concerned, Janet Altman's *Epistolarity: Approaches to a Form* (1982) and Joe Bray's *The Epistolary Novel: Representations of Consciousness* (2001) are the most compelling studies. Altman's book, in particular, has remained the standard reference work of epistolary criticism up to today. No one else has investigated the epistolary form as minutely and comprehensively as Altman. Bray's work, too, is recommended to those interested in the narratological potentials of the epistolary mode, even though as we will elaborate in the second part of this volume, his findings are no longer fully applicable to the epistolary fiction of the twentieth and twenty-first centuries.

The two most recent book-length studies on epistolary fiction are Kym Brindle's *Epistolary Encounters in Neo-Victorian Fiction: Diaries and Letters*, published in 2014, and Rachel Bower's *Epistolarity and World Literature, 1980–2010*, published in 2017. Brindle is interested in those contemporary epistolary novels that engage thematically as well as in terms of narrative technique with nineteenth-century Victorian epistolary novels (e.g. Bram Stoker's *Dracula*). Unlike classic Victorian examples of epistolary fiction, which use letters for exposing authentic documents and enabling direct access to truth, Brindle argues, letters in Neo-Victorian fiction are used for deconstructing stable notions of truth (cf. Brindle 2014: 3). While Brindle's approach sheds light on hitherto neglected epistolary phenomena, she does not distinguish between diaries and letters, a distinction which is essential to the understanding of epistolary fiction underlying this volume.

The latest publication in the field, Rachel Bower's *Epistolarity and World Literature, 1980–2010*, considers a great diversity of postcolonial epistolary novels ranging from the well-known *The Color Purple* by Alice Walker, to Monica Ali's *Brick Lane*, John Berger's *From A to X*, and Michael Ondaatje's *In the Skin of a Lion*. Bower argues that the revival of epistolary forms in the late twentieth century is directly linked to "ideals relating to dialogue and human connections" (Bower 2017: xi). Her work is extremely inspiring, not only because of her focus on epistolary texts from the late twentieth century, but also because, working with Bourdieu's 'literary field', she is interested in both the form of these epistolary texts as well as the contexts of their production and reception and offers compelling close readings of several contemporary epistolary novels.

Despite the significant amount of research into epistolary fiction that has been carried out in the past few years, and given the prevalence of Anglophone epistolary fiction in the last few decades, it is surprising that with the exception of the 'new epistolary classics', Alice Walker's *The Color Purple* and Saul Bellow's *Herzog*, contemporary Anglophone epistolary fiction has received so little attention. It seems as if the neglect of contemporary epistolary fiction stems from the ongoing misconception among literary scholars that the epistolary genre belongs to the past and that research in this field is saturated. The more radical among these scholars even posit the death of the genre after its eighteenth-century heyday. Among them is Elaine Showalter, who argues that "the epistolary novel, despite the prestige of Richardson and Rousseau, was obviously a technical dead end" (Showalter 1972: 121). Showalter belongs to the camp of literary scholars who have treated the popularity of the epistolary genre in the seventeenth and eighteenth centuries as a means to an end. Since the epistolary mode was the narrative technique of the first novelistic form, it is perceived by those scholars to be nothing more than the primitive predecessor of the narratologically more complex third-person novel. Brandtzæg (2013: n. pag.), for instance, refers to the epistolary novel as "the novel form in embryo – a nascent and formally awkward warm-up to the more sophisticated novel narrated in the third person" (Brandtzæg 2013: n. pag.). The tendency to dismiss the epistolary novel as only the first step in the evolution of the 'real' novel, the third-person novel, has led to the unsatisfying state in current scholarship where scholars either neglect the epistolary novel entirely or focus primarily on its traditional examples from the seventeenth and eighteenth centuries, believing that recent examples have nothing new to offer.

The present study aims at redressing this unsatisfying state in epistolary scholarship and attempts to prompt an epistolary renaissance, which has already taken place in fiction, in epistolary criticism as well. What has been particularly lacking so far is a comprehensive narratological study of the forms and functions of epistolary fiction as it has evolved in the last few decades. In the following chapters, we shall therefore address important aspects of epistolarity as they arise with regard to contemporary epistolary fiction, thus keeping pace with the renewed interest of authors in the rich aesthetics of this narrative form. This volume aims at filling, at least partly, the lacunae of epistolary research by, on the one hand, focusing exclusively on contemporary Anglophone epistolary fiction, and, on the other hand, by transcending the categories which previous studies of epistolary fiction have relied on. Thus, the present study not only transgresses genre boundaries through its consideration of epistolary novels, short stories and new media genres, but it also expands the notion of the 'epistolary' by including texts that rely on traditional letters *alongside* texts that use e-mails, tweets and text messages. While these digitalized forms of epistolary fiction have managed to attract the interest of critics, they have so far not been explored in depth alongside conventional epistolary texts.

3 Overview: The Chapters

The structure of this volume reflects the genre-transgressing approach of this study and foregrounds its focus on recent developments in epistolary writing. The book is divided into four sections, with Part I ("Contemporary Epistolary Fiction: New Approaches") setting the epistemological frame by presenting the main generic premises of epistolary fiction in the twentieth and twenty-first centuries as well as theoretical parameters for the study of contemporary epistolary fiction.

The second part is devoted to the 'epistolary short story', a sub-genre that has hitherto received almost no attention but that nonetheless constitutes an important part of the epistolary renaissance. It is for this reason, and because we wanted to counterbalance previous trends in research, that the section on the short story immediately follows the introductory section. Four essays pay tribute to the potential of the epistolary short story, focusing on stories or investigating epistolary forms in the short story alongside epistolary novels. Maria Löschnigg's "The Epistolary Short Story and the Representation of History" is the opening contribution to this part. Arguing that the epistolary mode "cater[s] to a modern understanding of historical knowledge, which questions the claim of objective representation and tends to favour multiple perspectives, including those of the marginal and the 'insignificant'", Löschnigg discusses different kinds of epistolary stories, examining in particular how the format of the letter in short stories is employed to render revisionist, alternative glimpses of history. Through close readings of six short stories by authors such as Graham Swift, A. W. Wells and Julian Barnes, Löschnigg not only makes a case for the suitability of the letter story for the mediation of historical content but also offers a synoptic view of the epistolary short story in Anglophone literature. In contrast to Löschnigg's more panoramic approach, Rebekka Schuh's contribution discusses the letter stories of a single author: Canadian Nobel Prize winner Alice Munro. In "Enveloped in Epistolary Illusion: The Aesthetics of Reading and Writing Letters in Selected Short Stories by Alice Munro", Schuh explores the power of letters to viscerally affect the protagonists and make them indulge in extensive daydreaming about their correspondent, their future life together, and other events suggested by the letters. Introducing the concept of 'epistolary illusion', Schuh argues that this emotional and imaginative state is reminiscent of 'aesthetic illusion', a concept from reader-response theory which explains the state of immersion triggered during the reading of fiction.

The third contribution introduces another cultural context of epistolary short-story writing and brings in a new angle by looking at epistolary short stories alongside epistolary novels. Maximilian Feldner's "Epistolarity in Twenty-First-Century Nigerian Short Fiction" looks at a variety of epistolary fiction from writers of the Nigerian diaspora, discussing, alongside short stories such as Chimamanda Ngozi Adichie's "The Thing Around Your Neck" (2009) and Sefi Atta's "Yahoo Yahoo" (2010), compelling examples of letters and e-mails in contemporary Nigerian novels. In the first part of his contribution, Feldner focuses on the importance of letters in narrating the experience of diaspora, while in the second he examines literary renderings of the practice of advance fee fraud (commonly referred to as 419), thus discussing texts which have their finger on the pulse of the time. Kym Brindle's chapter "Wish I Was There: Economies of Communication in Annie Proulx's *Postcards* and 'Brokeback Mountain'" concludes the short story section. Segueing neatly into the following section, Brindle focuses on postcards in Proulx's eponymous novel and compares them to the postcards used in "Brokeback Mountain". She is interested in how postcards subvert iconographic ideas of an American landscape tamed and reduced to national images or romanticised pastoral settings and how, specifically in *Postcards*, they visually organise a fragmented tale of travel and separation.

Part III of this volume, which takes account of 'The Contemporary Epistolary Novel', opens with Wolfgang Hallet's inspiring exploration of epistolary forms in the multimodal novel. Hallet distinguishes between the traditional word novel, in which letters are rendered only verbally, and the multimodal novel, which reproduces letters in their original shape and materiality. Authored and produced by fictional characters, Hallet argues, the reproduction of epistolary forms draws the reader into communicative, social and sometimes also material practices in the fictional world. Lisa Kazianka's contribution to this volume, in turn, provides insight into a particularly prolific sub-genre of epistolary writing: young adult fiction. In "Isolation, Participation and Communication in Young Adult Epistolary Fiction", Kazianka not only presents provocative arguments for the appeal of the epistolary mode for Young Adult readers but also offers compelling readings of Stephen Chbosky's *The Perks of Being a Wallflower* and Annabel Pitcher's *Ketchup Clouds*. Using the example of these two novels, Kazianka argues that the letter form, through its repeated references to the temporal and spatial setting of the letter writer, is particularly suited to represent the letter-writing characters' state of isolation and loneliness, while at the same time prompting the letter writers to reflect on their emotional state. Isolation and loneliness also figure prominently in Cecilia Ahern's fiction, which is in the focus of Ingrid Pfandl-Buchegger's chapter. Ahern's probably best-known novels, *PS, I Love You* and *Where Rainbows End*, are both epistolary novels but, as Pfandl-Buchegger shows, employ letters to different ends. In *PS, I Love You*, the letters serve as a form of trauma counselling and help the young widow and protagonist of the novel overcome her grief over her deceased husband in the first few months after his death. In *Where Rainbows End*, in turn, Ahern uses a plethora of communicative forms (including electronic media) to describe the long road to self-discovery and happiness in the life of her female protagonist against the backdrop of her Irish family and friends, thereby painting a vivid picture of Irish life and behaviour. The fourth chapter in this section is undoubtedly the most extraordinary of all, reflecting on the letters in Nick Bantock's *Griffin and Sabine* while written as a letter itself. Ames Hawkins's experimental essay focuses on the visuality and materiality of the correspondence in the first installment of the *Griffin and Sabine* series. A self-proclaimed creative-critical scholar, educator, and art activist, Hawkins explores how the materiality of mail impacts the telling of an epistolary story and how this opens queer possibility. The section on the contemporary epistolary novel ends with a look at contemporary epistolary fiction from yet another angle by exploring its didactic value. In "The Epistolary Revenant: Teaching Against Linearity", Toni Bowers presents the pedagogical benefits of beginning an undergraduate university course on 'Epistolary Fiction before 1800' with contemporary examples of the genre. Among the numerous advantages of such an approach, Bowers insists, are that contemporary epistolary writings more easily reach students and that their reading experience of these novels better equips them to understand the epistolary classics of the eighteenth century.

The fourth and final part of this volume, "Electronic Correspondence", explores different kinds of 'new epistolary fiction', that is, fiction which uses e-mails, tweets and/or text messages as a mode of narrative transmission. It is surely a section that most readers would expect to be part of a volume on the epistolary renaissance and, concluding from the echo we received upon inviting prospective contributors to this volume, it is obviously the form most critics focus on in their research on contemporary epistolary fiction.

The opening chapter of Part IV, Thomas O. Beebee's "E-Mail Epistlemologies", asks important questions about the epistemology of e-mail fiction and the conventional epistolary novel. His analysis of four quite distinct examples of the e-mail novel, Paula Danziger and Ann Martin's *Snail Mail No More* (2000), Paige Baty's *E-Mail trouble. Love and addiction @the matrix*, Matt Beaumont's *e*, and Michael Betcherman and David Diamond's *The Daughters of Freya*, centers on the following questions: can e-mail replace the letter as a form of mutual dialogic self-fashioning, or does it possess the inner contradictions that always remind us of our incapacity for such? Is the e-mail novel always a nostalgic, post-modern pastiche of the epistolary novel? Do the material conditions for the creation, transmission, reception, and archiving of e-mail affect the content in ways analogous to what we find in the epistolary novel?

In the following chapter, Silvia Schultermandl provides a glimpse into the teenage lives of Angela, Maddie and Zoe and their chatroom pseudonyms SnowAngel, Maddie and zoegirl in Lauren Myracle's *Internet Girls* Series. Schultermandl argues that the aesthetic response of 'stuplimity', a somewhat paradoxical combination of boredom and astonishment which these novels generate, functions as a social commentary on quick media usage. In Silke Jandl's contribution, the focus shifts back to conventional letters but stays in the realm of online lives. "In the Age of Vlogging: Functions of the Letter in YouTubers' Fiction and Non-Fiction" explores the trend towards letters and other forms of materiality in the books of YouTubers. Jandl regards the fact that YouTubers and other social media stars have turned to the publishing of books in addition to working on their online presence as an indicator that there is a demand for the creation and consumption of physical objects. The fact that YouTubers frequently include letters to add authenticity or create historicity in these publications is part of this trend. The next chapter takes a comparative approach to epistolary fiction, examining the relation between an epistolary 'classic', Henry Fielding's *Shamela*, and Gary Shteyngart's dystopian e-mail novel *Super Sad True Love Story*. Elizabeth Kovach's "E-pistolary Novels and Networks: Registering Formal Shifts between Henry Fielding's *Shamela* (1741) and Gary Shteyngart's *Super Sad True Love*

Story (2010)" sheds light on how these novels indicate the distinct infrastructural, technological, social, economic and political forms of their times.

The volume closes with a chapter by Gerd Bayer entitled "The Right Sort of Form for 'The Right Sort': David Mitchell's Tweet-Story". In terms of the epistolary form examined in this chapter, Bayer's contribution is undoubtedly the most forward-looking one. As Bayer demonstrates, "The Right Sort", which consists of tweets only, is a modern-day epistolary text at its best, while at the same time stylistically evoking the telegraph system. With this, Bayer contends, Mitchell questions what remains of the letter in the digital age, a question that is also at the heart of this volume. In sum, the chapters collected here both present the fascinating variety of epistolary fiction in the twentieth and twenty-first centuries and represent innovative and creative ways of exploring epistolary fiction. Thus, we hope that this study is relevant for researchers and teachers of (epistolary) literature as well as for students interested in the new appearances of epistolary fiction in the twentieth and twenty-first centuries.

Works Cited

Altman, Janet Gurkin. 1982. *Epistolarity. Approaches to a Form.* Columbus: Ohio State University Press.
Barnes, Julian. 2007/1996. "Evermore". In: Babara Korte & Ann-Marie Einhaus (eds.). *The Penguin Book of First World War Stories.* London: Penguin. 345–361.
Beebee, Thomas. 1999. *Epistolary Fiction in Europe 1500 – 1850.* New York: Cambridge University Press.
Bowers, Toni. 2009. "Epistolary Fiction". The Literary Encyclopedia.
    <https://www.litencyc.com/php/stopics.php?rec=true&UID=350> [accessed 21 January 2018].
Brandtzæg, Siv Gøril. 2013. "The Epistolatory Novel". Oxford Bibliographies Online: British and Irish Literature.
    <http://www.oxfordbibliographies.com/view/document/obo-9780199846719/obo-9780199846719–0079.xml> [accessed 26 November 2014].
Bray, Joe. 2003. *The Epistolary Novel. Representations of Consciousness.* Oxon: Routledge.
Bower, Anne. 1997. *Epistolary Responses. The Letter in 20th-century American Fiction and Criticism.* Tuscaloosa and London: University of Alabama Press.
Bower, Rachel. 2017. *Epistolarity and World Literature, 1980–2010. New Comparisons in World Literature.* Basingstoke, UK: Palgrave Macmillan.
Brindle, Kym. 2014. *Epistolary Encounters in Neo-Victorian Fiction.* New York: Palgrave Macmillan.
Cook, Elizabeth Heckendorn. 1996. *Epistolary Bodies: Gender and Genre in the Eighteenth-Century Republic of Letters.* Stanford: Stanford University Press.
Favret, Mary. 1994. *Romantic Correspondence: Women Politics and the Fiction of Letters.* Cambridge: Cambridge University Press.

Gilroy, Amanda & W. H. Verhoeven (eds.). 2000. *Epistolary Histories. Letters, Fiction, Culture.* Charlottesville and London: University Press of Virginia.
Goldsmith, Elizabeth (ed.). 1989. *Writing the Female Voice. Essays on Epistolary Literature.* London: Pinter.
Harris, Oliver. 2001. "Review: Out of Epistolary Practice: E-Mail from Emerson, Post-Cards to Pynchon". *American Literary History* 13.1: 158–168.
Hornby, Nick. 2009. *Juliet, Naked.* London: Penguin.
Nünning, Ansgar & Jan Rupp. 2013. "Media and Medialization as Catalysts for Genre Development: Theoretical Frameworks, Analytical Concepts and a Selective Overview of Varieties of Intermedial Narration in British Fiction". In: Michael Basseler, Ansgar Nünning & Christine Schwaneke (eds.). *The Cultural Dynamics of Generic Change in Contemporary Fiction: Theoretical Frameworks, Genres and Model Interpretations.* Trier: Wissenschaftlicher Verlag Trier. 201–234.
Showalter, Elaine. 1972. *The Evolution of the French Novel: 1641–1782.* Princeton: Princeton University Press.

Part I: **Contemporary Epistolary Fiction:
New Approaches**

Maria Löschnigg, Rebekka Schuh
Epistolarity
Theoretical and Generic Preliminaries

Abstract: Contemporary epistolary fiction calls for new critical approaches which do justice to the specificities of the form as it has emerged in the wake of the epistolary renaissance. This chapter therefore provides an overview of the central narratological issues of epistolarity. These include a generic distinction between the letter and the diary (which cannot be separated from the question of the presence/absence of the figure of the internal reader), the temporal and spatial complexity of epistolary fiction, multiperspectivity, and the fragmentation of linear storylines. The impact of digital forms of communication on the novel/short story as well as variants of partially and occasionally epistolary fiction will be further issues addressed in this chapter. The final part is devoted to the epistolary short story as a distinct literary form.

1 Introduction

While many aspects of epistolarity have already been addressed by Altman, Beebee, Bray and others (see "Introduction"), this chapter focuses on the specificities of contemporary epistolary fiction in novel and short story form. Bearing in mind that "novels written entirely in letters have become comparatively rare" (Bowers 2009: n. pag.) and that the re-emergence of the epistolary form in the late twentieth and the early twenty-first century is linked to a trend towards partially epistolary fiction, it is necessary for narrative theory to do justice to this shift. Following modern definitions of epistolary writing, which include hybrid forms where the epistolary voice is no longer limited to the letter but "unfolds through multiple forms of communication that have descended from the letter" (Bowers 2009: n. pag.) and which is combined with other (non-epistolary) narrative voices, this volume draws attention to the elasticity and adaptability of epistolary fiction, which, among other factors, has contributed to the form's survival and renaissance. This is also confirmed by Linda Kauffman (1992: xiv), who argues that the "very looseness of its [the epistolary mode's] conventions has made it resilient, adaptable, and relevant in diverse historical epochs". The fact that a number of contemporary works of epistolary fiction, and especially epistolary short stories, "use a mixed mode, in which letters carry not all of the narrative" (Beebee 1998: 385) renders it necessary to distinguish between the term 'epistolary fiction' on the one hand (i.e. narrative literature which includes epistolary modes that propel the plot and are essential for the structural denotation of meaning), and the various epistolary modes (including letters, postcards, and digital forms of communication) integrated into the narrative on the other. In fact, the integrated elements which are (usually) visually marked as separate texts assume a dual status as they constitute an autonomous meaning-making unit while simultaneously adopting a different semantic status as soon as they are deciphered as parts of the whole narrative. What Altman (1982: 169) says about letters in this context is similarly applicable to the different digital modes staged in a large number of contemporary epistolary novels: "Within the epistolary work the letter has both a dependent and an independent status. Like tesserae, each individual letter enters into the composition of the whole without losing its identity as a separate entity with recognizable borders". However, no matter whether we encounter an all-epistolary, a partially epistolary or an occasionally epistolary work of fiction (cf. Bowers 2009: n. pag.), in all cases the intrinsic features of epistolarity have to be considered with regard to the assembled or interpolated epistolary units and their aesthetic effects.

This chapter will thus first offer a narratologically based distinction between epistolary and diary modes and discuss it against the backdrop of the letter novel's long-lasting status as an ideal narrative medium for rendering subjective consciousness. Meta-narrativity as well as the temporal and spatial complexity of the epistolary novel and short story will also be addressed in this theoretical approach. Other genre-specific aspects of epistolary fiction such as multiperspectivity, the breaking up of linear story lines and the frequent use of editor or collector characters will be discussed with regard to their potential to challenge the myth of coherent and unified identities and of notions of subjectivity independent from the impact of social, cultural and political influences. In addition to considering new functions of epistolary fiction that result from contemporary experiments with this form as well as from the specific ideological, social and cultural context of the late twentieth and the early twenty-first century, this chapter will also address the impact of new media on narrative fiction and the definition of epistolarity. A typology of different epistolary functions employed in contemporary epistolary fiction, ranging from I-related to you-related manifestations of epistolarity, as well as a communicative model of contemporary epistolary fiction will offer applicable and adaptable categories for the further study of epistolary literature. While most of the parameters elaborated in the following four sections apply to both the novel and the short story, there are aspects of epistolary short fiction which demand specific consideration. The chapter therefore closes with an approach to epistolary short fiction as a distinct literary form.

2 Epistolarity and the Instance of the Internal Reader

As mentioned before, contemporary epistolary fiction more often than not appears in tandem with other narrative forms (diary, figural third-person narration, retrospective first-person narration, authorial narration). However, it is paramount all the same to identify the epistolary mode used in these novels or short stories as a distinct form of narrative expression defined by clear generic markers. In this context, Janet G. Altman (1982: 200) rightly criticizes tendencies to focus mostly on thematic concerns, pointing out that "all studies of the epistolary genre, whatever their approach, depend most fundamentally on some concept – intuitive or systematic – of the genre's structural constituents". Agreeing with Altman (1982: 88) that the most essential genre-determining feature of epistolary discourse is the presence of an intratextual addressee shaping the content, style and purpose of the epistolary text, it follows that clear distinctions must be made between the diary and the letter (or other addressee-related forms of communication). Even though, as Bayer notes, "criticism has found it cumbersome to differentiate between the two narrative modes" (2009: 173), it cannot be ignored that this blurring of boundaries between the diary and the letter (or its electronic equivalents) prevents an appropriate assessment of the different narrative potentials of both modes. Given that the "letter writer simultaneously seeks to affect his [sic!] reader and is affected by him [sic!]" (Altman 1982: 88), epistolary writing can never be the "transcribing [of] uncensored streams of consciousness" or "thinking out loud", as Ruth Perry (1980: 128) puts it.

Obviously, there *are* numerous features which diary fiction and letter fiction have in common: both are first-person narratives which are usually characterized by a minimal distance between or even near coalescence of the experiencing and narrating self, both fragment linearity through division into autonomous textual entities, and both are frequently "shown as collected, exchanged, edited and published", thus "account[ing] for their own origins" (Beebee 1998: 385). However, a number of features remain which decisively distinguish these two modes and testify to the individual letter's unique discursive status as a specifically crafted hypotext. The most important of these distinctive features is the presence of an intratextual addressee in epistolary texts. One should add here that in the case of confessional letters, especially those which are addressed to a reader who is already dead or who is never meant to receive the letters in the first place, the epistolary mode does indeed lean towards the diary mode without, however, entirely coalescing with it. A novel where this becomes evident is, for example, T. R. Richmond's *What She Left* (2015). Here, Jeremy Cooke's confessional letters to his friend Larry do not only continue when, at one point, Jeremy finds out that his friend is dead, but they also show that the envisioning of a concretized internal reader continues to affect the content as well as the style of these letters. Another example is Charlie from Stephen Chbosky's coming-of-age novel *The Perks of Being a Wallflower* (1999), who writes letters to an unknown recipient whom he chooses as a confident because he hears that this person is 'nice'. The letters serve a therapeutic function for the fifteen-year-old, and he stops his letter writing as soon as he comes to terms with the traumatic experiences of the past.[1] Again, it is by no means insignificant to whom the letters are addressed, which is similarly true for letters which are solely composed in the mind, or for 'dreamed letters', which appear for example in Alice Munro's short story "Accident". Many of these letters, which have a strong therapeutic function – especially those which also constitute an act of revenge or 'writing back' – show an interesting tendency to include the 'you' in the epistolary discourse, thus coming close to what Brian Richardson has referred to as the "autotelic form of second person narration" (2006: 30 ff.). This epistolary mode can be observed for example in Munro's story "Before the Change" (1998) and in Diane Schoemperlen's 'post-romantic novel' *At a Loss for Words* (2008), where the intratextual addressee repeatedly becomes an agent in the narrative. In both texts, the female protagonists grapple with broken relationships and deal with them by offering their former lovers their own stories, uncannily defamiliarized by being filtered through their female and feminist lens. While agency is thus given to the addressee, it is paradoxically the addresser who controls this agency through her appropriative act of 'writing back', thereby liberating herself from the oppressive impact of this experience.

In his article "Deceptive Narratives: On Truth and the Epistolary Voice", Gerd Bayer (2009: 173) shows, using the example of *Die Leiden des jungen Werthers*, that Goethe clearly differentiated between letter and diary. In a similar manner, Richard B. Wright's novel *Clara Callan* (2001) foregrounds the different narrative make-up of diary and letter. In this novel, the main character, Clara, is not only an assiduous writer of letters, but also keeps a diary. As the readers are in the privileged position of having access to both discourses,[2] they will find that the protagonist's accounts of events in her letters to her sister Nora not only radically

---

[1] For a close reading of the function of letter writing in Stephen Chbosky's *The Perks of Being a Wallflower*, see Lisa Kazianka's "Isolation, Participation and Communication in Young Adult Epistolary Fiction" in this volume.

[2] The reader is thus in a similar position to Clara's daughter Elizabeth, who discovers most of the correspondence many decades later and who features as the diegetic 'super-reader' in the novel.

differ from the narrativizing of the same events in the diary, but also that some events are entirely concealed from Nora. Epistolary discourse, as this novel compellingly shows, is edited and shaped for a specific reader, while diary narratives normally represent the uncensored thoughts of the writer. The presence of an intradiegetic addressee, as Altman and others have pointed out, is thus the most important defining feature of epistolary fiction, distinguishing it from diary fiction but also from other first-person narratives such as fictional autobiography, with its strongly retrospective character and the assumption of an implied reader (normally) situated on a different diegetic level, or from simultaneous first-person narration, where the showing-mode cancels out any conscious narrative purpose on the part of the focalizer.

Joe Bray's focus on 'representations of consciousness' in his 2003 book on the epistolary novel sheds light on the differences between the epistolary novel in the seventeenth and eighteenth centuries (which are the focus of Bray's study) and new forms that have emerged in the course of the renaissance of epistolary writing from the late twentieth century onwards. Bray starts out from Ruth Perry's claim that "the characters in such epistolary fictions were transcribing uncensored streams of consciousness" (Perry 1980: 128). At the same time, he clearly distances himself from assumptions that the epistolary novel "render[s] individual psychology" and "present[s] a relatively unsophisticated and transparent version of subjectivity" (2003: 1). Interestingly, however, his exploration of the potential for sophisticated and complex constructions of subjectivity (cf. 2; 137), which he attests to the letter novel, focuses almost exclusively on the intricate relationship between the experiencing and narrating self and the potential this creates for epistolary fiction to render something close to 'free indirect discourse'. In other words, Bray entirely eclipses the letter's intrinsic you-focus which – more radically than the distinction between experiencing and narrating self – complicates and defines the representation of consciousness in the epistolary novel and short story. While "the tensions that can be created between the letter writer's past and present selves, and the uncertainties about identity that arise as a result" (16) are also possible in other first-person forms (including the diary), it is in epistolary fiction alone that the narrative is additionally refracted through the presence of the envisioned addressee as well as the set of functions attributed to the respective letter.

While in eighteenth-century epistolary fiction the letter may indeed have been an important technique for rendering consciousness, this function has been taken over by other more effective techniques from the nineteenth century onwards. Thus, the focus on epistolary fiction "as a vital and immediate source for free indirect thought" (22) would be misleading with regard to contemporary epistolary writing. Even in predominantly confessional letters, the rhetoric in contemporary epistolary fiction is always defined by both the subjective consciousness of the writer as well as the rhetoric used *vis-à-vis* a specific reader. Contemporary epistolary fiction not only offers a plethora of different voices but also foregrounds the roles or different selves we adopt in society, depending on the envisioned reader and also, especially in medialized forms of epistolary writing, on whether it is a private or public discourse. Thus, we may argue, the impression of subjectivity rendered in epistolary fiction must be distinguished from the impression of subjectivity rendered in diary novels or through other techniques for rendering consciousness, as epistolary fiction is always influenced, deferred, and fractured by the presence of the intratextual reader. Contemporary novels such as *What She Left* or *Clara Callan*, among many others, are memorable examples illustrating that the expressed 'subjectivities' are rhetorically shaped with regard to the respective addressee. Through this, the contemporary epistolary novel becomes a powerful tool to represent and critically explore the social masks which we consciously or unconsciously wear. Bearing this in mind, it is difficult to apply Ian Watt's observation that the letter form offered Richardson "a short-cut, as it were, to the heart" (Watt 1957: 195) to new epistolary forms. In fact, the letter-mode (including medialized forms of epistolarity)[3] can never compete with the mode of the interior monologue or even with free indirect discourse with regard to the apparent access it provides to unmediated (and thus uncensored) subjective consciousness. Even if we take into consideration that a modern understanding of subjectivity acknowledges its fluidity and multiplicity, the external reader must always read epistolary texts not only as such, but also read them in a double way as texts written to a specific addressee with a specific purpose and agenda in mind.

If we consider seventeenth- and eighteenth-century epistolary novels as vehicles for rendering subjective consciousness in a more sophisticated and convincing way than was possible in authorial or autobiographical first-person narration, it is not surprising that a decline of the letter novel went hand in hand with the development of figural narration towards the end of the nineteenth century – with forerunners such as Jane Austen in the early nineteenth century. Free indirect discourse, interior monologue and other forms where showing dominates over telling obviously proved to be more powerful narrative forms for providing 'short-cuts to the heart' of characters. In fact, Bray's (2003: 22f.) argument is that free indirect discourse evolved from epistolary fiction, whose "style, and especially the way it represents consciousness, significantly influenced the

---

[3] Not even the diary, which after all demands a writer who consciously arranges his/her words on paper, could be such a convincing form of rendering uncensored thoughts and feelings.

novel" (Bray 2003: 132). While this assumption may have some relevance, Bray does not take into account that with the establishment of more effective *non*-epistolary forms of rendering consciousness in narrative fiction, the epistolary mode was no longer required to fulfil this purpose. Using the novel *Herzog* (1964) by Saul Bellow to show "how apt the letter is at representing internal struggle and turbulent conflict" (2003: 132), Bray seems to neglect that in this particular novel it is actually the intricate *combination* of the letter mode with sections of figural third-person narration which foregrounds the protagonist's mental turmoil. In other words, the turbulences of Herzog's mind are conveyed rather in the *non*-epistolary segments, while the epistolary segments induce or even force the letter-writer to adapt his discourse to suit the respective addressee and the purpose of the letter. Indeed, Bellow's novel, which Bray uses in order to support his argument, really only serves to counter it. The novel foregrounds the letter's you-related rhetoric while leaving the rendering of the protagonist's precarious mental state to the framing *non*-epistolary passages in third-person, first-person or even second-person narration. The following passage, featuring a letter to Ramona, the woman Herzog dates during his letter-writing phase (which is also the novel's present of narration), and the subsequent reflection on this letter in free indirect discourse, demonstrates the different narrative functions of these two techniques:

> *Dear Ramona, you mustn't think because I've taken a powder, briefly, that I don't care for you. I do! I feel you close about me, much of the time. And last week at that party, when I saw you across the room in your hat with flowers, your hair crowded down close to your bright cheeks, I had a glimpse of what it might be to love you.*
>
> He exclaimed mentally, Marry me! Be my wife! End my troubles! – and was staggered by his rashness, his weakness and by the characteristic nature of such an outburst, for he saw how very neurotic and typical it was. We must be what we are. That is necessity. And what are we? Well, here he was trying to hold on to Ramona as he ran from her. (Bellow 1965: 72)

Herzog's inner conflict, as becomes obvious in the passage quoted above, is most visibly manifested in his thoughts, those he does not write down, and those he does not address to anybody. It is here that Herzog's conflicted self is most radically exposed, showing his inner struggles, and his almost pathological penchant for self-reflection and self-doubt.

In other letters Herzog tries to get even with people, or rather to come to terms with "the anger, the pervasive indignation" (108) he feels with regard to people such as the Monsignor, who converted his wife. Again it is above all the discrepancy between letter and free indirect discourse which lays open Herzog's inner turmoil: The letter itself seems quite civil and organized: "*I am the husband, or ex-husband, of a young woman you converted, Madeleine Pontritter, the daughter of the well-known impresario. Perhaps you remember, she took instruction from you some years ago and was baptized by you. A recent Radcliffe graduate, and very beautiful...*" (108). Again, the epistolary discourse is juxtaposed with Herzog's interpolated thoughts mediated through free indirect discourse: "Was Madeleine really such a great beauty, or did the loss of her make him exaggerate – did it make his suffering more notable? Did it console him that a beautiful woman had dumped him? But she had done it for that loud, flamboyant, ass-clutching brute Gersbach" (108). While it is, of course, possible in principle to put everything one wishes in a letter, this is normally not how it works, as the envisioned addressee always to some extent demands the camouflage of social decorum and thus usually puts a restraint on the form and content of a letter. Herzog is very much aware of the specificities of the epistolary medium, which forces the writer to balance what he/she wants to express with what is appropriate and expedient with regard to the addressee. Thus, sometimes, Bellow's protagonist has to start all over again, discarding and reformulating what he has written: "*So Edvig,* Herzog wrote, *you turn out to be a crook too! How pathetic!* But this was no way to begin. He started over. *My dear Edvig, I have news for you.* Ah, yes, much better this way" (Bellow 1965: 59).

In general, Bellow's novel is an ideal text to showcase the epistolary form as a unique narrative technique. It accentuates the different functions and facets of the letter and juxtaposes them in an eye-opening manner with non-epistolary forms of focalization in third-, first-, and second-person discourse. Moreover, Herzog's urge to analyse his life through his imaginative correspondences with others foregrounds the dependence of the self on society. In fact, the success of Herzog's grand project of self-therapy results from his adoption of different positions within the web of social relations that have defined his life. Interestingly, the process of healing, in his case, involves not only the typical therapeutic letter, defined by 'writing back' to those who have caused the pain, but also includes letters of apology, thank-you-letters, advisory letters, and argumentative letters about social, political and philosophical questions. On the diegetic level of the novel, the letters help Herzog to overcome his crisis, which is indicated by Herzog's knowledge, at the end of the novel, "that he was done with these letters. Whatever had come over him during these last months, the spell, really seemed to be passing, really going" (348). For the extratextual reader, the epistolary passages addressed to a wide spectrum of different imagined readers shed light on Herzog's personality as defined via his interaction with others, while it is through their consistent juxtaposition with non-epistolary passages that Herzog's "violent contradictions of subjectivity" (Bray 2003: 136) are exposed. Bray's claim that "Herzog's letter-writing both expresses and is a result of his inner frenzy and turmoil" (2003: 136) therefore has to be approached with caution, as it is rather the intricate *combination* of you-related discourses with revelations of his consciousness through other narrative channels which produces this effect.

We may thus conclude that letters are rhetorical instruments which contemporary writers of fiction employ in order to present their characters as individuals who constantly need to position themselves within their social web. Letters are verbal instruments that only rarely offer 'short-cuts' to the heart, while they may affect the heart of another by means of their highly rhetorical and often manipulative structure. As new forms of rendering consciousness became prominent especially in the wake of modernism, both the narrative make-up as well as the functional dimensions of epistolary fiction shifted. Contemporary epistolary fiction fans out and renders more complex concepts of fictional subjectivity, foregrounding subjectivity or rather the (written) expression of subjectivity *vis-à-vis* an 'other' as dependent on this other; in other words it showcases subjectivity – or the communication thereof – as a cultural and social product. This also conforms with what Linda S. Kauffman (1992: xxi) observes about the external factors of subjectivity: "What we define as individual experience is shaped externally as well as internally. Subjectivity seems to arise solely from personal experience, but what one perceives as subjective are in fact material, economic, and historical interrelations". It is, in fact, one of the unique strengths of contemporary epistolary fiction that it is able to "highlight[...] the partiality [...] of all constructions" (Kauffman 1992: xxii), defined, as they are, by the relationship between addresser and addressee, by the purpose of the letter, and by situational as well as cultural and social factors.

3 Meta-Narrativity, Temporal and Spatial Displacement and the Position of a 'Super-Reader'

Apart from the reciprocal impact of the internal writer and reader in epistolary fiction, another noteworthy feature is what Altman refers to as the "*mise-en-abyme* of the writer-reader relationship",[4] which makes epistolary fiction one of the most strongly meta-discursive literary genres:

---

[4] See also Linda S. Kauffman (1992: xix): "The dialogue within the letter novel between letter writer and addressee is doubled by the dialogue between writer and reader".

> By its very *mise-en-abyme* of the writer-reader relationship, the epistolary form models the complex dynamics involved in writing and reading; in its preoccupation with the myriad mediatory aspects involved in communication, in the way that it wrestles with the problem of making narrative out of discourse, in its attempts to resolve mimetic and artistic impulses, epistolary literature exposes the conflicting impulses that generate all literature. (Altman 1982: 212)

Meta-narrativity as a genre-specific feature of epistolary fiction is also manifest in its tendency to narrativize the writing and reading processes. Altman's claim that "[t]he letter novel [...] resembles many of the experimental forms of the twentieth century that question the subordination of medium to message" (1982: 211) is even more relevant for medialized forms of epistolary fiction, as here the variety of different modes and their critical juxtaposition is multiplied, now including also (staged) collective and public forms of electronic communication. This "metafictional self-reflexivity", as Nünning and Rupp (2013: 215) note with regard to the impact of the Internet on the novel, is used not only to "disclose literary fictionality but also to direct attention to the border crossings which turn up every time one tries to translate real events into verbal or medial narratives – or into medial formats of any kind".

There are two other genre-specific features of epistolary narratives that appear essential: first, the spatial distance between correspondents, which prevents actual dialogic exchange (cf. Koepke 1990: 265), and, second, the temporal displacement in the turn-taking process, which (seemingly) prolongs the validity of the letter for the respective recipient. As a result of spatial distance, one may argue that letters draw their power from the fact that they exclude all non-verbal signals that are usually present during a face-to-face encounter and thus leave ample room for imaginary constructions.[5] Paradoxically, it would seem that through this displacement, "[l]etters permit an intimacy impossible in speech" (Mullan 2006: 256), where the addresser and addressee actually face one another. In this context, John Mullan (2006: 257) states with regard to Antonia Byatt's *Possession* (1990), which he quite accurately regards as "a novel about letters", that the author "has learnt that a letter is alive when it imagines the intended reader, the single person who will examine it. [...] Letters are where the heart cannot be stilled". The time lag, in turn, encourages the recipient of a letter to take something which is already past as present and to fix fluent entities as something permanent. This feature is especially relevant with regard to the

---

[5] In "Enveloped in Epistolary Illusion: The Aesthetics of Reading and Writing Letters in Selected Short Stories by Alice Munro" in this volume, Rebekka Schuh introduces the concept of 'epistolary illusion' to describe these imaginary constructions.

power of the letter to 'carry away'[6] the recipient, as it "makes the past persist into the present with all the illusion of reality, when no real present comes to reveal the past as past" (Altman 1982: 131). These two features of temporal and spatial displacement contribute particularly strongly to the 'larger-than-life dimension' created by epistolary communication. Wulf Koepke describes these mechanisms as follows:

> [O]rdinary figures, objects and situations are beautified and aggrandized und thus projected into a larger, more decorative, more elevated environment. Such beautification through elevation involves, by necessity, a dissolution of realistic details into mere suggestions and perception, a creation of 'Leerstellen' which the readers are invited to fill with the processes of imagination. The reader can thus project personal wishes and fears into the sketchy picture, indeed, project the self and a vicarious life into such a text. (1990: 271f.)

While the spatial distance of the correspondents is similarly relevant for the conventional letter as it is for the new media, the temporal distance is minimized in the medialized form, thus possibly revealing, in some cases, a movement towards dialogic communication. In consequence, Mullan (2006: 252) ascribes to e-mails a "baldness and a lack of intimacy that robs them of the voltage that letters can possess", adding that "their very informality is likely to make them less interesting than letters to a novelist". The fact that in the twenty-first century, letter writing has become virtually extinct as a common practice, while the literary use of letters still flourishes, may indeed be seen as further evidence of the letter's unique literary potential.

In addition to the other features mentioned, it is also the position of the extratextual reader which makes epistolary discourse so attractive for both the fiction-writer as well as the actual reader. The role of the reader of epistolary fiction is necessarily a voyeuristic one, as he/she reads something which, on the diegetic level of the text, is explicitly addressed to someone else. While this may well be one of the factors explaining the appeal of epistolary fiction, another may be its unique potential for producing discrepancy of awareness between the characters in the text and the extratextual reader. However, in a great number of epistolary novels and short stories the position of a "Super Reader" (Altman 1982: 94) is already anchored on the diegetic level of the text by the "presence of a reader-/editor-figure whose collecting of letters is part of the action of the narrative" (Altman 1982: 110). This structural device, which makes the "exegesis part of the die-

---

[6] See Maria Löschnigg. 2017. "Carried Away by Letters: Alice Munro and the Epistolary Mode". In: Janice Fiamengo & Gerald Lynch (eds.). *Alice Munro's Miraculous Art. Critical Essays.* Reappraisals: Canadian Writers. Ottawa: University of Ottawa Press. 97–113.

gesis" (Altman 1982: 201), can be observed for example in T.R. Richmond's *What She Left*. A *mise-en-abyme* of the receptive act is particularly apparent in novels with an internal editor figure. Like the internal 'Super Reader', the actual reader of the novel also reads and evaluates texts from different writers to different readers from his/her privileged position. In turn, the disadvantaged position of the epistolary characters, who have no knowledge of the entire correspondence and are bound to draw (often mistaken) conclusions from their fragmented knowledge, exposes the fallacies of meaning making processes on the extratextual level.

Through this narrativized foregrounding of the impossibility of having access to the 'whole' story, however, the reconstructive act of the editor-character as well as that of the actual reader is also paradoxically called into question. Due to its fragmented and multiperspectival distribution of information, which often leaves causal and semantic lacunae, epistolary fiction not only actively involves the reader in the process of creating meaning. At the same time, it also thematizes the inherent fallacies of all meaning-making processes, based as they always are on the abstract notion of a totality that is never really accessible. The foregrounding of reconstructive processes is particularly frequent in stories and novels with a marked polyphonic structure and applies most accurately to those works of epistolary fiction which feature an editor-figure. At the same time, the discrepancy of awareness that results from the superior knowledge of the extratextual reader/diegetic 'Super Reader' on the one hand, and the limited knowledge of the intratextual correspondents on the other, shows some affinity with the effect of character-configuration in drama. In both genres, the specific orchestration of this discrepancy of awareness constitutes a powerful technique for creating suspense and 'dramatic' irony. Through its intrinsically polyphonic structure[7] and fractured narrative voice(s), epistolary fiction most radically defies the "epic wholeness of an individual", which according to Bakhtin (1981: 37) "disintegrates in a novel". In fact, the "active polyglossia of the new world" (12), which is characterized by "openendedness, indecision, indeterminacy" (16) and disintegration and which has made epic authority obsolete (cf. 16), finds its most congenial narrative form in the fragmented structure of the epistolary novel/short story. One may even go so far as to claim that the disintegration of wholeness and certainty which defines our age even more than previous ones is iconically represented in the multi-vocal and composite structure of the epistolary novel. In analogy to Bakhtin's claim that the form of the novel resulted from a cultural turn that became most visible in the eighteenth century, one

---

7 The only exception here would be the rare case of the one-letter story.

could argue that the new penchant for fragmented narrative forms such as epistolary and multimodal fiction may be linked to the cultural turn brought about by the upsurge of the digital age.

4 Medialized Epistolary Fiction

When epistolary fiction started to reappear in the 1960s – first reluctantly and then, from the 1990s onwards, more rapidly – it had changed its guise. It now displayed not only a broad panoply of narrative forms, ranging from all-letter fiction to stories or novels where letters play a quantitatively minor role but can still be identified as defining elements of the narrative text, but it also decisively surrendered its function as a mode of rendering (uncensored) consciousness. Moreover, through the inclusion of staged forms of digital media, the orchestration of narrative modes into ever new constellations of meaning-making has reached a new climax. It can thus be claimed that the unabated rise of epistolary fiction since the 1990s is inextricably linked to the catalytic impact of the Internet on fiction. At the same time, one has to be aware that the inclusion of digital forms constitutes but an "imitation by a medium of the resources of another medium" (Ryan & Thon 2014: 10). In other words, the paperbound book cannot actually render the electronic medium 'Internet' (cf. Hallet 2009: 132f.; Elleström 2010: 32), yet the seeming multimediality which is achieved by the staged integration of electronic media into printed novels produces a significant reciprocal effect: on the one hand, the integration of Internet formats into the novel changes the generic landscape of narrative fiction, while on the other hand medialized fiction in book form "reinstalls the physicality and materiality of semiotic practices" (Hallet 2009: 146). Through this process, an element of implicit medial countering is introduced, in addition to the more explicit function of "cultural self-inspection" (Nünning & Rupp 2013: 202).

While there are several characteristics which 'medialized epistolary fiction' (see Löschnigg 2018) has in common with contemporary epistolary fiction that does without staged digital forms of communication, there are several constitutive structural features which are specifically relevant to the medialized epistolary novel, even though many of them mark a difference in degree rather than mode. Thus, medialized epistolary fiction – to a greater extent than the more conventional letter-novel – shares some features with the multimodal novel, which Wolfgang Hallet (2009: 130) defines as "the systematic and recurrent integration of non-verbal and non-narrative elements in novelistic narration". One such element, which also plays a role in (medialized) epistolary fiction, is the significance of typographical devices, the function of which is elucidated by Hallet as follows:

> Typography visualizes textual 'difference' and identifiable textual elements, voices, ways, styles and modes of writing, but it also represents the material side and the technologies of writing, from the fountain pen, the typewriter and book print to the digits of electronic and multimedial hypertexts. (Hallet 2009: 138 f.)

Through the frequent inclusion of elements such as fan websites or personal playlists (accessible to other Internet users), medialized epistolary fiction also features autonomous *non*-narrative units. However, these still retain elements of epistolarity as they are part of a process of self-stylization *vis-à-vis* a collective other. As in the multimodal novel, the reader is confronted with 'texts' produced by a character in the fictional world, which makes the character not only "move closer to the reader's real world" (Hallet 2009: 144), but also allows the reader insight into the "literary character's ways of 'world-making', into their ways of looking at the world and conceiving or structuring it" (Hallet 144 f.). Medialized epistolary fiction – like multimodal fiction – thus employs new and complex techniques of characterization. As opposed to most multimodal novels, however, all staged modes in (medialized) epistolary fiction, from conventional letters and e-mails to twitter messages and blogs and fan websites, are, in fact, not only written and read by characters in the novel, but are produced with a certain addressee/group of addressees in mind. Like no other novelistic genre, therefore, they foreground the influence of others (be it a specific individual, a group of friends, or a vaguely defined social collective) on the display of our self/selves.

To sum up, it can be said that medialized epistolary structures engender new forms of characterization as the reader is offered direct access to private and public forms of expression, communication and self-stylization. While this is also true, to some extent, of conventional epistolary novels, the medialized form, characterized as it is by a high degree of multimodality, not only broadens the range of available (imitated) textual formats and channels but also thematizes and questions new cultural and communicative practices. The task of the critic with regard to such 'fictions of the internet' (cf. Löschnigg 2018: 327–31) is thus to explore and describe the functions of various modes of information presentation and their interaction with each other within the narrative framework of the whole novel. Despite their structural differences, the receptive skills demanded by medialized epistolary novels are similar to those required for the multimodal novel, and are referred to as "multimodal literacy" (2008: 7) by Bateman and as a "multi-literate act" (2014: 168) by Hallet. While 'multimodal literacy' is to a large extent a consequence of the dramatically increasing medialization of our daily lives, it is the task of the literary critic to show how this combination of Internet-based presentational modes with more conventional modes results in new potentials for creating meaning and contributes to a generic transformation of the novel.

5 Partially and Occasionally Epistolary Fiction

The study of epistolarity should include not only the investigation of narratives which clearly fall into the category of epistolary fiction but should also focus on the function of correspondence such as letters, e-mails and postcards in novels and stories which are only 'partially' or 'occasionally epistolary' (cf. Bowers 2009: n. pag.). These are texts in which the quantitative proportion of the epistolary is rather limited and where epistolary segments are not essential for the basic plot of the narrative, yet where the impact of such segments on the aesthetic effect of narrative transmission is nonetheless considerable. In fact, the proliferation of contemporary novels and short stories which integrate epistolary elements testifies to authors' recognition of the unique narrative possibilities inherent in the epistolary mode. John Mullan (2006: 252) notes in this context that it "is remarkable that more than half of the contemporary novels on which [he has] focused in [his] book [*How Novels Work*] print letters", and rightly concludes that the "letter has, in truth, fictional uses [...] that have little to do with letters in real life". More than ten years after the publication of Mullan's book, this situation has remained unchanged despite the overwhelming impact of digital media on our everyday culture, a fact which confirms the unique signification created by including the specific structure and rhetoric of letters in narrative. In addition to conventional letters, however, e-mail has now been fully adapted to literary use, and it seems that e-mail, too, is developing its own distinct literary form of expression deviating from the e-mails we write in our daily lives.

In the following, we would like to briefly discuss some examples that provide insight into the multifaceted literary use of letters/postcards and e-mails. In Zadie Smith's novel *On Beauty* (2005), for instance, the entire first chapter consists of e-mails sent by American student Jerome Belsey, who is on an internship in London, to his father Howard, Professor of Art Theory at a prestigious (fictional) university near Boston. This expository use of e-mails not only allows Smith to render Jerome's first-person voice in an otherwise heterodiegetic narrative, but also has a number of additional effects. First, the e-mails function as a kind of exposition, introducing the contrast between the conservative and liberal professors Monty Kipps and Howard Belsey, whose positions are elaborated and critically questioned in the novel. Second, the e-mails prove an effective tool for characterization, offering a detailed description of the Kippses from the point of view of the enthusiastic Jerome, which reveals much about the young man and his psychological needs. It seems Jerome really cherishes the "negativized image" (Smith 2005: 4) he has of his family's home, which, in contrast to the Kipps household, is obviously not characterized by "home-cooked meal[s]" (6) and clear religious affiliations. In this connection, the e-mails also provide a first glimpse into Jerome's troubled relationship with his father, which is later shown to echo that between Howard and his own father Harold. Above all, however, it is the specific temporal structure of epistolarity which Smith exploits in the exposition to her novel. In his e-mail dated 19 November, Jerome writes:

> I have no idea how you're going to take this one! But we're in love! The Kipps girl and me! I'm going to ask her to marry me, Dad! And I think she'll say yes!!! Are you digging on these exclamation marks!!!! (7)

In chapter three, when Howard is already in London and on the way to the Kippses to sort out what he thinks must be a mistake, his wife Kiki reads another e-mail from their son, dated 21 November:

> Dad – mistake. Shouldn't have said anything. Completely over – if it ever began. Please please please please don't tell anybody, just forget about it. I've made a total fool of myself! I just want to curl up and die. (26)

Howard, who does not receive this message, still takes the 'truth' of the first e-mail for granted, and his blundering when he arrives at the Kippses to talk about Jerome and Victoria's 'engagement' turns out to be symptomatic of his life in general. On a surface level, the misunderstanding which arises from the temporal displacement of epistolary communication (and from Howard's refusal to use a cell phone) is a plot element which causes dramatic irony. On a deeper level, however, it stands symbolically for Prof. Howard Belsey's difficulties (or unwillingness) to relate adequately to his environment. As John Mullan (2006: 252) observes with regard to Philip Roth's *The Human Stain* (2000) and Martin Amis' *Yellow Dog* (2003), "it is the potential for error and misdirection that creates special fictional possibilities for emails". The speed and ease, and the possibility to reach any number of recipients at the same time that define electronic communication also make it extremely prone to far-reaching errors and render it an effective tool for literature. Speed and possible anonymity also contribute to e-mail's suitability for criminal activities, as is the case for example in Will Ferguson's novel *419* (2012), where the forged e-mails sent to Henry Curtis from Nigeria testify to the medialized epistolary mode's potential to serve as a mask.

An author who has successfully experimented with letters is Ian McEwan, who, for example, exploits the letter's functional repertory in the two first-person novels *Nutshell* (2016), which is in many ways a re-writing of *Hamlet*, and *Enduring Love* (1997). In *Nutshell*, the narrator is an unborn child who recounts, from inside the womb, his father's murder at the hands of his mother Trudy and his uncle Claude. In chapter nine, the fetus composes a mental letter to his father (cf. 83–85). This apostrophic text contains references to Shakespeare's sonnet cycle as well as including fragments from the news reports which the baby listens to through his mother and which readers will recognize as actual occurrences from the recent past. Like Louis MacNeice's famous poem "Prayer before Birth", written during the Second World War, McEwan's novel thus obliquely (and most effectively) comments on contemporary reality. What is particularly important in the context of the novel's use of epistolarity, however, is the specific impetus and rhetoric of this letter, which sets it off from the rest of the I-/we-narrative. The main incentive of the letter is an appeal to the father, who is implored by the unborn baby to remember the poem he once recited (Shakespeare's "Sonnet 29"?) and to recognize his son's love before he dies, or better, follow his son's warning and decline to drink the poisoned milkshake which the baby's mother and uncle have prepared for him. The unborn son's fear of rejection (cf. 84) and his revelation that he is "foolishly in love" (84) with life despite its brutality is emotionally charged through its being rendered in epistolary form, that is, through its staging as a direct appeal of a (baby) son to his father. What Mullan (2006: 256 f.) says about Byatt's *Possession* in this respect can similarly be applied to *Nutshell*: "If readers have found this deeply academic novel moving, it is because of the letters that do not get read, or sometimes do not get sent".

In McEwan's *Enduring Love*, in turn, letters fulfil an essential function as a counter to the authority of Joe Rose's first-person narrative. The novel features two letters from Joe's 'stalker', Jed Parry, which provide insight into the latter's pathological mindset by revealing how the delusional Jed interprets everything Joe does or does not do as a token of Joe's love for him:

> When you came out of your house yesterday evening and you brushed the top of the hedge with your hand – I didn't understand first. [...] Then I got it. You had touched them in a certain way, in a pattern that spelled a simple message. Did you really think I would miss it, Joe! So simple, so clever, so loving. (McEwan 1998: 96)

Through Jed's letters it becomes clear that what Joe regards as his rejection of and passivity towards Jed is interpreted as the exact opposite by the stalker. Jed, who suffers from de Clérambault's syndrome, transfers agency to Joe ("You've drawn me into your daily life and demanded that I understand it",

95), thus turning upside down – through his delusional logic – Joe's way of seeing things. In the third letter included in the novel, Joe's wife Clarissa tries to explain to her husband how she experienced his change of personality. If one regards Jed's letters as an antithesis to Joe's story, then Clarissa's letter, which appears towards the end of the novel, can be seen as the synthesis: Accepting now that Jed is mad, she still makes it clear that she could "understand how he might have formed the impression that [Joe was] leading him on" (218). The letters in *Enduring Love*, through their extreme focus on Joe as the intratextual addressee, serve as a mirror on and alternative version to Joe's narrative (the 'main' story), thus foregrounding discrepancies between how we see ourselves and how we are seen by others.

The dissolution of narrative authority is even more prominent in Margaret Atwood's first historical novel *Alias Grace* (1996), which revolves around the story of Grace Marks, a woman convicted of having helped in the murder of her employer in Canada in 1843. Featuring a patchwork of different texts (including documentary) and techniques (including references to quilting patterns), this multimodal novel also contains a great number of letters. These letters, however, do not contribute to the clarification of the case (i.e. the extent of Grace's involvement in the crime and the question of whether she was of sound mind), but like all the other narrative elements in this novel rather emphasize the elusiveness of the narrator-protagonist and undermine notions of historical objectivity.

In Graham Swift's *Wish You Were Here* (2011), the integration of epistolary elements serves yet another narrative and aesthetic function. While the two integrated postcards constitute only minimal textual segments in the novel, they nonetheless fulfil a decisive function for the characterization of the protagonist Jack Luxton. Written by him, they denote his limited ability to communicate in general. In fact, it could be argued that the limited space of the postcard (together with the sparse semantic substance of Jack's messages) iconically represents the 'prison of silence' which defines Jack's life and relationships. Numerous other examples of partially or occasionally epistolary fiction could be cited here, yet what is important at this point is how the different degrees and functional manifestations of epistolarity can be approached from a narratological point of view. Before investigating the narrative and aesthetic function(s) of epistolary modes within a novel or story, it is expedient to identify and categorize the functional motivation of each of the epistolary units integrated into a work of fiction. The following typology will therefore serve as a first model for the classification of epistolary discourses, representing a dynamic model open to expansion and modification:

I-focused letters	you-focused letters	
therapeutic	advisory	
confessional	appellative	
apologetic/appreciative	manipulative/deceptive	forged
	emotive	
	informative	
	argumentative	

Depending on how strongly and genuinely the writer mediates his/her own sensibilities or how strongly the focus is on the envisioned recipient, letters as (semi-)autonomous hypotexts in epistolary fictions can be categorized along a scale ranging from a strong I-focus to a strong you-focus. On one end of the scale there is the therapeutic letter, which instrumentalizes the epistolary mode for processes of healing. Interestingly, even though this functional variant of epistolary writing is most strongly focused on the letter-writer him-/herself and on the change the act of writing will prompt, it is also the form which most frequently and most strongly features the 'you' as an agent in the letter. Especially in therapeutic letters addressed to the person held responsible for the emotional/psychological crisis the writer finds him-/herself in, the autotelic you-form becomes a powerful tool for the act of 'writing back'. Brian Richardson (2006: 30 f.) uses the term 'autotelic second-person narration' for you-forms where, in contrast to the standard variant of you-narration, "the narrator is quite distinct from the narratee" (Richardson 2006: 31). While most literary examples of the autotelic form are written in the present tense and render the impression of addressing the actual reader, the use of the 'you' who becomes an agent in the text in epistolary fiction always designates the internal reader and engages with common past experiences rather than suggesting an identical temporality between narration and reception (cf. Richardson 2006: 31). However, despite the prominence of the 'you' in the narrative structure of many therapeutic letters, the functional focus is still always entirely on the writer him-/herself. The confessional letter is again strongly focused on the writer, but in this case, the addressee's position of a confident is of paramount importance. Letters of apology and thank-you-letters, in turn, are difficult to place, as they definitely aim at an effect on the recipient. At the same time, however, as the writer's need to express his/her apologies or gratitude is usually stronger than the prospective addressee's need to receive the message, we have placed such letters within the I-focused modes. Most 'typical' love-letters would fall into the category of the emotive letter, in which reciprocal sensibilities move to the foreground. In both the confessional and the emotive letter we may again have a strong appearance of the 'you'. However, in these cases the purpose is to confirm the bond of trust between addresser and addressee (confessional letter) or to engage in imaginative fantasies about the addressee in the case of the love letter (emotive letter). The most neutral variants are the informative and the argumentative letter, which, in literature, only rarely appear isolated from any other functions. The focus clearly shifts to the addressee with the advisory letter, whereas letters with the predominant purpose to have an effect on the reader or even instigate him/her to some action could be subsumed under the heading of appellative epistolary discourse. The more we move in the direction of you-focused letters, the more the writer disappears behind a 'rhetorical' mask, especially in the case of the manipulative letter which morphs into the deceptive letter as soon as true motives are clearly veiled. The forged letter, in which the true identity of the writer is concealed by a fake identity, could, in fact, assume any of the other forms. It has to be added here that this typology only works as long as the boundaries between the different types remain permeable and as long as we use the types only to denote the most dominant mode in a letter. It also has to be noted that this typology is open for expansion and that in most cases there will be a combination of two or more functions, albeit usually with one dominant function. Epistolary hypotexts are also rich sources for implicit characterization. Interestingly, the more the functional drive moves from I-centred to you-centred modes the less the epistolary text works as a tool for characterization in the diegesis of the novel. Whereas manipulative, deceptive, and forged letters are extremely expressive sources for the external reader, the internal reader – due to his/her limited information – is denied this form of implicit characterization.

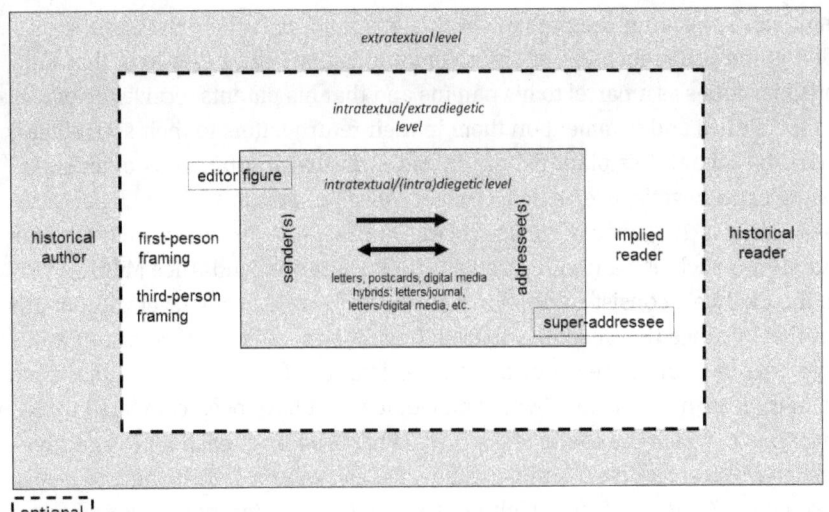

Based on Neumann and Nünning's (2008: 27) communication model for narrative texts, and using Gérard Genette's terminology, this model illustrates the various levels of communication in epistolary fiction, highlighting in particular the boundary-transgressing qualities of letter fiction. Letter communication in fiction usually takes place on the (intra)diegetic level, where individual characters write and read different kinds of epistolary discourses. Sometimes, but not always, the (intra)diegetic level is mediated by narratorial figures on the extradiegetic level, be it in the form of first- or third-person narrators or editor-figures, and addressed to an implied reader or super-addressee. As the model shows, the editor-figure as well as the super-addressee can be on both the intra- as well as the extradiegetic levels, thus transporting the letter communication that has taken place on the (intra)diegetic level onto the extradiegetic level. Rohinton Mistry's short story cycle *Tales from Firozsha Baag* is a case in point, for it is here that both the editor-figure and the super-addressee cross the diegetic boundary from the intra- to the extradiegetic level. As we learn in the final story "Swimming Lessons", Kersi – whom the reader has met as a character and narrator in previous stories – is the author of the entire story cycle, including "Swimming Lessons". Now a permanent resident in Canada, he has mailed these stories back to his parents in Mumbai in a parcel. His parents, who turn out to function as super-addressees of the stories, are also familiar to the extratextual reader as characters in previous stories. In *Tales from Firozsha Baag*, the transcending of the boundary between intra- and extradiegetic level is metaleptic since in "Swimming Lessons" Kersi's parents are at one and the same time characters who send letters to their son *and* the readers of this very story, thus paradoxically reading themselves. In this example, it is the extradiegetic level which is the prime location of letter communication, since it is here that Kersi sends his stories as a parcel to his parents and that his parents receive the parcel, read the stories and comment on them in their return letters to their son. What is remarkable about epistolary fiction, however, is that in numerous other examples the extradiegetic level is non-existent. All-letter novels such as Lionel Shriver's *We Need to Talk about Kevin* and Mark Dunn's *Ella Minnow Pea*, and all-letter short stories such as Sandra Birdsell's "The Bird Dance" and Alice Munro's "Before the Change", consist solely of letters on the (intra)diegetic level without any narrative instance that mediates these letters. It is because of this lack of a mediator and thus the absence of *the* crucial feature of narrative texts that such epistolary texts are associated with 'immediacy' and have been compared to dramatic texts in which the characters – instead of speaking to each other on stage – write letters to each other. An interesting case in point is T. R. Richmond's epistolary novel *What She Left*, which does without a framing narrative while still featuring an editor figure. Prof. Jeremy Cooke, who collects and arranges all the texts produced by the characters in order to publish them as a book, can be identified as the editor figure only through his own epistolary texts exchanged on the diegetic level of the narrative. In fact, the intricate interplay between the extra- and intradiegetic levels of narrative, between frames and hypotexts, and between intra- and extratextual reader-figures is one of the most appealing and powerful features of epistolary fiction and the basis for the genre's exceptional meta-discursive potential.

6 The Epistolary Short Story as a Distinct Literary Form

While the epistolary fiction of the late twentieth and the early twenty-first century has been of comparatively little interest to literary scholars, it is undoubtedly the sub-genre of the epistolary short story that has received the least attention. Claiming that "[t]he return to epistolary conventions has arguably been most marked in longer prose works, and in focusing on these I have had to leave aside the short stories and verse works using epistolary conventions during this period" (Bower 2017: 20–21), Rachel Bower is so far the only author of a book-length study on epistolary fiction to even consider the existence of non-novelistic forms of epistolarity. However, in contrast to Bower, this volume insists that the epistolary renaissance marks not only a renaissance of the epistolary long form but also the (re-)birth of the epistolary short story, even if it has been significantly less visible in literary criticism. Scholars of epistolary fiction and other attentive readers will rightfully object that Henry James already wrote epistolary stories, for example, "The Point of View" (1882) and "A Bundle of Letters" (1878). However, considering the Canadian literary landscape, for example, epistolary stories significantly increased only in the wake of the epistolary renaissance at the end of the twentieth century. In the late 1980s, the 1990s and the early 2000s, the epistolary short story boomed in Canada. A major writer of epistolary stories during this time was Nobel Prize laureate Alice Munro with as many as twenty-two letter stories in her oeuvre. She is joined by other contemporary short story authors such as Austin Clarke, Olive Senior, Rohinton Mistry and Emma Donoghue.[8] Outside of Canada, in US-American, Latin-American, Anglophone African and British literature, the letter story has also been thriving. Gail Pool's edited anthology of letter stories, *Other People's Mail* (2000), offers a great selection of international letter stories published in the second half of the twentieth century by authors such as Julio Cortázar, Nadine Gordimer and Doris Lessing. Sandra Cisneros's "Little Miracles, Kept Promises" about letters left at shrines and places of pilgrimage, Elizabeth Jolley's "Wednesdays and Fridays" about the changing relationship between a mother and her grown-up son, and Joyce Carol Oates' "Dear Joyce Carol," and "Dear Husband," are other singular examples from the rich field of contemporary Anglophone letter stories.[9]

The fact that there is a certain reluctance in short story criticism to consider such phenomena is also connected to the still inferior position of the short story in comparison to the novel and the fact that short story writing continues to spark significantly less research than novel writing (cf. Löschnigg 2014: 3; Nischik 2017: 2). Thus, whereas critics are eager to identify new sub-genres of the novel, short stories tend to remain mere short stories and are hardly listed as examples of the existence of thematic genres such as gothic fiction or historical fiction, even though the short story offers stimulating examples in these and other sub-genres. Instead, much of short story criticism continues to grapple with the question of what a short story really is. Adrian Hunter's notion of the short story as 'minor literature' opens up a completely new and compelling perspective on this 'inferiority complex' of short story criticism. 'Minor literature' is a concept taken from Gilles Deleuze and Félix Guattari's *Kafka: Toward a Minor Literature*

---

[8] For further information on the epistolary short story in Canada see: Rebekka Schuh. 2018. "Stories in Letters – Letters in Stories: Epistolary Liminalities in the Anglophone Canadian Short Story". Unpublished PhD Dissertation, University of Graz.

[9] Due to the prominence of epistolary stories in Canadian literature and our expertise in this field, however, the following examples are taken from Canadian literature.

(1986). In this book, Deleuze and Guattari (1986: 16) develop the concept of 'minor literature', as opposed to 'major literature', to refer to the writing "which a minority constructs within a major language". The main characteristics of minor literature are a deterritorialization of language, a political agenda and a collective value. Minor literature is not about individual concerns but always stands for a larger group (cf. Deleuze & Guattari 1986: 16–17). Hunter (2004, 2007) applies this concept to describe and re-evaluate the peculiarities of short story writing:

> The interrogative story's 'unfinished' economy, its failure literally to express, to extend itself to definition, determination or disclosure, becomes, under the rubric of a theory of 'minor' literature, a positive aversion to the entailment of 'power and law' that defines the 'major' literature. (Hunter 2007: 140)

He emphasizes that minor literature celebrates its minority status by highlighting its oddities in relation to major literature (cf. Hunter 2004: 220–21). It does not want to become major but rebels against major forms of expression to "self-consciously maintain[...] its ec-centric, 'minority' position" (Hunter 2004: 221). In short, minor literature embraces its minor status rather than aiming to produce yet another master-narrative, for that would mean not merely acquiescing to the rules of power battle but also reproducing them.

Thinking of the short story in terms of minor literature, according to Hunter, highlights the strengths and potentials of the short story's characteristics. It "provides for a more creative way of thinking about deficit, curtailment, lacking, the markers of 'minority'" (Hunter 2007: 140) so frequently connected to the short story. As Hunter (2007: 140) stresses, characteristics of the short story that have previously been treated as the genre's deficiencies – its openness, ambiguity, and versatility – become positivized under the framework of minor literature. The short story's minority character, however, is not inherent in the genre but created and perpetuated by writers and their particular emphases (cf. Hunter 2007: 140).

Since many of the generic characteristics of epistolary fiction discussed in the previous sections also apply to the epistolary short story, this section is devoted to a brief elaboration of the ways in which the epistolary short story stands out as a genre in epistolary renaissance fiction. As is typical of contemporary epistolary fiction in general, the epistolary short story, too, frequently integrates single letters into stories that are narrated from an overall first- or third-person perspective. However, while the letter mode in the form of letters, e-mails, or blog entries in epistolary novels usually dominates over other narrative modes so that the relevance of these letters for the creation of meaning is more marked, epistolary short stories create epistolarity with much less. The relative brevity of short stories and their compression of meaning make it possible that only a few letters or even a single letter can create enough epistolarity to imbue the entire short story with meaning much in the same way as an all-letter structure can. However inconspicuous on the printed page, a single letter in André Alexis's "My Anabasis" is the main propulsion for the plot and triggers a number of uncanny events, including several encounters with doppelgängers. In other stories, the letters are not as relevant for the plot as such but nonetheless open up a unique perspective on the themes of the narrative. In Alice Munro's "Material", it is only through a short letter that is eventually broken off that the first-person narrator voices her true thoughts about her ex-husband's public image as a writer. In Dede Crane's "What Sort of Mother", a single letter at the end of a story which has been fully focalized through the mother, Nancy, is the only insight we get into the perspective of Nancy's daughter and her response to Nancy's leaving the family; and in Elyse Gasco's "Mother: Not a True Story" a fake letter written by the adoptive mother in the voice of the biological mother does exactly what the title promises: It reveals the mother myth as "[n]ot a true story", as a fantasy and a construction.

Of course, there are also numerous examples of letter stories which conform to the traditional understanding of epistolarity and are written in letters exclusively or to a great extent. Alice Munro's "A Wilderness Station", one of the comparatively well-known letter stories, for example, consists of a series of eleven letters and one article published in the Carstairs magazine *Argus*. All the letters as well as the article have been collected by Leopold Henry, a historian from Queen's University, Kingston, a hundred years after they were written. They center around the death of Simon Herron in the backwoods of Huron County in 1852 and the mysterious circumstances under which he died. Through the different perspectives given in the individual letters, the story provides five different versions of his death, some of which are more plausible than others but all of which compete to be accepted as the truth. Austin Clarke's "Waiting for the Postman to Knock" is another example of the 'traditional' type of letter story and renders the life of a West Indian domestic in Canada, who came to Toronto via the Domestic Scheme in 1955. While its surface structure – a series of letters embedded in a first-person narrative – is not very remarkable for a letter story, it is quite outstanding in other respects. One of strengths of the story is the adroit juxtaposition of the oral dialect of the protagonist Enid and the first-person narrator, who invites the reader to "lissen to the letter Enid write" (Clarke 2013: 27), "cause it is something to hear" (Clarke 2013: 32), with the distance and formality of Canadian business letters:

> *Dear Mr. Landlord,*
> *I am a sick woman. I barely crept out of my room yesterday to go to the bank to see what happened to that cheque I wrote for you. Well, I can tell you, Mr. Landlord, that I don't understand how my money could disappear so fast from that Royal Bank. [...]*
> *Well, Mr. Landlord, you listen to me now, sir. I am only telling you a few of the things that happens to black people in this country to let you know that it ain't no honeymoon living in this place. [...]*
> *Respectfully yours,*
> *Miss Enid Scantlebury* (Clarke 2013: 27–30, italics in original)

Another type of the all-letter story, which is in a way its purest form, is the single-letter story. Single-letter narratives are unique to the short story and, as Maria Löschnigg shows in a separate chapter, this form has quite peculiar qualities.

The epistolary short story occupies a special position in the renaissance of epistolary forms also because, in contrast to the trend of medialized epistolary forms in recent novels, newer forms of epistolary communication, such as e-mails and text-messages, are comparatively rare in epistolary stories. One of the few e-mail stories is Steven Heighton's "Noughts & Crosses: An Unsent Reply" (2012). In this story, Heighton returns to one of the earliest and still prevailing kinds of letter, the love letter, and re-interprets it in an e-mail story about the shattering affair of two women. Having received a disappointing e-mail from her lover that she "needed to reflect a little" and that "it is hard when we are always in dialogue" (Heighton 2012: 123), Arnella dissects every sentence of this e-mail trying to understand the sudden turn of events and in passing cynically comments on the advantages of being left via e-mail: "Oh and another nice thing about email: you are always sitting down to read it. No more Puccini swoons, buckling to the floor with the farewell letter clinched in one hand, the other cupping the brow. Instead, you settle deeper in your chair" (Heighton 2012: 130). Doretta Lau's "God Damn, How Real is This?" (2014) consists of several text messages sent to the first-person narrator from her own future self, warning her about potential illnesses: "THAT MOLE ON YOUR LEFT ARM THAT YOU'VE BEEN IGNORING? GET THEE TO A DOCTOR" (Lau 2014: 9) and "HEY TRICHO-SLUT, GET YOUR MAN HANDS OUT OF OUR HAIR. I HAVE A LAKE MICHIGAN-SHAPED BALD SPOT FORMING ON THE BACK OF MY HEAD. STOP PLUCKING. IT'S STARTING TO LOOK LIKE A PENIS" (Lau 2014: 9). While the narrator's doctor diagnoses her with "Münchausen by proxy" (Lau 2014: 13), the texts the narrator and some of the narrator's friends receive from their future selves seem to be a lightminded critique of the ever-expanding place that modern technology occupies in people's lives. This is particularly suggested by the narrator's reaction to the "cacophony of phones beeping and bleeping" (Lau 2014: 12) in her doctor's waiting room: "If I knew how to code a virus, I would direct my future self to send the inventor of communicative time travel a diseased email to avert this reality" (Lau 2014: 12).[10] Given the great variety of epistolary stories in the Anglophone literary scene and the semantic potential of these stories, it is quite surprising that they have received so little attention as a distinct genre. The following section in this volume, which is entirely devoted to the epistolary short story, tries to compensate for this lack of critical attention.

Works Cited

Alexis, André. 2001. "My Anabasis". In: George Bowering (ed.). *And Other Stories*. Vancouver: Talon Books. 15–40.
Altman, Janet Gurkin. 1982. *Epistolarity. Approaches to a Form*. Columbus: Ohio State University Press.
Bakhtin, Mikhail. 1981. "Epic and Novel: Toward a Methodology for the Study of the Novel". In: Michael Holquist (ed.). *The Dialogic Imagination: Four Essays by M. M. Bakhtin*. Austin and London: University of Texas Press. 3–40.
Barnes, Julian. 2007/1996. "Evermore". In: Babara Korte & Ann-Marie Einhaus (eds.). *The Penguin Book of First World War Stories*. London: Penguin. 345–361.
Bayer, Gerd. 2009. "Deceptive Narratives: On Truth and the Epistolary Voice". *Zeitschrift für Literaturwissenschaft und Linguistik* 154. 173–187.
Beebee, Thomas O. 1998. "Epistolary Novel". In: *Encyclopedia of the Novel*, ed. Paul Schellinger. Chicago, London: Fitzroy Dearborn Publishers. 384–388.
Bellow, Saul 1965. *Herzog*. Harmondsworth: Penguin.
Bower, Rachel. 2017. *Epistolarity and World Literature, 1980–2010*. New Comparisons in World Literature. Basingstoke, UK: Palgrave MacMillan.
Bowers, Toni. 2009. "Epistolary Fiction". *The Literary Encyclopedia*. <https://www.litencyc.com/php/stopics.php?rec=true&UID=350> [accessed 21 January 2018].
Bray, Joe. 2003. The Epistolary Novel. Representations of Consciousness. Oxon: Routledge.
Cisneros, Sandra. 1991. "Little Miracles, Kept Promises". In: Sandra Cisneros. *Woman Hollering Creek and Other Stories*. New York: Vintage. 116–129.
Clarke, Austin. 2013/1971. "Waiting for the Postman to Knock". In: *They Never Told Me And Other Stories*. Holstein, ON: Exile Editions Ltd. 26–57.
Crane, Dede. 2008. "What Sort of Mother". In: *The Cult of Quick Repair*. Regina, Saskatchewan: Coteau Books. 175–208.
Deleuze, Gilles & Félix Guattari. 1986. *Kafka: Toward a Minor Literature*. Minneapolis and London: University of Minnesota Press.
Elleström, Lars. 2010. "The Modalities of Media: A Model for Understanding Intermedial Relations". In: Lars Elleström (ed.). *Media Borders, Multimodality and Intermediality*. Basingstoke: Palgrave Macmillan. 11–48.

---

[10] For more examples of medialized epistolary short fiction see Maximilian Feldner's chapter "Epistolarity in Twenty-First Century Nigerian Short Fiction".

Gasco, Elyse. 1999. "Mother: Not a True Story". In: *Can You Wave Bye, Bye, Baby?* Picador: New York. 189–238.
Hallet, Wolfgang. 2009. "The Multimodal Novel: The Integration of Modes and Media in Novelistic Narration". In: Sandra Heinen & Roy Sommer (eds.). *Narratology in the Age of Cross-Disciplinary Narrative Research*. Berlin/New York: Walter de Gruyter. 129–53.
Heighton, Steven. 2012. "Noughts & Crosses: An Unsent Reply". In: *The Dead Are More Visible*. Toronto: Knopf Canada. 123–138.
Hornby, Nick. 2009. *Juliet, Naked*. London: Penguin.
Hunter, Adrian. 2007. *The Cambridge Introduction to the Short Story in English*. Cambridge: Cambridge University Press.
Hunter, Adrian. 2004. "Story into history: Alice Munro's minor literature". *English* 53. 219–238.
Jolley, Elizabeth. 1986. "Wednesdays and Fridays". In: Elizabeth Jolley. *Woman in a Lampshade*. London: Penguin. 150–156.
Kauffman, Linda S. 1992. *Special Delivery. Epistolary Modes in Modern Fiction*. Chicago: University of Chicago Press.
Koepke, Wulf. 1990. "Epistolary Fiction and Its Impact on Readers: Reality and Illusion". In: Frederick Burwick & Walter Pape (eds.). *Aesthetic Illusion: Theoretical and Historical Approaches*. Berlin: Walter de Gruyter. 263–74.
Lau, Doretta. 2014. "God Damn, How Real Is This?" In: Doretta Lau. *How Does a Single Blade of Grass Thank the Sun?* Gibson, BC: Nightwood Editions. 9–15.
Löschnigg, Maria. 2018. "Medialization as a Catalyst of Generic Change: Exploring Fictions of the Internet in Nick Hornby's *Juliet, Naked* (2009) and T.R. Richmond's *What She Left* (2015)". In: Vera Nünning & Ansgar Nünning (eds.). *The British Novel in the Twenty-First Century. Cultural Concerns – Literary Developments – Model Interpretations*. Trier: Wissenschaftlicher Verlag Trier. 327–42.
Löschnigg, Maria. 2017. "Carried Away by Letters: Alice Munro and the Epistolary Mode". In: Janice Fiamengo & Gerald Lynch (eds.). *Alice Munro's Miraculous Art. Critical Essays*. Ottawa: University of Ottawa Press. 97–113.
Löschnigg, Maria. 2014. *The Canadian Short Story in English. Continuity and Change*. Trier: Wissenschaftlicher Verlag Trier.
McEwan, Ian. 2016. *Nutshell*. London: Jonathan Cape.
McEwan, Ian. 1998/1997. *Enduring Love*. London: Vintage.
Mistry, Rohinton. 1987. *Tales from Firozsha Baag*. London: Faber and Faber.
Mullan, John. 2006. *How Novels Work*. Oxford: Oxford University Press.
Munro, Alice 1995/1994. "A Wilderness Station". In: Alice Munro. *Open Secrets*. London: Vintage. 190–225.
Munro, Alice. 1985/1974. "Material". In: Alice Munro. *Something I've Been Meaning to Tell You*. London: Penguin Books. 30–49.
Nischik, Reingard. 2017. *The English Short Story in Canada. From the Dawn of Modernism to the 2013 Nobel Prize*. Jefferson, NC: McFarland and Company.
Nünning, Ansgar & Jan Rupp. 2013. "Media and Medialization as Catalysts for Genre Development: Theoretical Frameworks, Analytical Concepts and a Selective Overview of Varieties of Intermedial Narration in British Fiction". In: Michael Basseler, Ansgar Nünning & Christine Schwaneke (eds.). *The Cultural Dynamics of Generic Change in*

Contemporary Fiction: Theoretical Frameworks, Genres and Model Interpretations. Trier: Wissenschaftlicher Verlag Trier. 201–34.

Neumann Birgit & Ansgar Nünning. 2008. *An Introduction to the Study of Narrative Fiction.* Stuttgart: Klett.

Oates, Joyce Carol. 2009. "Dear Joyce Carol,". In: Joyce Carol Oates. *Dear Husband,. Stories.* New York: Harper Collins. 227–237.

Oates, Joyce Carol. 2009. "Dear Husband,". In: Joyce Carol Oates. *Dear Husband,. Stories.* New York: Harper Collins. 316–326.

Perry, Ruth. 1980. *Women, Letters, and the Novel.* New York: AMS.

Pool, Gail (ed.). *Other People's Mail. An Anthology of Letter Stories.* Columbia and London: University of Missouri Press.

Richardson, Brian. 2006. *Unnatural Voices. Extreme Narration in Modern and Contemporary Fiction.* Columbus: Ohio State University Press.

Richmond, T.R. 2015. *What She Left.* London: Penguin Random House.

Ryan, Marie-Laure & Jan-Noël Thon. 2014. "Storyworlds across Media: Introduction". In: Marie-Laure Ryan & Jan-Noël Thon (eds.). *Storyworlds across Media: Towards a Media-Conscious Narratology.* Lincoln/London: University of Nebraska Press. 1–21.

Smith, Zadie 2005. *On Beauty.* New York, Toronto, London: Penguin.

Wright, Richard B. 2003/2001. *Clara Callan.* New York: Harper Perennial.

Part II: **The Epistolary Short Story**

Maria Löschnigg
The Epistolary Short Story and the Representation of History

Abstract: While authors have repeatedly chosen the narrative format of epistolary short fiction for rendering literary perspectives on historical events, this sub-genre has so far received no critical echo in discussions of theoretical and generic aspects of historical fiction. Taking a look at a wide range of epistolary stories addressing different historical periods, this chapter aims at contributing to closing this lacuna. It offers a narratological investigation into the specific narrative and communicative make-up of the epistolary form, exploring its potential for revisionist, alternative glimpses at history as it unfolds its specific aesthetic effect within the confined textual space of the short story. With its focus on the one-letter story, the framed letter story and the narrative use of postcards and telegrams, the chapter not only considers the great variety of epistolary short fiction, but also means to offer a useful narratological framework for the appreciation of epistolary short fiction as a unique literary vehicle for the mediation of historical content.

1 Introduction

As genres for the representation of historical and political events, neither the short story nor the epistolary form as a mode of narrative expression have received much critical attention. As far as the short story is concerned, this is due to the genre's lack of panoramic scope, which may explain why the dominant narrative forms to define what Aleida Assman (2010: 99) calls the "working memory" have been memoirs and novels, while short fiction has been deferred to the sphere of "reference memory", that is, the cultural reservoir. As Ann-Marie Einhaus has shown in her monograph *The Short Story and the First World War* (2013), this is definitely the case with regard to short fiction's relatively marginal position in the cultural memory of the First World War. Apart from the snapshot character of the short story, another reason for its marginalization is its stronger degree of literariness and experimental appeal, which not only reduces the extent of potential readership but has also often been linked to a lack of realist detail and credibility.

Scepticism with regard to the use of the epistolary mode for historical fiction dates back to Sir Walter Scott (cf. Beebee 1999: 169f.; Bower R. 2013: 57, 63), who problematized the genre's lack of objectivity and of "distinguishing between important and unimportant events" (Bower R. 2013: 5). These alleged 'deficiencies' are, however, exactly the features which cater to a modern understanding of historical knowledge, which questions the claim of objective representation and tends to favour multiple perspectives, including those of the marginal and the 'insignificant'. While Scott obviously *did* see the expressive capacities of the letter-form when he recognized the "faculty of the letter [to] facilitate[…] the creation of full, human characters" (Bower R. 2013: 63), arguing that the letter affords "the opportunity of placing characters, each in their own peculiar light, and contrasting their thoughts, plans and sentiments" (Scott 1968: 42), the general conventions of historical writing in the nineteenth century were just not receptive yet for these alternative and more dynamic approaches to history. Since Scott, it seems, criticism has more or less avoided paying attention to the intersection of epistolary writing and historical focus. While with regard to the novel, an increasing interest is discernible as to how "the unique structure of letters can open up historiographic possibilities" (Bower R. 2013: 59), epistolary short fiction constitutes a general lacuna in criticism. One of the few critics who have investigated the adequacy of the letter-form for narrating historical events is Rachel Bower. In her insightful interpretation of Michael Ondaatje's historical novel *In the Skin of a Lion*, she demonstrates compellingly how the "epistolary form lends itself to an interrogation of questions of history and temporality" (2013: 58). The fact that despite this scholarly ignorance concerning the short story in general and the letter-mode in particular, writers in the twentieth and twenty-first centuries have repeatedly turned to both the genre as well as the mode and have combined them successfully in historical epistolary stories shows that writers have recognized this genre's unique aesthetics of expression and effect. It also testifies to a conceptual shift concerning literary approaches to history, a shift that makes possible the appreciation of the rich narrative spectrum the epistolary form can offer.

To do justice to an intriguing generic variety of historical fiction and to make up for its marginalization in criticism, this chapter undertakes a narratological exploration of the subgenre of the epistolary short story with regard to the mediation of historical content. As will be shown on the example of epistolary stories addressing different historical periods, the letter, with its specific narrative and communicative make-up, offers valuable formats for revisionist, alternative glimpses at history and unfolds a specific aesthetic potential within the confined textual space of the short story. Moreover, the engagement with this critically marginalized literary form also contributes to its transference from the cultural reservoir to the working memory (cf. Einhaus 2013: 21). As the canon which defines the working or active memory includes works of art "which are repeatedly reread, appreciated, staged, performed and commented" (Assmann 2010: 99), the focus on works and genres which have held a place in the passive realm of the reference memory fulfils an important function as it enhances "the dynamics of cultural memory and keeps its energy flowing" (Assmann 2010: 104).

Letters are texts which are shaped by a specific addressee. In other words, not only the mere presence of an intratextual reader, who "alone distinguishes the letter from other first-person forms" (Altman 1982: 87) is to be considered, but also the respective identity of this internal addressee and the nature of his/her relationship with the internal writer. While the reaching out to a 'you' has an impact on the style and tone of the epistolary text, the letter as a whole actually becomes a material space that emblematically stands for a spatial/ideological/political/emotional gap while simultaneously being the medium that bridges this divide. "Epistolary language", as Altman (1982: 189) points out, "is polarly generated. We have noted throughout that the letter is both a reflection of the gap and an instrument for gap closing". In epistolary stories which address political issues and historical events, this aspect demands particular attention as the letter is a metonym for the distance that has been *forcefully* created between individuals who used to be close and can no longer communicate face-to-face.

Connected to the letter's polar signification, another aspect that needs consideration with regard to historical epistolary fiction is the letter's impact as a rhetorical and material form of agency in situations of restricted freedom (cf. Bower A. 1997: 12). In her monograph *Epistolary Responses*, Anne Bower wonders why "letter fiction's frequent focus on restricted freedom to communicate [...] and on the difficulties of communication" has not led to "encourage scholarly attention to contemporary epistolary fiction" (1997: 12). Indeed, one must agree with Bower on this issue, as authors *have* repeatedly used the letter-form to render situations of oppression, war and imprisonment, while there is hardly any criticism on the function of epistolary discourse with regard to the mediation of the above-mentioned issues. As Bower makes clear, "absence/presence is *so* essential to letters – an agonizing pull between here and there, intimacy and separation, bonds and barriers, time present and future (or past and present), the tangible and the intangible" (Bower A. 1997: 16; cf. also Altman 1982: 13–15) that its instrumentalisation for narratives of crisis is not surprising. In short fiction where moments of crisis are rendered in a concentrated form, the letter with its implied gap lends itself particularly well to foreground the effects of political conflict on social relationships.

Apart from the letter's unique aesthetic function, which ensues from the impact of the internal reader as well as from its status as a multivalent communicative act denoting agency, letters also yield a high degree of authenticity. Letters not only render the illusion of encountering a genuine document from the respective time, thus enhancing the aura of historicity, but are also defined by a high degree of immediacy. This results from a dominance of the experiencing self and the narrativization of the present of narration, that is, the here and now out of which the epistolary discourse emerges. The 'authentification' of epistolary fiction, as Altman puts it, can be related "to the phenomenon of 'presentification' [...], whereby the writer tries to create the illusion that both he and his addressee are immediately present to each other and to the action" (1982: 202). At the same time, the conflation of internal and external addressee, which Altman has referred to as the "*mise-en-abyme* of the writer-reader relationship" (1982: 200), caters to the metaleptic illusion of transcending time and space, thus drawing the reader into the respective historical context. The letter thus, paradoxically, creates authenticity and historicity while simultaneously foregrounding the construed nature of historical narrative, as it is always clear that the account we get is written by a certain 'involved' person and affected by the presence of an internal reader.

In the following, the range of aesthetic expressions that result from the above-mentioned features of the epistolary mode will be investigated with regard to the genre of the short story and with a view to their functionality for a literary representation of history. I shall first explore the one-letter story as a specific form of epistolary discourse and its signification of meaning in Graham Swift's "Haematology" and Ken Saro-Wiwa's "Africa Kills Her Sun". Even though the historical sites featured in these stories could not be further apart – one relating to the English Civil War in the seventeenth century, the other to the Ogoni war in Nigeria in the 1990s – there are many similarities as to the function of epistolary discourse with regard to the narrative depiction of history. The second focus will be on the First World War, one of the most prominent sites of memory internationally, and one which has assumed renewed interest with the 2014–18 centenary. The short story, as Ann-Marie Einhaus has pointed out, offers a "wide range of different fictional interpretations [...] that can challenge and add depth to the myth of the war and its literary canon" (2013: 6). As opposed to one-letter stories such as "Haematology" and "Africa Kills Her Sun", letters in First World War stories hold a seemingly minor position. However, the epistolary short story is not defined by the spatial prominence of letters in the text but rather, as will be shown, by their importance for the overall effect of the story, for their impact on the characters and the plot against the backdrop of the experience of the war.

2 The One-Letter Story as a Vehicle of Historical Impact and Political Intent

The one-letter story seems to pose a paradox: while it may be taken to represent the 'purest' form of the epistolary story as the letter actually *is* the story, the absence of the voice of the addressee might at the same time suggest an affinity to diary narratives. However, as opposed to the diary, one-directional epistolary narrative is always strongly shaped by the addressee, who informs the style and content of the letter, thus definitely fulfilling one of the most important generic criteria of epistolary discourse (cf. Koepke 1990: 263; Altman 1982: 88). Thus, even those letter-stories that lack any dialogic structure refute Ruth Perry's claim that epistolary fictions transcribe "uncensored streams of consciousness" (1980: 128). The addressee-inclined definition of the letter indeed challenges the letter's "long tradition of adding veracity to a fictional narrative" (Bayer 2009: 174). One may even claim that with the inherent "persuasive element" (Koepke 1990: 263) which derives from the focus on a 'you', the epistolary mode is one of the most unreliable forms of first-person narration. However, the issue of reliability in most letter narratives is suspended by the specific communicative structure of the letter and by the transparent exhibition of its purpose and discursively enacted reality.

Letters come "in the shape of an edited version of reality" (Bayer 2009: 175) which is defined by the nature of the relationship between letter writer and intended reader. Apart from those letters specifically designed to deceive the reader[1], the envisioned addressee does normally not affect the truthfulness or credibility of a letter, but rather determines the *how* of mediation, including the careful selection and distribution of information. This reader-centredness thus highlights and makes visible the socially determined variability of subjectivity. Moreover, it merges the depiction of historical/political reality with the dimension of human relationships. Gerd Bayer describes this 'phatic function' of letters, which should by no means be underestimated, as follows:

> What characterizes a letter is not the relationship it might have to reality, but rather the nature of the relationship between the author and the reader, or rather between the epistolary narrator and the epistolary narratee. This implicit inclusion of the narratee most significantly shapes the tone of the letter. (2009: 176)

---

[1] Examples of such deceptive letters are Alice Munro's "Hateship, Friendship, Courtship, Loveship, Marriage" (2001) or "The Jack Randa Hotel" (1994), as well as the spy story "Giulia Lazzari" (1928) by W. Somerset Maugham.

With regard to the use of letters for historical short fiction, this yields an interesting narrative potential. In the stories discussed in this chapter, internal author and reader are separated by political circumstances. Even though the letters also disclose factual information about their specific historical periods their main value lies in the foregrounding of the impact these political events have or had on social relationships. Two aspects, in particular, are responsible for this genre-specific approach to history. First, reflection and analysis dominate over report or, as Altman elaborates, "many of [the letter's] narrative events may be nonnarrated events of which we see only the repercussions" (1982: 207). Second, the relationship between internal narrator and narratee also defines the performative function of letter narratives. Through their performativity, letter narratives, in particular those which do without a frame, display a high degree of "discursive self-consciousness" which "is overtly challenging the novel's [and short story's] traditional narrativity" (Altman 1982: 211). Altman explains this phenomenon as follows:

> The complexities of the interrelationship between *histoire* and *discours* are particularly visible in epistolary fiction, where *histoire* can be generated only through *discours*, and where the actions constituting *histoire* are not simply narrated but often enacted, and occasionally nonnarrated. (1982: 210)

In addition to the letter's potential to reflect on and/or enact 'events' rather than reporting them, another issue that deserves attention is the question with whom the reader of an epistolary discourse identifies (cf. Altman 1982: 193). While in most first-person forms the (implied) addressee remains vague and anonymous, the integration of a clearly identifiable internal reader offers an explanatory foil for the refraction of perspective on the part of the narrator. In other words, the internal reader, even though he/she is denied a voice in these one-letter stories, constitutes an additional interpretive instance, a frame of reference against which the content and style of the epistolary story is evaluated. At the same time, the unframed relating to a 'you' endows the addressee with a shape and identity encouraging a dual receptive process which involves identification with both internal writer *and* internal reader. Identification with the internal reader, in particular, is engendered by a direct and systematic addressing of a 'you' which, diegetically, remains within the world of the story, but has a tendency towards metaleptic transgression, thus affecting and involving the extratextual reader in a way not comparable to other narrative modes.

Concerning the aspect of authenticity which, after all, plays a considerable role for historical fiction, it must again be emphasized that in many epistolary narratives language is used "to present a seemingly unmediated transcription of internal and external reality" (Altman 1982: 194). In the stories discussed in this section, the authors integrate yet another element of trustworthiness by using epistolary narrators who render the impression of being authorized – by their historical validity, their social position or their insider knowledge of the related content – to mediate the story. In the following, the intersection of the generic features introduced in this section with the mediation of historical content will be further discussed on the example of two representative one-letter stories.

Graham Swift: "Haematology"

The story "Haematology" (2014)[2] by Graham Swift consists of one single letter composed by William Harvey, physician of the late King Charles I, and addressed to his cousin Ned, who has risen to the position of Colonel Edward Francis in Oliver Cromwell's regime. The letter is written a week after Charles' execution – "the seventh day" of the creation of "a new world" (35), as William Harvey sarcastically remarks – and focuses on the absurdity of civil war (or war in general), which makes enemies of people who actually have much more in common than what separates them. The letter, being "a both-and, either-or phenomenon, signifying either bridge or barrier, both presence and absence" (Altman 1982: 189), proves to be an ideal format for rendering this situation. The letter's main purpose is its phatic function of re-connection, which constitutes an important element of the 'action' of the story. The persuasive rhetoric which the writer, William Harvey, employs in order to bring about this performative act is already suggested by the title, and involves various implications of blood.

By using the word 'cousin' in his address as well as in his signature, and highlighting the familial bond and shared past by frequent references to a 'we', their 'blood relation' is emphasized while simultaneously exposing their political enmity as absurd. The story's title, "Haematology", also refers to William Harvey's profession as a physician and to the historical William Harvey's seminal contributions to anatomy and the study of blood physiology. In fact, Harvey's groundbreaking theories published in 1628 and commonly referred to as *De Motu Cordis*, turn out to be a rich meaning-making subtext, which the letter writer consciously employs for his persuasive rhetoric. Harvey's discovery of the phases of the heart's motion (contraction and expansion) as well as of the movement of blood as a circulation system are linked to the "fortunes of men, an ebb

---

[2] Graham Swift (2014). "Haematology". In: G. S. *England and Other Stories*. London and New York: Simon & Schuster. 31–42. (Page references are to this edition.)

and flow, a rise and fall" (33), suggesting, among others, that also Cromwell's new regime will be subject to change. Interestingly, the historical Harvey's findings unwittingly led to a de-mystification of the assumed superiority of 'Royal blood' thus implicitly questioning Charles I's divine right and supporting the enemy camp. In the story, this irony strengthens Harvey's argument that he is "charged with the King's body, not with the body politick" (38).

The other important analogy is that of the composition of blood, which in all human beings shows more similarities than differences. Drawing from this, the absurdity of war and of killing due to politically created enmities is radically exposed:

> But was it not proven when that royal blood – may we even call it that? – spurted forth but a week ago at Whitehall? And is it not proven when any man's head or limb is severed from his body, as has been the lot of many men – nay, of women and children – in these late times? A king is but a man like any other. Has it needed seven years of war and a trial by Parliament to determine the matter, when any such as I might have attested to it? Anatomy is no respecter. I have dissected criminals and examined kings. Does it need any special statute to claim the one might be the other? (32)

As this passage shows, "Haematology" definitely renders verifiable facts and details from the period of the English Civil War. It also renders reliable facts about the correspondent himself, like references to his studies in Padua (cf. 34) or his marriage to Elizabeth Browne, daughter of Elizabeth I's and James I's physician. However, we do not turn to literature for factual accounts of historical events. What literature can offer are interpretations of the past which provide perspectives and insights that are not transferrable by factual discourses and which make the past relatable for later generations. While the novel may provide more comprehensive views on history, it is the short story's strength to highlight and scrutinize specific facets. In the case of the one-letter story, this is the envisioning of an internal perspective vis-à-vis another. Many passages are philosophical and argumentative rather than narrative, thus reflecting the repercussions of historical events rather than the events themselves.

The most important 'event' of the story, that is William's attempt to reconnect with his cousin, is enacted by a strong foregrounding of the pronoun 'you', frequently merging in the collective 'we', thus highlighting commonalities rather than difference. In other words, William offers Edward not only his cousin's own story[3] – a feature very common in epistolary discourse – but he also

---

[3] See for example: "There was a smile on your lips, but there was a smouldering in your eyes. You poured another cup of ale" (37).

serves him their *common* story, not only from the time before the civil war has torn the country as well as families apart, but also in a present and anticipatory way: "I was never a man of arms, but I am haunted by the dream, Ned, that we face each other on a field of battle. I have no potion to drive away the stubborn vision. We both have swords drawn. They are not wooden rulers. It is not apples and orchards. It has come to this" (41). Apart from these fear-ridden speculations about possible future encounters, William also refers to the actual day of execution which they both attended as representatives of two different political camps: "Yet tell me, did we see each other? And tell me, might we yet, in the time remaining to us, see each other again? We are kinsmen and, whatever the divisions between us, we are now old men" (42). The letter ends with an appeal to his cousin, an invitation to come and join him at his brother's house and live with him: "We should sit and be at peace, Ned, and talk, as old men are given to talk" (42). These passages definitely confirm Altman's observation that "underlying the epistolary dialogue are common memories and often common experiences" (1982: 119), as well as Bayer's emphasis on the phatic function of the letter, which is often "not meant to communicate reality but to endear the letter writer to the addressee" (2009: 176). Moreover, the focus on the 'you' leads to a fleshing out of the internal reader, thus facilitating what I have earlier referred to as dual receptive process, that is, the reader's identification with both, internal narrator *and* reader. While the repeated use of the informal name 'Ned' accentuates the familiarity between the cousins, the 'you' that punctuates the text functions as a vortex that draws the reader into the story, leading to an ontological conflation of intra- and extratextual levels.

Considering, as Nünning (1993: 153) claims, that many of Swift's stories and novels demonstrate and thematize the insurmountability of chasms between individuals, "Haematology" constitutes an exception in the oeuvre of the British author. By choosing the format of the letter, the story is staged as a performative act to overcome the crisis of communication between individuals torn apart by external events. The internal author William Harvey actively shapes the letter for his specific reader, Colonel Edward Francis, with the phatic aim of (re-)establishing a bridge and with the appellative aim of persuading him to reconnect again. At the same time, this fictionalized historical persona offers his cousin (and the external reader) his interpretation of history, which, in turn, is rhetorically instrumentalized to speak out against the divisive power of politics and to achieve reconciliation. The ending of the story – as of most one-letter stories – has the effect of a mystery that is never resolved, as we never find out what impact William Harvey's letter has on his cousin. Creating this communicative gap encourages the reader to evaluate the letter on two levels, the historical level, according to its possible effects on Harvey's cousin, and a contemporary level with regard to its effect on the external reader himself/herself. The performative aim of the letter to elicit a response is further heightened by the strong interrogative structure of the letter.

By using a historical figure of the time of the English Civil War and employing him as an epistolary narrator addressing his cousin, Swift creates the illusion of actually listening to a voice of the time. While this establishes authenticity and enhances the historical impact of the story, Harvey's rhetoric transcends the seventeenth-century armed conflict between Royalists and Parliamentarians and exposes the absurdity of politically designed enmities and ensuing violence. Shaping his literary depiction of the English Civil War in the form of a letter, and exploiting the letter's implication of separation and bond as well as its specific communicative appeal for the extratextual reader, Swift allows for innovative approaches to a conflicted period of the past.

Ken Saro-Wiwa: "Africa Kills Her Sun"

In a similar manner as Graham Swift, Nigerian author, activist and political martyr Ken Saro-Wiwa employs the format of the unidirectional letter story in "Africa Kills Her Son" (1989)[4] in order to highlight politically imposed separation and isolation. However, while Graham Swift looks at history from the distance of several centuries, Saro-Wiwa was actually personally involved in the conflict to which his story relates. In fact, his embroilment in the power struggle "with the Nigerian military government over the rights of the Ogoni and the degradation of their environment by international oil companies" (Gikandi 2009: 482) resulted in his execution in 1995 through the military government of General Sani Abacha, an execution which, according to Charles E. Larson, was "swift and brutal, a travesty of human rights and a failure of international diplomacy" (1998: 210). "By the time of his execution", as Gareth Griffiths remarks, "Ken Saro-Wiwa had earned a reputation as one of Nigeria's most prolific, and talented writers" (2000: 198). His position as a writer rests, above all, on his novel *Soza Boy* (1985), which focuses on the Nigerian Civil War/Biafran War (1967–70). Having experimented with many different genres, including popular ones, Saro-Wiwa also published two collections of short fiction, one of them, *Adaku and Other Stories* (1989), including the epistolary narrative "Africa Kills

---

[4] Ken Saro-Wiwa (1997/1989). "Africa Kills Her Sun". In: Charles R. Larson (ed.). *Under African Skies. Modern African Stories.* New York: Farrar, Straus and Giroux. 212–221. (Page references are to this edition.)

Her Sun". Historically, the story focuses on the military dictatorship of Ibrahim Banangida (1985–1993), characterized, as most of the other dictatorships that determined the political life of the country since its independence in 1966, by corruption, human rights violations and environmental degradation. In particular, Saro-Wiwa's story relates to the protest of representatives of the Ogoni people against the irreversible devastation of their region in the Niger Delta by *Shell* and other oil companies. The story envisions the time before Saro-Wiwa founded the non-violent *Movement for the Survival of the Ogoni People* (MOSOP) and published the *Ogoni Bill of Rights* in 1990, and before the conflict escalated when, between 1992 and 1994, the government killed hundreds of people and wiped out 30 villages, leaving about 30.000 Ogoni people homeless (cf. *Global Nonviolent Action Databse*, n. pag.). Knowing about Ken Saro-Wiwa's execution a year later makes it difficult not to see the fact that Bana, the main character and epistolary narrator of the story, writes his letter in prison on the night before his execution as a gloomy anticipation of the real author's own – hauntingly similar – fate.

Structurally, Swift's and Saro-Wiwa's stories display many similarities, yet while the aesthetic effect of "Haematology" is based most strongly on the prominent focus on a 'you', "Africa Kills Her Sun" relies for its effect, first, on its foregrounding of the present of narration and, second, on the material function of the letter. The former is achieved through the correlation of story time and discourse time, that is, the epistolary narrative actually captures the night before Bana's execution and is also narrativized as the time he needs to write his letter to his friend of youth, Zole. This also confirms Altman's observation that "the pivotal time in epistolary discourse is [...] the present, and the pivotal tense is the present of narration (*Erzählzeit*)" (1982: 123). Even though in a number of external analepses, Bana refers to Zole's and his shared past, and to past political events which are causally connected to the even more distant (pre-)colonial past when their forebears "sold their kinsmen into slavery for minor items such as beads, mirrors, alcohol and tobacco" (217), and to the future in a proleptic passage envisioning his execution, the core story is that of Bana in his cell, writing a letter a few hours before his execution. Remarks such as, "Time is running out, Zole. Sazan and Jimba are awake now." (219), "Day has dawned and I haven't finished my letter" (220), and "My time here expires and I must send you all my love" (221), ensure that the reader retains the impression of immediacy and urgency that in turn support the aura of authenticity and create a strong appeal on the external receptive level. The use of the present tense and the suggested simultaneity of recording and recorded event create the illusion of a merging of experiencing self and narrating self. Even though, as Bray explains, there will always be a gap between time of narration and narrated time, no matter how slight, entailing that "the two selves of the first-person letter writer [...] remain distinct" (Bray 2003: 20), this slight delay seems to me irrelevant as soon as we talk about the effect of the closeness between narrating/experiencing self and between narrated time/time of narration. In fact, in statements such as, "Time is running out, Zole. Sazan and Jimba are awake now." (219), the writing of this line and the actual running out of time are indeed coextensive. What still remains distinct, however, are the two selves, that is, Bana's self as a recorder and Bana's self as the one who feels the passing of time. As this distinction, however, is reduced to a minimum, and as temporally the two selves are indeed connected in parallel, the aesthetic effect is that of 'writing to the moment', thus underlining what Altman has referred to as the 'presentification' (cf. 1982: 202) of action, writer and reader. Together with the "*mise-en-abyme* of the writer-reader relationship" (Altman 1982: 212), this makes possible an aesthetic effect on the reader which, in this manner and urgency, is not to be achieved through other forms of narrative. The fact that the format of the one-letter story holds a particular appeal for the external reader is shown by actual readers' responses to "Africa Kills Her Sun" on the Internet, where they have published letters in reply to the fictitious character of Bana, signing it with Zole.[5]

The second prominent function of the letter-mode in Saro-Wiwa's story is its material representation of the epitaph which the narrator Bana wants his friend Zole to erect. In fact, this request is one of the main purposes of Bana's letter, and also an important story element which, as could already be seen in Swift's story, is again *enacted* through the appellative structure of discourse rather than *told*. At the beginning of his letter, Bana mentions his central concern only in passing, putting the emphasis rather on Zole's role of a confident:

> I still remember you, have always remembered you, and it's logical that on the night before tomorrow, I should write you to ask a small favor of you. But more important, the knowledge that I have unburdened myself to you will make tomorrow morning's event as pleasant and desirable to me as to the thousands of spectators who will witness it. (212)

Towards the end of the letter, the actual request moves centre stage: "And now I come to what I consider the most important part of this letter. My epitaph" (220). Considering again the cliffhanger quality of one-letter stories, we do not know

---

5 See, for example "After Sunset (A Reply to Ken Saro-Wiwa's Africa Kills her Sun)" (http://www.wamathai.com/2012/08/22/after-sunset-reply-to-ken-saro-wiwas-africa-kills-her-sun/#comments); or "Our Sons Kill Africa: A Reply to Ken Saro_Wiwa's Africa Kills her Sun" (http://the-divine-bandit.com/2012/08/16/our-sons-kill-africa-a-reply-to-ken-saro-wiwas-africa-kills-her-sun/) [both accessed 8 September 2017].

whether Zole ever receives the letter and whether she succeeds in fulfilling Bana's wish. Metaphorically, however, the letter already stands for this epitaph as well as representing the "microphone" (218) Bana would like to have in the stadium where they will be executed, "a microphone that will reverberate through the Stadium, nay, through the country as a whole!" (218) The letter literally contains the epitaph (twice): "'Africa Kills Her Sun.' A good epitaph, eh? Cryptic. Definite. A stroke of genius, I should say. I'm sure you'll agree with me. 'Africa Kills Her Sun!' That's why she's been described as the Dark Continent? Yes?" (221). Most of the letter, in fact, is an explication of the epitaph in the form of a black satire of corrupted Nigeria, where the common connotations of life and death, of freedom and imprisonment are radically reversed.

Not least, the story is also a defense: even though Bana does not care about what the corrupt court thinks of him, he wants to make sure that those who care should know the truth, know about the political weight of his death, know that he is not a murderer. Zole metonymically stands for the world, for all those whom the fictive letter-writer Bana as well as the historical author Ken Saro-Wiwa means/meant to reach. Sending this letter gives his death a purpose: "As this night dissolves into day, Sazan, Jimba and I shall be free. Sazan and Jimba will have left nothing behind. I shall leave at least this letter, which, please, keep for posterity" (217). By having chosen the letter-form for this story, the author has opted for a narrative mode that, as has been shown, "is a congenial method to make characters and the historical context out of which they write tangible for the reading audience", or, as Rachel Bower puts it, to "*make the past present* for a future reader" (2013: 62).

3 Epistolary First World War Stories

Addressing the traumatic experience of the First World War, several authors have turned to the genre of the short story and have integrated letters, notes, telegrams and field postcards in order to enhance the aesthetic effect of their narratives. "Short stories", as Ann-Marie Einhaus observes, "often use the war as plot intensifier and have greater interest in formal characteristics, whereas other, especially non-fictional war texts have little interest in form beyond its relationship to the perceived authenticity of a text. War as a topic appears to demand realism, genre demands artistry" (2013: 27). Through their different focus, which results from the idiosyncratic structural parameters of short fiction, First World War stories "challenge and complement existing cultural assumptions about the war" (Einhaus 2013: 8). Agreeing with Einhaus (2013: 7) that "exploring the short-story genre as a new field of writing about the war contributes to opening up new avenues for critical inquiry", I should like to add that this endeavor is particularly rewarding with regard to an exploration of the use of the epistolary mode in war stories.

In letter stories addressing the First World War, epistolary formats are embedded in the larger framework of first- or third-person narratives and thus seem to hold a minor position in comparison to the one-letter story discussed in the previous section. However, following more recent concepts of epistolarity, the epistolary genre in this chapter – as in fact throughout the whole volume – is not defined according to quantity but quality, that is, according to the prominence of the aesthetic effect produced by letters, notes, cards etc. In the stories which are in the centre of this subchapter, the aesthetic effect results to a large extent from the meaning-making reciprocal relationship between the frame and the integrated epistolary hypo-structures. While the framed letter story shares some features with the one-letter story, as for instance the letter's material evidence of lives torn apart by political circumstances, there is also a set of functions and effects which results from the frame, from the more concrete textual manifestation of the internal reader and from the multi-vocal structure of such stories. Indeed, the letter-induced polyvocality of these stories complexifies the narrative voice of the frame through seemingly authentic first-person voices, or, as in multidirectional epistolary stories, through rendering different perspectives (often contrasting the home front with the battlefront). The fragmentation suggested already by the slice-of-life quality of short fiction is further enhanced by the disruption of linear storylines ensuing from the inclusion of epistolary passages. Through this, the epistolary short story mirrors, on the discursive level, the disruption of lives torn by the dynamics of war.

Stories Written During or Shortly After the Great War

A number of authors who published war stories between 1914 and the beginning of World War II have turned to the letter for their narrative mediation of experiences of the First World War. Letters play a role, for example in Edgar Jepson's "Albert's Return" (1919), or in Richard Marsh's "Scandalous" (1916), where the "[y]oung protagonist Ethel receives a letter from the front, left in an abandoned overcoat and posted to her by a young soldier who found the coat" (Einhaus 2013: 92). In "An Autumn Gathering" (1918) by Alec Waugh, a young English officer comes upon Pieter's last letter to Gretchen, which makes him reflect on the absurdity of war.

In "Giulia Lazzari" (1928) by W. Somerset Maugham, in turn, the letter is a tool of deception, creating a suspenseful spy story, but also highlighting the atmosphere of suspicion and distrust which is a consequence of nations at war. The story has been collected in Maugham's *Ashenden, Or, The British Agent*, featuring the recurring figure of agent Ashenden, who "frequently finds himself in situations where he has to suppress natural feelings of sympathy and compassion in order to do his job, and counter espionage and the thwarting of enemy plans are here no longer presented as straightforward patriotic acts" (Einhaus 2013: 123). In "Giulia Lazzari", Ashenden's task is to get a hold of the Indian Spy Chandra Lal, who works for the Germans, through the (enforced) help of his girlfriend Giulia. While the story is largely told from the point of view of agent Ashenden, Chandra's voice is mediated via his intercepted letters. One of Chandra's letters, which Ashenden reads out to Giulia, is paraphrased by the agent and commented upon from his point of view. The emotional intensity of the letter, which "was eager and passionate" and full of "hot fire that burned the pages" (Maugham 2007: 149) contrasts painfully with Ashenden's official discourse and function, which forces the agent not only to ignore the 'human' aspect of Chandra's identity but also to exploit it for catching the spy. The dramatic epistolary effect is further enhanced by the disturbing violation of the voice of Giulia, who is forced to write letters to her lover, dictated by Ashenden, which are meant to entice Chandra to come and see her and thus walk right into the trap laid out for him. Ashenden's devilish plan succeeds, but Chandra manages to kill himself before being tried and executed.

An extremely disturbing story which also relies on the impact of letters, is John Galsworthy's "Told by the Schoolmaster" (1926). It is the story of not yet sixteen-year-old Jim Beckett, who, in the summer of 1914, fakes his age in order to be accepted by the army. The reader meets Jim again in September 1915, when he proudly tells the schoolmaster not only that he will be going to France on the next day, but also that he and his 16-year-old girlfriend got married. While Jim's letters to Betty are partly paraphrased by the schoolmaster, it is another letter, namely that of Betty's mother to Jim, which proves to have fatal consequences for the young soldier. Telling Jim that his wife will soon give birth, Jim resolves to ask for leave, "but they wouldn't give it" (221). When Jim lingers on after the birth of his son, in July 1916, "when the Somme battle was at its height" (220), his wife gets nervous and talks to the constable in order to prevent her husband from getting into trouble. As a consequence, and to Betty's utter dismay, Jim is taken to France and court-martialled for "[d]eserting in the face of the enemy" (222). While the reader is denied the letters the schoolmaster writes to the authorities on behalf of his former pupil Jim Beckett, the letter the schoolmaster receives in return from the chaplain is included in full:

> Dear Sir,
> The boy Jim Beckett was shot to-day at dawn. I am distressed at having to tell you and the poor child his wife. War is a cruel thing indeed.
> [...]
> Private considerations count for nothing in such circumstances – the rule is adamant. (Galsworthy 2007: 223)

The guilt-ridden schoolmaster, who tells the story and cannot forgive himself for not having revealed Jim's true age while it could still have made a change, aptly concludes the story: "A little ironical though, that his own side should shoot him, who went to fight for them two years before he needed, to shoot him who wouldn't be legal food for powder for another month!" (Galsworthy 2007: 223). The official letter highlights the incompatibility of private and public concerns in times of war. The absurdity of war which renders the killing of a child 'necessary' is made more radically visible by contrasting the voice of the chaplain (through his official letter) with the emotional first-person voice of the schoolmaster.

Even more radically than in "Told by the Schoolmaster", the narrator's guilt motivates the story in A. W. Wells' "Chanson Triste". With its setting at the border between Bulgaria and Macedonia and the unusual situation depicted in the story, "Chanson Trieste" is also a memorable example of the short story's contribution to a more multifaceted cultural memory of the Great War. The story features an English soldier's fraternizing with the Bulgarian enemy soldier Nicolas Dimitri, who hides in a hut in the hills and with whom the narrator communicates via the exchange of books, letters, gifts and photographs. The letters, parts of which are paraphrased in the story, are material evidence for the war-induced barrier between the two men, while at the same time enacting a strong bond: "All that I seemed to live for, at that time, was the weekly letters, hidden under the large, flat boulder in the little straw-thatched hut" (Wells 2007: 115). As I have shown elsewhere (cf. Löschnigg 2017), the impossibility of face-to-face contact nourishes the correspondents' fantasies, which are further supported by their drawing on commonalities, in this case, by their seeing each other as "apostles of the new world that is to arise from all this crimson chaos" (Wells 117). In retrospect, the narrator reflects on their 'epistolary' fraternization as follows:

> I leave it entirely to the psychologists to explain the strange compelling attraction, the almost romantic glamour, that sometimes pervaded this friendship of ours, right from the very beginning. Times there must have been, of course, when both of us must have reflected that what we were doing was utterly wrong and deceitful: that we were committing a crime for which, had they discovered it, the countries whose uniforms we wore would immediately have had us shot, and buried like so much loathsome carrion; and yet, speaking for my-

self, I can only say that always uppermost in my mind was a feeling of stupendous glamour about our association [...]. (Wells 2007: 115)

This 'glamour' comes to an abrupt end when Dimitri leaves a note saying, "Shall be going from here end of this week, [...] hope we shall meet sometime", and the narrator answers by urging Dimitri to dare an encounter: "Wednesday, midnight. Come, I shall be here. I shall not fail" (Wells 2007: 117). Through this note, the narrator unwittingly leads his friend to his death, as his own English comrades, having become suspicious, send a patrol exactly to their prospective meeting place. Dimitri is shot, and before he dies the narrator has the feeling that he looks at him and recognizes him and will die thinking that he, "the man whom he had hailed as an affinity of a nobler, cleaner world, had lured him to that death" (118). Letters in this story are the medium to create deep friendship while at the same time becoming the instrument of the brutal mechanisms of war. Giving the letter in this story this two-fold function proves to be a compelling narrative tool to highlight the dehumanizing incompatibility of private feelings and military duties.

The epistolary effect of the story, however, is not limited to the exchange of letters within the framed tale, which is triggered by a scenario in the narrator's present, that is, a couple of years after the end of the First World War. Attending a concert with his wife, the narrator rashly leaves the concert hall when the orchestra plays Tschaikovsky's "Chanson Triste", the tune which he once heard Dimitri whistle. Hearing "Chanson Triste" elicits the actual core story, which in turn frames the fatal notes exchanged by the two enemy soldiers. Even though the story, at first sight, seems to be a typical first-person narration, the excessive addressing of the 'you' as well as the occasional narrativizing of the writing process reveal a strong affinity to the epistolary form.[6] When the troubled narrator writes, "[a] thousand times still, I am afraid, my mind must rehearse and endure it again" (117), we are reminded of Coleridge's "Ancient Mariner", condemned to tell his story again and again to make up for his crime. At the same time, however, the writing down of the story and addressing it to an anonymous but still strongly accentuated implied reader, seems to suspend the 'curse' in "Chanson Triste" and put the narrator's mind at ease (cf. Wells 2007: 111).

Even though Wells' story lacks the clearly identifiable addressee that is a generic marker of the one-letter story, the narrative nonetheless unfolds the aesthetic effect typical of this genre: reaching out to an unnamed reader on the die-

---

6 See for example: "And I would have you imagine..." (Wells 2007: 112), "I wish I could convey to you..." (113), "But I will not trouble you with these" (115), "and even now as I write" (116).

getic level, a reader who is repeatedly addressed and interwoven into the narrative, leads to the semi-coalescence of internal and external reader that, as we have seen in the previous section, defines one-directional epistolary discourse. The actual reader is put in the role of the confident and feels directly spoken to. Apart from this effect on the receptive level, the story also thematizes the function of narrative with regard to the extreme experience of war. Einhaus captures this function as follows:

> The narrator touches upon two crucial points with respect to the relationship between mourning and writing about war: first, the potentially therapeutic effect of writing about one's own war experience ('I have sometimes thought that if I put it all down on paper, precisely and exactly as it occurred, my mind might become easier'), and second, the comforting nature of being able to relate these experiences to those of others through the medium of narrative, denied to the narrator by a lack of literary counterparts to his own experience. (Einhaus 2013: 90)

"Chanson Triste" is a particularly compelling example of the narrative potential of the letter form for stories depicting war scenarios. The story fully exploits the letter's double status as a token of bond as well as of separation. It further makes ample use of the letter's "potential to 'carry away' the recipient emotionally or to serve as a trigger for imaginary worlds" (Löschnigg 2017: 98). In addition, the epistolary make-up of the whole story not only points to the therapeutic function of writing but also produces a strong appeal for the external reader.

Looking Back on the First World War from a Distance

As Ann-Marie Einhaus has noted, "rather than offering narrative models for actual memories and experiences, later literary commentators on the war engage with issues of remembrance and historicity, or make use of the war as a defining event in British popular consciousness that can serve numerous purposes as a plot intensifier, reference point or metaphor for futility" (2013: 144). This observation also holds true for epistolary war stories, where letters serve as triggers for the act of remembering, enhance the historicity of the content as well as the illusion of listening to authentic voices from the past, and function as material evidence of lives torn apart. The letter as memory-trigger is used by Elizabeth Bowen in "The Demon Lover" (1945), in which Mrs. Drover "is suddenly confronted with her past through a ghostly letter from her former fiancé, who was to the best of her knowledge killed twenty-five years previously in the summer of 1916" (Einhaus 2013: 143). Two contemporary epistolary stories, in which commemoration plays a role, are Hazel Gaynor's "Hush" (2016) and Julian Barnes' "Evermore" (1996). The focus, here, will be on "Evermore" due its unique exploitation of the minimalist aesthetics of military postcards.

"Evermore", as Einhaus elaborates, "addresses the issue of mourning and remembrance in a more remote, self-conscious manner and can be read as a detached sociological and psychological study of mourning rather than an attempt to interpret and alleviate grief for a readership still caught up in the emotions that accompany bereavement" (2013: 144). For fifty years Miss Moss, the protagonist and focalizer of the story, has used her holidays for a tour of the cemeteries of the Western Front to mourn the death of her brother Sam buried at Cabaret Rouge. On these tours she always carries with her Sam's last three field postcards: "On the day itself, she would unknot the bag and trace her eyes over the jerky pencilled address, the formal signature (initials and surname only), the obedient crossings-out. For many years she had ached at what the cards did not say" (345).[7] Frank Davey (2018 forthcoming) describes this form of truncated communication as follows:

> These military postcards resembled the pre-1902 British picture postcard, with no message being allowed on the address side and the message replacing the picture. The French and German cards used censorship to control the message, while the British and Canadian ones provided a pre-printed message which in some ways resembled a blank cheque. The soldier was invited to insert his signature, his service number, and in some cards to add or delete a limited amount of prescribed information. But unlike the cheque, the card threatened its own destruction should excess information be inserted.

In the story, the "brutal choices" (345) these postcards dictated and which "also erased any indication of thought" (Davey 2018 forthcoming), signify the erasure of private identity which, in the case of Sam, prefigure his actual extinction. The standardized field postcard with its drastically limited choices achieved by erasure, textually mirrors the systematic war machinery of destruction (cf. Davey 2018 forthcoming). Through the 'staging' of such a military postcard in his story "Evermore", Barnes has employed a compelling technique to convey the restriction brought forth by martial law. At the same time, the integrated card functions as a strong marker of historicity.

As far as Miss Moss in "Evermore" is concerned, the minimal and maimed communicative value of these postcards forces her to focus on the writing itself, on the way the letters are formed, the thickness of the pencil line used for era-

---

[7] Julian Barnes. 2007/1996. "Evermore". In: Barbara Korte & Ann-Marie Einhaus (eds.). *The Penguin Book of First World War Stories*. London: Penguin. 345–361. (Page references in brackets are to this edition.)

sure etc., in order to squeeze some meaning out of the 'message'. Through her zooming gaze, the focalizer also forces the reader to follow the "large looping S with a circling full stop after it" (346) and interpret it as an iconic representation of the abrupt and premature end of a life cycle. On one card, though, the mourning sister finds a digression, where Sam has added two elliptic sentences, which miraculously have escaped censorship: "50 yds from the Germans. Posted from Trench" (346). Given the brutally restrictive corset of the card, this short piece of information adopts monumental importance. Not only *what* Sam has written but also *why* he has written it becomes the subject of the focalizer's repeated concern. Also, the fact that this forbidden message is not written in pencil is thoroughly scrutinized: "And in ink, too. Was it code for something else? A premonition of death?" (346).

The field postcards, or rather the gaps they represent, are closely linked to Miss Moss's obsession with commemorating her brother. Not knowing but only guessing with never a chance of actually finding out, is suggested as one possible motivation for her incessant mourning. Absence, namely the absence of information, is also why Thiepval, the great monument for the missing of the Somme, is the most disconcerting for her.[8] Through Miss Moss's prolonged state of mourning, the story addresses and problematizes the process and function of mourning itself. "Rather than attempting to forget and move on with her life, Barnes' mourning sister clings to grief as if it were a professional occupation, in defiance of the fact that life and history move on" (Einhaus 2013: 146). Miss Moss not only "refuses to shift her loyalties from the dead to the living" (Einhaus 2013: 146), she even resents the dead of World War Two, as they seem to reduce the impact of the Great War. With the strong prominence of the rhetoric of absence and erasure foregrounded above all through the field postcards, but also through Miss Moss's disapproval of Thiepval, the story accentuates the blotting out of individuality and information as a central and delicate aspect of private mourning.

As opposed to "Evermore", which is set about fifty years after the First World War, the temporal setting of the contemporary war story "Something Worth Landing For" (2016)[9] by Jessica Brockmole is October/November 1918, that is,

---

[8] The title of the story, in fact, refers to the inscription on Thiepval's Stone of Remembrance, "THEIR NAME LIVETH FOR EVERMORE".

[9] Jessica Brockmole. 2016. "Something Worth Landing For." In: *Fall of Poppies. Stories of Love and the Great War.* New York: HarperCollins. 157–202. (Page references in brackets are to this edition.) In fact, three out of the nine stories assembled in *Fall of Poppies* (2016), a collection of rather sentimental pieces of short fiction written specifically for the centenary of the Great War, contain letters.

the final days of the war. Through her ample use not only of letters but also of telegrams, Brockmole integrates another minimal form of correspondence and fruitfully exploits its aesthetic effect. Brockmole's war-romance is narrated from the point of view of John Wesley Ward (Wes), a young American pilot stationed in Pruniers in France and about to be "flying out with the squadron" (197) for the first time. Apart from this prospect, which utterly scares him, he has to come to terms with the shadow of his brother Val, a flying ace and the pride of his parents, who "Fell. Crashed. Flew himself into an early grave" (165). On the day before he leaves for active service as a war pilot, he meets a young French woman, pregnant and crying, and out of pity and kindness, but also out of a need to have somebody to think of him when he is in the air, he offers to marry her. They engage in a messy wedding ceremony, sealed with a fleeting kiss and with Victoire's promise to write to her husband each day. In turn, she makes him "promise not to write in return" (173), as she does not want to lose her heart to someone who will most likely be dead in no time.

Following the convention of romance, however, what happens is that in the course of their unidirectional correspondence they both fall in love. Wes receives the first of eleven letters from Victoire on October 29, 1918. In her letters, Victoire discloses more and more about her life, increasingly including Wes in her envisioning of him as husband and father of her child. While Victoire's growing affection is rendered in the text by the change of her salutations from *"Dear Mr. Ward"*, to *"Dear John Wesley Ward"* and *"Dear Wes"*, and her signature from *"Your wife, Victoire Donadieu Ward"*, to *"Your wife Victoire"* to *"Victoire"*, Wes' transformation can be explained by what Rebekka Schuh has referred to as "epistolary illusion".[10] His liminal situation in conjunction with his very fragmented knowledge of his wife trigger his imagination, which is nourished by her letters and aggrandized by the temporal and spatial displacement of their epistolary communication and the gaps this engenders.

"The soldier's sweetheart", as Einhaus notes, "was a recurring figure in magazine fiction [on the Great War] and constituted a concept appealing to men and women alike" (2013: 91). Brockmole clearly draws on this convention in "Something Worth Landing For"[11] and exploits the war-context as a plot intensifier for her sentimental romance. However, through her skilful juxtaposition of the format of the love letter with the pragmatic functionality of the telegram she manages to enrich her story with interesting aesthetic effects. While the eleven letters

---

10 See Rebekka Schuh's "Enveloped in Epistolary Illusion: The Aesthetics of Reading and Writing Letters in Selected Stories by Alice Munro" in this volume.
11 She also does so in her best-selling epistolary war-novel *Letters from Skye* (2013).

written by Victoire to Wes as well as the letter written by Wes on Armistice Day to his wife's guardian, Father Benoît, are full of hope and developing love, the telegram's pragmatic and elliptic style becomes emblematic of the defective relationship between Wes and his mother. The correspondence starts when Wes begs his mother to send his birth certificate, which he desperately needs to make his marriage legal:

> NEED BIRTH CERT PRONTO= ARMY STUFF= WES+I (180)
> WHAT KIND OF SON TELEGRAPHS HIS MOTHER= VAL WROTE THE NICEST LETTERS+ (181)
> YOU FORGET I'M THE DISAPPOINTING SON= STILL NEED BIRTH CERTIFICATE+ (185 f.)
> SPEAKING OF DISAPPOINTING ARE YOU FLYING YET= VAL SHOT DOWN ENEMY AIRCRAFT AND STILL FOUND TIME TO WRITE HIS MOTHER ONCE A WEEK+ (186)
> BIRTH CERTIFICATE PLEASE= ALSO SOME MONEY WIRED+ (187)

There follow a number of more of such telegrams, making the reader wonder about the cold-heartedness of Wes' mother. However, as the last telegrams reveal, the problem is not really a lack of care or feelings, but rather a lack of being able to communicate these feelings. When his information that he is "BEING SENT UP TOMORROW" (197) is answered with "IT'S ABOUT TIME" (197), Wes almost cracks and wires, "YOU ALWAYS TOLD VAL TO BE CAREFUL= IN EVERY SINGLE LETTER YOU SENT= WHY HAVE YOU NEVER SAID THAT TO ME+" (197). His mother's answer to this filial outcry betrays the first hint of feelings for her second son and even indicates a superiority to his idolized brother Val: "BECAUSE YOU ARE THE ONE SMART ENOUGH TO SURVIVE+" (197). When on 11 November Wes sends his last telegram, imploring his mother to send the certificate, his mother's answer, "HAVE FAITH= I SENT IT THE FIRST DAY YOU ASKED+" (200), discloses the painful discrepancy between her feelings and the difficulties she has expressing them.

The typographic contrasting of the telegrams (in austere capitalized letters) and the letters (in unobtrusive italics) visually foregrounds the differences which define the relationship between Wes and Victoire on the one hand, and Wes and his mother on the other. In addition, the staging of twelve letters and eighteen telegrams disrupts the linearity of the text and, as has been mentioned before, structurally mirrors the disruptive experience of the war. Moreover, the epistolary form facilitates the rendering of a multiplicity of voices. First, Wes' first-person voice is fanned out by his telegram-voice used for his mother as well as by his epistolary voice used in his letter to Victoire's guardian. Second, a further perspective is introduced by the voice of Wes' mother via her telegrams. Third, another female voice is introduced through Victoire's letters. In view of the prominence in canonical texts of "military or military-related experience of the conflict, [t]he challenge lies in complementing them to gain a better view of the whole picture" (Einhaus 2013: 4). Through her inclusion of female voices and her skilful use of epistolary forms, Jessica Brockmole has offered a fresh and accessible perception of the war.[12]

4 Conclusion

The epistolary short story, as has been shown in this chapter, offers a wide spectrum of genre-specific features which facilitate literary perspectives on historical events not possible in this manner through other narrative forms. The one-letter story draws for its aesthetic effect on the prominence of the internal reader and creates the impression of immediacy and authenticity by foregrounding the experiencing self as well as by its performativity, that is, its enactment of some of the events. The dual emblematic status of the letter as barrier and as bond as well as its tendency to produce the illusion of a conflation of internal and external constellations of the writer-reader-relationship, can be listed as further features which prove to have a strong impact on the receptive level and are intrinsic features of both the one-letter story and the framed epistolary story. Letters, moreover, enhance the historicity of the narrative, rendering the impression of being confronted with actual documents from the past. With regard to framed letter stories, the aspect of polyvocality is uppermost, as is the disruption of linear storylines through the integration of typographically marked hypotexts. The intrinsic revisionary element of epistolary fiction, moreover, renders it an ideal form for catering to modern understandings of the 'making of history'. As Rachel Bower (2013: 65) points out, "The *inter*subjective communication of epistolary exchange both necessitates the continual revision of consciousness and reaches out to another. This takes place both within and without the text". In combination with the generic brevity of the short story, as has been outlined, the features intrinsic to epistolary writing lead to unique effects. Taking a closer look at historical epistolary short fiction therefore brings to light not only the essence of narrative diversity regarding literary approaches to history, but also the importance of acknowledging this diversity in critical writing.

---

[12] Other epistolary First World War stories which offer female perspectives are Jennifer Robson's "All for the Love of You" (2016), Hazel Gaynor's "Hush" (2016) and Alice Munro's "Carried Away" (1994).

Works Cited

Altman, Janet Gurkin. 1982. *Epistolarity. Approaches to a New Form*. Columbus: Ohio State University Press.
Assmann, Aleida. 2010. "Canon and Archive". In: Astrid Erll (ed.). *A Companion to Cultural Memory Studies*. Berlin: De Gruyter. 97–107.
Barnes, Julian. 2007/1996. "Evermore". In: Babara Korte and Ann-Marie Einhaus (eds.). *The Penguin Book of First World War Stories*. London: Penguin. 345–361.
Bateman, John A. 2008. *Multimodality and Genre: A Foundation for the Systematic Analysis of Multimodal Documents*. New York: Palgrave Macmillan.
Bayer, Gerd. 2009. "Deceptive Narratives: On Truth and the Epistolary Voice". *LiLi: Zeitschrift für Literaturwissenschaft und Linguistik* 39.154: 173–187.
Beebee, Thomas O. 1999. *Epistolary Fiction in Europe 1500–1850*. Cambridge: Cambridge University Press.
Bower, Anne. 1997. *Epistolary Responses. The Letter in Twentieth-Century American Fiction and Criticism*. Alabama: University of Alabama Press.
Bower, Rachel. 2013. "'Yes, but ... Have you read his letters?': Epistolary Correspondence with the Past in Michael Ondaatje's *In the Skin of a Lion*". *Canadian Literature* 219 (Winter): 57–74.
Bray, Joe. 2003. *The Epistolary Novel. Representations of Consciousness*. London and New York: Routledge.
Brockmole, Jessica. 2016. "Something Worth Landing For". In: *Fall of Poppies. Stories of Love and the Great War*. New York: HarperCollins. 157–202.
Davey, Frank. 2018. "From the Erasure 'Art' of World War I Canadian Postcards to Art in the Age of Mechanical Reproduction". In: *The First World War Then and Now. Literature, Theatre and the Arts*, ed. Sherrill Grace, Martin Löschnigg & Waldemar Zacharasiewicz. Focus Issue: *Anglistik: International Journal of English Studies* 29.2. (forthcoming).
Einhaus, Ann-Marie. 2013. *The Short Story and the First World War*. Cambridge: Cambridge University Press.
Galsworthy, John. 2007/1926. "Told by the Schoolmaster". In: Babara Korte & Ann-Marie Einhaus (eds.). *The Penguin Book of First World War Stories*. London: Penguin. 214–223.
Gaynor, Hazel. 2016. "Hush". In: *Fall of Poppies. Stories of Love and the Great War*. HarperCollins. 319–354.
Gikandi, Simon. 2009. "Ken Saro-Wiwa". In: S. G. (ed.). *The Routledge Encyclopedia of African Literature*. London and New York: Routledge. 482.
Griffiths, Gareth. 2000. *African Literatures in English. East and West*. Harlow: Pearson Education.
Hallet, Wolfgang. 2014. "The Rise of the Multimodal Novel: Generic Change and Its Narratological Implications". In: Marie-Laure Ryan & Jan-Noël Thon (eds.). *Storyworlds across Media: Towards a Media-Conscious Narratology*. Lincoln/London: University of Nebraska Press. 151–172.
Koepke, Wulf. 1990. "Epistolary Fiction and Its Impact on Readers: Reality and Illusion". In: Frederick Burwick & Walter Pape (eds.). *Aesthetic Illusion. Theoretical and Historical Approaches*. Berlin: Walter de Gruyter. 263–274.
Larson, Charles E. 1998. "Ken Saro-Wiwa". In: C. E. L. (ed.). *Under African Skies. Modern African Stories*. New York: Farrar, Straus and Giroux. 210–211.

Löschnigg, Maria. 2017. "Carried Away by Letters: Alice Munro and the Epistolary Mode". In: Janice Fiamengo & Gerald Lynch (eds.). *Alice Munro's Miraculous Art: Critical Essays*. Ottawa: University of Ottawa Press. 98–113.

Maugham, W. Somerset. 2007/1928. "Giulia Lazzari". In: Babara Korte & Ann-Marie Einhaus (eds.). *The Penguin Book of First World War Stories*. London: Penguin. 140–161.

Munro, Alice. 1995/1994. "Carried Away". In: A. M. *Open Secrets*. New York: Vintage. 3–51.

Nünning, Ansgar. 1993. "Erzählen als Mittel subjektiver Sinnstiftung. Individualität, Skeptizismus und das Problem der *(un-)reliability* in Graham Swifts Kurzgeschichten". *Anglistik & Englischunterricht* 50. 153–174.

"Ogoni Struggle with Shell Oil, Nigeria, 1990–1995". *Global Nonviolent Action Database*. <http://nvdatabase.swarthmore.edu/content/ogoni-people-struggle-shell-oil-nigeria-1990–1990> [accesses 7 September 2017].

Perry, Ruth. 1980. *Women, Letters, and the Novel*. New York: AMS Press.

Robson, Jennifer. 2016. "All for the Love of You". In: *Fall of Poppies. Stories of Love and the Great War*. New York: HarperCollins. 77–116.

Saro-Wiwa, Ken. 1997/1989. "Africa Kills Her Sun". In: Charles R. Larson (ed.). *Under African Skies. Modern African Stories*. New York: Farrar, Straus and Giroux. 212–221.

Scott, Walter. 1968/1827. "Samuel Richardson". In: Ioan Williams (ed.). *Sir Walter Scott on Novelists and Fiction*. London: Routledge & Kegan Paul.

Swift, Graham. 2014. "Haematology". In: G. S. *England and Other Stories*. London and New York: Simon & Schuster. 31–42.

Wells, A. W. 2007/1925. "Chanson Triste". In: Babara Korte & Ann-Marie Einhaus (eds.). *The Penguin Book of First World War Stories*. London: Penguin. 111–119.

Rebekka Schuh
Enveloped in Epistolary Illusion

The Aesthetics of Reading and Writing Letters in Selected Short Stories by Alice Munro

Abstract: Meta-epistolarity is a central element of epistolary fiction. Characters repeatedly comment on the writing of letters, on the reading of letters, and even on the feelings triggered by waiting for a letter. In Alice Munro's short stories, the depiction of these events points to the peculiar power of letters to viscerally affect the characters' lives. In addition to their strong emotional investment in the letter correspondence itself, epistolary characters frequently indulge in extensive daydreaming about their correspondent, their future life together, and other events suggested by the letters. The dissociative and emotional state of imagination that is triggered by letters is reminiscent of aesthetic illusion, the concept in reader-response theory which describes the mental response to the perusal of representations. In this chapter, I investigate how aesthetic illusion is a fruitful concept to examine the intratextual response to reading and writing letters in Alice Munro's short stories. In analogy to aesthetic illusion, I call this response 'epistolary illusion'. I end with the proposition that as a microcosm of literature, the letters in the intratextual world of Alice Munro's stories, along with their effects and uses, provide insight into the effects and uses of literature in real, extratextual life.

1 Introduction

Epistolary fiction is full of meta-commentary on the writing, reading, or finding of letters, on the excitement upon the arrival of a letter or the disappointment upon not receiving a letter, on the opening of letters, the first reaction upon reading a letter, attempts at interpreting a letter, and so on and so forth (cf. Altman 1982: 88). Considering the epistolary stories by Alice Munro more specifically, it is striking that the rendering of these events repeatedly points to the peculiar power of letters to viscerally affect the lives of the protagonists – to the extent that the letters fundamentally overturn these characters' lives. Thus, the mere prospect of a letter from a young man makes Edie, the first-person narrator of

"How I Met My Husband" (*SMT*[1]) overturn her daily routine in order to organize it around the arrival of the postman:

> [I] concentrated on waiting for my letter. The mail came every day except Sunday, between one-thirty and two in the afternoon [...]. I would get the kitchen all cleaned and then go up to the mailbox and sit in the grass, waiting. I was perfectly happy, waiting. [...] It never crossed my mind for a long time a letter might not come. I believed in it coming just like I believed the sun would rise in the morning. (*SMT*: 67–68)

In a similar vein, the mailbox becomes "the central object" governing the narrator's life in the story "Tell me Yes or No" (*SMT*). For Gail, the protagonist of "The Jack Randa Hotel" (*OS*), Johanna, the protagonist of "Hateship, Friendship, Courtship, Loveship, Marriage" (*HS*), and Louisa, the protagonist of "Carried Away" (*OS*), the arrival or absence of a letter from a beloved man is reason enough to uproot their lives. These women all quit their jobs, move away from their homes, and leave behind their loved ones to either follow the man who has written them letters, or to hide from him if his letters were a disappointment.

Along with their strong emotional investment in the correspondence, the protagonists of these stories each develop a tendency to indulge in daydreams about their correspondent or their future life together. These imaginings function either as a self-protective response to disappointment in a man, or as a pleasurable daydream in which the protagonists fantasize about how much better their lives will be once they are with their letter writers. Thus, for example, the women imagine the death of the epistolary lover in order to deal with the disappointment of no longer receiving letters, or they imagine going on trips to their correspondent's hometown; they imagine that their correspondent proposes to them, or that he unexpectedly shows up at their door; they even imagine running into and having a conversation with the man who had written them letters, decades after his death. While this imaginative behaviour in Alice Munro's stories is predominantly a female behavior[2], there is also one male correspondent who devel-

---

[1] Alice Munro's short story collections will be abbreviated as follows: *SMT* for *Something I've Been Meaning to Tell You* (1974) and *OS* for *Open Secrets* (1994).

[2] Löschnigg (2017: 105) has convincingly argued that it is only Munro's female characters who are capable of constructing an imaginary world, as a feminist stance in Munro's writing: "Slightly modifying Coral Ann Howells' statement that all of Munro's characters 'share the sense that life can be lived simultaneously in two different dimensions or experienced from two perspectives, with the result that her protagonists are not split subjects but pluralized subjects' (170), I would argue that this is true mainly for Munro's female characters, who live their fantasies *and* continue with their here-and-now realities. Munro's heroines may be carried away by letters, as the intricate epistolary make-up of these stories convincingly shows, but they still resist 'becoming estranged from the material spaces of their everyday worlds' (Howells 170). This skill to

ops fantasies as a result of a letter correspondence: Jack Agnew, a character in the story "Carried Away".

Appropriating the title of this very story, "Carried Away", Maria Löschnigg (2017) describes the ability of the letter to viscerally affect the correspondents' lives as "[t]he letter's potential to 'carry away' the recipient emotionally or to serve as a trigger for imaginary worlds" (Löschnigg 2017: 98). These worlds are "idealized imaginary worlds that often radically contrast with the reality they [the characters] inhabit" (Löschnigg 2017: 99). Within the wide range of Alice Munro's epistolary stories, there are numerous such examples in which letters 'carry away' the protagonists on several levels, sometimes ending in a total loss of control. However, the focus of this chapter is on a specific way of being 'carried away', a state in which 'carried away' is taken literally, and which describes the pleasurable state of 'dissociation' that the characters fall into in the course of their correspondence. This dissociative state, which is prominent in several of Munro's stories, but also in other epistolary works, is reminiscent in both quality and function of what reader-response theorists call aesthetic illusion:

> Aesthetic illusion is a basically pleasurable mental state frequently emerging during the reception of representations (texts, artefacts or performances). [...] [It] consists primarily of a feeling, of variable intensity, of being imaginatively and emotionally immersed in a represented world and of experiencing this world in a way similar (but not identical) to real life. [...] [A]esthetic illusion can satisfy our thirst for experience by offering various 'off-line' experiences and wish-fulfilments in a 'harmless' context without exposing us to potentially serious consequences. [...] [I]t instructs us how we (and others) would feel if recentred in such situations as emotional and thinking beings with certain potentials and limitations, what it would be like to act in certain ways or remain passive, and what it would be like to experience the consequences that could arise for ourselves and others. (Wolf 2013: 51–53)

While aesthetic illusion is a concept from reader-response theory that explores the relationship between literature and the reader on the *extra*textual level, what Löschnigg (2017) calls "carried away by letters" is an *intra*textual response to reading, writing, or waiting for letters. Thus, there is an undeniable discrepancy in the realms from which these two concepts originate. Nonetheless, I will establish a connection between them by using the extratextual and theoretical concept of aesthetic illusion in order to illuminate the impact of letter writing and reading on the intratextual correspondents. This appropriation of aesthetic illusion for epistolary discourse is based on the following considerations. In ad-

---

reconcile fantasy with reality is one of many implicit feminist markers of Munro's writing [...]" (Löschnigg 2017: 105).

dition to the strong similarity between the quality and function of the intratextual state of being 'carried away by letters' and the extratextual concept of aesthetic illusion, my claim that the intratextual mental response to letters is reminiscent of aesthetic illusion is based on two other premises: first of all, the observation that the state of being 'carried away by letters' in Alice Munro's stories is, to different extents, shown to intersect with the mental responses triggered by the intratextual reading of novels, and second of all, that the connection between letters and literature has been made in earlier scholarly discussion of epistolary fiction and of Munro's stories.[3] Janet Altman (1982: 212), for instance, observes the following:

> [T]here is a very real sense in which it [epistolary literature] metaphorically 'represents' literature as a whole. By its very *mise-en-abyme* of the writer-reader relationship, the epistolary form models the complex dynamics involved in writing and reading; [...] In fact, what makes this form so intriguing to study [...] is the way in which it explicitly articulates the problematics involved in the creation, transmission, and reception of literary texts. (Altman 1982: 212)

Schmidt-Supprian (1993) expands on this when she says,

> The dynamic [of epistolary fiction] is based on the fact that there is, within the narrated world, an identical process 'en miniature' between the producer, text and the recipient as on the level of the narrator and anticipated reader and on the highest communicative level between author and historical reader. (Schmidt-Supprian 1993: 113, my translation)

She continues,

> Seen from this angle, the communicative event 'novel' is in a way a complicated mirroring of the integrated letter correspondence. (Schmidt-Supprian 1993: 116, my translation)[4]

This very observation, i.e. the similarity between the communicative process of letter correspondence and the communicative process 'literature', opens up several interesting fields of investigation. While Altman (1982: 212) concludes that

---

3 See Moore, Lorrie. 2002. "Artship". Issued by *The New York Review of Books*, January 17. <http://www.nybooks.com/articles/2002/01/17/artship/> [accessed 18 August 2016].
4 Original quote in German: "Die Dynamik liegt vor allem darin, daß sich innerhalb der erzählten Welt, sozusagen 'en miniature' ein artgleicher Prozeß zwischen Produzent, Text und Rezipient abspielt wie auf der Ebene des Erzählers und antizipierten Lesers und auf der letzten Kommunikationsstufe zwischen Autor und historischem Leser" (Schmidt-Supprian 1993: 113). "Der Kommunikationsvorgang 'Roman' bildet so gesehen gewissermaßen eine Art kompliziertere Spiegelung des integrierten Briefvorgangs" (Schmidt-Supprian 1993: 116).

"the *mise-en-abyme* within the novel of the writer-reader relationship invites *speculation* about the relationship of the real writer and reader to each other and to the text" (emphasis on 'speculation' mine),[5] Schmidt-Supprian (1993: 116) goes a step further and proposes, "Therefore, remarks about the writing and reading of letters, or about letters as texts, can *undoubtedly* be read as earnest or ironic allusions by the author to the production of the novel or as hints for its reception" (my emphasis and translation)[6].

Building on these arguments, to consider how letters – their writing and receiving, but also their qualities as material objects – affect the correspondents in the intratextual worlds of Alice Munro's stories is to seek insight into how literature on a larger scale – its writing and reading, but also its material existence in the form of books[7] – impacts those parties involved in the extratextual communicative process that is literature: the real, historical author and the real, historical reader. Thus, they too establish a connection between the *extratextual* responses to literature and the *intratextual* responses to letters. My argument that there is a relation between the intratextual state of being 'carried away by letters' and how extratextual readers respond to the reading process (in theoretical terms, to aesthetic illusion) is then a continuation and specification of Altman's and Schmidt-Supprian's findings.

In what follows, I will use the term 'epistolary illusion' to refer to the intratextual mental responses to letters in Alice Munro's stories, and 'aesthetic illusion' only when I refer to the theoretical concept of reader-response theory on the extratextual level. In doing so, I propose that epistolary illusion is *related to* aesthetic illusion; however, I do not propose that epistolary illusion can or should be *equated with* aesthetic illusion. Rather, I argue that since both states describe the mental and emotional responses to a (written) artefact, and since these responses share a strong resemblance, the parameters that have been used to describe aesthetic illusion are fruitful for a description and elucidation of epistolary illusion. Whether this connection is also beneficial in the reverse,

---

[5] Altman's use of "mise en abyme" needs elaboration. Wolf (1993: 296, my translation) defines mise en abyme as "the mirroring of a macro-structure of a literary text in a micro-structure of the same text". In epistolary fiction, however, the mirroring occurs not between two diegetic levels in the story, as is the common usage of mise en abyme, but rather between the intratextual diegesis and the extratextual world of the reader.
[6] Original quote in German: "So können zweifellos Bemerkungen zum Briefschreibeakt, zur Briefrezeption oder zu Brieftexten als ernst gemeinte oder ironisch gebrochene Anspielungen des Autors auf die [...] Romanproduktion oder als Rezeptionshinweise gelesen werden [...]". (Schmidt-Supprian 1993: 116)
[7] See Altman 1982: 212: "[...] the relationship [...] to the text".

that is, whether reader-response theorists can use the narratological approach to the intratextual renderings of epistolary illusion as a basis to explore the manifestations of aesthetic illusion is beyond the scope of this chapter, but might be a promising subject for future research. In the following section, I will briefly present the concept of aesthetic illusion as theorized by Wolf (2013), which will then serve as the basis for introducing the concept of epistolary illusion and its application to Alice Munro's "Carried Away" (*OS*) and "Tell me Yes or No" (*SMT*).

2 From Aesthetic Illusion to Epistolary Illusion

Aesthetic illusion is the abstract theoretical counterpart to a common feeling among readers of literature: the feeling of immersion into the fictional world of a literary text, a film, an image, a sculpture, or any other kind of representation (cf. Wolf 2013: 51–52). It is a predominantly imaginative and emotional mental response, and refers to experiencing an imaginative world and everything that happens in that world as if it were real. Aesthetic illusion therefore offers what Wolf (2013: 11) calls "[q]uasi-experience[s]". Triggered by an "external, material stimulus" (Wolf 2013: 10), this state of immersion is unstable and gradable, and while fluctuating between "complete immersion" and "total rational distance" (Wolf 2013: 18) (without ever reaching either of these extremes), aesthetic illusion requires the constant awareness of the recipient that what they are experiencing is not real, but a product of their imagination. Moreover, aesthetic illusion is directly dependent on the content and suggestions of the artefact that triggered it, rather than jumping arbitrarily from one association to the next (cf. Wolf 2013: 8).

The qualities of aesthetic illusion can also be applied to epistolary illusion, the intratextual aesthetic illusion, in which the readers and writers of letters in Alice Munro's short stories are enveloped. Epistolary illusion, too, is an emotional and imaginative mental response to the reception of a representational artefact, a letter. It begins as a strong emotional response and gradually becomes imaginative. Indeed, the process of exchanging letters has several structural characteristics that facilitate the creation of illusions. The spatial distance between the communicators, for instance, comes with a loss of "all non-verbal signals that usually go with a face-to-face encounter and thus leave ample room for imaginary constructions" (Löschnigg 2017: 5). The time gaps (i.e. the time of epistolary inactivity between the sending of a letter and the arrival of a response letter) and time lags (the difference between the present of writing a letter and the present of reading it) between the correspondents can function like a cliffhanger, and not only increase suspense but also enhance the imaginative participation of the reader (cf. Fröhlich 2015: 15–16). Finally, the addressee-directedness of letters can easily manipulate the reader into taking the reality represented in the letter(s) at face value, rather than considering the processes of aggrandizement at play (cf. Koepke 1990: 271–272).

The imaginative dimension of epistolary illusion differs slightly from aesthetic illusion in terms of the connection between the letter writing and reading characters' imaginings and the content of the letters. Wolf (2013: 8) emphasizes that a *sine qua non* criterion for aesthetic illusion is "a close relation between the artefact and the imaginative experience, a relation in which the artefact is more than a mere trigger". He (2013: 9) elaborates that, as part of aesthetic illusion, the imaginings produced in the mind of the recipient must be "similar if not identical to the specific worlds or world elements represented (or suggested) by the artefact in question". Epistolary illusion also results in a connection between the content of the letters and the imaginings of the reader, and this connection, too, goes beyond the former being a trigger of the latter. However, the imaginative aspects of epistolary illusion are not as strongly dependent on the content of the letters themselves, since they are supplemented by anticipation. Particularly when a correspondent has been waiting too long for a letter, they start to fill in what Wolfgang Iser calls '*Leerstellen*', i.e. the gaps that would explain the absence, by *imagining* why there has been no response. These fantasies can be related to events suggested by previous letters, or to the occurrence of an event that the character who is in a state of epistolary illusion intended to bring about with the arrival of their letter.

The third characteristic feature of aesthetic illusion, its gradable and unstable nature, also applies to epistolary illusion. Epistolary illusion too fluctuates between full immersion and rational distance, and while there are moments in which the characters seem to lose control of themselves, they soon regain an awareness of the artificiality of their experiences, if they have not maintained this awareness throughout. Thus, epistolary illusion, like aesthetic illusion, is not only gradable, it is also unstable. It too can be destroyed by contextual factors, or it can end regardless of changes in the context, work or recipient. This is primarily the case when the desire underlying the 'quasi-experience' reaches satisfaction, so that the epistolary illusion becomes functionless. Thus, epistolary illusion is more self-directed and self-controlled than aesthetic illusion. While the fulfilment of human desires also plays a role in aesthetic illusion, it seems to be more of a side effect. Epistolary illusion, on the other hand, is strongly need-driven. It is directly dependent on a frustrated desire which can be sated by epistolary illusion. Thus, in "Carried Away", epistolary illusion serves Louisa's desire to actually see the face of her lover and to know who he is/was; in "Tell me Yes or No", the imaginings of the first-person narrator satisfy her desire to explain why her lover stopped sending her letters.

3 Imaginative Women: "Carried Away" and "Tell me Yes or No"

"Carried Away" and "Tell me Yes or No" are the two letter stories by Alice Munro that contain the best examples of the state of epistolary illusion. In both stories, epistolary illusion begins with a strong emotional connection – the women fall in love with their correspondents – and transforms into an imaginative response when their correspondence with their lovers ends. While in "Tell me Yes or No", the protagonist is in a state of epistolary illusion throughout the story, in "Carried Away" the imaginative dimension fully emerges only in the final part of the story. It is here that the specific nature of epistolary illusion fully comes into effect. Louisa 'falls into' epistolary illusion when she reads the name of her former epistolary correspondent and lover, whom she has never met in real life. While experiencing epistolary illusion, Louisa constantly maintains an awareness that she is indulging in her daydreams, and that she is doing so to get over the fact that she has never seen her epistolary lover.

"Carried Away" consists of four sub-sections, all of which are narrated from a figural point of view. The story opens with a section entitled "Letters" and with Louisa opening a letter that arrived that day. It is February, 1917. This letter is addressed to "The Librarian, Carstairs Public Library, Carstairs, Ontario" and was written by Jack Agnew, a regular visitor to the library, who is now a soldier writing from the hospital. Jack is looking for some distraction. Even though he is not badly injured, the atrocities of war bother him, and writing this letter is a way of coping with it: "What has landed me here in hospital is not too serious. I see worse all around me and get my mind off of all that by *picturing things* and wondering for instance if you are still there in the Library" (*OS:* 4, my emphasis). Indeed, Jack consciously chooses letter writing as a means of facilitating the "picturing [of] things" (*OS:* 4), and he is quite creative in doing so. Louisa, on the other hand, remains rational, distanced, and uninvolved, both on an emotional level and in terms of her imaginings.

Apart from Jack's flirtatious comments, they exchange information about their favourite books and authors, Louisa's being "Thomas Hardy, who is accused of being gloomy but I think is very true to life—and Willa Cather" (*OS:* 6), while Jack favours non-fiction books about history or travel. Only when Jack asks for Louisa's picture does Louisa take a step back from her rationality, but even then, it is only temporary (*OS:* 10). When Jack declares that he loves her, Louisa does not react overly emotionally. All she does to suggest that she reciprocates his feelings for her is respond to his letters, send him a picture of herself, and confess that she had been disappointed by a man before, but now "believe[s] that it was all for the best" (*OS:* 10).

That Louisa has, contrary to what her letters suggest, become immensely emotionally invested in her correspondence with Jack only becomes apparent in the second section of the story, "Spanish Flue", which is set shortly after the war has ended. Louisa expects Jack to visit her after the soldiers have returned from the war. The uncertainty about whether or not Jack will approach her in combination with Louisa's waiting in uncertainty has the effect of a cliffhanger, both intensifying her emotional response and triggering her imagination as to what is keeping him:

> When she entered the Town Hall she always felt he might be there before her, leaning up against the wall awaiting her arrival. Sometimes she felt it so strongly she saw a shadow that she mistook for a man. She understood now how people believed they had seen ghosts. Whenever the door opened she expected to look up into his face. [...] And then she fancied that he might be across the street on the Post Office steps, watching her, being too shy to make a move. (*OS:* 17)

At some point, however, Louisa loses her patience, and the epistolary illusion fades. As a result, she also loses her interest in reading: "It was at this time that she entirely gave up on reading. The covers of books looked like coffins to her, either shabby or ornate, and what was inside them might as well have been dust" (*OS:* 17). Thus, the pleasure she takes in reading and books diminishes in parallel to the pleasure she took in her correspondence, which supports my claim that aesthetic and epistolary illusion are connected. In fact, throughout their correspondence, books play a prominent role in Louisa and Jack's relationship: their mutual interest in books is what connects them from the beginning. Jack opens the correspondence by writing about how he admires the way Louisa reorganized the library. They discuss their favourite authors, and Jack writes about the books he last borrowed from the library. It soon becomes clear that the library and reading are two of the main things that connect Louisa and Jack, and that this fact distinguishes them from the community. For example, Jack asks Louisa to keep their correspondence a secret since "people would laugh at me for writing to the Librarian as they did at me going to the Library even" (*OS:* 6). Even though their letters gradually expand to different topics, reading and books are still the overarching themes of the story. Not only is Louisa a librarian, a profession that is also featured in other Munrovian letter stories, but the words "Library" and "Librarian" are also always capitalized, not only in the characters' letters, but also in the parts of the story that are mediated by third-person figural narration. Being a reader or not being a reader is a definitive trait when it comes to interpersonal relationships in Carstairs. Arthur Doud, for instance, only gets closer to Louisa when he becomes a library user. When Louisa reads about Jack's marriage to a Miss Grace Horne in the newspaper, the fact that she is "Not a library user" (*OS:* 17) is also important:

> She read a short notice of his marriage to a Miss Grace Horne. Not a girl she knew. Not a library user. The bride wore fawn silk crêpe with brown velvet streamers. There was no picture. Brown-and-cream piping. Such was the end, and had to be, to her romance. (*OS:* 17–18)

The first thing we learn is that Grace Horne is "[n]ot a girl she knew. Not a Library user" (*OS:* 17) and therefore uninteresting. This is followed by a description of the bride's dress and: "There was no picture. [...] Such was the end, and had to be, to her romance" (*OS:* 18). The modification of the verb from "*was* the end" to "*had to be* the end" points to the difficulty of ending this platonic relationship, while the fact that "[t]here was no picture" (*OS:* 18) points to the reason for Louisa's difficulty ending the relationship, and turns out to be a key sentence. While Jack had seen Louisa even before she sent him the picture, Louisa never gets to see him.

The next section, "Accidents", starts with Jack's death in a tragic, possibly self-inflicted accident, in which his head is cut off at his workplace. Arthur Doud, Jack's boss, and the one who picked up Jack's head and brought it back to his body, returns some of Jack's books to the library, and, in doing so, meets Louisa. Louisa is primarily interested in Jack's appearance, asking Arthur, "What did he look like?" (*OS:* 37). Arthur, however, "could not bring any picture of Jack Agnew to mind" (*OS:* 37). Jack Agnew's appearance remains an enigma, and continues to bother Louisa decades after his death. Even though the story shows that Louisa manages to move on with her life and falls in love with a new man, the fact that she has never seen Jack Agnew keeps the epistolary illusion intact. It is this lack of knowledge that fuels it, while, at the same time, also satisfies her desire in the final part of the story, "Tolpuddle Martyrs". Louisa is now in her sixties; it has been almost forty years since Jack wrote her the first letter, and thirty years since his death. Reading about a trade union event, where a Mr. John (Jack) Agnew will speak, Louisa gets a "jumpy pulse" (*OS:* 41) and "was beginning to feel a faintly sickening, familiar agitation" (*OS:* 43), even though "[t]he coincidence of the name was hardly even interesting. Neither the first name nor the last was all that unusual" (*OS:* 43). She goes to the event, and what happens there is "gloomy" like Thomas Hardy's work, yet also "very true to life" (*OS:* 6). Waiting at a bus stop, Louisa closes her eyes, only to look right into Jack Agnew's face when she opens them. Even though she says, "'I don't recognize you [...]'" (*OS:* 45), there is no doubt that the Jack Agnew who wrote to her decades ago is speaking to her. As in their letters, their conversation is ordinary: Louisa asks about his wife and daughter, and tells him about her marriage to Arthur Doud. That Louisa is in a state of epistolary illusion shows in her awareness of the impossibility of this event. Jack tells her stories about his life and family, which naturally conflict with what Louisa knows to have happened since his death: "How could Louisa begin to correct him? Could she say, No, your wife Grace got married again during the war, she married a farmer, a widower" (*OS:* 46). They have a casual conversation until Jack leaves. Throughout the conversation, Louisa is aware that what is happening is paradoxical. Not only does she acknowledge that Jack Agnew is "a dead man" (*OS:* 48), but she also questions whether what has just happened was real: "[S]he was not sure that he [Jack Agnew] had listened to all of this, and in fact she was not sure that she had said all of it." (*OS:* 48) At the same time, she is aware of her role in constructing the fantasy: "Oh, what kind of a trick was being played on her, or what kind of trick was she playing on herself!" (*OS:* 49). With her comment that, "You would think as you get older your mind would fill up with what they call the spiritual side of things, but mine just seems to get more and more practical, trying to get something settled" (*OS:* 48), she also expresses that she is aware of the function of the imagination: to settle something. The quality of the epistolary illusion she experiences is metaphorically represented as a wave:

> No wonder she was feeling clammy. She had gone under a wave, which nobody else had noticed. You could say anything you liked about what had happened—but what it amounted to was going under a wave. She had gone under and through it and was left with a cold sheen on her skin, a beating in her ears, a cavity in her chest, and revolt in her stomach. It was anarchy she was up against—a devouring muddle. Sudden holes and impromptu tricks and radiant vanishing consolations. (*OS:* 50)

Even though epistolary illusion also entails certain negative physical responses, the state in general seems to be pleasurable. Cox (2004: 84) argues that Munro emphasizes "narrative pleasure": "Like drink, drugs or sex, storytelling induces an altered state, grounded in the body. [...] [S]he suggests that we construct multiple selves, switching, in fantasy and in reality, between parallel lives" (Cox 2004: 84).

Such switching between parallel lives also figures prominently in "Tell me Yes or No". In this story, the relationship between the first-person narrator and her lover is, in large part, conducted through letters, and it is the absence of a letter in addition to the lack of an explanation for this absence that drives the first-person narrator into a state of epistolary illusion, imagining a scenario to explain her lover's silence: "I persistently imagine you dead" (*SMT:* 107). In contrast to "Carried Away", the correspondence that led to the epistolary illusion took place in the past, outside of the story, so that the story in its entirety reflects the narrator's epistolary illusion, while we learn about the causes of this state only retrospectively.

Although literature and the reading of fiction do not play as prominent a role as in "Carried Away", they are definitely themes of this story. The epistolary lover is a journalist; his wife, a librarian. Reading fiction has always played an important role in the narrator's life, and it continues to do so in her imagination. When she met the man who would later become her lover, she was in the habit of "reading and falling asleep on the couch" (*SMT:* 107); even further in the past, her reading of D.H. Lawrence shaped her ideas about sex (*SMT:* 108). The moment she fell in love with the "you" in the story is also tied to reading: "[W]hen I was reading on the couch, I felt myself drop a lovely distance, thinking of you, and that was the beginning, I suppose, the realization of what more there could still be. So I said to you, 'I was in love.'" (*STM:* 110). Finally, when the narrator is in pain about the absence of a letter, she turns, or imagines turning, to women's magazines (*SMT:* 117).

The opening sentence of the story, "I persistently imagine you dead" (*SMT:* 107), not only paves the way into the narrator's epistolary illusion, but, by addressing a "you", also suggests that there is an addressee involved. Since this "you" comes up again and again, and the relationship between the "I" and the "you" had been, in large part, lived out in letters, several scholars argue that the story itself is also an unwritten letter to this lover (cf. Duncan 2011: 16; Gadpaille 1988: 66; Heble 1994: 80). This further classifies the story as epistolary (in addition to the thematic dominance of letters and the inserted letters towards the end), but it also supports my reading of the story: As I see it, "Tell me Yes or No" not only testifies to the state of epistolary illusion, it also emphasizes its need-driven nature, and shows that the illusionary state remains active until the underlying need – in this case the absence of a response – has been explained.

Moreover, "Tell me Yes or No" highlights the time lag in epistolary correspondence as a main contributor to the emergence of epistolary illusion. The time lag in epistolary communication leads to the recipient of a letter perceiving something that is past as present. Thus, what the recipient takes as his/her present reality in relation to the correspondent is an illusion in itself, for it no longer corresponds with the letter *writer's* present. In Altman's words:

> The epistolary situation, in which both time lags and absence play such a large role, lends itself to the temporal ambiguity whereby past is taken for present. The only possible present is the most immediate past—be it the last contact or the last letter. In narrative whose action is the recovery from unrequited love, the lover will continue to 'love in the past tense' until a more immediate present effaces that past. (Altman 1982: 132)

In the case of "Tell me Yes or No", what seems to have been an unexpected termination of the couple's correspondence makes the narrator hold on to the 'present' reality that her lover's last letter represents. At the same time, the longer she waits for a new letter, the more she begins to question the validity of this reality. Forced to try to explain why he stopped sending letters, the narrator creates a new, if imagined, present for herself, in which her lover has died. This present, too, is tied to a letter written in the narrator's mind, the letter that is the story "Tell me Yes or No".

That the entire story about the correspondent's death is the product of the narrator's imagination is suggested by the first sentence ("I persistently imagine you dead", *SMT*: 107). However, the question of where to draw the line between the narrator's imaginings and actual events, that is, those events that in the intratextual world are accepted as real, is more difficult to determine. The story repeatedly jumps back and forth between what seems to have been the narrator's past with her lover, and her present strategy of coping with his silence by "killing [him] off" (Heble 1994: 83) in her imagination. Héliane Ventura (1992: 105) observes that, even though "[t]he world of fantasy and the world of fact keep impinging upon each other to the point of dissolution", the two story strands "are carefully differentiated by the use of tense" (Ventura 1992: 105). The passages written in the present tense form the narrator's imagined present, whereas the passages in the past tense are facts about their past (cf. Ventura 1992: 105–106).

While it is true that the past events narrated in the story are also the product of the narrator's memory of what this past was like (and thus the narrator's *imaginings* of this past), what I refer to as epistolary illusion in this story are the passages written in present tense. It is here that the ontological border between fact and fantasy is crossed, as the narrator moves from emotional involvement to the self-created imaginative world in which she is able to explain the end of her correspondence with her lover. Throughout her state of epistolary illusion, the narrator is aware of the imaginative quality of her experience, as the numerous meta-comments show. The events written in past tense, on the other hand, describe how and why she was gradually lured into this state of epistolary illusion.

With this in mind, we can see that the cause of the narrator's epistolary illusion was her affair with a journalist. Both the journalist and the narrator were married when they began their relationship, which was, apart from a few visits, largely conducted in letters. Their affair goes smoothly until the narrator realizes and then covers up the fact that she is more deeply attached to the relationship than her lover. With this realization, the continuation of the affair, represented metonymically by the continuation of their correspondence, seems increasingly improbable to the narrator, so that every letter from her lover has the effect of a cliffhanger, and only intensifies her emotional engagement:

> From the beginning, of course, I knew that this was a dangerous way to live. At any moment the ties may be cut [...]. Always before, at the last moment, rescue arrived. My brief wild letter, final desperation, and then your letter of humorous, somewhat tender, apology, which tells me there was never any danger. It was on solid ground all the time, you never left. (*SMT*: 117)

Eventually, however, no letter of rescue arrives, and the wait becomes too long and too exhausting. This is when the border between fact and fantasy is crossed, and her epistolary illusion changes from a primarily emotional to an imaginative involvement:

> I am in the habit of carrying around your last letter in my purse. When the next letter comes, I replace it, I put it with all the earlier letters in a box in my closet. While it is fresh in my purse I like to take the letter out and read it at odd moments, for instance if I am sitting having coffee in some little café, or waiting at the dentist's. Later on I never take the letter out at all, I grow to dislike the sight of it, folded and dog-eared reminding me of what weeks, what months, I have been waiting for the new letter. But I leave it there, I don't put it in the box, I don't dare.
> Now, however, [...] I go home and remove this letter, this last letter, from my purse, put it with the others and shove the box out of sight. [...] I continue with my life. (*SMT*: 110–111)

Even though this passage is written in the present tense and would, according to Ventura (1992), thus constitute part of the story's fantasy, I argue that it is on the edge between fact and imagination. The use of "Now, however, [...]" (*SMT*: 111) introduces a turning point, and implies a stark contrast to the previous statements, indicating that it is at this point that the narrator realizes that the last letter was also the final letter. It is this realization and the acceptance thereof that leads to her fantasies. To continue with her life, as she resolves, she needs a solid story that will enable her to move on, "[s]he needs to kill him off the way a writer of fiction or television scripts often kills off a character – and she needs to make his death 'solid'" (Osachoff 1983: 77).

The killing off in her imagination takes the shape of an epistolary illusion. Not only is it triggered by and shaped according to the narrator's desire for an explanation, but it also shifts back and forth between immersion and distance. The narrator gradually slips in and out of the epistolary illusion, alternating between experiencing it and creating it. In the beginning, her role as the *creator* of the fantasy is foregrounded, while, later on, her immersion and her role as an experiencing object become dominant. Here, her own agency in creating this imaginative trip is less conspicuous than in the first part of the story. Upon visiting her ex-lover's house, she speaks to him directly and says, "Imagine this real, a real house [...]" (*SMT*: 118), as if correcting the belief that the house in her imagination can be determined deictically, when really it is just any house, an empty signifier. Later she speaks of "a story, a true story" she has read "in a magazine" (*SMT*: 118), emphasizing the contrast to her own, untrue story. Only towards the end does it become explicitly clear that the trip, like her lover's death, is the product of her imagination: "In this *city of my imagination* I walk past stone walls up and down steep hills, and *see in my mind* that girl Patricia" (*SMT*: 124, my emphasis). The narrator then ends the story somewhat impatiently, declaring that everything, past and present, was simply her imagination:

> Never mind. I invented her. I invented you, as far as my purposes go. I invented loving you and I invented your death. I have my tricks and my trap doors, too. I don't understand their workings at the present moment, but I have to be careful, I won't speak against them. (*SMT*: 124)

The narrator's description of her inventions as "tricks and [...] trap doors" (*SMT*: 124) emphasizes once more the self-directed, need-driven nature of epistolary illusion. Like Louisa in "Carried Away", the first-person narrator of "Tell me Yes or No" also describes epistolary illusion as a trick, and she, too, highlights that she is the creator of the trick as much as its beneficiary. Thus, in Heble's (1994: 80) words, the story emphasizes "the way in which invention may be motivated by a deep psychological need or desire" (Heble 1994: 80).

4 Conclusion

According to Altman (1982) and Schmidt-Supprian (1993), correspondence in a fictional work can be seen as a small-scale model of the communicative acts involved in the production and reception of literature, so that the correspondence is a mise en abyme of literature as communication. Therefore, both Altman (1982) and Schmidt-Supprian (1993) point to the possibility of using the remarks about responses to the writing and/or reading of letters as data for an investigation of responses to the writing and/or reading of literature in the extratextual, 'real' world. In line with these arguments, I have used the theoretical framework of Wolf's (2013) theory of aesthetic illusion in order to examine intratextual manifestations of epistolary illusion, which, I have shown, shares undeniable similarities to aesthetic illusion. I have, therefore, proposed that epistolary illusion is related to aesthetic illusion, and can be seen as a variant of the latter. Due to the similarities in the emergence, quality, and function of epistolary illusion and aesthetic illusion, it would be interesting for future research to investigate whether the connection I have made between these two states can also be used to explore extratextual manifestations of aesthetic illusion. This would be in line with Wolf's own recommendations for future investigations of aesthetic illusion: "[W]hat can be consulted is at best indirect evidence: written reception testimonies as well as aesthetic reflections [...] and last but not least the artefacts themselves, in particular where they metareferentially thematize or play with aesthetic illusion or 'imagination'" (Wolf 2013: 29–30).

If letter writing and reading in Alice Munro's short stories is a mise en abyme of writing and reading literature, then whatever they suggest about the effects or uses of letter writing/reading on and for the protagonists provides insight into the effects and uses of literature in real life. The effect that is foregrounded in the stories discussed in this chapter is that letter writing/reading carries the protagonists away into an emotional and imaginative state reminiscent of aesthetic illusion, which I have referred to as epistolary illusion. The use or function of this state is that it helps the protagonists overcome problems and caters to their desires. It follows, then, that these are also two of the major uses of literature in the extratextual world. In this sense, these stories are, in Nicholas Frangipane's words, a case of "fiction-affirming fiction":

> for these characters to truly understand their lives and make sense of the world the facts alone are not enough; they must explore every unlived possibility, if only in their imaginations, to live fully, to live comfortably, to understand their world and themselves. [...] Ultimately, this technique [...] allows Munro [...] to make an argument for the importance of fiction, and its role in society. (Frangipane 2008: 134)

Works Cited

Altman, Janet. 1982. *Epistolarity. Approaches to a Form*. Columbus: Ohio State University Press.

Duncan, Isla. 2011. *Alice Munro's Narrative Art*. New York: Palgrave Macmillan.

Frangipane, Nicholas. 2008. "A Reason to Read: Fiction-Affirming Fiction in Alice Munro's Open Secrets". *Undergraduate Review. Bridgewater State University*. 4.24: 133–139.

Fröhlich, Vincent. 2015. *Der Cliffhanger und die serielle Narration. Analyse einer transmedialen Erzähltechnik*. Bielefeld: transcript Verlag.

Gadpaille, Michelle. 1988. *The Canadian Short Story*. Toronto: Oxford University Press.

Heble, Ajay. 1994. *The Tumble of Reason: Alice Munro's Discourse of Absence*. Toronto: University of Toronto Press.

Koepke, Wulf. 1990. "Epistolary Fiction and Its Impact on Readers: Reality and Illusion". In: Frederick Burwick and Walter Pape (eds.). *Aesthetic Illusion. Theoretical and Historical Approaches*. Berlin/New York: Walter de Gruyter. 263–274.

Löschnigg, Maria. 2017. "Carried Away by Letters – Alice Munro and the Epistolary Mode". In: Janice Fiamengo & Gerald Lynch (eds.). *Alice Munro's Miraculous Art. Critical Essays*. Ottawa: University of Ottawa Press. 97–113.

Moore, Lorrie (2002, January 17,). "Artship". *The New York Review of Books*. <http://www.nybooks.com/articles/2002/01/17/artship/> [accessed 18 August 2016].

Munro, Alice. 1995/1994. "Carried Away". In: Alice Munro. *Open Secrets*. London: Vintage. 3–51.

Munro, Alice. 1974. "How I Met My Husband". In: Alice Munro. *Something I've Been Meaning to Tell You*. London: Penguin Books. 50–69.

Munro, Alice. 1974. "Tell me Yes or No". In: Alice Munro. *Something I've Been Meaning to Tell You*. London: Penguin Books. 107–124.

Osachoff, Margaret Gail. 1983. "'Treacheries of the Heart': Memoir, Confession, and Meditation in the Stories of Alice Munro". In: Louis K. MacKendrick (ed.). *Probable Fictions. Alice Munro's Narrative Acts*. Downsview, Ontario: ECW Press. 61–82.

Schmidt-Supprian, Alheide. 1993. *Briefe im erzählten Text. Untersuchungen zum Werk Theodor Fontanes*. Europäische Hochschulschriften. Frankfurt am Main: Peter Lang.

Ventura, Héliane. 1992. "The Setting Up of Unsettlement in Alice Munro's 'Tell me Yes or No'". In: Theo D'haen & Hans Bertens (eds.). *Postmodern Fiction in Canada*. Postmodern Studies 6. Amsterdam: Rodopi. 105–123.

Wolf, Werner. 2013. "Aesthetic Illusion". In: Werner Wolf, Walter Bernhart & Andreas Mahler (eds.). *Immersion and Distance. Aesthetic Illusion in Literature and Other Media*. Rodopi: Amsterdam, New York. 2–63.

Wolf, Werner. 1993. *Ästhetische Illusion und Illusionsdurchbrechung in der Erzählkunst*. Tübingen: Max Niemeyer Verlag.

Maximilian Feldner
Epistolarity in Twenty-First Century Nigerian Short Fiction

Abstract: The epistolary mode plays a considerable role in twenty-first century Nigerian fiction, as Nigerian writers often depict the practice of writing letters in their fiction and incorporate the letter's generic properties into their narrative prose. This chapter explores Nigerian epistolary fiction and particularly focuses on two major narrative functions letters have in this literature. Analysing the use of the epistolary mode in Ike Oguine's novel *A Squatter's Tale* (2000), Sefi Atta's short story "News from Home" (2010), Chimamanda Ngozi Adichie's short story "The Thing Around Your Neck" (2009) and Adichie's novel *Americanah* (2013), the chapter will first discuss the way experiences of diaspora are narrativized in this literature. These examples show that letters often also indicate the extent to which a character is still attached to their homeland. Secondly, letters in Sefi Atta's short story "Yahoo Yahoo" (2010) and in Adaobi Tricia Nwaubani's novel *I Do Not Come To You By Chance* (2009) allow for an intricate examination of the practice of advance fee fraud (commonly referred to as 419) as well as the sociocultural context that forces people into 419.

1 Introduction

Contemporary Nigerian writers often depict the practice of writing letters in their fiction and incorporate the letter's generic properties into their narrative prose. Referring to epistolarity as the creation of meaning in narrative literature through the formal features of the letter (cf. Altman 1982: 4), this chapter explores epistolary Nigerian fiction and particularly focuses on two major narrative functions letters can have in this literature. First, as many current Nigerian novels and short stories are diasporic, with their characters located abroad, letters are presented as a means of staying in touch with the home that was left behind. E.C. Osundu's "A Letter from Home" (2010) takes the shape of a Nigerian woman's letter to her son who has left Nigeria. The short story presents a satirically exaggerated account of the hopes and expectations that are associated with emigration. In this story, presenting only the mother's perspective, the attempt at communication appears to be unsuccessful. In other examples of Nigerian epistolary fiction, by contrast, letters are featured as an important facilitator of communication and often indicate a diasporic character's degree of connection with

https://doi.org/10.1515/9783110584813-005

Nigeria. In Ike Oguine's novel *A Squatter's Tale* (2000) the migrant protagonist remains in close contact with his home. This, however, keeps him on the fringes of society for most of his first year in the United States, and it is only when the ties are broken through a series of letters that he can fully arrive in the new country. In Sefi Atta's short story "News from Home" (2010) letters help the protagonist, also a migrant in the United States, to maintain connections with her home in Nigeria, serving as an anchor for her identity and enabling her to take part in her hometown's political struggles. Finally, in Chimamanda Ngozi Adichie's short story "The Thing Around Your Neck" (2009) and her third novel *Americanah* (2013), letters indicate a reorientation for diasporic characters towards Nigeria, often culminating in their return home. Letters therefore not only provide a possibility of narrativizing the broad range of diasporic experiences in Nigerian literature, but also signal the extent of a character's continuing attachment to their old home as well as of their process of arrival in and adaptation to the new place. As a second function letters in Nigerian fiction allow for an intricate examination of the practice of advance fee fraud (commonly referred to as 419). In Sefi Atta's short story "Yahoo Yahoo" (2010), Adaobi Tricia Nwaubani's novel *I Do Not Come To You By Chance* (2009), and Teju Cole's novel *Every Day is for the Thief* (2007), letters, which are the characters' main instrument for their e-mail scams, serve as a starting point for the depiction of the fraudsters' sociocultural contexts, illuminating possible reasons and motivations for their fraudulent activities.

2 Letters in Nigerian Diaspora Literature

E.C. Osundu's "A Letter Home" (2010)

"My Dear Son, / Why have you not been sending money through Western Union like other good Nigerian children in America do? You have also not visited home. Have you married a white woman?" (Osundu 2010: 45). This is the opening of a story by Nigerian writer E.C. Osundu, published in his short story collection *Voice of America* (2010) and entitled "A Letter from Home". As is immediately visible in the use of the salutation and the direct addresses to a recipient 'you', the story is written in the form of a letter from a Nigerian mother to her son in America. In the mother's attempt to reach a son who seems to have been silent and unresponsive to previous letters, the aim of her letter is to communicate across distances, a purpose that is fundamental to letter correspondence. Her letter may fail to connect her to her son but on the extradiegetic level, i.e. as a story, "A

Letter from Home" nevertheless expresses a number of central concerns of Nigerian diaspora fiction.

The story addresses the spatial distance between the letter writing mother and the addressed son, and thus points towards the Nigerian diaspora, a phenomenon amply fictionalized in contemporary Nigerian literature.[1] In her letter the mother outlines the trajectories, successful and unsuccessful, of several acquaintances who, like her son, have left the country, and thus the letter demonstrates the possible scope of migratory experiences in the context of the Nigerian diaspora. Among her examples the most accomplished migrant is Ogaga's son, who went to Germany, was soon able to buy his father a BMW and is now building hotels. Other positive examples are Odili's son, who made his way to Europe across the Sahara to come back a rich man, or Obi's daughter, who worked as a prostitute in Italy but has become successful and respectable enough for people to overlook her past. As negative examples she mentions Kaka's son, who, after having been sent to America with the community's fund, married a white woman and now ignores his family, or Okolosi's son, who failed in America and has, after his return, become the village's madman.

In the hope that her son will follow the positive examples, the mother financially supported her son's migration by selling her market stall. Not having heard from him for a while, her biggest worry seems to be her own status at home rather than her son's well-being, imploring him to remember "your promise to buy me a car and get me a driver, so I can proudly sit in the owner's corner like the wife of a top civil servant" (Osundu 2010: 46). It is statements like these that point to the central function of the letter in this story. Rather than using the letter for sentimental purposes, "A Letter from Home" exploits the epistolary form for its satirical possibilities. The very first question in the letter addresses the money the son has failed to send, instead of inquiring about his well-being as would be expected. Due to the limited perspective of a single letter, readers do not learn about the son's reasons and motivations for his continued absence and silence, or indeed, whether the mother's charges are even justified. This is fitting, as the mother appears less interested in his experiences than in the effects of his actions on her reputation and thus the letter reflects the mother's one-sided interests. As the letter continues in the vein of its opening, the epistolary mode effectively exposes the mother's self-centeredness in a satirical

---

[1] For a more detailed discussion of contemporary Nigerian literature, including in-depth examinations of several of the texts discussed in this chapter, see Maximilian Feldner. 2017. "Narrating the Diaspora – Transmigration and Socio-Cultural Imaginaries in 21st Century Nigerian Literature". Unpublished PhD Dissertation, University of Graz.

manner. She repeatedly reminds her son, for example, of the bride she has chosen for him to improve the family's standing in the community.

E.C. Osundu's interesting literary experiment thus conveys the potential of epistolary storytelling in contemporary Nigerian fiction. In his story the letter format makes possible a combination of seemingly disparate elements. It links an account of various experiences and outcomes of migration, of the hopes and expectations that surround the migration to America, and of the way familial relationships can be affected by diasporic experiences, with the satirical depiction of a mother's obsession with her status in society and the resulting exaggerated expectations for her son and his success abroad. Imitating the voice of this mother, the format of the letter, moreover, incorporates in a limited space a great number of references to the wider cultural context of the mother. For instance, certain folk beliefs are visible when she threatens to force her son back to Nigeria with a spell or when she alludes to a possible family curse. Also, the folktale with which she closes her letter indicates a cultural context in which fables and proverbs play an important discursive role.

Ike Oguine's *A Squatter's Tale* (2000)

Since the letter is a form of communication across "a distance between correspondents which makes a direct dialogue impossible" (Koepke 1990: 265), a main function of letters in Nigerian literature is to serve as a connection between Nigeria and its diaspora. While E.C. Osundu's story presents the point of view of one who stayed behind, more typically the stories and novels of the Nigerian diaspora use the epistolary mode to narrate the experiences of the migrants. Ike Oguine's novel *A Squatter's Tale* (2000), for example, tells the story of Obi, a young Nigerian who migrates to the United States in the early 1990s in order to escape the political instability and low employment prospects in Nigeria. It traces the conflicts and disappointments with which Obi grapples as he attempts to build an existence in the new country. Having followed the lure of America he soon realizes that the promises of the "land of opportunity" (Oguine 2000: 37) are mostly hollow. Instead of being paved with gold he finds that the streets "were depressing: they struck me as places from which hope and ambition had been wrung out" (Oguine 2000: 29). Obi struggles to make a living without a valid visa and work permit and remains at the margins of society for most of his first year.

A major reason for his inability to adapt and to become an integrated member of society is his homesickness, which is particularly expressed in his long and expensive telephone conversations with his girlfriend Robo. This situation is decisively changed by a break-up letter she sends him:

> Disaster struck the week after, in the shape of a letter delivered by DHL [...]. "... I'm sorry to write you this kind of letter so close to your birthday, but believe me, Obi, I think it will be even more unfair to keep putting it off. Since you left for America I have thought about us a lot and I think it will be better for the two of us to end this relationship. Being in a relationship where the other person is so far away has been very difficult for me." (Oguine 2000: 180)

This letter, a consequence of the distance between the two, sends Obi into a feverish state of despair that lasts more than two weeks, despite the fact that he himself had not bothered to stay faithful to Robo. Unable to reach her on the phone, he keeps arguing with her in his mind: "Those feverish pleas addressed to a sheet of cream writing paper lasted all day, interrupted by desperate, unsuccessful, attempts to get through to Robo's house by phone" (Oguine 2000: 186). He does not actually send her a letter, but his notes do have a positive effect in that they help him to dispense with the memories that tie him to Nigeria. Although Robo's message at first is devastating for him, it has a beneficial effect, as it enables him to find closure and to fully accept his new life in the United States: "Robo's letter had set me free, as free as a lunatic or a dead man" (Oguine 2000: 187). In a short and carefully composed letter he eventually *does* send to Robo he lets her know that he accepts her decision.

The contrast between his feverish and rambling thoughts and the letter he sends her, which is comparatively generous and conciliatory, demonstrates the possibility of carefully composing one's thoughts in a letter. As opposed to the rash and impulsive words he might have spoken to her in direct conversation, the letter allows him a more graceful ending: "I glowed after I had sent off the letter. I had shown dignity and maturity. My life had begun on an honourable note" (Oguine 2000: 197). While the novel's ending remains open, there is a strong indication that Obi has a future in America, something that is not a given throughout most of the novel. Together with other changes in his life, such as a stable job and his own apartment, the reading and composition of letters help him to arrive, to move from the edges to the centre of society:

> Though inside it [America], I had remained at the margins – for the previous year I really hadn't been living in America but in a sort of halfway country, a sort of satellite life outside the life that went on, tenuously linked to the American way of life by work and a common currency, shops and television. Now, though I would always be in a sense apart from it, always be more Nigerian than American, I had also had to strive for a place inside it; I had a way to be both apart from and part of this vast country. (Oguine 2000: 196)

Sefi Atta's "News from Home" (2010)

While in *A Squatter's Tale* letters vitally contribute to the main character's orientation away from Nigeria and towards a new dedication for building a life in the United States, in other examples of Nigerian diaspora literature letters help to maintain connections with the old home. In Sefi Atta's aptly titled "News from Home" (2010) a letter demonstrates the close links the protagonist still upholds to her native village in Nigeria. Eve, the first-person narrator and protagonist of the short story, is a young Nigerian woman who moved to the United States where she works as a nanny for a rich Nigerian American family. The story mainly pursues two concerns: On the one hand, it depicts Eve's migratory experiences in America, on the other, it represents the extraction of oil in her home village and its negative effects on its environment and inhabitants.[2]

A recent arrival to the United States, Eve critically compares her new home to Nigeria. Like other Nigerian migrants she had high expectations, having "thought that going to America was as fantastic as going to Heaven" (Atta 2010: 187). The actual experience of the country is underwhelming, like the flowers which "are pale compared to hibiscus and bougainvillea, muted like the rest of the house" (Atta 2010: 170). In her worst moments she even thinks "that living in America was exactly what it was like to live in a mortuary" (Atta 2010: 173). Still, Eve intends to stay, planning to get a visa and a better job. A letter from her friend Angie confirms that there is no point in coming back: "Eve, you can't come back. There is nothing here for you. You must take your nursing exams while you're there. I hear that they need nurses over there in America. You can always come home to visit" (Atta 2010: 196). Despite having graduated from nursing school, Eve is unable to get a job in Nigeria. The only jobs, few and hard to get, are provided by the foreign oil company that dominates the region. "News from Home" tells of the negative social and environmental consequences of oil production, including the impoverishment of Eve's home village, the destruction of the environment, the constant gas flares and the oil-polluted water.

Eve does not miss the irony of the fuel-guzzling cars in America, while many Nigerians grapple with gas shortages and intermittent electricity provision. Even from afar she is invested in her hometown's protests against the oil company's intrusion into their habitat. Usually she has to rely on the rare article in an American newspaper for information, but feels that they misrepresent the struggle, for

---

[2] For a more extensive discussion of literary representations of the destructive consequences of oil extraction in the Niger Delta, see my article, "Representing the Neocolonial Destruction of the Niger Delta: Helon Habila's *Oil on Water* (2011)" (Feldner 2018)

example, when a *New York Times* article falsely claims that according to local custom women would strip naked as a shaming gesture. Eve thinks that "the newspaper report was a hoax, designed to ridicule Africans and trivialize our protest" (Atta 2010: 170). More reliable, accurate and detailed information about the planned protests comes in form of her friend Angie's letter:

> We will block their airstrip, jetty, helicopter pad and storage depot. We will demand that they give us electricity, clean water, better roads, schools, clinics, jobs. Pregnant women, too, and mothers, with babies on their backs. She said Summit Oil may send the security forces to stop us, but we will not be stopped. We will carry nothing but palm leaves in our hands and respond to their threats with songs. (Atta 2010: 196)

The letter serves as a means of keeping in contact with family and friends in Nigeria. At the same time, by informing her about the protesters' plans, it also involves Eve in the struggle against the oil company, at least in spirit. The letter's function in the story is therefore a vital one. It is not only presented in its entirety and is greatly valued by Eve, who has "read it many times before" (Atta 2010: 195), but it also provides the link that makes possible the story's narrative interweaving of the protagonist's migratory experiences with an exploration of the situation at home. Because it effectively connects the two strands of the story, it allows Eve to reconcile her diasporic situation with her wish to participate in her hometown's struggles.

Chimamanda Ngozi Adichie's "The Thing Around Her Neck" (2009)

In the fiction of Chimamanda Ngozi Adichie, letters serve as a trigger for a return to Nigeria. In the short story "The Thing Around Your Neck" (2009), Akunna, a young Nigerian woman, has moved to the United States after winning the visa lottery, but is plagued by loneliness and thinks about home a lot. Her alienation from her host culture is expressed in critical observations about American ways of life, for example, when she notices that "people left so much food on their plates and crumpled a few dollar bills down, as though it was an offering, expiation for the wasted food" (Adichie 2009: 118).

The story employs epistolarity to convey Akunna's loneliness, when she composes long letters home in her head but never sends them off:

> [...] you chose long brown envelopes to send half your month's earnings to your parents at the address of the parastatal where your mother was a cleaner; [...] Every month. You wrapped the money carefully in white paper but you didn't write a letter. There was nothing to write about. (Adichie 2009: 118)

The assertion that she has nothing to write about, however, is inaccurate, as Akunna has a lot to tell. She "wanted to write because [she] had stories to tell" (Adichie 2009: 118), stories about her life in the United States and about the differences she observes between Nigerians and Americans. The reason she cannot bring herself to write home is likely her sense of failure. She understands that the "trick was to understand America, to know that America was give-and-take. You gave up a lot but you gained a lot, too" (Adichie 2009: 116). However, Akunna has gained very little, as the promises of the American Dream have failed to materialize, something she shares with other migrants depicted in Nigerian diaspora literature, such as Atta's Eve and Oguine's Obi. She was told that in America she would immediately get a good job, a big car and a large house, but instead she works as a waitress in a diner somewhere in Connecticut, barely getting by. She cannot bring herself to admit to family and friends at home that she could not fulfil their unrealistic expectations concerning her life in America. In addition, she feels the pressure of certain obligations when getting in contact with people at home:

> It wasn't just to your parents you wanted to write, it was also to your friends, and cousins and aunts and uncles. But you could never afford enough perfumes and clothes and handbags and shoes to go around and still pay your rent on what you earned at the waitressing job, so you wrote nobody. (Adichie 2009: 118–119)

The epistolary mode here reveals much about the expectations and motivations that can be connected to migration, but also provides insights into the migrant's mindset. In Akunna's case, the medium of the letter fails her, not helping her to express herself. It is a marker of her solitude as well as of the distance she experiences between the different worlds of Nigeria and the United States. Notably, the story is written in the second-person narrative mode. The you-narration, which can heighten readers' identification with the protagonist, closely resembles the epistolary mode, "the *I* of epistolary discourse always having as its (implicit or explicit) partner a specific *you* who stands in unique relationship to the *I*" (Altman 1982: 117, original emphasis). If Akunna is unable to use the letter to communicate her situation, it could be argued that the story itself represents a kind of letter to herself that supports her in the processing of her experiences. By the end of the short story, Akunna's loneliness and unhappiness, which manifest themselves as the eponymous thing around the neck (cf. Adichie 2009: 119), have been alleviated by her boyfriend. She has managed to settle down in the United States, and the "thing that wrapped itself around your neck, that nearly choked you before you fell asleep, started to loosen, to let go" (Adichie 2009: 125). Still, the story ends with Akunna boarding a flight to Nigeria, after finally having sent home a note with her address and having learned about her father's death. It is therefore her mother's reply, a letter she wrote "herself; you knew from the spidery penmanship, from the misspelled words" (Adichie 2009: 127), that causes Akunna to return to Nigeria.

Chimamanda Ngozi Adichie's *Americanah* (2013)

In Adichie's third novel *Americanah* (2013), letters are similarly involved in the protagonist's return home. The novel tells the story of Ifemelu, who, after having lived in the United States for thirteen years, decides to move back to Nigeria. She has gained citizenship and successfully built a life and career for herself. Nonetheless, she increasingly gravitates back towards Nigeria and Obinze, the boyfriend she separated from when moving abroad. Even though she has several relationships with American men, Obinze retains a central role in her life. Overall, their love story provides the main narrative arc of the novel and their eventual reunion marks its endpoint.

Letters, in the shape of e-mails, help them to tentatively get reacquainted after hardly having been in touch for thirteen years. It is in an e-mail that Ifemelu tells Obinze about her plans to return:

> Ceiling, *kedu?* Hope all is well with work and family. Ranyinudo said she ran into you some time ago and that you now have a child! Proud Papa. Congratulations. I recently decided to move back to Nigeria. Should be in Lagos in a week. Would love to keep in touch. Take care. Ifemelu. (Adichie 2014: 19)

Ifemelu has obviously planned her return before getting in contact with Obinze, but her use of "Ceiling", her term of endearment for him, signals the significance he has had in her decision-making process. Before they meet again in Nigeria, their e-mails help them to successfully rekindle their relationship, after a few failed attempts at establishing contact earlier. These happened at times when the distance between them was the greatest: Ifemelu struggling with depression in her first years in the United States, and Obinze trying to survive in England as an illegal immigrant. Their e-mail exchange a few years later, by contrast, provides them with the opportunity to get close again, among other things by talking about Obinze's mother's death.

Ifemelu is the novel's primary protagonist, but long stretches of the novel are also narrated from Obinze's perspective. In several instances the switch from a chapter where Ifemelu is the focalizer to one of Obinze's chapters is accompanied by an e-mail, as if the narrative perspective were transferred from one to the other via that e-mail, in most cases from Ifemelu to Obinze. Most of their e-mails are therefore perceived through Obinze's perspective. Together with him, it seems, the external readers read Ifemelu's messages, note his reactions to them and observe him writing his responses:

> When Obinze first saw her e-mail, he was sitting in the back of his Range Rover in still Lagos traffic [...]. First, he skimmed the e-mail, instinctively wishing it were longer. [...] He read it again slowly and felt the urge to smooth something, his trousers, his shaved-bald head. (Adichie 2014: 19)

How important this message is to him shows in his reaction upon receiving it, but also in his careful composition of his response e-mail, which he "wrote and rewrote" (Adichie 2014: 35), as well as in his anxiously waiting for her to write back: "Obinze checked his BlackBerry often, too often, even when he got up at night to go to the toilet, and although he mocked himself, he could not stop checking. Four days, four whole days, passed before she replied" (Adichie 2014: 369). In addition to the e-mails conveying the characters' investment in their love story, writing e-mails to Ifemelu also helps Obinze to come to terms with his experience of living in England as an illegal immigrant for a few years. He had been deported just before he was able to go through with a sham marriage that would have provided him with a visa and allowed him to stay permanently.

> He began to write to her about his time in England, hoping she would reply and then later looking forward to the writing itself. He had never told himself his own story, never allowed himself to reflect on it, because he was too disoriented by his deportation and then by the suddenness of his new life in Lagos. Writing to her also became a way of writing to himself. (Adichie 2014: 372)

As a result, e-mails are not only an instrument of re-establishing contact, but also have a therapeutic function, as Obinze can finally rid himself of his disappointment about the forced return and address the difficulties he had during that period.

3 419 – Scam Letters: Teju Cole's *Every Day is for the Thief* (2007), Adaobi Tricia Nwaubani's *I Do Not Come To You By Chance* (2009) and Sefi Atta's "Yahoo Yahoo" (2010)

Letters in Nigerian epistolary fiction also play a role in the literary depiction of internet fraud. In Teju Cole's novel *Every Day is for the Thief* (2007), the narrator, a Nigerian American on a visit in Nigeria, sits in an Internet café and suddenly recognizes what the bustling online activities around him are about. He feels as if having "discovered the source of the Nile or the Niger" and the "the origin of the world-famous digital flotsam" (Cole 2014: 26), because he realises that many of the café's patrons are engaged in Internet fraud, popularly called '419' or 'Yahoo Yahoo'. 419, named after Section 419 of the Nigerian criminal code, refers to advance fee fraud schemes, which involves letters or e-mails sent to extracted e-mail addresses. These e-mails typically ask the addressees for their support in the retrieval of a large sum of money that supposedly lies frozen on a Nigerian account, for which they are promised a sizeable part of that money. The narrator's excited shock about his discovery in Cole's novel quickly abates and is replaced with annoyance and criticism: "Yahoo yahoo are on the front lines of their own shadow war, mangling what little good name their country still has" (Cole 2014: 27). Because Cole's narrator is largely an outsider and an almost journalistic observer, he remains on the surface of the phenomenon. Two other Nigerian works of fiction approach the same topic, but examine it in more detail: Sefi Atta's short story "Yahoo Yahoo" (2010) and Adaobi Tricia Nwaubani's novel *I Do Not Come to You by Chance* (2009). Both detail the proceedings of the fraud business as they centre on a young Nigerian who is being introduced to 419. They stage their protagonist's conflict about whether to give in to the temptation of quick and easy money or to resist it for the sake of their families, and thus explore the circumstances and reasons that might drive young men into careers as fraudsters.[3]

Sefi Atta's "Yahoo Yahoo", the last and longest story of her collection *News from Home* (2010), depicts the day on which her first-person narrator, Salami, becomes introduced to the business when a smooth-talking acquaintance tries to

---

[3] An outside perspective on the practice of 419 can be found in the Canadian travel writer Will Ferguson's novel about Nigeria, *419* (2012). In this novel, a North American woman travels to Nigeria to confront a young Nigerian, whose fraudulent activities have driven her father into suicide.

recruit him. The story traces his interest in and excitement about 419, as well as his increasing awareness of its implications. He is attracted by the opportunity to make a lot of money that could relieve his family's poverty. Adaobi Tricia Nwaubani's novel *I Do Not Come To You By Chance* similarly deals with the induction of its protagonist Kingsley into the world of 419. But Kingsley faces higher odds than Salami, who is not under any immediate pressure to make money because he still goes to school and lives with his parents. Kingsley, by contrast, is his family's *opara*, the eldest son and charged with the obligation to provide for his family. Although he is highly educated and well-qualified he is unable to find a job. The costs of his father's illness and eventual death place a great financial burden on the family, while his fiancée leaves him in order to get married to a rich man. For him money is therefore also the decisive incentive to get into 419. At first he only wants to pay the most pressing bills, but soon he starts to enjoy the advantages of having money, a position whose seductive lure is extensively demonstrated in the novel. Both, Nwaubani and Atta show the structural reasons that cause young and well-educated people to become pawns that contribute to and perpetuate the social ills that pervade Nigerian society.

An example of such a fraudulent e-mail can be found in *I Do Not Come To You By Chance*, where Kingsley uses the name of the widow of General Sani Abacha, the military leader who in the 1990s ruled Nigeria with an iron fist, in order to attract possible victims for his scheme:

> Subject: Request for urgent humanitarian assistance/
> Business proposal
> Dear friend,
> I do not come to you by chance. Upon my quest for a trusted and reliable foreign business man or company, I was given your contact by the Nigerian Chamber of Commerce and Industry. I hope that you can be trusted to handle a transaction of this magnitude.
> [...]
> Sometime ago, I deposited the sum of $58,000,000.00 cash (fifty eight million USD) of my late husband's money in a security firm whose name I cannot disclose until I'm sure that I can trust you. I will be very grateful if you could receive these funds for safe keeping. For your kind assistance, you are entitled to 20% of the total sum.
> [...]
> Yours sincerely,
> Hajia Mariam Abacha (Nwaubani 2009: 178–180)[4]

---

4 Salami, in Atta's story, is presented with a similar example: "In my department, we discovered an abandoned sum of $25.5 million [...]. [We decided] to make this business proposal to you and release the money to you as the next of kin [...]. We agree that 30% of the money will be for you as a foreign partner, in respect to the provision of a foreign account, 10% will be set aside for

If the recipients of such an e-mail show interest, they are usually prompted to transfer smaller sums to make possible the main transaction. These bogus fees, such as "registration fees" or "fund transfer repatriation fees", piling up while the promised sum never materializes, are the actual aim of the fraudsters.[5]

The e-mails, as presented in these stories, are therefore not sent with the intention of establishing contact or communication, but with the primary aim to trick foreigners in paying money. The writers of the letters don various masks to deceive the recipients and create numerous scenarios to disguise their fraud e-mails as honest and authentic requests. As Atta puts it, some 419ers "would print fake certificates and letterhead paper, rent a government office and furnish it if necessary. They would put on any charade. Any" (Atta 2010: 246). In one memorable exchange Kingsley realises that a victim from whom he has already received substantial sums has become suspicious. He writes him another e-mail as the director of the "Economic and Financial Crimes Commission" in Nigeria who, he claims, is working together with the FBI in the fight against fraud. He informs the victim that they have caught the perpetrators and will return the money, but claims that "to facilitate the process of retrieving your funds, we would require a payment of $5,000 U.S. dollars for the International Collaboration fees [sic]" (Nwaubani 2014: 358). This is one example of the boundless inventiveness of the fraudsters, who send thousands of e-mails in the hope that among the recipients some are gullible and greedy enough to fall for their ruse. In *Every Day is for the Thief*, Teju Cole's narrator argues that the stories used in the scams "are such enterprising samples of narrative fiction that I realize Lagos is a city of Scheherazades. The stories unfold in ever more fanciful iterations and, as in the myth, those who tell the best stories are richly rewarded" (Cole 2014: 27).

The unnamed narrator in Cole's novel is clearly critical of the scammers but he also blames the gullibility of those who are tricked by 419, noting that there "is a sense, I think, in which the swindler and the swindled deserve each other. It is a kind of mutual humiliation society" (Cole 2014: 27). Similar lines of argumen-

---

expenses incurred during the business, and 60% will be for my colleagues and I. [...] You must apply first to the bank as next of kin of the deceased, indicating your bank name, bank account number, your private telephone and fax number for easy and effective communication" (Atta 2010: 222–223).

5 One character in Nwaubani's novel, for example, pays "$16,000 for lawyer's fees, $19,000 for a change of beneficiary certificate, $14,500 for a security company tariff, $21,000 for transfer of ownership, $ 11,900 for courier charges, $23,000 for customs clearance, $17,000 for Hague authorization, $ 9,000 for ECOWAS duty, and $ 18,700 for insurance fees" (Nwaubani 2009: 270), before eventually getting wary.

tation are used in the 419er's attempts at defending their actions. In Atta's short story, when voicing concerns about his victims Salami is told by his friends that he is "not deceiving them. You're just telling them exactly what they want to hear" (Atta 2010: 270–271). The reasoning is that those that fall for his scams, *Mugus*, deserve it due to their prejudices, greed and corruption:

> *Mugus* were not only fools, he said, but they were also the victims of their own vices. Those who sent money in response to our begging letters were somehow relieving their guilt about how extravagant their lives were, or they were prejudiced about Africans and believed we were all desperately in need. Those who sent money to claim lottery proceeds were plain greedy, and anyone who responded to transfer-of-funds letters had to be corrupt as hell. (Atta 2010: 246)

In Nwaubani's novel there is likewise a lot of space given to the fraudsters' self-justification, for example, when Kingsley argues that the 419ers are supporting local youth and orphans and thus styles them as modern-day Robin Hoods. Most of the justifications for 419 turn conventional notions about the morality of the scammers on their head. They accuse their victims of racism, ignorance, greed, corruption and economic imperialism, while referencing in their own defence the history of slavery and colonialism, reversed imperialist and racist logic as well as the notion that fraud contributes to Nigeria's development (cf. Dalley 2013: 21–24).

Although both Atta's story and Nwaubani's novel evince a certain admiration for the proceedings, they do not romanticize the 419ers. The narratives include numerous objections to the activities of the scammers, not least from their own families. Salami is afraid of his father's reaction, and decides not to join the business. Kingsley's girlfriend leaves him when she finds out about his involvement, and the punishing silence of his mother forces him to at least build a veneer of respectability before she accepts him again. Moreover, the fact that both protagonists are homodiegetic narrators provides Atta and Nwaubani with ample opportunity to present their protagonists' motivations, problems and inner conflicts in complex and detailed ways, rendering them sympathetic characters without hiding their flaws. Both texts therefore present a complex and ambiguous stance towards the 419ers. Neither making excuses for the scammers, nor demonising them, they acknowledge the issue as a serious problem but also show the contexts, circumstances and motivations behind 419 and thus depict it as a complex social matter, an endeavour for which the narrative employment of the letter format proves to be vital.

4 Conclusion

In her influential book, *Epistolarity. Approaches to a Form* (1982), Janet Altman notes that in "numerous instances the basic formal and functional characteristics of the letter, far from being merely ornamental, significantly influence the way meaning is consciously and unconsciously constructed by writers and readers of epistolary works" (Altman 1982: 4). As demonstrated in the examples above, epistolarity is salient in Nigerian fiction. Narrative literature that depicts the phenomenon of 419 naturally revolves around e-mails, which serve as the main instrument in the form of advance fee fraud that involves tricking the addressees into transferring large amounts of money. Sefi Atta's short story, "Yahoo Yahoo" and Adaobi Tricia Nwaubani's novel, *I Do Not Come To You By Chance* present insightful examples of how 419 scams are narrativized in recent Nigerian fiction. In the context of these narratives, letters can also be seen as a starting point for explorations into the contexts of the 419ers and the possible reasons and motivations behind their fraudulent activities.

In the case of diasporic fiction, letters provide insights into a character's migratory experience but often also mark pivotal points in a migrant's trajectory. Letters can reveal the connectedness a character might still feel with their homeland, as in Sefi Atta's "News from Home", where her friend's letter enables the protagonist to participate, to a certain degree, in the struggles at home while living abroad. Letters can indicate the state of despair, sense of failure and loneliness of a character like Akunna in Chimamanda Ngozi Adichie's "The Thing Around Your Neck", who wants to write home but cannot bring herself to actually do it. In Adichie's novel *Americanah*, letters prepare the protagonist's return to Nigeria after many years in the United States by facilitating her attempts at establishing contact with her former boyfriend. Finally, letters can signal a new beginning, such as in the case of Ike Oguine's *A Squatter's Tale*. In this novel a letter from home reveals the protagonist's continued attachment to his girlfriend and Nigeria while also initiating his process of disengagement, at the end of which he is able to truly start his life in the United States.

However, the role of letters in Nigerian literature is not restricted to diasporic fiction and depictions of 419 but can have further functions. In Helon Habila's *Measuring Time* (2007), for example, one character leaves Nigeria in order to participate in military conflicts in other African countries. Throughout the novel he sends letters to his twin brother, a budding historian who has stayed behind, to tell him about his war experiences, but also to communicate the political ideas he is encountering abroad. In Chika Unigwe's novel *Night Dancer* (2012) a Nigerian woman has to come to terms with her mother's death, and she does so with a series of her mother's letters written for her. The letters connect two generations of Nigerian women and help the protagonist to reacquaint herself with her two parents, as she learns more about her family's history. Similarly, in Yewande Omotoso's *Bom Boy* (2011), a Nigerian man writes letters from prison to his South African-born son to impart Nigerian traditional knowledge and folklore to him, telling him about a curse that has afflicted the family. As can be seen, the epistolary mode in Nigerian literature is also used to communicate war experiences and political ideas or serves to transmit cultural and historical knowledge. Considering the multiple functions letters have and the variety of contexts to which they can be applied, there is therefore no doubt that epistolarity plays a major role in contemporary Nigerian literature.

Works Cited

Adichie, Chimamanda Ngozi. 2009. *The Thing Around Your Neck*. London: Fourth Estate.
Adichie, Chimamanda Ngozi. 2014/2013. *Americanah*. London: Fourth Estate.
Altman, Janet Gurkin. 1982. *Epistolarity. Approaches to a Form*. Columbus: Ohio State University Press.
Atta, Sefi. 2010. *News From Home*. Northampton, Mass.: Interlink Books.
Cole, Teju. 2014/2007. *Every Day Is for the Thief*. London: Faber & Faber.
Dalley, Hamish. 2013. "The Idea of 'Third Generation Nigerian Literature': Conceptualizing Historical Change and Territorial Affiliation in the Contemporary Nigerian Novel". *Research in African Literatures* 44.4: 15–34.
Feldner, Maximilian. 2017. "Narrating the Diaspora – Transmigration and Socio-Cultural Imaginaries in 21st Century Nigerian Literature". Unpubl. PhD dissertation, University of Graz.
Feldner, Maximilian. 2018. "Representing the Neocolonial Destruction of the Niger Delta: Helon Habila's Oil on Water (2011)". *Journal of Postcolonial Writing*, doi: 10.1080/17449855.2018.1451358
Ferguson, Will. 2013. *419*. London: Head of Zeus.
Habila, Helon. 2007. *Measuring Time*. New York: Norton.
Koepke, Wulf. 1990. "Epistolary Fiction and Its Impact on Readers: Reality and Illusion". In: Frederick Burwick & Walter Pape (eds.). *Aesthetic Illusion. Theoretical and Historical Approaches*. Berlin: Walter de Gruyter. 263–274.
Nwaubani, Adaobi Tricia. 2009. *I Do Not Come To You By Chance*. New York: Hyperion.
Oguine, Ike. 2000. *A Squatter's Tale*. Oxford: Heinemann.
Omotoso, Yewande 2011. *Bom Boy*. Athlone, South Africa: Modjaji Books.
Osondu, E.C. 2010. *Voice of America*. New York: HarperCollins Publishers.
Unigwe, Chika. 2012. *Night Dancer*. London: Jonathan Cape.

Kym Brindle
Wish I Was There

Economies of Communication in Annie Proulx's *Postcards* and "Brokeback Mountain"

> "I went to the little two-by-four post office and wrote my aunt a penny postcard. We went back to the gray road."
>
> Jack Kerouac, *On the Road* (1957)

Abstract: Annie Proulx exploits the narrative possibilities of the picture postcard in the novel *Postcards* (1993) and in the celebrated short story "Brokeback Mountain" (1999). Ideas of place, landscape, journeying, and longing for home are encapsulated in picture postcards that symbolise geographic distance and emotional alienation. Postcards, freighted with extra-textual meaning derived from picture and place, symbolise spatial and emotional distance between sender and addressee: they are testimony to restless fragmented lives on the road. Proulx exploits structural irony with messages that symbolise the inescapable pull of home and a need to connect whilst remaining largely empty of any truth of experience. Avoidance and liberation from conventions of epistolary exchange are necessary functions for Proulx's regional narratives of exile and alienation.

1 Introduction

American novelist, Annie Proulx exploits the narrative possibilities of the picture postcard in her first novel *Postcards* (1993), which was the first novel written by a woman to win the PEN/Faulkner award. A postcard is also significant in Proulx's short story "Brokeback Mountain", which became part of the 1999 collection *Close Range: Wyoming Stories* and was then adapted for film in 2005.[1] Both novel and story develop the pictorial and souvenir possibilities of postcards. The form's self-reflexive potential is more prominent in the novel and is therefore more extensively explored in this essay. Postcards may, as Jeffrey Meikle observes, be "an ephemeral category of material artefact" (Meikle 2009: 112), but as an embedded epistolary strategy they serve two essential narrative functions for Proulx. Firstly, they subvert iconographic ideas of an American landscape tamed and reduced to national images or romanticised pastoral settings and,

---

[1] The story was originally published in *The New Yorker* in 1997.

https://doi.org/10.1515/9783110584813-006

secondly (specific to *Postcards*), they visually organise a fragmented tale of travel and separation. Proulx's regional narratives of exile and alienation stem from her observation that "the story will come from the landscape" (Skow 1999: n. pag.), and both texts discussed here typically focus on place, landscape, and journeying. Proulx evokes tensions between an idealistic tourist gaze and the harsh reality that subjugates those compelled to scrape an agrarian living from unforgiving territory. This chapter will consider the role of postcards for journeying, which I propose draws energy from the American road narrative. Postcards are epistolary emblems of travel; as Daniel Gifford observes, "postcards are almost instinctively imagined as by-products of travel" (Gifford 2013: 5) and, as such, they testify to restless lives "on the slow move" (Proulx 1993: 254) for Proulx's protagonists, Loyal Blood in *Postcards*, and Ennis Del Mar and Jack Twist in "Brokeback Mountain".[2] For Loyal, abruptly severed from roots and home, a sheaf of identical picture postcards symbolises his fugitive status where "you don't get anywhere except to a different place" (*PC:* 195). For Ennis, a souvenir picture postcard testifies to one special place – a paradise lost, whilst others in the story illustrate the hazards and delays of postal communication. This chapter will consider the ways in which the postcard – that most condensed of epistolary forms[3] – contributes to contemporary conceptions of America and its myths of road, travel, and self-discovery.

Road fables have a long-standing presence in popular American culture, as noted by Ronald Primeau (1996: 1), who claims that "since the 1950s readers have been fascinated by who goes on the road as well as why, when, and where they go and what they discover along the way". Theodore Dreiser's 1916 *A Hoosier Holiday* is usually identified as the first 'automobile road book', but, of course, the most well-known example is Jack Kerouac's 1957 American Beat generation novel, *On the Road*, with its iconic counterculture celebration of individualism. Travel stories tend to focus on the romance of the road, developing ideas of adventure and freedom, often with a focus on masculinity and liberation. The genre is grounded in pioneering ideals of 'going West' supported by the pervasive ideology of the American Dream that includes "the importance of: individual and national freedom, independence, and mobility; democratic space in a simultaneously present and vanished frontier" (Slethaug and Stacilee 2012: 4). Notions of freedom and individualism, and ideas of spiritual growth and quest are a driving force in road tales founded on frontier mythology, with the frontier famously explained by Frederick Turner in 1893 as "the outer-edge of the wave – the meet-

---

2 Hereafter referred to parenthetically as (*PC*) and (*BM*).
3 With the possible exception of the telegram.

ing point between savagery and civilization" (Turner 1893: n. pag.) Proulx's insistent preoccupation with Turner's unstable line between savagery and civilisation challenges the myths associated with the American frontier. Her fiction subverts ideals of frontier conquest dismantling notions of a mythological West of opportunity and personal freedom. "Brokeback Mountain", with its deterministic depiction of "country boys with no prospects" (*BM:* 284), highlights the failure of key concepts of the American Dream, as does the struggle of the Blood family in *Postcards* who haplessly watch the disintegration of family and farm.

Proulx aligns postal culture with the tradition of the American road narrative. Post and road are indeed inextricably linked; as Esther Milne (2014: 306) observes, "metaphors of transportation and travel, of arrival and departure, of traversing distance and imagining presence define the epistolary register". On their introduction in the late nineteenth century postcards offered a cheap and fast form of communication. Plain cards evolved in Austria and Germany in the 1870s, with picture postcards spreading across Europe and reaching England in 1894. They provided a new and condensed physical space for text that demanded a different style of writing and economic use of language. The 1893 Chicago Exposition stimulated the first widespread use of privately printed picture postcards in the United States, with Rural Free Delivery established in 1898. As Rosamond Vaule (2004: 48) points out, "at a time when the telephone was not yet an integral part of the American household, postcards provided both a visual and written link, whether from across town or across the nation". Rise in popularity of the picture postcard reflects the expansion of the United States from small town rurality to an urban, consumerist superpower.[4] Postcards were, as Allen Freeman-Davis (2002: 1) argues, very much part of the "emerging world of consumption, advertising, and accelerated communication". Davis further suggests that "to travel and not buy postcards is almost to deny that you went on a trip. Postcards enabled the tourist to preserve the memory of travel, and to put those memories in order" (Davis 2002: 4). There were concerns that the postcard's missing envelope exposed the epistolary message to potential unauthorized reading; postcards may have gained the convenience of brevity, but they lost confidentiality and the postcard had to be accepted as an open form of communication that mutates the epistolary privacy pact. The key fact that postcards offer a semi-public form of address that is personal, but not private is not, however, a problem for Proulx's reticent men of few words.

---

4 George Eastman's development of photographic equipment fuelled the postcard boom and cards became widely available in general stores across the country. Kodak facilitated the printing of private photo cards and the tourist industry, encouraged by the railways, promoted souvenir cards.

Typically succinct and often evasive, postcards are an ideal epistolary vehicle for Proulx's 'dirty realist' representation of tough, terse masculinity. Outlined in 1983 by Bill Burford, dirty realism was explained as a new type of writing with "a different scope" that focussed on "the belly side of contemporary life", "devoted to the local details, the nuances, the little disturbances in language and gesture [...] strange stories: unadorned, unfurnished, low-rent tragedies" (Burford 1983: 4). What is particularly pertinent for this discussion is Burford's claim that the genre's stylistics are characterised by sentences "stripped of adornment, [...]; it is what's not being said – the silences, the elisions, the omissions – that seem to speak most" (Burford 1983: 5). Elisions and omissions are also essential characteristics of postcard communication, with limited space offering ready excuse for those who prefer to say little. David Henkin (2006: 174) points out that "the postcard tendency was the reduction of correspondence to formal gestures", a point echoed by Bernard Siegert, who argues that "in principle, the postcard was therefore nothing but a stamp that could be written on; it reduced the materiality of communication to its bare economy" (Siegert 1999: 154).

Significantly, Proulx explains that postcards were a narrative device that enabled her to "enlist the aid of the reader in filling in the blanks" (Bray 1992: n. pag.). Here, the narrative possibilities of the postcard as an epistolary medium become clear: truncated missives promote strategies of close reading inviting recipients to read between the lines and speculate beyond limited content. In this way, readers piece together a tale of separation and perceive different realities and viewpoints. As Janet Gurkin Altman argues "the narrative discontinuity inherent in the epistolary form affords interesting possibilities for elliptical, allusive writing, the creation of suspense, and juxtaposition of contrasting views or episodes" (Altman 1982: 183). Postcards frame sections of narrative and provide context for each chapter as well as visually highlighting epistolary relations to similarly sustain a focus on distance, travel and separation throughout the novel. The postcards frame chapters in dissimilar ways to epigraphs, which tend to make room for voices of historical authority or literary intertexts. They are examples of Gérard Genette's paratexts: "More than a boundary or a sealed border, the paratext is, rather, a threshold" (Genette 1997: 1). As "thresholds" visually distinct from the body of text, but narratively informative, they cause, as Bernard Duyfhuizen suggests, "the framing narrative and the framed tale to merge in interpretively significant ways" (Duyfhuizen 1992: 159). Abbreviated messages and abstracted meaning frustrate recipients and leave them puzzling over what is not said rather than simply accepting the economy of sparse words on the card. In this way, Proulx organises themes of alienation and distance – both geographic and emotional.

2 Postcards – Fragmentation and Irony

In Proulx's novel, material images of postcards form one element of a fragmented narrative. The novel depicts the decline of a farming family in post-war America. The first chapter opens with a murder scene and is headed by a postcard dated 1944; a final card dated 1988 prefaces the penultimate chapter. Forty-nine of the fifty-eight chapters are, in fact, prefaced with an image of a postcard. (These are mostly handwritten and often difficult to read.) Ten intermittent chapters, all with the same title "What I See", do not have a preface, and one further chapter is framed by an extract from a Fire Marshall's Report instead of a postcard; two more postcards appear mid-chapter. The Report extract is perhaps afforded preface privilege because, as Proulx's explains, the novel was, in fact, inspired by a Vermont fire marshal's report from the 1930s in conjunction with an actual picture postcard. A stack of cards with pictures of escaped convicts originally circulated as sheriff alerts was given to Proulx by a friend. In interview with Rosemary L. Bray of *The New York Times*, Proulx states: "I had a few and found them haunting, absolutely disturbing" (Bray 1992: n. pag.). The character Loyal Blood was spurred on by the "arresting" face on one particular card and her fictional "character jumped forward at once" (Bray 1992: n. pag.).

As prefaces, cards in *Postcards* are written by various correspondents ranging from officials and doctors, to an opportunist neighbour turned realtor, and a relative of murdered Billy's querying her disappearance. All the Blood family write postcards at some point, with eleven signed by Loyal and a further unsigned anonymous card in his handwriting. The postcards provide snapshots of individual family characters: aggressive, blunt communication from violent, bullish patriarch Mink Blood, indicative of his "monotonous ideas and narrow corridors of toil" (*PC:* 19); (see Figure 1).

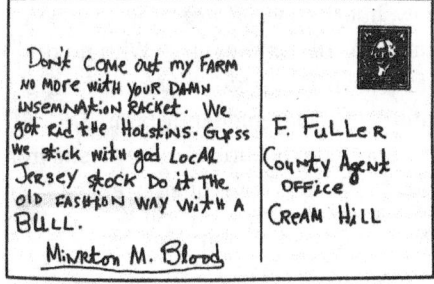

Figure 1 "Mink's Revenge"

His wife, Jewell Blood, "crushed [by him] into a corner of her life" – a domestic life of "profound sameness" (*PC:* 143) – writes despairingly to her eldest son, "Come home" (*PC:* 124). Brother Marvin (Dub), ironically the son with "wandering habits" (*PC:* 18), reveals "pent rage" (*PC:* 55) at Loyal's abandonment of responsibility for farm and family to him; cards detail a spell in prison, a subsequent dubious rise in fortunes, and then "tax problems" that cause these to fall again. And for sister Mernelle, desperate for love and connection beyond the farm, postcards are eagerly awaited, a joyous anticipation of the wider world and passport to a different life; she corresponds first with a pen-pal and then conducts an epistolary romance with a "lonely hearts prisoner" (*PC:* 132) who advertises in the newspaper for a wife. The ironies multiply as the family all receive marketing cards offering wry advertisement for a new consumerist America: "the fancy arm. The prosthesis" (*PC:* 49) for Dub, who lost a limb jumping from a moving freight train; electric fences for Mink – unrealised promise of modernisation for the farm that might have saved it and him; "Rudy's Car City" (*PC:* 237) for Jewell, who finds brief freedom on the road before a car accident results in her death.

In this way, postcards organise the dark thread of irony that stitches the fragmented novel together. As Linda Hutcheon (1994: 35) explains, "irony is a 'weighted' mode of discourse in the sense that it is asymmetrical, unbalanced in favor of the silent and the unsaid". As a narrative strategy, postcards realise Proulx's fascination for "watching for the historical skew between what people have hoped for and who they thought they were and what befell them" (TMR 1999: n. pag.). The 'skew' takes shape with irony realised as the "silent and the unsaid" of postcards' elliptical gaps. Bleak, typical Proulx mischance forces swift and unpredictable change for Loyal Blood, who echoes pioneer ideology when he abruptly announces his departure from the family farm: "we're pullin' out and going out west, someplace out there, buy a farm, make a new start" (*PC:* 10). This is dishonest and ironic, on all levels. The novel has opened with a murder – possibly accidental – we never know, but this event forces Loyal's involuntary exile from the farm he loves to an unhappy life on the road.[5] With no desire to venture further than the fence line of his own property – it was, in fact, girlfriend Billy, who longed to escape a future "on your goddamn farm" (*PC:* 81), holed-up in a world she scorns. Now dead and secretly buried by Loyal, she ironically stays behind on the land that Loyal loves and is consequently exiled from.

---

5 Details of the tragedy remain ambiguous to the end of the novel: we know that Billy suffocated in the mud during sexual intercourse/rape, but it is unclear whether this was because Loyal blacked out or succumbed to the "The Blood temper" (*PC:* 18).

In rare internal recognition of irony, Loyal sets out "down on the town road he thought it was a sour joke how things had turned out" (*PC:* 13).

Postcards highlight a contradiction between appearance and reality by revealing a gulf between Loyal Blood's life as represented in infrequent messages home, and the reality of the world he, in fact, experiences on the road – the world we read about in the main body of text. Irony is further developed as readers become privy to unrecognised catastrophes in the world he writes back to. With no dreams of freedom or frontier, Loyal's road narrative is less quest and more dismal recording of estrangement from home. With no itch to escape (unlike brother Dub, and sister Mernelle), no desire for travel or new experience, he suffers greatly from what Proulx has elsewhere termed "the substitution of the steering wheel for the curve of the earth" (Proulx 2008: 23). In permanent exile, he is condemned to a restless geographic odyssey with no planned destination. "He didn't think where he was going, just heading out. It seemed to him there didn't have to be a direction, just a random travelling away from the farm. It wasn't the idea that he could go anywhere, but the idea that he had to go somewhere, and it didn't make any difference where" (*PC:* 26). He did not want to leave his rural heritage – his ambition and identity are bound and fixed with the farm, and he remains forever 'loyal' to the memory of it. Alienated from home and family, the road for Loyal is hence always identified as the "wrong road"; "a back road"; "a dusty road;" "empty dirt roads"; a "lonely road".

Proulx's neo-Regionalism comprehensively distorts the road narrative tradition. For Loyal, what becomes of his life and what forms the bulk of the narrative is not the lost family farm or the soured dream of a new one, but his perpetual journeying: "He's not sure where he is. So many roads look the same, the repetitive signs, the yellow stripe to the horizon. The same cars and trucks are repeated over and over" (*PC:* 308). In a discussion of travel and landscape, Proulx reveals distaste for the automobile:

> The invention and manufacture of the automobile and paved high-ways provided the national psyche with a surrogate frontier. By 1927, 26 million cars stank and jarred around the country, each driver a pioneer. For the following generation, the mythic drive from coast-to-coast became a rite of passage; and the road book, an important American literary form. (Proulx 2008: 17)

Unsurprisingly, therefore, the protagonists of her fiction are focussed on survival rather than redemptive travel experience. Poverty and hardship remove them from ideals of social protest and they take to the road purely for economic survival. The "unsecured scaffolding" (*PC:* 253) of Loyal's rootless wanderings include prospecting for uranium; trying to scrape a bare living as a bone digger, then trapper, and a brief experience of farming his own land. Realising the cherished dream of land ownership goes literally up in smoke, as his farm, just like his home, burns to the ground uninsured. "Brokeback Mountain"'s "pair of deuces going nowhere" (*BM:* 285) similarly depicts economic plight and, more significantly, social and cultural outlawing of taboo love. These are dirty realism's "stories not of protest but of the occasion for it" (Burford 1983: 5).

3 Postcards – Function and Form

Altman's point that "within the epistolary work the letter has both a dependent and independent status" (Altman 1982: 167) is similarly applicable to the postcard. Dependently, they work to contextualise chapters and fill gaps in the main narrative, but independently, and visually, they remind of distance – literal and metaphorical. The content of the cards may initially appear somewhat random, but, as prefaces, they organise Proulx's distinctive black irony – the "discomforting and sometimes elusive irony" that Burford identifies as the stylization of dirty realist stories (Burford 1983: 4). Independently, they offer minimal information in coded messages that require active, close, and speculative reading alert to sub-textual messages; they promote a style of reading that may generate misreading on very little information. Dependently they are linked to the topic of each chapter signalling often abrupt shifts in direction to emphasise that this is a work of textual fragments. As fragments, they offer no overt continuity, but Loyal's do chart a broad chronological guide to a wandering life: his eleven postcards plot a simple linear (if deceptive path) through an unhappy life in exile. They are marked by repeated expressions of ironic hope that the farm is "doing good" (*PC:* 56), illustrating stark irony between postcard sentiment and reality. His postcard messages barely skim the surface of a chaotic world of random misfortune on the road, and lack of exchange leaves him blind to home disasters: fires, lost farms, lost babies, both parents lost to suicide and accident – incalculable loss and no gain – dirty realism's strange and fated stories.

As Loyal's only link with home, postcards provide fragmented and deceiving testimony. Dufhuyizen posits that "the framed tale, we often discover, is centered on questions of human contact and transmission" (Dufhuyizen 1992: 158). In this case, Proulx's focus is on motion and movement away from the centre, with the postcard a slender and unsatisfying transmission of human contact. A shuffle of illgotten postcards – all with the same image of the "thick-bodied bear with a red snout coming out of the black trees" (*PC:* 33) become Loyal's only point of contact with his family. For Loyal, the road stretches longer, places become many, and connection with home more and more distant, but the bear postcard remains con-

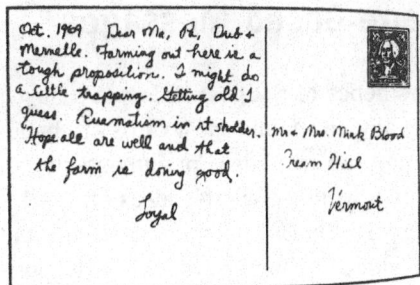

Figure 2: "Shotguns"

stant. As intermittent, but persistent contact with family, the card's epistolary journey is always homeward and it repeatedly drops into the Blood family mailbox. Gifford argues that postcards seldom carried a substantial linear message and Loyal's reflect this with spare and evasive messages that throw new emphasis on the picture. The bear represents Loyal's enduring psychic return to an unbearable, profound loss. The relationship between sender and image thus provides a symbolic and material medium for the condition of exile. Hunted and "unbalanced in mind" (*PC*: 36), the bear was a popular tourist attraction before suddenly disappearing from view. Captured on film by an amateur photographer, the bear, as a postcard image, signifies careless consumer sentiment – the natural world unsympathetically hijacked by a greedy, unthinking tourist gaze. The history of the card is explained in a brief dedicated chapter entitled "A Short, Sharp Shock", with a postcard preface dated 1926. The card closes a narrative gap to explain the bear's disappearance – a victim of rural modernisation, the information that the bear is electrocuted exemplifies the function of the postcard as preface (see figure 3).

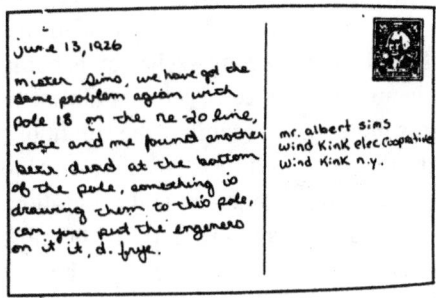

Figure 3: "A Short, Sharp Shock"

4 Picture Postcards – Image Based Messages

As visual media, postcards supply an aesthetics of the post in Proulx's novel; there are no postmarks, but dates are usually given, and most cards are handwritten. Handwriting has always been bound up with ideas of authenticity (an abiding concern of Proulx's). Simulated handwriting emulates ideas of a verifiable trace of paper to body; as Johanna Drucker (1995: 62) maintains, "'personal writing' is always an inscription of the individual within the symbolic". The postcard bear symbolises Loyal's alienation from his natural habitat, where "the smooth fields were echoes of himself in the landscape" (*PC:* 85). His brief, undetailed, and dissembling written messages are not explicit and the postcard image is misunderstood and not read symbolically or even sympathetically by family addressees. The handwritten cards may visually suggest "inscription of the individual" (Drucker 1995: 62), but fundamentally they accentuate a paradox of contact and separation. Their multiplicity and constraints of epistolary form further add to their frustration: "another bear postcard for Jewell, written in Loyal's handwriting, so small it was a nuisance to read it" (*PC:* 40–41). Cards begin with the signature, "son Loyal", later condensed to "Loyal", and eventually reduced forty-three years later to an impersonal "L.B" – an erosion of 'loyalty' and 'blood' ties that indicates widening material, if not emotional, distance.

"Brokeback Mountain"'s postcards are the epistolary means of closing what is in many ways an insurmountable social and geographic distance. The text is less overtly structured by postcards than the novel, but they do supply the necessary epistolary medium to organise Jack and Ennis's long-distance, thinly-stretched relationship. For a love affair marked by hiatus, postal communication is vital to arrange infrequent meetings that barely bridge "the great gulf" (*BM:* 287) between the lovers.[6] A fragile epistolary chain of communication typifies a relationship characterised by delay, waiting, anticipation, with time lapses often felt interminable: "never enough time, never enough" (*BM:* 307). In this way, the story's cards draw on a more traditional epistolary exchange, echoing strong links to sentimentality and the genre of romance of letter tradition in its early formation. In this guise, postcards more closely manifest the conditions of epistolary presence and absence, what Anne Bower suggests is "*so* essential to letters – an agonizing pull between here and there, intimacy and separation, bonds and barriers, time present and future (or past and present), the tangible and the intangible" (Bower 2014: 16; original emphasis). It is by postcard that ab-

---

[6] Jack's first contact with Ennis after a four-year gap is by letter. Postcards are their means of communication thereafter.

sence is made final and barriers become permanent when Ennis learns of Jack's death by post: "Ennis didn't know about the accident for months until his postcard to Jack saying that November still looked like the first chance came back stamped DECEASED" (*BM:* 311; original emphasis). Such abrupt closure of epistolary presence as third-person impersonal despatch of devastating news is similarly emphasised in *Postcards*, when Jewell and Mernelle write in a vain attempt to Loyal to let him know that his father has died, with a card addressed to "Mr. Loyal Blood (works at mines) General Delivery, Colorado" (*PC:* 124). The card is unsurprisingly returned: "ADDRESS UNKNOWN" (*PC:* 124; original emphasis), a poignant illustration that Loyal truly is "lost out in the world" (*PC:* 128).

In different ways, therefore, both texts reflect ideas of epistolary presence, as posited by Esther Milne (2010: 2):

> presence is a term that need not refer always to *material, corporeal* presence. Rather presence is an effect achieved in communication (whether by letters, postcards or email, for example) when interlocutors imagine the psychological or, sometimes, physical presence of the other.

However, this argument is based on epistolary dialogue – a component missing from the Blood family postal transaction. With no return address (excepting the final vague "Coffee Pot, Michigan", (*PC:* 330), the bear image consistently anonymises location, thereby denying presence and continually frustrating recipients: "'How come he don't put no return address on these things,' asked Jewell, turning the postcard over and frowning at the bear. 'How does he expect us to answer him? How are we supposed to tell him anything that's went on'" (*PC:* 42). As the family disintegrates and the farm is destroyed by fire, all Loyal's immediate family rail against the 'empty' communication of his postcards

> 'Bloods been running on empty since Loyal lit out. Damn him, sends his damn postcards every year or so but never lets us know where to write. You realise he don't even know Pa's dead? ... Sends his dumb bear postcards. How many of those bears have we got to see? What makes him think I want to hear from Him? I don't care about his damn postcards'. (*PC:* 249)

The key difference between Loyal Blood's multiple "dumb bear postcards" and Ennis Del Mar's single picture postcard is the absence of location; the two texts therefore diversify ideas of the image based message. Unlike Loyal's stack of postcards, Ennis buys just one. Declaring "one's enough" (*BM:* 317), his card is not destined for postal transaction like Loyal's, but is kept and treasured as a souvenir of place to support imagination and memory. Ennis's card, to borrow Mark Asquith's phrase is "landscape reduced to postcard sublimity" (Asquith 2009: 29) that fixes nostalgic memory and idealisation of place and the past.[7] It is treasured as an *aide-memoire* that in some small way closes an impossible gap in space and time. Susan Stewart suggests, "the souvenir speaks to a context of origin through a language of longing, for it is not an object arising out of need or use value; it is an object arising out of the necessarily insatiable demands of nostalgia" (Stewart 1993: 135). Materially embodying symbolic meaning and fashioning memory as a sacramental object that feeds nostalgia, the picture postcard is all that remains of the "imagined power of Brokeback Mountain" (*BM:* 316). In this way, the absolute focus on place for Ennis's souvenir image contrasts with Loyal's absent location and denial of postal contract.

In dissimilar, and less material ways, cards nonetheless function as a metaphor to tie memory to place in *Postcards*. On the day that Loyal unwillingly sets out on the road, he 'fixes' the familiar landscape in his memory with a final glance at the farm. Place is already reshaping in the form of a tourist image suggestive of an elemental trinity of sky, water, and land framed as an idealised postcard image. This will shape memory as narrative to be revisited again and again over long time:

> The place was as fixed as a picture on a postcard, the house and barn like black ships in an ocean of fields, the sky a membrane holding the final light, and there were the blurred kitchen windows and up behind the buildings the field, the rich twenty-acre field propped open toward the south like a Bible, the crease of the water vein almost exactly in the centre of the ten-acre pages. (*PC:* 14)

The production processes of nostalgic memory are thus made visible. Loyal believes that "the unsecured scaffolding of his life rested on forgetting" (*PC:* 253), but the imagined picture postcard is imprinted on his memory as a story-book memory of the past. It illustrates pure landscape unpolluted by the highway and Proulx's "stinking and jarring" automobiles. It reflects Hutcheon's outline of nostalgia whereby "the simple, pure, ordered, easy, beautiful, or harmonious past is constructed (and then experienced emotionally) in conjunction with the present – which, in turn, is constructed as complicated, contaminated, anarchic, difficult, ugly, and confrontational" (Hutcheon 1998: n. pag.). Perpetually in motion, Loyal's 'home' on the road is a contaminated, difficult, and ugly present: an anarchic jangling of sounds far removed from the elegiac lost landscape: "cowboy bars were his living rooms and he had a thousand from Arizona to Montana"

---

[7] Actual picture postcards were subject to much reshaping of reality. Hyperreal colours fed technicolour memories putting a bright slant on what might have been a less vivid reality. See Jeffrey Meikle (2016) on the Curt Teich company's production of linen postcards.

(*PC:* 253); their sounds – "jukebox, click of cues, cooler door slamming, chair leg scrape, talk" were "home sounds for him" (*PC:* 254). Hutcheon suggests that nostalgia is "rarely the past as actually experienced, of course; it is the past as imagined, as idealized through memory and desire" (Hutcheon 1998: n. pag.). Shaped by unhappy journeying, Loyal idealises the past in nostalgic (but deceptive) memory and the present and the road are purely an extended passage of mourning for his loss.

The final one of ten naturalistic chapters entitled "What I see" revisits the postcard-styled image that Loyal retains in memory. In the beginning the land was shaped as a biblical narrative, but at the end of his life it is his one time travelling companion, Blue Skies, and the palimpsest of his book – "the Indian's book. His book" (*PC:* 109) – that rewrites landscape as "the close-stitched earth, the root, the rock" (*PC:* 340). This text is a more authentic record than the unadorned framework of his postcards. He tentatively becomes confident to write: "things he planned to do, song lyrics, distances travelled, what he ate and what he drank" (*PC:* 109), as a more detailed, honest, and private record of journeying than the sparse, allusive postcards with their mystifying symbolism.

5 Conclusion

Postcards occupy a special place in epistolary culture forging connections between letter writing and digital communication. The brevity of reduced, often cryptic messages anticipates adaptations of epistolary culture that have become commonplace in subsequent texting and message technologies. Postcards may be freighted with extra-textual meaning derived from picture and place, but they are also in many ways imperfect and flawed motifs of epistolary communication. Any epistolary transmission is inherently fragmented, but further fragmentation of the message is driven by the spatial constraints of postcards, which compel writing to be modified for a condensed postal transaction. As Altman observes "epistolary narrative is by definition fragmented narrative. Discontinuity is built into the very blank space that makes of each [postcard] a footprint rather than a path" (Altman 1982: 169). Brevity of form and typical one-way communication may, in fact, come to symbolise geographic distance and emotional alienation as much as reinforce connection between sender and addressee. The gestures and economy of postcard writing therefore dovetail with the halting and evasive style of communication that tends to characterise Proulx's torturous relationships. In a rough-and-ready western world that comprehensively debunks the Western mythology of the cowboy, the frontier, and pioneer spirit, personal relationships are typified by the restricted formality of postcard epistolary transaction. Moreover, Proulx's ready acknowledgement of a writing strategy of elision where "the reader writes most of the story" (Bray 1992: n. pag.) readily coincides with the gaps and delays of postcard transmission. Proulx's theme of landscape and dirty realist techniques draw on epistolary strategies as clear links to travel, home, and the land seen from the perspective of those who suffer and work it, emphasising, as Ennis del Mar concludes, "if you can't fix it you've got to stand it" (*BM*: 318). Failing this, take to the unhappy road.

Works Cited

Altman, Janet Gurkin. 1982. *Epistolarity. Approaches to a Form*. Columbus: Ohio State University Press.
Asquith, Mark. 2009. *Annie Proulx's "Brokeback Mountain" and Postcards. Continuum Contemporaries*. London: Continuum.
Bower, Anne. 2014. *Epistolary Responses. The Letter in Twentieth-Century American Fiction and Criticism*. Tuscaloosa: University of Alabama Press.
Bray, Rosemary. 1992. "The Reader Writes most of the Story". *New York Times Books*. <http://www.nytimes.com/books/99/05/23/specials/proulx-postcards.html> [accessed 20 July 2017].
Burford, Bill. 1983. *Granta 8: Dirty Realism. New Writing from America*. Middlesex: Penguin Books.
Davis, Allen F. 2002. *Postcards from Vermont. A Social History, 1905–1945*. Hanover: University Press of New England.
Drucker, Johanna. 1998. *Figuring the Word. Essays on Books, Writing and Visual Poetics*. New York: Granary Books.
Duyfhuizen, Bernard. 1992. *Narratives of Transmission*. London: Associated University Presses.
Genette, Gerard. 1997. *Paratexts. Thresholds of Interpretation*. Trans. by Jane E. Lewin. Cambridge: Cambridge University Press.
Gifford, Daniel. 2013. *American Holiday Postcards. 1905–1915. Imagery and Context*. Jefferson, NC.: McFarland & Company.
Henkin, David. 2006. *The Postal Age. The Emergence of Modern Communications in Nineteenth-Century*. Chicago: University of Chicago Press.
Hutcheon, Linda. 1994. *Irony's Edge. The Theory and Politics of Irony*. London: Routledge.
Hutcheon, Linda. 1998. "Irony, Nostalgia and the Postmodern". <http://www.library.utoronto.ca/utel/criticism/hutchinp.html> [accessed 2 February 2017].
Kerouac, Jack. 2000/1957. *On the Road*. London: Penguin.
Meikle, Jeffrey L. 2009. "Pasteboard Views: Idealizing Public Space in American Postcards, 1931–1953". In: Miles Orvell & Jeffrey L. Meikle (eds.). *Public Space and the Ideology of Place in American Culture*. Amsterdam: Rodopi. 111–133.
Meikle, Jeffrey L. 2016. *Postcard America. Curt Teich and the Imaging of a Nation, 1931–1950*. Texas: University of Texas Press.
Milne, Esther. 2010. *Letters, Postcards, Email. Technologies of Presence*. London: Routledge.

Milne, Esther. 2014. "Postcards". In: Merriman & Mimi Sheller (eds.). *The Routledge Handbook of Mobilities*. London: Routledge. 306–315.

Primeau, Ronald. 1996. *Romance of the Road. The Literature of the American Highway*. Ohio: Bowling Green State University Popular Press.

Proulx, Annie. 2003/1993. *Postcards*. London: Fourth Estate.

Proulx, Annie, 2000/1999. *Close Range Wyoming Stories*. London: Fourth Estate.

Proulx, Annie. 2008. "Dangerous Ground: Landscape in American Fiction". In: Timothy R. & Wendy J. Katz (eds.). *Regionalism and the Humanities*. Lincoln: University of Nebraska Press. 6–25.

Siegert, Bernhard. 1999. *Relays. Literature as an Epoch of the Postal System*. California: Stanford University Press.

Skow, John. 1999. "On Strange Ground". *Time Magazine* May 17. <http://content.time.com time/magazine/article/09171,990992,00.html> [accessed 13 February 2017].

Slethaug, Gordon E. & Ford Stacilee. 2012. (eds.). *Hit the Road, Jack: Essays on the Culture of the American Road*. Montreal: McGill-Queens University Press.

Staff at TMR, 1999. "Interview with Annie Proulx". *The Missouri Review* 22. <http://www.missourireview.com/index.php?genre=Interviews&title=Interview+with+Annie+Proulx> [accessed 13 February 2017].

Stewart, Susan. 1993. *On Longing. Narratives of the Miniature, the Gigantic, the Souvenir, the Collection*. Durham: Duke University Press.

Turner, Frederick Jackson. 1893. "The Significance of the Frontier in American History". *Modern History Sourcebook*. <http://www.fordham.edu/halsall/mod/1893turner.html> [accessed 13 February 2017].

Vaule, Rosamond B. 2004. *As We Were. American Photographic Postcards, 1905–1930*. Boston: David R. Godine.

Part III: **The Contemporary Epistolary Novel**

Wolfgang Hallet
Epistolary Forms as Semiotic and Generic Modes in the Multimodal Novel

Abstract: The integration and representation of epistolary forms in the novel is by no means a new phenomenon or narrative strategy. However, the traditional word novel, as a rule, transforms them into the verbal sign-system of narrative discourse and its linearity. By contrast, the multimodal novel tries to reproduce the original shape, material features and textual organization of epistolary forms, be they personal handwritten or formal and typed business letters, postcards, notes or e-mails, in recognizable ways. Thus, they are not only bounded texts in their own right that constitute the polyphony of narrative discourse, but they are also artefacts and objects that offer the reader direct access to personal utterances and ways of establishing interpersonal relations in the fictional world. Authored and produced by fictional characters, the reproduction of epistolary forms draws the reader into communicative, social and, sometimes, also material practices in the fictional world.

1 Semiotic Modes in the Traditional and in the Multimodal Novel

The rise of the multimodal novel, mainly and increasingly from the beginning of the 1990s, is directly connected with and constituted through the use of various textual and symbolic forms in novelistic narration. As compositional elements, they remain recognizable in terms of their original shape, wording and materiality, if only in imitated, reproduced form (as, e.g., print reproductions of hand-drawn sketches, handwritten letters or diary entries, or of photographs or maps). Such textual and other semiotic elements are thus displayed as clearly bounded texts, artefacts or objects in the fictional world on the one hand, but are fully integrated into, or framed by, the narrative discourse on the other. Like handwritten letters, postcards, notes or e-mails, they are all texts in their own right that are able to produce and carry meaning, establish interpersonal relations and show characteristic textual features in distinct cultural contexts. The reader is thus directly presented with ways of communicating and producing meaning in the fictional world. Obviously, this type of narrative discourse also affects the act of reading substantially: the reader is urged to interconnect the various single modes and semiotic artefacts in the novel, including verbal narration, and process them into a more or less coherent meaning of the novel. Thus, although the multimodal novel may be composed of a range of distinct texts and other semiotic elements, the act of (hypertextual) reading turns the multimodal novel into one whole bounded text and "a single, multi-layered, multimodal communicative act, whose illocutionary force comes about through the fusion of all the component semiotic modes" (van Leeuwen 2005: 121).

By contrast, the traditional word novel in printed form has to present and represent such other semiotic forms merely in verbal form: a newspaper clipping cannot be reproduced but has to be paraphrased, and instead of representing places and distances in a cartographic map, as the multimodal novel might do, the traditional novel has to resort to describing places and spaces in verbal form. Photographs as artefacts and objects in the fictional world are a case in point, too. They can only be integrated into the traditional novelistic narrative if they are 'translated' into words, i.e. by providing the reader with a neat ekphrastic description of the objects and persons in the photograph. Also, its composition, i.e. the way the content of a photograph is presented and arranged in this visual artefact, can be conveyed to the reader in verbal form only. In the case of a colour photograph, the colours would also have to be 'translated' by giving the reader an idea of the shades of colour, their combination, their interplay with the objects and persons in the photograph. Therefore, the traditional novel is a case of the monomodal concept of communication, in which "language was (seen as) the central and only full means for representation and communication" (Kress & Van Leeuwen 2001: 45).

Thus, from a semiotic perspective, verbal narration may be regarded as a complex act of semiotic translation that transforms various semiotic modes into the discursive mode of the word novel. It may even be argued that the metaphorical language of fiction is deeply rooted in this need to 'translate': in order to convey the shapes, forms and the textual or aesthetic organization of an artefact or the looks of a person or object to the reader, the author (and the narrator) often resort to metaphors and similes, since otherwise it would be almost impossible to evoke in the reader a precise impression or imagination of the original (material) objects or artefacts.

All of this applies to epistolary forms in the traditional novel, too. Since the original letters and epistolary messages are not or cannot be represented in their full material, medial and visual form, there are different strategies of representing and integrating them into the narrative discourse of the traditional novel. The simplest form would be reported speech, authored by the narrator or one of the characters in the novel. In this case, the original letter would not occur at all; instead, it would be presented in completely discursive form, with no specific representation of the different mode in which it was first created. Thus, the semiotic mode that the reader is presented with is either written discourse or a written transcript of the original written mode, as is the case with handwritten letters or messages.

Quoting a sentence or a passage from the letter, with quotation marks signalling and confirming to the reader that these are (genuinely) the original words in the letter, would be another representational strategy. In case a whole letter is quoted, paragraphing would be a textual strategy, suggesting that the part of the narrative discourse in question that is set off from other parts of the text was not authored by the narrator, but by one of the characters in the novel, i.e. the sender of the letter. Often, the use of different font types is another indicator of an originally different semiotic mode, symbolizing that the letter was either hand-typed or e-mailed. Italics are often used to represent handwriting, such as in personal letters or on postcards or in informal notes. Apart from typography, layout may be a form of symbolic representation that makes it possible to convey to the reader the typical textual structure of a letter, with lines for the date, the reference or the salutation. This way, an epistolary novel that is almost exclusively composed of a series of letters may look rather conventional by employing traditional typing and print technologies only (cf. fig. 1), as opposed to a mimetic photographic reproduction of 'the original' letter or postcard.

The personal handwritten postcard may serve as a particularly striking example that the traditional word novel is semiotically limited when it comes to representing artefacts of a specific design. The front side, as a rule, displays a photograph or picture or another kind of graphic design. The verso of the postcard has a specific layout that defines it as a specific mode and genre, dividing the page into a field for a stamp, lines for the postal address and usually half of the page for the handwritten message. If addressed in the word novel, the graphic front must be described in great detail to enable the reader to imagine the original picture, and the back side with the message can only be represented if the layout of the book page mimics the specific organization of this side of the postcard and the handwritten characters of the textual message. However, the original visual form of the stamp cannot be represented or imitated; the narrator (and the author) need to provide the reader with an extremely detailed verbal description (ekphrasis) of the content, colours and contours in order to evoke a mental image in the reader.

The postcard is also an interesting instance of how semiotic modes and culturally established genres always also constitute communicative, social and cultural practices. As a rule, a postcard is part of a situation in which the sender is temporarily away from their regular social environment and in a context that is different from this person's everyday routines (e.g. holiday). The postcard is often meant to signal to the addressee that the sender seeks to sustain personal

20 • MARIA SEMPLE

pause and revisit the rules outlined in the Galer Street handbook. (Italics mine.)

Section 2A. Article ii. There are two ways to pick up students.
By Car: Drive your vehicle to the school entrance. Please be mindful not to block the loading dock for Sound Seafood International.
On Foot: Please park in the north lot and meet your children on the canal path. *In the spirit of safety and efficiency, we ask that parents on foot do not approach the drive-up area.*

It always inspires me that we have such a wonderful community of parents who are so engaged with one another. However, the safety of our students is always top priority. So let's use what happened to Audrey Griffin as a teachable moment, and remember to save our conversations for coffee, not the driveway.

Kindly,
Gwen Goodyear
Head of School

*

Emergency-room bill Audrey Griffin
gave to me to give to Mom

Patient name: Audrey Griffin
Attending Physician: C. Cassella

WHERE'D YOU GO, BERNADETTE • 21

Emergency Room Visitation Fee	900.00
X Ray (Elective, NOT COVERED)	425.83
Rx: Vicodin 10MG (15 tablets, 0 refills)	95.70
Crutch Rental (Elective, NOT COVERED)	173.00
Crutch Deposit:	75.00
TOTAL	1,669.53

Notes: Visual inspection and basic neurological examination revealed no injury. Patient in acute emotional distress, demanded X ray, Vicodin, and crutches.

*

From: Soo-Lin Lee-Segal
To: Audrey Griffin

I heard Bernadette tried to run you over at pickup! Are you OK? Should I come by with dinner? WHAT HAPPENED?

*

From: Audrey Griffin
To: Soo-Lin Lee-Segal

It's all true. I needed to talk to Bernadette about her blackberry bushes, which are growing down her hill, under my fence, and invading my garden. I was forced to hire a specialist, who said Bernadette's blackberries are going to destroy the foundation of my home.
Naturally, I wanted to have a friendly chat with Bernadette. So I walked up to her car while she was in the pickup line. Mea culpa! But how else are you ever going to get a word with that woman? She's like Franklin Delano Roosevelt.

Fig. 1: A double page from *Where'd you go, Bernadette* (Semple 2013: pp. 20–21), displaying a head teacher's note sent to the parents (top left), an "emergency room bill" and two e-mails.

ties, and apart from the personal message it also carries additional information either in pictorial or in verbal form on the front side. In light of the omnipresence of digital communication, the postcard also stands out as a material object that has to be transported, delivered and retrieved from a 'real' mailbox and held in a person's hands while it is being read. These socio-pragmatic implications of communicative artefacts are part of the genre concept as explained in more detail in the following section. In any case, it has already become obvious that, in contrast with the traditional novel, by reproducing and presenting (some of) the characteristics of the original artefact the multimodal novel allows the reader to access the fictional world directly, i.e. there is no act of verbal mediation and no narrator between the (fictional) artefact and the reader. The reader is able to look at and study texts, images, maps and other semiotic products (objects and existents) that originate from the fictional world.

2 Letters as Semiotic and Generic Modes

In order to better understand the substantially different way of representing the fictional world in the novel and of involving the reader in it, it is helpful to explain in more detail the cultural, social and semiotic work that all of the artefacts mentioned above do. It was M.A.K. Halliday who, in Systemic Functional Linguistics, first defined genres from a functional perspective as elements of discourse that organize and structure social and cultural life symbolically: "The various genres of discourse, including literary genres, are the specific semiotic functions of text that have social value in the culture" (Halliday 1978: 145). The social semiotics approach to genre has emphasized this social function of texts further, focussing on "what people do to or for or with each other by means of text" (van Leeuwen 2005: 123) and by studying how they are embedded in or connected to social and communicative practices in a given social or historical context.

For epistolary forms, it is particularly relevant that they are conceptualized and theorized as texts in their own right which can be regarded as fully developed, conventionalized semiotic modes. In Systemic Functional Linguistics and in Social Semiotics a semiotic mode is defined as "a socially shaped and culturally given resource for making meaning in representation and communication" (Kress 2010: 53). If such a mode "is used in recognisably stable ways as a means of articulating discourse" (Kress & van Leeuwen 2001: 25) in everyday communication, it is identified as a type of text, a genre. Like all genres, epistolary forms are more or less conventionalized modes and semiotic resources. As such, they are "culturally and historically specific forms of communication", "templates for doing communicative things" (van Leeuwen 2005: 128).

The kind of 'communicative work' that such types of text and generic forms do is described as being defined by three different categories termed linguistic metafunctions by M.A.K Halliday (cf. Halliday 1978: 128–130). The ideational (or: representational) function refers to the content that is typically conveyed by a certain generic form. Thus, by convention, a business letter is supposed to address business matters only, as opposed to personal issues which are regarded as alien to this genre. In a similar vein, the interpersonal function (or meaning) of a business letter defines into what kind of social interaction the sender and the addressee of the letter enter or involve each other. The specific kind of personal relation that is expected to be determined by business purposes and the economic field, is opposed to, for instance, private or social ties that are established or sustained in a personal letter to a member of the family, except in cases of family businesses/corporations, which might blend clear boundaries. The third category, the textual meaning of an utterance, refers to the specific way in which a generic form of utterance is typically organized. As a rule, and by convention, "[a] genre consists of a series of 'stages' which are given functional labels" (van Leeuwen 2005: 127). This textual function or the sequence of stages in a given text or utterance "realizes a particular strategy for achieving an overall communicative goal" (van Leeuwen 2005: 127). For epistolary forms, these stages are often highly conventionalized, even in terms of their linguistic form, such as 'salutation' or presenting a personal experience in the main part of a private letter.

Thus, when studying letters in the context of the fictional world of a novel, Halliday's meta-functions (or van Leeuwen's three "characteristics of content, form and function"; van Leeuwen 2005: 123) provide us with foci that make it possible to relate them to other components of the storyworld and analyse their role and purpose in a given social context or a particular personal relationship. In addition, these categories make it possible, if not mandatory to identify and describe cultural and communicative practices that become manifest in them in order to understand how and to what end characters make use of semiotic resources and options that are available or conventionalized in the culture. From such observations, it may even be possible to determine a character's position in its social and cultural field or domain (cf. section 3).

This way, every single semiotic form that is part of the novel and its overall narrative discourse can be and must be regarded and analysed as an individual text or artefact that has a specific contribution to make to both the constitution of the storyworld and to the way in which this world unfolds in the narrative discourse. Since in the multimodal novel a letter or a personal message is often presented in its original material or medial form, the semiotic work of its material or physical quality and the way it is perceived, or the practices in which they are embedded also needs to be studied and analysed. In particular, letters are always directly related to their authors, i.e. one of the characters in the novel, and to the addressee of the letter. This way, a letter always adds a different perspective to the way events, actions or experiences are presented to the reader.

Texts and artefacts are also characterized by the specific semiotic potential (termed affordance; cf. van Leeuwen 2005: 4–5) that they offer in acts of communication and representation. On the one hand, the affordance of the linguistic form (and sign system) of a letter is specific as compared to visual or graphic modes of communication; the way a photograph or a map communicate is considerably different from how a linguistic text produces and conveys meaning. On the other hand, epistolary forms are particularly suited to convey meaning and to engage in a specific kind of interaction as compared to other linguistic forms of communication. For instance, as opposed to a newspaper article or a pamphlet, the personal letter always constitutes a closer and private, sometimes intimate, tie between the sender and the receiver and is particularly suited to express subjective views, individual concerns and experiences as well as personal feelings. By presenting them as identifiable representations of a character's thoughts and feelings and authenticating them as produced by the hands of a literary character, this specific affordance is foregrounded and provides the character in the novel with a textual voice of its own. Narratologically speaking, unlike a quote from, or a paraphrase of, a letter in the traditional novel, a letter that is fully reproduced and presented in the multimodal novel constitutes an additional narrator or narrative voice. In *Miss Jane* (Watson 2016), the novel discussed in more detail in section 3, the letters exchanged between two medical doctors, Dr. Eldred O. Thompson and Dr. Ellison Adams, introduce independent narrative voices of the autodiegetic kind into the otherwise heterodiegetic narrative. Thus, every letter that is presented as an independent, bounded textual unit contributes to the multiperspectivity of the overall narrative, which implies that Thompson's experiences, thoughts and questions are also perspectivized in Adams's letters, a character who is otherwise absent from the story.

However, the most conspicuous feature of the multimodal novel in its developed form is the integration of a whole range of different modes, including the words of the narrator. For instance, *The Curious Incident of the Dog in the Night-Time* (Haddon 2003), apart from letters and the narrator's discourse, is composed of photographs, maps, mathematical formulae, algorithms, hand-drawn sketches and diagrams and many more semiotic modes. Thus, the letters that take on a decisive role in the course of events in the novel are perceived as a very particular and conspicuous kind of communication, since the narrator resorts to visual artefacts and graphic storytelling whenever possible (see section 4). This multimodality poses particular challenges to the reader and the act of reading. Whereas in the word novel the narrative is rendered in linear form, the multimodal narrative directs the reader's attention to various other semiotic elements on the page or double page and it is left to the reader to try and integrate them into the whole of the narrative and construct a transmodal coherent meaning. This, of course, implies that, whereas reading the traditional novel requires solely alphabetic literacy, the multimodal novel presents the reader with a range of other sign systems in the codes of which the reader needs to be proficient in order to decode them and 'read' them as a part of the narrative as a whole.

3 Epistolary Textual Worlds as Social Spheres and Cultural Domains

As pointed out in section 2, Social Semiotics pay particular attention to the field and social context in which a semiotic artefact or utterance is embedded. Epistolary forms in a multimodal novel can therefore be expected to not only communicate some relevant kind of content, but also to represent the sociocultural world in which they are written. Brad Watson's (2016) unusual novel *Miss Jane* is a case in point. The novel presents the story of Jane Chisolm who is born in 1915 in east-central Mississippi with a genital and urological defect resulting in incontinence. Thus, her mobility is limited and, to a good degree, she is excluded from the social life which girls and young women traditionally lived at that time. Thus, young Jane has to spend most of the time on her parents' farm near the small city of Mercury. For a number of years, Dr. Eldred O. Thompson is her only connection to the world beyond the farm. He becomes a true friend of hers and, contacting Dr. Ellison Adams, a colleague of his at Johns Hopkins University School of Medicine in Baltimore and long-time friend, he engages in medical research in order "to find out if there's the possibility of sphincter construction or repair, which would at least allow her to be in social situations without embarrassment" (*Miss Jane:* 99), as Ed Thompson writes. Since in terms of distance and travel time the two doctors "are what seems almost worlds apart" (*Miss Jane:* 100), they engage in regular letter writing to get in touch and discuss options for the girl's medical or surgical treatment.

The letters in *Miss Jane* can be regarded as mimicking the cultural function and functionality of letters at the beginning of the twentieth century quite realistically. They serve to bridge the spatial distance between two friends and colleagues and make it possible for them to keep in touch; they are a semiotic tool to negotiate serious issues, and they are a means of articulating personal sympathy and affection. In light of the Social Semiotics approach introduced in section 2, the letters that the two medical doctors exchange are an interesting case in point, since in terms of content and personal interaction one would expect them to be professional letters embedded in the specialized medical discourses of the time and negotiations between experts. This is certainly true for the series of letters presented (in italics as a typographical signal that they are handwritten), but a closer scrutiny reveals that the domain of medical care and surgery fuses with two other worlds. These three domains can be described and characterized as follows:

The scientific domain of medical treatment and surgery dominates the series of letters, mirroring the original purpose and the professional negotiations between two doctors. There is even a third, more specialized expert introduced, Dr. Young, whom the other two consult. His specialization and expertise is highly appreciated by the other two and, as Ed Thompson states, he is expected to continue "to make great strides in this field" (*Miss Jane:* 46). The professional domain is also represented by scientific terminology ("urological condition", "blockages", "fistulas"; *Miss Jane:* 45) and by quite a matter-of-fact professional style and register. This way, these letters serve to shortcut two socially and culturally distant cultural domains and social spheres, juxtaposing the academic world of medical research, progress and high technology in an urban environment on the one hand, and the rural antediluvian world of the Chisolms' farm life which has almost no access to the urban world and the cultural and scientific knowledge that it generates on the other. It is this juxtaposition that sheds very sharp light on the socially and educationally small, limited and limiting world of Jane Chisolm's family and the very uncomfortable social situation that the girl faces: It is a world of shame, discrimination and segregation from which the girl, due to her physiological handicap, suffers.

However, the Chisolms' small world of the family and the rural world of farming feature quite prominently in the letters because Ed Thompson shows great interest in the girl's fate. He continuously characterizes the family's way of life and the girl's ways of coping with her situation. In doing so, Thompson displays a lot of sympathy for Jane and engages in assessing her intellectual and social progress. Also, he keeps discussing the prospects of her future life as a woman "with romantic love – full-on or chaste" (*Miss Jane:* 99), revealing that he is deeply committed to the girl's and young woman's well-being and personal development. The limitations of rural life quite strongly contrast with Jane's decision to leave the farm and live in the city when she is sixteen. This can be seen as the young woman's act of emancipation, liberating herself from the restraints of farm life and also becoming economically independent from her parents. The letters thus continuously present one of the main character's views and comments on the protagonist, rendering additional characterizations of the family's life on the farm and establishing a meta-level of personal and social judgements in addition to the narrator's rendition of Miss Jane's life story.

The third social sphere addressed in the letters is that of the two doctors' and friends' private lives, which are apparently only in parts identical with their family life. They frankly discuss their scepticism regarding their marriages and regularly give very personal, and sometimes intimate advice to each other. In these parts of the letter, the tone changes towards a very personal, private tone between friends and contrasts firmly with the scientific and rational way of thinking and of considering medical or surgical solutions for the girl's condition in other parts. It is of particular interest to observe how in these passages pragmatic medical expertise is complemented and balanced by very uncertain considerations and tentative thoughts or pieces of intimate advice like this one after the death of Thompson's wife: "You take care, now, Ed. Living alone, there, you take care not to over-indulge in your favourite vices" (*Miss Jane:* 112).

This brief analysis reveals that these letters are not just a generic realization of communicative acts in terms of content, textual form and interaction, as social semiotics would have it. Of course, they are also semiotic modes of communication, representation and interaction and a medium of contact between two friends and colleagues. However, in the multisemiotic narrative they are much more: To a good extent they constitute important parts of the complex storyworld of the novel by establishing cultural domains (Dr. Adams' scientific world of medical care and surgery, the Chisolms' rural life of a farmer family) and social spheres like a country doctor's middle class life in a small city and Miss Jane's adult professional life in a small-town office. Furthermore, in these letters (and merely in them) these different worlds are brought into contact and interconnected, and in and through them Dr. Thompson takes on the role of a go-between. He is the only character with ties to all of the domains and spheres that are addressed in the letters. It is through him that these domains and spheres are brought into contact, and this is why, in a sense, he is the covert protagonist of this multi-layered sociocultural storyworld.

Thus, a multitextual and multisemotic novel like *Miss Jane* turns out to construct and represent the storyworld as a network of interconnected texts and artefacts which stimulate or enable the reader to imagine the social and cultural world that is implied in every single text and semiotic mode, but also in the storyworld as a whole since it is composed of a series of interconnected texts and narratives. Thus, as Alison Gibbons points out with reference to cognitive Text-World-Theory, the textual units and the printed words of a multimodal novel function "as a sort of portal into the imagined world of the novel, that is, into the text-world itself" (Gibbons 2012: 35) on the one hand, and into each of the different worlds (spheres, domains) to which every single text belongs on the other.

4 Semiotic Dysfunctions: 'Dead letters'

In the semiotic approach to communication and representation, a letter is always more than content in verbal form. As the series of letters in *Miss Jane*, with their potential to evoke a whole world, have already indicated, there is always a person's life and their way of thinking and feeling attached to or implied in it. But beyond that very close interrelatedness of the sender and the letter, there is much more to it: there is a whole number of personal and social practices involved in letter-writing, if it is only using pen and paper, putting a stamp on the envelope or mailing the letter or retrieving it from a mailbox. This material and pragmatic dimension of letter-writing may seem to be trivial, but seemingly banal actions and practices turn out be particularly crucial if they are not or cannot be properly performed. Since fiction, in many cases, is not interested in simply replicating lifeworld practices, but rather in exhibiting deficiencies and counter-realities, or extraordinary, dysfunctional sides of human interaction, some of the most striking examples of letter-writing are those in which this kind of communicative and social interaction is inhibited or even impossible. If such dysfunctional sides are thematised and narrated in the novel, they can be expected to be particularly pertinent and meaningful in the world that is unfolded in the novel.

'Dead letters', the metaphor in the title of this section, quotes a chapter heading from the successful Holocaust youth novel *The Book Thief* (Zusak 2005: 97). Liesel, a Jewish girl who is hidden from Nazi persecution by foster parents, tries to keep in touch with her mother by exchanging letters with her. However, she is desperate on the one hand since she has not received any mail from her mother for a long time; on the other hand, she has not been able to send any letters because she simply does not have enough money to buy a stamp. These complications affect the girl's everyday life and her emotional status substantially because of their existential implications in Liesel's "sudden realization [...] that [...] her mother would never write back and she would never see her again" (*The Book Thief*: 99). 'Dead letters', therefore, are always a sign of deep social or emotional or even societal disruption, as in the case of the Holocaust in *The Book Thief*. In this book in particular, the term almost loses its metaphorical quality since it is a person's death that the dead letters symbolize.

It is this direct intertwinedness of people's social lives and their letters that attributes to them a pivotal role in the narrative discourse of the novel and the plot that unfolds. In *The Curious Incident of the Dog in the Night-Time* (Haddon 2003), a whole bundle of letters turns out to be central in every respect: in the very middle of the novel Christopher, the adolescent autodiegetic narrator, finds a box full of letters written by his mother whom he believed to be dead; they are 'dead letters' that never reached Christopher because his father stuffed them away in order to hide them from his son. In what can be read as one of the most emotional experiences and moments in the novel, these letters present a totally different narrative that reveals to the young narrator that the world that his father's stories have built around him was all lies. Counter to what his father told him, his mother was not dead, but had left her family and begun a new life with another man in London after her husband's affair with a neighbour. What is more, these letters also lead to his father's confession that he killed the dog, the mystery of whose death Christopher wants to solve in the manner of a detective. It is therefore more or less logical that these dead letters mark a turning point in the whole story: after 'the curious incident of the dog' has been solved, Christopher leaves his father and joins his mother in London in order to begin a new and different kind of family life. Thus, these letters were not only, as Christopher and the reader learn at that point of the plot, his mother's failed attempt to stay in touch with him, but they also set Christopher's whole world in turmoil, destroying a seemingly sound social and familial environment in which Christopher believed to live, including the very close relationship with his father that Christopher had developed. In this sense, these dead letters are indexical of the death of his family.

In Mark Z. Danielewski's (2000) *The Whalestoe Letters*, disruption and disorder in both the social and the mental sense are the general condition that the letters establish from the beginning. This fictional collection of letters, a number of them originally contained in Danielewski's (2000: 586–644) big multimodal novel *House of Leaves* (as also contended by the anonymous editors) were discovered by Walden D. Wyrha, an Information Specialist working at "The Three Attics Whalestoe Institute" (*The Whalestoe Letters:* xi), a psychiatric facility. The letters were all written by Pelafina H. Lièvre, the mother of Johnny Truant, the protagonist of *House of Leaves*. While they are an impressive series of love letters to her son, their status is dubious since "there is no direct evidence that any were actually sent" (*The Whalestoe Letters:* ix), nor is there any sign of Johnny Truant ever answering one of them. In firm contrast with the communicative and interpersonal function of personal letters, Pelafina's letters remain totally self-referential in terms of both their content and the pretended addressee. Instead of assuring her son of her deep love and affection, these letters obviously serve to ascertain Pelafina herself of her feelings of true love for her son. Since Pelafina's mental state is also doubtful, these letters are a representation of her need to constantly re-affirm herself of a loving relationship with a person whom she never sees nor reaches. Counter to the cultural and communicative functions of letters, they are a manifestation of the mentally and socially self-contained world in which Pelafina lives.

As the collection of Whalestoe letters is presented in chronological order, this interpersonal and semiotic dysfunction gradually also materializes in a disintegration of the textual elements and the conventional structure of letters, thus not only violating the rules of their textual organization, but finally also abrogating linguistic structures and even the semantic function of the alphabetic code (see fig. 2).

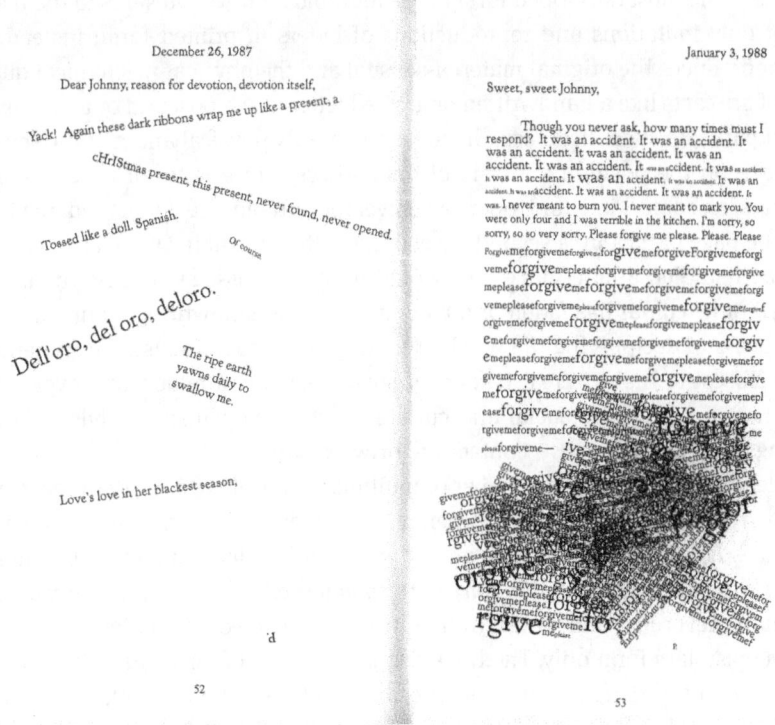

Fig. 2: A double page from *The Whalestoe Letters* (Danielewski 2000: 52–53)

In the novels in question, 'dead letters', the ones that are never sent or never read, turn out to be particularly powerful textual signs of interpersonal disruptions, social disintegration and even, as in *The Book Thief*, of the extinction of millions of people.

5 Envelopes and Postcards: The Material Presence of Epistolary Artefacts in Multimodal Novels

One of the affordances of the multimodal novel, as opposed to the word novel, is its ability to integrate other artefacts in the narrative discourse that remain perceivable and experienceable as such. This is why it can be concluded "that the practice of reading multimodal literature can be seen as closer to our experiential processing of reality when compared to more conventional novels" (Gibbons

2012: 39). The most developed form of the multimodal novel presents to the reader not only imitations and reproductions of letters in printed form; instead, it fully reproduces the original material-sensual and the physical-mechanical qualities of artefacts like a handwritten or a typed letter or the postcard or a note on a slip of paper. In such instances, the reader, in a truly physical and motoric sense, will take on the position and role of the addressee of a letter or an epistolary message of some kind and open an envelope, unfold the letter and read it, turn the page or pick up a second sheet of the letter to read it. Often, after having read and studied a letter once, one would re-read a passage because the ink is blurred or its colour has faded or the irregularities of handwriting require a careful process of deciphering the words. This way, the reader's sensual experiences come closest to those of real readers of such epistolary artefacts and evoke the imagination of a whole social and cultural world of which such kinds of letter writing and communicative contact are or were part.

Meanwhile, there are a number of multimodal novels which offer their readers such material and physical experiences of reading letters. One of the early instances is a rather small book and short novel by Nick Bantock (1991), titled *Griffin and Sabine. An Extraordinary Correspondence.*[1] It is a story of two persons who have never met and whose (rather mysterious) personal relationship develops in epistolary form only. The book displays a series of postcards with beautiful artwork of graphic design reproduced in colour on the recto placed on one book page, and the verso with the handwritten message and address on the following page in precisely the same position. In addition to these pages that are composed of one side of a postcard only, with no hetero- or autodiegetic narrator and no narrative discourse at all, there are four letters in an envelope that are interspersed between the postcard pages, two typed ones by Griffin and two handwritten ones by Sabine. In order to be able to read these letters, the envelopes have to be opened and the letters in full A4 size have to be retrieved from the envelopes and unfolded.

A more recent novel, *S. Ship of Theseus. By V.M. Straka* (Abrams & Dorst 2013) is a complete reproduction of the (fictional) original library copy of a novel which, apart from the words of the novel itself, also reproduces two student readers' dialogue about the story in handwritten commentaries and questions in the margins. Thus, the novel itself is turned into a medium of epistolary exchange between Eric, a PhD student, and Jen, a graduate student; this way, the fictional readers' interactions with the text become an integrated part of the

---

[1] See also Ames Hawkins's "An Open Letter to Nick Bantock OR Letters and/as Ephemera(l): Desire, Transposition and Transpoetic Possibility with/in Epistolary Form" in this volume.

Epistolary Forms as Semiotic and Generic Modes in the Multimodal Novel — **139**

novel. The empirical reader's interaction with *Ship of Theseus* thus constantly operates on two different levels. Moreover, the empirical reader will also find copies of historical letters, i.e. the reproduction of letters that are recognizable as photocopies from the "Straka Arkiv Uppsala" (Abrams & Dorst 2013, n. pag.). In addition, the library book also contains long letters, handwritten by Jen and Eric, in which the two students render stories from their own (family) lives, so that once again various textual worlds are co-present in this multitextual and multisemiotic novel and which are, in the true sense of the word, spread out under the reader's eyes to be accessed and explored (see fig. 3).

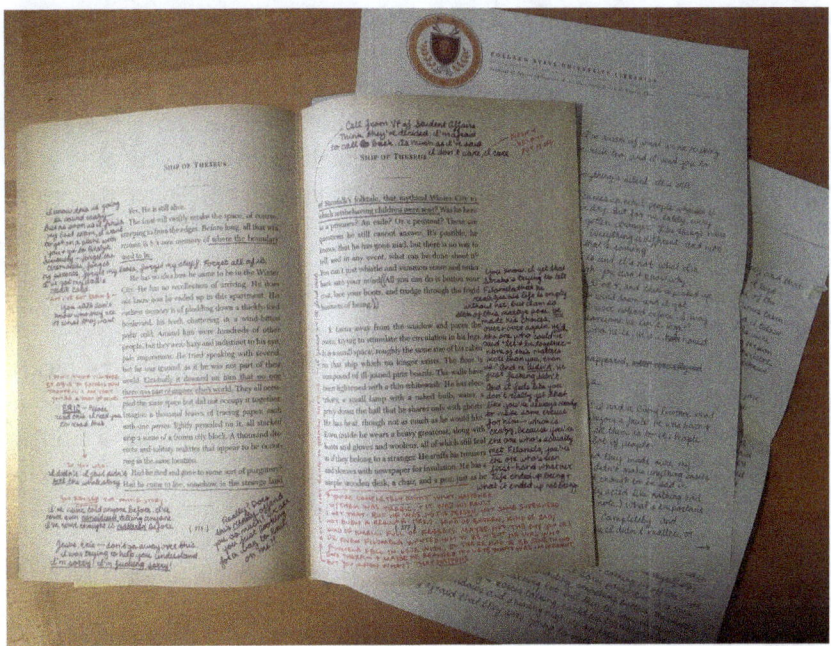

Fig. 3: A double page from *S. The Ship of Theseus* (Abrams & Dorst 2913: 376–377) with one of the inserted handwritten letters.

In Graham Rawle's multimodal novel *Diary of an Amateur Photographer. A Mystery* (1998; cf. Hallet 2018), an envelope and the message inside even take the most prominent position in the novel that any message can possibly have. Not only is the letter and its content reproduced in full material form, but the letter also urges the reader to make a decision and to contribute actively to the resolution of the case. This way, the letter and the message are key to the plot and the story since a small snippet from a book on the envelope, while warning the autodiegetic narrator (the amateur photographer) and the reader of this murder mystery that "it might be better for you not to know the full truth" (n. pag.), simultaneously offers them access to the resolution of the case. Since the narrator decides "not to open it, I don't want to know what's inside" (n. pag.), it is a dead letter, and the reader cannot learn the truth by simply reading on, but only through actively engaging in the epistolary practice of opening the envelope, retrieving a card from it and reading the paper snippets on the card. In this instance, the material object and the epistolary practice even constitute the plot which would otherwise remain open-ended and incomplete. Integrating objects into the novel this way and urging the reader to get actively involved, transforms the novel into a truly interactive story in which a dead letter can be brought back to life by the reader.

However, the completely reproductive and material (rather than mimetic) imitation of real-world objects has more to it than an added extra material to the verbal discourse of the novel. As Hans-Ulrich Gumbrecht (2004: 91–132) has pointed out, in the traditional hermeneutic approach, reading a novel in terms of aesthetic experience is first and foremost a process of meaning-making and an act of interpretation. The multimodal novel, by contrast, also offers experiences of the sensory and physical kind which are either evoked (e.g. in the printed reproduction of a handwritten letter) or can be directly experienced, as is the case if a letter is handed out to the reader or a postcard can be picked up from the novel, held in the hand and studied in detail. This kind of presentation (or: fictional replica) of a material object (its 'presence') leads to a different kind of experience, Gumbrecht contends, an experience which, to some extent, questions the semiotic approach in the humanities:

> Typologically speaking, the dimension of meaning is dominant in Cartesian worlds, in worlds for which consciousness (the awareness of alternatives) constitutes the core of human self-reference. And are we not precisely longing for presence, is our desire for tangibility not so intense – because our own everyday environment is so insuperably consciousness-centered? Rather than having to think, always and endlessly, what else there could be, we sometimes seem to connect with a layer in our existence that simply wants the things of the world close to our skin. (Gumbrecht 2004: 106)

In the type of epistolary novel discussed in this section, letters, notes and personal messages, apart from their textual and ideational dimension, remain visible and perceptible as material objects originating from and produced in the fictional world of the novel. This is one of the affordances which, compared to the word novel, is quite unique, not just in terms of an addition to the verbal text, but as a specific quality that cannot be accessed by readers in printed texts. This kind of multimodal novel comes closest to "the body's physical, sensory, and perceptual interactions within the world" (Gibbons 2012: 41) and to the medial and material practices in epistolary communication in the reader's non-fictional world.

6 The Multiplication of Types of Semiosis, Senses and Experiences in the Multimodal Novel

Most probably it is the loss of physical and sensory perceptions in the digital age that generates a new interest in the material forms of human communication and their medial carriers. In the digital age, the sign systems have materially dissolved and are experienceable only as digits and pixels on the screen. In the age of streaming technologies, this liquidification of all signs and codes makes it even impossible to possess and keep the products of communicative exchange in personal material archives. This may be one of the explanations for why direct, unmediated access to the original shape and qualities of epistolary novels develops a lot of fascination in contemporary fiction. Fiction, it appears, has the potential to refer the reader back to the (vanishing) mediality and materiality of the objects and practices in their lifeworld, and the affective dimension which materials also often constitute. Due to their often very personal implications, letters and postcards in their original material form can even be regarded and treated as beloved objects (Habermas 1996). This way, multimodal novels, and those in fully developed form like *Griffin and Sabine* and *S. Ship of Theseus* in particular, are also fictional imitations of cultural practices of collecting and worshipping material objects. In this light, digital epistolary forms like e-mails and chats, which could not be discussed in this essay, can be regarded as firmly contrasting with the material forms of communication. Material forms of communication vis-à-vis digital ways raise the kind of question that Nick Hornby (2009) negotiates in *Juliet, Naked*. In this novel, the juxtaposition of electronic communication and the material world leads to the question, where and in what manner a person develops and displays their true identity (cf. Kusche 2012: 113–115), and who the 'real' person is, and why the full material form of an artefact or a physical person may appear to be more reliable than those in electronic form.

In narratological terms, the integration of the full body of epistolary forms challenges the reader's reading habits acquired in encounters and interactions with linear texts. Clearly bounded or even independent textual entities and objects delinearize the narrative discourse that is now arranged in a hypertextual manner, with a particular emphasis on the meaning-making or communicative affordance of each of the various semiotic modes employed and an identifiable status in the social and cultural (sometimes historical) storyworld. In case multimodality is extended into multimateriality, conventional reading practices even become inadequate. They need to be expanded into a physical and sensory act of experiencing and exploring the material world of the book that reproduces the material quality of objects and artefacts in the lifeworld in order to present them as objects from the storyworld.

Works Cited

Abrams, J.J. & Dorst, Doug. 2013. *S. Ship of Theseus. By V.M. Straka*. New York: Hachette.
Bantock, Nick. 1991. *Griffin and Sabine. An Extraordinary Correspondence*. San Francisco, Ca.: Chronicle.
Danielewski, Mark Z. 2000. *House of Leaves. A Novel*. New York: Pantheon.
Danielewski, Mark Z. 2000. *The Whalestoe Letters*. New York: Pantheon.
Gibbons, Alison. 2012. *Multimodality, Cognition and Experimental Literature*. London & New York: Routledge.
Gumbrecht, Hans-Ulrich. 2004. *Production of Presence. What Meaning Cannot Convey*. Stanford: Stanford University Press.
Habermas, Tilmann. 1996. *Geliebte Objekte. Symbole und Instrumente der Identitätsbildung*. Frankfurt/Main: Suhrkamp.
Haddon, Mark. 2003. *The Curious Incident of the Dog in the Night-Time*. New York: Vintage.
Hallet, Wolfgang. 2018. "Multimodal Storytelling in Contemporary Fiction: Graham Rawle's *Diary of an Amateur Photographer. A Mystery* (1998) and Mark Haddon's *The Curious Incident of the Dog in the Night-Time* (2003)". In: Ansgar Nünning & Vera Nünning, (eds.). *The British Novel in the 21st Century: Cultural Concerns – Literary Developments – Model Interpretations*. Trier: WVT. 343–359.
Halliday, Michael A. K. 1978. *Language as Social Semiotic. The Social Interpretation of Language and Meaning*. London: Edward Arnold.
Hornby, Nick. 2009. *Juliet, Naked*. London: Penguin.
Kress, Gunter. 2010. *Multimodality. A Social Semiotic Approach to Contemporary Communication*. London & New York: Routledge.
Kress, Gunter & van Leeuwen, Theo. 2001. *Multimodal Discourse. The Modes and Media of Contemporary Communication*. London: Arnold.
Kusche, Sabrina. 2012. "Der E-Mail-Roman. Zur Medialisierung des Erzählens in der zeitgenössischen deutsch- und englischsprachigen Literatur". Unpubl. PhD dissertation, Stockholm University.
Semple, Maria. 2013. *Where'd you go, Bernadette?* New York: Little Brown.
van Leeuwen, Theo. 2005. *Introducing Social Semiotics*. London & New York: Routledge.
Watson, Brad. 2016. *Miss Jane*. New York & London: Norton.
Zusak, Markus. 2005. *The Book Thief*. New York: Knopf.

Lisa Kazianka
Isolation, Participation and Communication in Young Adult Unidirectional Epistolary Fiction

Abstract: Since the late twentieth century, the epistolary form has become increasingly popular in Anglophone adolescent literature. Scholarly discussions, however, have largely neglected the conventional letter-form, equating it with the diary novel or focusing on the 'new' epistolary using modern means of communication. The conventional letter-form, however, favours narrative strategies that enhance the degree of introspection and thus the depiction of identity and interiority, while increasing adolescent readers' involvement and engagement. The novels I analyse are *The Perks of Being a Wallflower* by Stephen Chbosky (1999) and *Ketchup Clouds* by Annabel Pitcher (2012). I venture that, in comparison to other first-person narratives, the letter-form draws increased attention to the character's state of isolation and loneliness. It allows for repeated references to the time and location of narrating, effectively constructing setting as both physical and symbolic space. Further, letter novels construct an overt narratee, who, I contend, plays a shaping role in the narrative and the protagonists' development. The two novels present highly introspective and complex characters that engage in self-analysis, self-reflection and self-discovery, while also observing/reflecting on their surroundings. They construct identity as dialogical, fragmentary and unstable, pointing to the role of isolation, participation and communication in the quest for self. This chapter highlights that letter novels offer a complex way to interrogate the dominant discourses of YA literature.

1 Introduction

In recent years, young adult (YA) literature has gained widespread popularity and influence, both in regard to readership and as a field of academic study. It has also increasingly become a space for authors to experiment with narrative modes, perhaps because, as Coats (2011) explains, it continuously "responds to and helps contextualize cultural trends for its readers" (320). The epistolary is one such key trend in twenty-first-century YA fiction (see also Cadden 2011) – although it is not 'new' in adolescent literature. The first novel with an adolescent letter-writing protagonist, *Daddy-Long-Legs*, written by American author Jean Webster, was published in 1912 – although at its time of publication it was aimed at an adult audience. It has remained in print since, which accounts for its lasting popularity. Throughout the twentieth century, but especially towards the end of it, letter narratives for young adults remained popular: Beverly Cleary's *Dear Mr Henshaw* (1984) won the Newberry medal, for example, John Marsden's *Letters from the Inside* (1991) met with acclaim, and Stephen Chbosky's *The Perks of Being a Wallflower* (1999) is today considered a literary classic. The twenty-first century has seen a dramatic expansion of the epistolary mode, moving in particular "from actual letters to text messages" (Cadden 2011: 308), as in Lauren Myracle's *Internet Girls* series (2004–2014).[1] Despite this new focus on modern communication technologies, however, the 'traditional' letter mode remains a popular means for authors to convey their stories to teen readers, and the number of adolescent novels employing this mode is growing.

2 The Appeal of the Epistolary for YA Literature

When the epistolary mode enjoyed its heyday in the seventeenth and eighteenth centuries, it was to a large extent because the period's "preoccupation with the creation of meaning and with questioning the received order was best conveyed in pluralistic, fragmented textual forms, such as encyclopedias, dialogues, and letters" (Beebee 2010: n. pag.). Epistolarity, Beebee (2010: n. pag.) explains, "therefore lent a seriousness and a moral context to fiction which the novel had been said to lack". YA fiction is often defined by drawing a demarcation line to children's literature on the one hand, and adult literature on the other (see e.g. Cadden 2011). Besides the obvious age correlation of the intended audience and the protagonist(s), Trites (2000) and Coats (2011) name the interrogation of "a closed moral universe" (Coats 2011: 322) as a defining characteristic of YA literature. This corresponds to the "questioning [of] the received order" (Beebee 2010: n. pag.) that led to the rise of the epistolary in the seventeenth and eighteenth centuries. This parallel might partially explain the growing importance of the epistolary in contemporary YA fiction. Another parallel can be drawn to letter fiction by/about women, in which protagonists "use the letter as a subversive and freeing agent" (Campbell 1995: 332). Just as feminist literature is traditionally concerned with gender-related power structures, literature for young readers focuses on the child/adult or teen/adult power hierarchy. The letter form seems to be an ideal means to explore such hierarchies.

---

[1] See Silvia Schultermandl's "Stuplimity and Quick Media Epistolarity in Lauren Myracle's *Internet Girls* Series" in this volume.

The trend of epistolary in YA fiction might further be related to the genre's primary concern with identity construction. Nikolajeva (2014: 252) explains: "Self-knowledge is central for our existence, and adolescence is a dynamic and turbulent phase of human life. YA fiction has a strong potential to offer readers accurate portrayals of selfhood." The YA novel evolved out of the *Bildungsroman* and focuses on character change and growth, issues of identity and self-discovery. It follows the teen protagonists as they try to make sense of new experiences, but also depicts how they learn to understand and exist within the power structures and "the social forces that have made them what they are" (Trites 2000: 3). In epistolary YA fiction, this journey of self-discovery, of learning how to make sense of the world and its power structures, emerges through letters, e-mails, chats and notes, through which the young protagonists communicate their feelings and thoughts, and process overwhelming, disturbing and traumatic events. The conventional letter mode, in particular, offers a form of personal narration that enables a high degree of introspection and thus has a great potential to portray growth and identity development.

Narratives can emphasise either character or plot. The YA novel is usually character-driven, and traditionally, the epistolary mode also prioritises the growth/development and emotional states of characters. In general, the novel is considered to "examine the consciousness of one or more characters", but in epistolary novels, this examination of consciousness is even more foregrounded, since "unfolding a story in letters automatically emphasizes the psychological angle of vision as no other narrative form does" (Perry 1980: 119). The letter-form thus brings us closer to the protagonist's consciousness. In the context of YA fiction, however, this is applied in an ironic manner. Cadden (2000: 146) points out the "irony of the use of 'authenticity'" in personal narration, "since the so-called adolescent voice is never – and can never be – truly authentic". It is thus crucial to remember that of course "we are dealing with an *adult* author's (re)construction of a young person's selfhood" (Nikolajeva 2014b: 142; emphasis added). Narrative situation, first-person perspective in particular, has become a widely researched subject within YA scholarship. Notably, children's literature critic Maria Nikolajeva has commented extensively on the implications of personal narration in adolescent literature (e. g. Nikolajeva 2014, 2014b). Nikolajeva explains that "personal perspective is a gratifying device to emulate interiority in young adult fiction" (2014b: 144). Considering the prominence of the personal perspective in YA fiction, it is suprising that scholarship has, so far, largely neglected to examine how this perspective is employed in epistolary texts for adolescents.

3 The Current State of Scholarship on YA Epistolary Fiction

In general, scholarship focusing on the epistolary has overlooked the genre of YA fiction, and research focusing on YA fiction has dealt with the epistolary only marginally. Critics have pointed out the 'usefulness' of the letter mode in the context of YA literature, particularly regarding the depiction of identity development (e.g. Wasserman 2003), but have neglected to pose the question *which* narratological devices/strategies render the letter mode useful and, more importantly even, what implications they may have for the adolescent reader. Further, the *variety* of the epistolary and each variant's possibilities/limitations needs to be acknowledged. I propose the following criteria for differentiation: (1) the prominence of the epistolary; (2) the medium of communication; (3) the number of correspondents. Each element impacts the structural and thematic constituents of an epistolary narrative and thus also the way a reader goes about interpreting the respective text. A YA novel that integrates e-mails between different correspondents into third-person omniscient narration will have a different structure, create different effects, and employ different narrative devices than a novel that is told exclusively in chat messages or one that consists entirely of letters. Much recent commentary on the epistolary in YA fiction focuses on the role of new communication technologies and the changing nature of the epistolary (e.g. Coats 2011), neglecting the letter as a means of narration.

One main issue that contributes to the dearth of scholarship on YA novels in the conventional letter-form is that they are often only included or briefly mentioned in discussions of the diary novel under the assumption that the two modes are so similar that they need not be treated separately. Indeed, there are structural similarities between diary and letter novels, and the two forms are regularly combined within narratives. As Martens (2009: 77) writes, both are "particularly suited to the description of events that took place in the recent or immediate past and to the expression of present thoughts and feelings". Sometimes, letters can seem "almost indistinguishable" from diaries because they are so private (Bower 1997: 5). Nevertheless, it is important to make the distinction, and to make it primarily based on the presence of an internal reader. The diary novel does not usually presuppose an internal, fictive reader, since diaries are private per definition. Letters, on the other hand, are addressed to a recipient and most scholars agree that the presence of this recipient is the main factor that distinguishes the epistolary from other first-person narration.[2]

The adolescent narratives I analyse in this chapter act exclusively as epistolary texts and use the letter as a medium of communication. They are *unidirectional* epistolary narratives, in which a single protagonist is writing letters to a non-replying addressee. The two novels are: *The Perks of Being a Wallflower*[3] by Stephen Chbosky, published in 1999 and adapted for the screen in 2012, and *Ketchup Clouds*[4] by Annabel Pitcher, published in 2012. In *Perks*, the protagonist is fifteen-year-old Charlie, who writes letters to an undisclosed recipient referred to as "Dear Friend". In his letters, he reflects on his daily family and school life and his experiences with his newfound friends, seniors and stepsiblings Patrick and Sam. He recounts memories that are of relevance to him, offers opinions on general subjects, and records his mental struggles. Over the course of the novel Charlie goes through 'typical' adolescent experiences, such as dating and alcohol abuse, but also uncovers repressed traumatic memories that lead him to remember how his late aunt Helen – whose death he feels guilty about – sexually abused him as a child. In *Clouds*, fifteen-year-old Zoe (a pseudonym for her real name, Alice[5]) sends letters from England to Stuart Harris, a prisoner in the US, whose contact details she found on a Death Row website. She writes to him with a clear intention to confess: Zoe feels responsible for the death of Max, a boy she dated, and on whom she cheated with his brother, Aaron – although it becomes clear at the end that the boy's death was an accident. She hopes that sending her story to a criminal, someone who might relate to her struggle, will make her guilt disappear. Death and sexuality, two common rite-of-passage themes in YA fiction play an important role in both novels.

Scholarly work on YA epistolary literature needs to combine a discussion of the form with a discussion of how the form interrogates the discourses *specific to* adolescent literature. In this chapter, I focus on the adolescent protagonists' position between isolation and participation, and their desire to communicate, explicating how the letter form enables an in-depth exploration of such topics that are of high relevance for adolescents, their identity and development. Traditionally, the letter writer in epistolary literature "feels alone and must feel alone in

---

[2] McCallum (1999: 225) coins the term "epistolic-diary narration" for diary novels in which the protagonist "is to some extent aware of an addressee, either implicit or explicit", even if this addressee might be the diary writer's future self.
[3] Henceforth abbreviated as *Perks*.
[4] Henceforth abbreviated as *Clouds*.
[5] Her character will be referred to as Zoe throughout this chapter, since she uses this name until her final letter.

order to write" – this is vital "to the epistolary urge" (Campbell 1995: 338). In *Perks* and *Clouds*, the theme of isolation gains a new dimension, as it exists in relation to and in negotiation with participation in society and a desire to communicate – a struggle that young adult readers can relate to. Adolescence is a period in which close friendships and romantic relationships are assigned a particularly high value, but it is also a time of experiencing loneliness and isolation (cf. Matthews et al. 2016: 340). Both states have associations with depression and other mental health issues that also emerge in the two novels, in which the letter-writing protagonists are cut off from society for different reasons. In their letters, they describe their state of isolation, how it contributes to their understanding of themselves and the world around them. Nikolajeva (2005) writes that "[s]etting can illuminate the character" (133). Indeed, in *Perks* and *Clouds* time and place enhance characterization, by creating a heightened sense of the protagonists' state of physical and emotional isolation. The letter-form draws attention to the adolescent protagonists' struggle to find a middle ground between inward-focus – caused by and resulting in isolation – and participation. The selected novels postulate that both are part of growing up and relevant for the construction of identity in adolescence, but that eventually, participation should be given preference.

4 Desire for Participation in *The Perks of Being a Wallflower* vs Voluntary Withdrawal in *Ketchup Clouds*

Charlie in *The Perks of Being a Wallflower*, begins to engage in letter-writing on the eve of his transition to high school, because he is "really afraid of going" (Chbosky 1999: 7). In 'real' life, he does not have anyone to confide in: his best friend Michael committed suicide a year earlier; his aunt Helen, whom he describes as his favourite person, died when he was a child; his siblings neglect him; and he cannot talk about important things with his family. In addition, his fear of becoming socially alienated at school quickly turns into reality. According to Trites (2000: 3), family and school belong to the institutions, or "social forces", that shape adolescents and require them to "negotiate the levels of power" that exist within society. Chbosky's novel defines these two 'institutions' as the central spaces in which the protagonist moves between isolation and participation, negotiating his roles as active participant and passive observer. Charlie's letters serve as a space for him to explore and communicate these negotiations. Although chosen as a means of *communication*, the letter-writing does not offer Charlie a way out of isolation; it rather encourages it. This can be envisaged as a circle: the lack of participation leads to isolation, which increases the protagonist's desire to communicate, but because he does not receive any replies, the letter-writing again leads back to isolation. Leaving this state can only be achieved through 'real-life' participation.

From his very first letter, the narrator-protagonist demonstrates his preoccupation with friendships and loneliness. However, the term 'participation' and Charlie's obsession with it start to permeate his writing only after a conversation with his English teacher Bill, who is initially the only person paying attention to him. He asks Charlie questions about his life, encouraging him to spend less time (over)thinking and more time 'participating'. It is important to consider what an adult means or intends by calling on a child/teen to 'participate'. When Bill uses the term, he refers to dancing at school events and going on dates (cf. Chbosky 1999: 26), naming typical high school experiences – experiences that are part of the transition from child to adolescent, of growing up. Bill is thus an adult who is using his empowered position to urge a teen character towards maturity – even if it is with the best intentions in mind. Charlie frequently mentions Bill in his letters, demonstrating his respect and admiration for him. He also expresses his happiness over the fact that Bill "forgets that [he is] sixteen", and makes him feel "like a grown-up" (Chbosky 1999: 177, 114), displaying the common adolescent desire of being treated more like an adult. Throughout the novel, Bill acts as "a wise adult to guide a confused adolescent" – a discursive practice that is commonplace in YA literature (Trites 2000: 80). Bill's advice to Charlie indeed has an important impact; in fact, it is a major propelling force behind the narrative. Towards the end, Charlie offers his own definition of 'participation': "I think the idea is that every person has to live for his or her own life and then make the choice to share it with other people. Maybe that's what makes people 'participate.' I'm not really certain" (Chbosky 1999: 182). His expression of uncertainty, however, demonstrates that he is still trying to discover the meaning of the term.

Adolescents, Trites elaborates, experience school "as a site in which they are simultaneously repressed by authority and peers and in which they are liberated by socializing with their friends and by learning new ideas" (2000: 35). Liberation through socialisation becomes possible for Charlie once he makes friends with Patrick and Sam – the latter being the girl he then falls in love with. However, despite the developing friendship, the protagonist continues to experience isolation. In such periods, one of Charlie's main coping strategies is to take on the role of an 'observer' of society. Coats (2011) writes that "[c]haracters who operate on the social rim situate themselves as observers not fully integrated into the culture they tend to view with equal parts longing and disdain" (319). In

Perks there is no disdain on Charlie's part, but rather a curiosity about the people surrounding him:

> I walk around the school hallways and look at the people. I look at the teachers and wonder why they're here. If they like their jobs. Or us. And I wonder how smart they were when they were fifteen. Not in a mean way. In a curious way. It's like looking at all the students and wondering who's had their heart broken that day, and how they are able to cope [...]. (Chbosky 1999: 153)

Such passages reveal Charlie's desire to understand others – both his peers and authority figures. They further emphasise his inward-focus, which dramatically increases whenever he is not actively participating. For the dynamic of the plot, Charlie's isolation is advantageous, since it is in this state that he reveals his deepest fears and worries, which give the reader insights into his consciousness. In addition to his observations at school, Charlie comes up with a personal project that involves observing people in malls in order to "figure out why [they] go there" (Chbosky 1999: 155). The school and the mall – two *social* spaces – thus become spaces of isolation for Charlie.

Matos (2013) describes Chbosky's narrator-protagonist as "a passive participant in his environment who observes and learns from the people around him" (87). He argues that Charlie "avoids becoming an active member of his community", taking on an "inactive role" (87). While this is indeed the case, such a statement neglects to consider that Charlie does not intentionally avoid being an active member, but is denied this opportunity despite his attempts to integrate. He actively tries to participate within his home and to engage with family members who regularly reject him – sometimes intentionally, sometimes because they are oblivious to his needs. Charlie also makes an effort with his friends; his only fault is that he is too naïve and inexperienced to understand how friendships and dating work. His traumatic past, that is uncovered later, further explains his difficulties in relationships. While Charlie does often take on a passive role in society, his isolation at home and at school is not self-induced but grows out of his circumstances and the lack of people he can communicate with. Whenever Charlie actively wishes to remain unseen, it is because he desires protection from judgement:

> I pretended [my friends] were in the car with me. [...] if anybody saw me talking out loud when I was alone in the car, their looks might convince me that the something that's wrong with me might be even worse than I thought. (Chbosky 1999: 159)

In such moments, he is overcome by a fear of being labelled as 'different' or 'Other', commonly experienced by adolescents. Charlie's concern with how others perceive him is intensified by his awareness of his mental health issues.

Identity construction in *Perks* is clearly tied to the idea of belonging. Throughout Charlie's letters, the reader gets a sense of how crucial friendships, company and participation have become for him, with these topics increasingly permeating his writing. His identity, development and state of mind are heavily influenced by his connection with others – or, conversely, the lack thereof. Coats (2011: 318) writes how contemporary fiction featuring male protagonists no longer follows "[t]he 1970s myth of the lone male standing against peer pressure and shaping his own destiny". Rather, today's YA fiction acknowledges "that identities are in fact shaped by our participation in groups, rather than our standing apart from them" (Coats 2011: 318). Chbosky's novel echoes this sentiment: Charlie's friendships and his relationship with his parents and siblings indeed have a considerable impact on his self-perception and development.

While Charlie craves company and resents his isolation, Zoe desires this status. This is reflected in the fact that little of her letter-writing deals with her present social life; references to school concern almost solely Zoe's panic attacks, her hiding attempts, and the increasing superficiality of her relationship with her best friend. Instead, the time and location of Zoe's letter-writing are foregrounded. The protagonist repeatedly describes her nightly retreat to the family's garden shed, which offers her the isolation she requires to share her story. The setting is indeed a powerful device in this novel, in which the shed becomes a symbol for Zoe's voluntary withdrawal from society. While Zoe is temporarily isolated due to her own choices, her recipient will spend the rest of his life in imprisonment and hence isolation. This fact is at the forefront of Zoe's thoughts: she frequently refers to Stuart's isolated existence in her letters, regularly mentioning his cell and envisioning his life there with no friends, freedom and purpose, and under constant control by guards. When Zoe discovers the resemblance in size between her addressee's cell and her shed, the parallel between the two spaces becomes even clearer to the reader.

The concept of prison, Foucault (1977: 232) explains, is based on the deprivation of liberty. Isolation has always been the foremost principle: "The isolation of the convict from the external world, from everything that motivated the offence, from the complicities that facilitated it" (236). In light of this statement, Zoe's withdrawal from society, demonstrated by her lack of desire to actively participate in and outside school, becomes a form of self-punishment. Zoe blames her desire to participate for the unfolding of the traumatic events that she relates in her letters. This becomes clear early on, when she describes her wish to make experiences, from which she is kept by her overprotective mother: "I was sick of missing out. Sick of listening to their stories. And jealous, really jealous, that I didn't have a few of my own" (Pitcher 2012: 12). Thus, after the traumatic incident, Zoe turns herself into a 'convict' as a form of self-punishment, isolating herself "from the external world, from everything that motivated the offence" (Foucault 1977: 236).

Prison, Foucault continues, is also "the place of observation of punished individuals" (1977: 249). Observation takes two forms: surveillance and knowledge about inmates (cf. Foucault 1977: 249). While Zoe's addressee is exposed to these two forms, Zoe's shed offers a place to *escape* from observation. In her letters, Zoe repeatedly emphasises the shed's suitability as a place to hide from prying eyes – and indeed, the only eyes watching her write her letters are those of animals:

> No eyes at all apart from eight on the spider, and they're not looking at me. [...] It'll be different tomorrow. The eyes will be back. Sad ones and inquisitive ones, some that stare and others that try not to look [...]. (Pitcher 2012: 22)

While Zoe is safe in her shed, she becomes a subject of observation/surveillance at school, falling victim to the curiosity and judgment of both peers and authority figures. Later in the novel, Zoe describes a situation in which she would have loved "to be a fly on the wall" (Pitcher 2012: 90), reminding us of the limitations of her first-person account, which is restricted to her own knowledge and viewpoint. This reference to a fly then draws the protagonist into the present moment of writing:

> Funnily enough there's an actual fly on the actual wall right now. Sort of. A little black one is caught in the web on the shed windowsill, stuck in the silk and staring at the garden probably wondering what on earth happened to its freedom. (Pitcher 2012: 90)

The loss of the fly's freedom corresponds to Zoe's, as she locks herself into the shed night after night, the spider's web referring to her own web of lies that she has woven and is now trying to write her way out of. The use of the term 'fly on the wall' is also interesting, since it refers to an unnoticed observer – the reader of the novel, perhaps? Garcia (2013: 104) emphasises the role of voyeurism regarding diaries and letters in YA fiction, since such novels "position the reader as someone that has somehow come across a text that was not necessarily intended for him or her." As a result, he continues, "our reading of these texts is a peek into a world we were not necessarily invited into" (Garcia 2013: 104).

Zoe's letters reflect her desire to remain hidden from judgement – yet, she offers herself up for judgment to a stranger. The stranger, however, is someone that Zoe thinks will understand: "You killed someone you were supposed to love and I killed someone I was supposed to love, and we both understand the pain and the fear and the sadness and the guilt" (Pitcher 2012: 7). Zoe feels such high degree of responsibility for her boyfriend's accident that she equates herself with a murderer. Nikolajeva emphasises that it is crucial to consider the difference "between *being* guilty according to a given legislation [...] and *feeling* guilty, whether with or without reason" (2014b: 199; emphasis in original). Zoe's repeated comparisons between her own situation and the addressee's encourage readers to consider questions of guilt and morality, and to discern the difference between being and feeling guilty – a challenging task. The fact that Stuart is executed for his crime before he can receive Zoe's final letter further prompts the reader to ponder capital punishment and its ethical implications.

Finally, Foucault emphasises the role of prison "as an apparatus for transforming individuals" (1977: 233). In isolation and solitude, convicts are forced to reflect and, by extension, repentance, which will eventually lead them on a path of transformation. The reader receives knowledge of Stuart's process of repenting through Zoe's comments on the poems[6] that he writes in his confinement, published regularly on the Death Row website: "I read your poem *Forgiveness* and how you *Regret taking a life With a carving knife Especially your wife*. Honest truth I think you deserve a chance to redeem yourself" (Pitcher 2012: 185; emphasis in original). The shed becomes Zoe's place for reflecting on her own guilt as well as Stuart's, for her repentance and transformation. Zoe's place of isolation might be her 'cell', her place of imprisonment during the night; she can, or rather must, however, leave it before dawn to prevent her parents from discovering her hiding/writing place. She is also free to *abandon* her 'cell', her 'imprisonment', once she has begun the process of transformation, whereas Stuart will never be able to participate in society again.

5 Writing as Talk? The Role of the Narratee in Unidirectional Epistolary Narratives

Fictional diarists feel the urge to express their thoughts; fictional letter-writers, however, write out of a desire to *communicate* their thoughts to someone other than themselves (cf. Altman 1982: 89). Thus, in contrast to diary fiction, the narratee/internal reader in an epistolary novel is not the narrator-protagonist's future self, but a specific addressee. Although there are differences between unidirec-

---

6 These are not included in the novel in their entirety but referred to in terms of their title, content or specific lines.

tional letter novels and letter narratives with two/multiple correspondents, the addressee always plays a significant role in the narrative.

Scholars dealing with Chbosky's novel commonly refer to Charlie's letters as a journal/diary (see e.g. Cadden 2011). However, the narrator-protagonist does not only view his letters as a place to pour out his thoughts, but craves a connection to his addressee, recommending books/songs, asking questions, and trying to make his experiences relatable to them. Charlie explicitly justifies his decision to write letters, stating that they are "better than a diary because there is communication and a diary can be found" (Chbosky 1999: 11). He thus clearly views his letter-writing as communication, despite not receiving any replies, and hence not having any information about his addressee, his or her feelings or reactions. The same applies to Zoe, who repeatedly refers to her letter-writing as 'talk', implying an element of dialogue/exchange – which, as in *Perks*, is of course missing. Isolated from society and provided only with a fake address, Stuart is unable to establish a correspondence with Zoe. However, he does communicate with the outside world through his poetry, from which Zoe construes his state of mind. Readers are tempted to interpret Stuart's poems as his way of 'talking' to Zoe, since he publishes them regularly and they could therefore be reactions to Zoe's letters – assuming, of course, that he reads them. Despite the lack of replies, Zoe is convinced that the correspondence is just as helpful for her recipient as it is for her, commenting repeatedly on Stuart's (assumed) need for her letters.

Altman (1982) argues that letter novels in which there is no "desire for *exchange*" (89; emphasis in original) are not epistolary narratives. She "insist[s] upon the fact that the reader is 'called upon' to respond" (Altman 1982: 89) – an element that is lacking in unidirectional novels. Nevertheless, *Perks* and *Clouds* are radically different from diary/journal narratives, since "awareness of a specific second-person addressee can alter the character and experience of the first-person writing itself" (Altman 1982: 91). In other words, "[r]eader consciousness explicitly informs the act of writing" (Altman 1982: 186). In epistolary novels, the depiction of narrated events – the content and extent of what is shared – very much depends on the narratee and the protagonist-narrator's relationship to them. In diary novels, "author, narrator and narratee are identical and thus unlikely to have motivation for deceit" (Bray 2003: 177). Letters, in contrast, are both a means to reveal and hide information. This is reflected, above all, in the (unidirectional) letter-writers' desire for anonymity, as well as the countless omissions/delays that characterise the narration. Altman (1982: 88) further writes that "[t]he letter writer simultaneously seeks to affect his reader and is affected by him". This again also applies to unidirectional letter novels, which, once more, emphasises the difference between epistolary and diary narratives and justifies a treatment of novels such as *Perks* and *Clouds* as the former.

The protagonists in unidirectional epistolary novels write the letters to be read, addressing them to specific people whose presence is invoked in the letters and thus contributes to the construction of meaning and the protagonist's identity – albeit to different extents. In *Perks* the internal reader admittedly loses their specificity so that sometimes the 'you' seems to coincide with the external reader. This is not the case in *Clouds*, in which the internal reader persona is much more specified/developed. The lack of response in both *Perks* and *Clouds* points to a lack of dialogue; however, it offers semantic gaps that require the audience to develop their own conclusions as to whether the recipient reads the letters or not, and if so, how they react.

In addition, and in relation, to the presence of the narratee, greeting and closing lines – formal elements specific to epistolary communication – add further possibilities for interpretation. They can reflect the mood of a letter, as well as the relationship/degree of intimacy between narrator and narratee, impos[ing] "upon the writer a gesture of *self-definition* vis-à-vis the addressee" (Altman 1982: 145–146). In *Perks*, the protagonist begins each letter with "Dear Friend", ending it with "Love Always, Charlie". Cadden (2000: 150) comments that this "professed love" can be viewed either as "a miscalculation of traditional closings" or "as indicative of the understanding [Charlie] craves from both the narratee and the implied audience". The limitation, however, is that the lines remain identical throughout the novel; hence, we do not receive additional information regarding the mood and narrator-narratee relationship of individual letters. *Clouds*, in contrast, makes use of this possibility. Zoe's changing greeting and closing lines reflect her increasing trust and feelings of 'friendship' towards the addressee. She begins the correspondence in an overly formal way, addressing her recipient with "Dear Mr S Harris" and ending the letter with a simple "From Zoe". The more of her story and thus herself she reveals, the more 'casual' the lines become, ranging from "Hi Stuart"/"From Zoe, x" to "My dear Stu"/ "Love, Zoe xxx". The closing line of her last letter, "Yours truly, ALICE JONES" (Pitcher 2012: 287) reflects her relief at finally signing off with her real name.

The presence of the addressee influences readers' experience and interpretations, since they are required to "read any given letter from at least three points of view – that of the intended or actual recipient as well as that of the writer and [their] own" (Altman 1982: 111). Interpretations develop from a negotiation of these viewpoints. Campbell (1995: 338) emphasises that this applies just as much to single-correspondent letter novels, since the reader nevertheless "comes to know the addressee". Discussions of epistolary fiction frequently address the role of the narratee; a treatment of the form in YA literature, however, has to consider additional questions: "Is the narratee a child or an adult?"; and if it is the latter, "[w]hat kind of adult?" (Nikolajeva 2014b: 147) In *Perks*[7] and *Clouds* the recipient of the letters is an adult. The reader thus cannot cognitively align with the narratee. It is obvious, however, that the novelists attempt to keep the external reader in mind. In her way of address, Zoe does not treat Stuart like an adult[8], as she refrains from explaining and referring to objects/concepts that adults would be familiar with. Additionally, she does not behave as if she were addressing a *male* adult, since she openly discusses her sexual experiences. Charlie also tends to treat his addressee like a teenager, explaining, amongst others, the act of masturbation. The desire to share their thoughts not with a peer but with an older, experienced addressee reflects the protagonists' yearning for being understood by someone who 'has been through this'.

The overt construction of a narratee, whether in the form of an adult or peer, is an important element of letter novels; it is particularly valuable in YA fiction, since this overt construction "denies implied readers a passive reading position" (McCallum 1999: 227). Further, as Genette (1980: 260) emphasises, "the existence of an intradiegetic narratee has the effect of keeping us at a distance, since he [or she] is always interposed between the narrator and us". Readers are thus offered another subjectivity that they cannot identify with, but whose position they can evaluate and make use of in their interpretations.

6 Conclusion

Both novels present highly introspective and complex characters that engage in self-analysis, self-reflection and self-discovery, while also observing/reflecting on their surroundings. In comparison to other first-person narratives, the letter form draws increased attention to the characters' state of isolation, alienation and loneliness. More than any other first-person form – except, perhaps to some extent the diary novel – the epistolary mode allows for repeated references to and descriptions of the time and location of narrating. Such references convey a sense of immediacy while reducing the distance between reader and the act of narration. They further draw attention to the setting as both physical and symbolic space. Indeed, the setting acts as more than just a 'backdrop' to the stories

---

[7] Although Charlie includes virtually no information about the addressee in his letters, we know that he or she is older than him and has been through the high school experience; technically, he or she is thus 'of age'.
[8] However, we must consider that Stuart is not the 'average' adult – he is powerless, stripped of all his rights and freedom.

and serves to enhance characterisation. It is inextricably linked to the characters' movement/negotiation between isolation and participation, their understanding of themselves and others. The letter mode further emphasises the young protagonists' desire for communication. Letter novels construct an overt narratee, who plays a shaping role in the narrative and the protagonists' development. The importance of the narratee increases, the more present he/she is in the letters and the more agency he/she has. The overt construction of an intradiegetic narratee, an internal reader, distinguishes epistolary from diary fiction; it keeps the external reader at a distance, while adding a third viewpoint that they have to evaluate and consider in their interpretations. This applies just as much to *unidirectional* letter fiction as it does to novels which feature an actual multidirectional correspondence. Most importantly, the novels point to the role of isolation, participation and communication in the quest for self. In this quest, the reader is the metaphoric 'fly on the wall' looking over the adolescent protagonist's shoulder as they put their struggles to paper – in isolation, but looking for connection.

Works Cited

Altman, Janet Gurkin. 1982. *Epistolarity. Approaches to a Form*. Ohio: Ohio State University Press.
Beebee, Thomas. 2010. "Epistolary Novel". In: David Herman, Manfred Jahn & Marie-Laure Ryan (eds.). *The Routledge Encyclopedia of Narrative Theory*. London: Routledge. <http://literature.proquest.com/searchFulltext.do?id=R04432089&divLevel=0&queryId=2981902471947&trailId=15 A891FA14B&area=ref&forward=critref_ft> [accessed 30 March 2017].
Bower, Anne. 1997. *Epistolary Responses. The Letter in 20th-Century American Fiction and Criticism*. Tuscaloosa: University of Alabama Press.
Bray, Joe. 2003. *The Epistolary Novel. Representations of Consciousness*. London/New York: Routledge.
Cadden, Mike. 2000. "The Irony of Narration in the Young Adult Novel". *Children's Literature Association Quarterly* 25.3: 146–154. <https://doi.org/10.1353/chq.0.1467> [accessed 27 March 2017].
Cadden, Mike. 2011. "Genre as Nexus: The Novel for Children and Young Adults". In: Shelby A. Wolf, Karen Coats, Patricia Enciso & Christine A. Jenkins (eds.). *Handbook of Research on Children's and Young Adult Literature*. New York/Oxon: Routledge. 302–313.
Campbell, Elizabeth. 1995. "Re-Visions, Re-Flections, Re-Creations: Epistolarity in Novels by Contemporary Women". *Twentieth Century Literature* 41. 3: 332–348. <http://www.jstor.org/stable/441856> [accessed 6 March 2017].
Chbosky, Stephen. 1999. *The Perks of Being a Wallflower*. London: Simon & Schuster.
Coats, Karen. 2011. "Young Adult Literature: Growing Up, In Theory". In: Shelby A. Wolf, Karen Coats, Patricia Enciso & Christine A. Jenkins (eds.). *Handbook of Research on Children's and Young Adult Literature*. New York/Oxon: Routledge. 315–329.

Foucault, Michel. 1977. *Discipline and Punish. The Birth of the Prison*, trans. Alan Sheridan. New York: Vintage Books.

Garcia, Antero. 2013. *Critical Foundations in Young Adult Literature. Challenging Genres.* Rotterdam: Sense Publishers.

Genette, Gérard. 1980. *Narrative Discourse*, trans. J.E. Lewin. Oxford: Basil Blackwell.

Martens, Lorna. 2009/1985. *The Diary Novel.* Cambridge: CUP.

Matos, Angel Daniel. 2013. "Writing through Growth, Growth through Writing: *The Perks of Being a Wallflower* and the Narrative of Development". *The ALAN Review:* 86–97. <https://scholar.lib.vt.edu/ejournals/ALAN/v40n3/pdf/matos.pdf.> [accessed 26 June 2017].

Matthews, Timothy, Andrea Danese, Jasmin Wertz, Candice L. Odgers, Antony Ambler, Terrie E. Moffitt & Louise Arseneault. 2016. "Social isolation, loneliness and depression in young adulthood: a behavioural genetic analysis". *Soc Psychiatry Psychiatr Epidemiol* 51: 339–348. DOI: 10.1007/s00127–016–1178–7 [accessed 26 May 2017].

McCallum, Robyn. 1999. *Ideologies of Identity in Adolescent Fiction. The Dialogic Construction of Subjectivity.* New York: Garland Publishing.

Nikolajeva, Maria. 2005. *Aesthetic Approaches to Children's Literature. An Introduction.* Lanham, MD: The Scarecrow Press.

Nikolajeva, Maria. 2014. "Voicing Identity: The Dilemma of Narrative Perspective in Twenty-First Century Young Adult Fiction". In: Catherine Butler & Kimberley Reynolds (eds.). *Modern Children's Literature: An Introduction.* London: Palgrave. 251–267.

Nikolajeva, Maria. 2014b. *Reading for Learning. Cognitive Approaches to Children's Literature.* Amsterdam/Philadelphia: John Benjamins Publishing.

Perry, Ruth. 1980. *Women, Letters, and the Novel.* New York: AMS Press.

Pitcher, Annabel. 2012. *Ketchup Clouds.* London: Indigo.

Trites, Roberta Seelinger. 2000. *Disturbing the Universe. Power and Repression in Adolescent Literature.* Iowa City: University of Iowa Press.

Wasserman, Emily. 2003. "The Epistolary in Young Adult Literature". *ALAN Review* 30.3: 48–51. <https://scholar.lib.vt.edu/ejournals/ALAN/v30n3/pdf/wasserman.pdf> [accessed 21 March 2017].

Ingrid Pfandl-Buchegger
From Ireland with Love

The Use of Epistolary Writing in Cecelia Ahern's Fiction

Abstract: Best-selling Irish novelist Cecelia Ahern is one of a number of contemporary writers who employ epistolary writing in their novels. Her use of letters, however, serves a different purpose than that of other, more radical innovators. Even though her fiction is about women and predominantly addressed to a female audience, Ahern uses letters to give a voice to both male and female characters. In her first novel, *PS, I Love You*, the letters serve as a form of trauma counselling: they are a legacy of the deceased husband to his wife to help her overcome her grief in the first months after his death. In her second novel, *Where Rainbows End*, a multi-perspectival narrative written entirely in epistolary style, Ahern uses a plethora of communicative forms (including electronic media) to describe the long road to self-discovery and happiness in the life of her female protagonist against a backdrop of her Irish family and friends, thereby painting a vivid picture of Irish life and manners.

1 Introduction

In an era of globalized communication and of constant readiness to communicate one's personal experiences, thoughts and feelings on social media, Samuel Richardson's expression 'writing to the moment'[1] has taken on a new, existentialist meaning. The focus on the present makes it all the more important to document the fleeting moment and to affirm our existence and consolidate our identity through 'physical' manifestations of writing in order to counteract the post-modernist feeling of the loss of the individual self in a global universe of mass phenomena. Writing and communicating have become existentialist necessities: 'I text, therefore I am'.

Considering the importance of 'writing' and thus 'self-fashioning' one's life and identity in contemporary society, it is no surprise that literature has also rediscovered a form of writing that was last popular in the seventeenth and eighteenth centuries and is associated with authors such as Aphra Behn, Samuel Richardson, Goethe, Montesquieu, Rousseau, Choderlos de Laclos, or even early

---

[1] As discussed, among others, in a letter to Lady Bradshaigh (Richardson 1965: 289).

https://doi.org/10.1515/9783110584813-009

Jane Austen – the epistolary novel. Since its beginnings, epistolary writing has been associated with women. The letter seems to be a particularly suitable form for the expression of women's innermost thoughts and feelings, especially with regard to the topic of love. The form allows for the creation of intimacy while at the same time establishing a certain distance from the addressee, allowing the writer to express in privacy what she would be too shy to express in the presence of another person in face-to-face communication. This confidential nature of epistolary communication even encourages confessional writing. As the title of a contemporary epistolary novel pointedly suggests, it is a 'closeness that separates' (see Katie Hall and Bogen Jones' novel of the same name, published in 2013), that seduces writers to pour out their hearts in an 'epistolary urge' without having to observe the physical reactions or facial expressions of their correspondent.

Epistolary literature has also been connected with a positive change in the status of women (already as early as the seventeenth and eighteenth centuries), the act of writing becoming a means of liberation from patriarchal (or, more recently, postcolonial) constraints and other-directed life-concepts and giving a voice to the writer's private considerations and intimate feelings. Not surprisingly, writing in the form of letters and diaries, or, of late, blogs or e-mails, has seen a revival in an age of informal and immediate communication enabled and made popular by social media, which mainly takes place without being face-to-face. Again, not surprisingly, it can predominantly be found in women's literature and young adult novels, providing women, adolescents, and marginalized or even mentally challenged people with the chance to reflect and re-write their lives and thus create an identity for themselves.

This kind of self-representation, free of the interference of authorial narrative voices, also speaks more immediately to the reader, offering psychological insight into the mind of the writer(s). The specific emotional appeal of epistolary writing with its characteristic traits of subjectivity, fragmentation, disregard of chronology and use of associative and informal language helps create a sympathetic 'closeness' between the writing subject and the recipient.

Such intimate closeness between reader and fictional character may be one of the reasons for the immense success and popularity of writers such as Irish novelist Cecelia Ahern, who also uses the epistolary style in some of her best-known novels, award-winning bestsellers that are being sold in over 40 countries. Her first two novels, *PS, I Love You* and *Where Rainbows End* (also published under the title *Love, Rosie*), which are written in the epistolary style, were also adapted quite successfully into motion pictures. Ahern writes love stories for a predominantly (young) female audience. In view of the age of her readership, she uses a contemporary form of epistolary communication that would appeal to a younger generation, allowing her characters to express their thoughts and feelings not only in the form of letters, but mainly availing themselves of electronic forms of communication such as e-mails and instant messaging.

In the following analysis, I will take a look at the different ways in which Ahern uses epistolary forms in her first two novels, *PS, I Love You* and *Where Rainbows End,* explore the impact epistolary writing has on her fiction, and discuss possible reasons why this format holds such an appeal for her as a writer and her subject matter. I will argue that although Ahern's novels continue the tradition of epistolary practice in many ways, they stand in contrast to more radical tendencies in contemporary epistolary writing. Using both unidirectional and multidirectional forms, her novels give voice not only to women, but also to male writers, as, for instance, in the rather unusual case of the husband in *PS, I Love You*. Additionally, the spontaneous informality and oral quality of epistolary exchanges perfectly complies with Ahern's endeavours to paint vivid linguistic portraits of her characters that contribute to the creation of a colourful tableau of Irish society and manners.

2 *PS, I Love You* – Epistolary Messages from the Beyond

> "As I write this letter/send my love to you/ remember that I'll always/be in love with you."
> (The Beatles, "P.S., I Love You")

PS, I Love You[2] was Ahern's first great success as a novel-writer, her debut novel, which she wrote in 2002 at the remarkably young age of twenty-one, and which was published in 2004 ("Cecelia Ahern" 2012, online). It falls into the category of trauma fiction, addressing, in this case, the trauma that the loss of a loved one often causes, and depicting the beneficial effects of epistolary memory in dealing with the 'healing' process, though differently than mainstream therapeutic letter-writing.[3] Written by a (young) female author for a distinctively 'female' audience of (young) female readers on the very romantic topic of lost love and the quest of its young female protagonist for a new meaning in life and an identity of her own, it additionally falls into the category of literature by and for women and

---

[2] Henceforth referred to as *PS*.
[3] For a discussion of the therapeutic function of letter writing in narrative fiction, see El Hamamsy (2010).

has many of the characteristics of an 'engendered' form. Generally categorised as typical Celtic 'chick-lit' (Ging 2008: 242) with its rather emotional 'Irish' mixture of tears and laughter, of dying and living on, it tells the story of a young woman who loses her husband and soul-mate due to a brain tumour and is overwhelmed with grief and virtually paralysed by helplessness and complete disorientation.

PS is certainly not an epistolary novel in the traditional sense, even though its title already suggests the importance of letter writing. The novel as such is written in the third-person form and follows (for the most part, with only four very brief exceptions) the point-of-view of the female protagonist, the young Irish widow Holly Kennedy. The over 500-page text contains only 10 letters (plus an accompanying cover letter), left by the recently deceased husband to his wife, and most of these are short notes rather than regular letters. Thus, in this case the bereaved person is not the letter writer, trying to come to terms with her grief by means of the epistolary practice, but the addressee of the letters. In spite of their brevity, these letters are not only omnipresent in the novel, they are also an essential component of the structure of the narrative, as they function as important triggers for the development of the plot, propelling the action forward by guiding the behaviour of the main character. According to Elizabeth Campbell's classification, such a novel could still be categorized as 'epistolary', "if the plot is determined, advanced or resolved by letters" (1995: 333).[4] In a way the whole narrative could be called a 'post-scriptum', the letters having been composed before the onset of the narrative action, which in turn is a consequence of and reaction to the content of these letters.

Holly learns of the existence of the letters about two months after her husband's death. They are enclosed in an envelope, or rather a "thick brown package" (*PS:* 30), addressed to Holly Kennedy but with no sender information, and had been posted by her husband, Gerry, to Holly's parents, who are, however, unaware of its contents, its sender, or of its importance for their daughter. The package contains a cover letter and one 'letter' for every month of the remaining year, starting with March (Gerry had died at the beginning of February). As the accompanying letter specifies in the postscript, "they must be opened exactly when labelled and <u>must be obeyed</u>" (*PS:* 33; emphasis in the text). Each envelope

---

4 Campbell follows Charles E. Kany (1937) in this, who describes an early Renaissance novel as epistolary that also contains only ten letters, which, however, play an important role in the development of the plot and the denouement. Campbell, in her paper, discusses several novels which do not include letters *per se*, but only references to these letters or unwritten letters: Ruth Prawer Jhabvala's *Heat and Dust*, Elizabeth Jolley's *Miss Peabody's Inheritance*, and Sylvia Molloy's *Certificate of Absence*.

bears an inscription, indicating the month in which the wife is supposed to open it, rather than an address or the name of an addressee. The accompanying letter is the only 'real' letter in terms of form, a letter of farewell addressed to "My darling Holly", thanking her for their time together and encouraging her to "go on alone" (*PS:* 32), and signed, with professions of everlasting love, "Your husband and best friend, Gerry". The enclosed tiny envelopes lack an address, they are only inscribed with the name of the month, and the messages they contain are very short notes, without a salutation; instead of a signature, there is always the same postscript: "PS. I love you …", which gives the name to the whole novel. The actual purpose of these notes is specified in the postscript in Gerry's covering letter – they represent "The List", a legacy that Gerry had once playfully promised to leave for his wife after his death to help her cope with the, at that time, rather mundane details of daily life, such as turning off the lights in the bedroom or remembering to buy some milk. The real list that Gerry composes during his progressing illness, unknown to his wife and friends, is concerned with more serious matters. Aware of his impending death, Gerry has put together guidelines for his wife, "a ten-step psychological guide to dealing with loss" (Ging 2008: 243), which is meant to enable her to overcome her trauma and to face life again with renewed courage. Gradually, these monthly guidelines lead her from utter dismay, depression, seclusion, neglect of her appearance and inability to work back to a 'normal' life for a thirty-year-old woman. The letters progressively set the wife tasks, starting with insider jokes such as buying a bedside lamp, going on to suggesting that she begin looking after herself, buy some new clothes, take up her social contacts again and go out and enjoy herself, encourage her to find a satisfying job (Holly had been working as a secretary, but never liked her work), and finally even to search for a new partner. Most of these notes are associated with a memorable occurrence in their life together, or with their friends, so that whenever Holly opens a letter, she in a way also 'opens' a memory, one of "a million, billion happy memories" (*PS:* 466) accumulated over the past fifteen years that she spent with her husband, which usually starts her 'daydreaming'. She imagines Gerry sitting at the table watching her and talking to her, or remembers the accompanying events (e.g. the list, their routine fights about turning out the light in their bedroom, the 'disco diva', or "the 'spensive white dress" stained with red wine by a drunken Holly, 13f., and others). Each time Holly holds an envelope in her hands she feels a connection with Gerry (*PS:* 78), as though he was not really dead. The letters give her the illusion that he is only on holiday and writing her letters (*PS:* 92), so these messages keep him alive for her and provide her with very precious moments of 'intimacy' and consolation ("now he was dead she was still living through him", *PS:* 468).

Not all of these memories are pleasant remembrances for Holly, however, nor are the things Gerry asks her to do easy for her to achieve. Yet these guidelines are, of course, instructions for Holly, a "sort of Bible" (*PS:* 467), Gerry's "Ten Commandments", as an exasperated friend calls them (*PS:* 458) – a legacy which she considers her moral duty to carry out, even if it provides a real challenge and compels her to conquer her weaker self. Sometimes Gerry's challenges are simply painful (asking her to dispose of all of Gerry's belongings in the house), sometimes they are embarrassing and require her to go beyond her comfort zones, as in the case of the karaoke competition for which Gerry had secretly entered her name. Having once made an absolute fool of herself at karaoke, Holly, who cannot keep a tune and has no sense of rhythm and melody, blankly refuses at first, but gives in after an imaginary conversation with Gerry and endures a disastrous performance, which, however, boosts her self-esteem and takes her one step ahead in building up enough self-confidence for Gerry's next task. After the summer, he suggests that she find a new job and "shoot for the moon" (*PS:* 291), and again Holly trusts in his 'superior' understanding and lands a job with a magazine, the first job that she really likes. As Holly's reactions to these epistolary messages show, the letters can – despite the correspondence's one-sided nature and the impossibility of exchange or an epistolary answer (due to the demise of her husband) – ultimately elicit a response, albeit a non-epistolary one.[5]

As opposed to a general tendency in epistolary literature (esp. in contemporary, e.g., postcolonial, literature), where letters are used to give women a voice of their own, Ahern uses letters to give a voice to the deceased husband, so Gerry can have a way, as one chapter written from his point-of-view tells us, "to remain with Holly even when he was gone" (*PS:* 462), to keep his memory alive and to help his wife get through the initial months after these traumatic events. His reasons for writing letters are not the wish or need to express his feelings, or to discover the nature of his feelings (as was the case with Richardson's Pamela and many of her female epistolary successors), but his serious concern for his partner and his desire to support her. Thus his letters do not express the immediate feelings of a man about to face death who is worried about his health, nor do they relate his fear of dying, or of suffering, or even feelings of self-pity and despair, and how he tries to cope with these through letter-writing. The feelings expressed in Gerry's letters are altruistic feelings, mainly of solicitude and love for his wife, and the letters are written in a highly positive vein to encourage her, challenge

---

[5] The earliest known instance of such letters without replies is Ovid's *Heroides*, while Goethe's *The Sorrows of Young Werther* is supposedly the best-known example in German literature.

her, raise her spirits, and frequently to make her laugh. An oft-mentioned function of epistolary writing, the possibility it gives to readers to obtain insight into the writer's mind and feelings and through this intimate acquaintance create empathy with a character, is only indirectly fulfilled in this case (we learn about Gerry mainly from Holly's memories and through her feelings for him). Instead, Gerry is given the privilege of one chapter in which the third-person narrative is focalised through his mind, which has an effect of immediacy similar to letter writing and is also apt to make the audience sympathize with a character by allowing them access to his/her thoughts and feelings. It is rather fitting that this is the chapter in which he is shown writing the final letter and assembling the package he will send to Holly, which provides a moving insight into the psyche of a dying man and his final preparations for leaving this world behind.

At first sight, the theme of a husband counselling or coaching his wife from beyond the grave would appear rather to reinforce traditional gender roles: the helpless female lost in her emotions, who is dependent on support and guidance from her dominant, rational partner from the next world in order to steady herself and take control of her life. What sounds and starts like a sentimental maudlin tale of love beyond death is, however, at least in part, saved by Ahern's talent in rendering the boisterous vital energy, humour and liveliness of her Irish homeland in her dialogues. The sentimental third-person narrative turns into a lively portrait of Irish life and behaviour, the rugged zest for life, and the solidarity and warmth within the family and among friends, as soon as it is interspersed with direct speech in the story. While the beginning of the novel is still heavy with vivid, partly anthropomorphic metaphors ("one day destiny greedily changed its mind", *PS:* 2; "She longed for the couch to hold out its arms to her", *PS:* 3) and intense physical reactions as expressions of Holly's limitless despair ("an overwhelming grief knotting her stomach and pulling at her heart", *PS:* 1; "Bile rose in her throat and she ran to the bathroom, where she collapsed to her knees before the toilet", *PS:* 1; "Holly drifted from room to room while she sobbed fat, salty tears, *PS:* 3), the introduction of the 'list' and the rather forceful intervention of her friend Sharon drag Holly out of her mute desolation and help her (and the narrative) to surface from the numbness and excessive desperation of her stream of thoughts and emotions to some wholesome, witty dialogues.[6]

Another sentimental element is the astounding ability of the husband to empathise with his wife and his exceptional knowledge of his partner, which allow

---

[6] See also Bernice Harrison's comment that "Ahern has a way with funny, sparkly dialogue" in her review of *PS, I Love You* in the *Irish Times* (2004: 62).

him to predict the stages through which she will be going and when, and how she will cope with her loss and her new situation in life. It is accounted for by the fact that Holly and Gerry are "best friends, lovers and soul mates, destined to be together" (*PS:* 2), establishing a connection beyond the grave, which obviously also gives Gerry the strength to prepare the letters unnoticed and even take a trip to the travel agency to book a holiday for his wife and her friends. Thus Holly is convinced that "Gerry would know exactly how she was feeling, he would know exactly what to say and exactly what to do" (*PS:* 89). As already mentioned, this sentimentality is counteracted by the boisterous humour and sometimes raucous wit of the verbal exchanges and by the inclusion of a number of slapstick scenes, which testify to the deft sense of the ridiculous and absurd as well as a love of practical jokes.[7] Holly's friends and family convulse with mirth during the public viewing of her brother Declan's award-winning video about Holly's drunken birthday party antics, and they virtually roar with laughter whenever they remember stories of the karaoke disaster, when Holly tripped over the steps and fell on her face, her skirt flying over her head and her underwear showing, and, worse still, broke her nose. The reactions of her husband and best friends are, to say the least, lacking in refinement: "Gerry lost his voice from laughing so loudly and Denise and Sharon helped matters by taking photographs of the scene of crime, which Denise then chose as the cover for her invitations to her Christmas party with the heading, 'Let's get legless!'" (*PS:* 120 f.)

In addition to the use of humour, which according to Frye's archetypal conceptual framework for literary modes disrupts the tendency towards idealization in the conventions of romance and thus destroys sentimental illusion (1966/1957: 225), Ahern also saves her novel from too glib a romanticism by avoiding a stereotypical happy ending. In an unexpected reversal, Holly's new friend and would-be suitor Daniel returns to his ex-girl-friend and Holly is left to take stock of her situation at the end of the year, while meeting a new (male) chance acquaintance for coffee: she feels confident, happy with her new job and ready for new experiences and memories, while cherishing her many happy memories of the past. Holly has resisted the temptation to rush into a new relationship, learned to live on her own and depend on her own judgement, and is ready

---

[7] The important role of humour is also emphasized by Marian Keyes, another famous representative of the genre 'chick-lit' (or "young female commercial fiction") in Ireland, who defines her own novels as "comic contemporary women's fiction". Similarly, Ahern's novels could also be categorized as such. Keyes' defence of 'chick-lit' equally applies to Ahern's fiction: "I have always used humour to survive my many, various forms of darkness. Things are really funny when they cut to the bone [when they cover] what it means to be human, and to be mortal, and to be fragile and imperfect." (quoted in O'Keeffe 2009, online).

for "more life" and perhaps "more love" (*PS*: 503). In this sense, *PS* could even be called an anti-*Dubliners* story – in Ahern's novel, the original paralysis that James Joyce described in his stories about Ireland's capital at the beginning of the twentieth century gradually leads to independence, and a self-determined optimistic view of life, showing that in the twenty-first century, Dublin's females have found the energy to "just live" their lives (*PS*: 503).

In Holly's case, this is certainly attributable in large part to the letters, even though she is not the writer, but the receiver of them. These letters fulfil a double function in terms of chronology, pointing both backward and forward. The narrative, which progresses over a time of nine months from beginning to end, is permeated with flashbacks in the guise of memories that are evoked by the letters. By referring back to significant events in the past they help to fill in important information on the background of the story going back some fifteen years to the time when Holly and Gerry met in school. On the other hand, they are also a means of pushing the plot forward by initiating new developments and encouraging the protagonist to look and move forward. Due to the largely straightforward narrative and the small number of letters, the novel does not suffer from the usual lack of chronology, fragmentation, or repetitiveness of more conventional 'genuine' epistolary novels, which makes it into a 'readerly' text in the positive sense. It is an easy, effortless, if lengthy, read that may be enjoyed and, according to a number of reviews cited in the flyleaf of the novel, will alternately move its readers to tears and laughter.[8]

3 *Where Rainbows End* – An Extended Tour-de-force Across (Several) Media

> "If you like a novel like a twitter narrative,
> go for it – otherwise steer clear."
> (Review on amazon.co.uk)

Ahern's second acclaimed novel, *Where Rainbows End* (2004)[9], is entirely conveyed in the epistolary style, though in a modified contemporary manner, both in the form of letters and electronic communication. The series of short documents composed by multiple correspondents uses various different

---

8 Or incite them to satirize the novel, as, e.g., in the *Guardian* ("PS, I Love You by Cecelia Ahern", online), which offers a "digested read", "[c]ondensed in the style of the original", making fun of the melodramatic plot and the rather stereotypical characterisation.
9 Henceforth referred to as *Rainbows*.

media: hand-written short notes and letters, e-mails, chat-room conversations, short instant messages, postcards, greeting cards, printed invitations (to weddings, birthday parties), faxes, newspaper clippings, bills etc. In contrast to *PS*, there is a real exchange of communications, between several correspondents: the main characters Rosie and Alex, Rosie's family, her daughter Katie, her parents and brother and sister, as well as her friends and partners. As the story covers a very long period of time (several decades in the lives of the two protagonists, Rosie Dunne and Alex Stewart, and their families and friends) and is elaborated over more than 400, sometimes 500 pages (depending on the edition), the handling of such a comprehensive collection of material requires skill, efficiency and elaborate planning with regard to information management. The extensive use of epistolary forms of communication makes it more difficult for the reader to follow the story line or work out the plot than in a straightforward linear narrative. As the novel comprises a selection of the most important experiences in the lives of the main characters, there are often extended time gaps (sometimes of several years), and the narrative shows all the characteristic traits of epistolarity, such as breaks in the chronology and logical structure, fragmentation, and repetitiveness. Even though the narrative itself unfolds in chronological order, the entries are not marked by a time or date, so that certain items of information have to be inferred by the reader, missing pieces to be put together as in a puzzle from several sources, while on the other hand different news is communicated or discussed by several correspondents, and it often adds to the humour of the novel to see different characters react to the same messages in their own idiosyncratic fashion. Ahern manages to give every character a distinct voice (even accounting for age, through changes in grammar and style in the children's exchanges, or by characterising Alex's and Katie's texts by their misspellings, e.g., rendering the word "know" as "no") and a distinctive personality that remains consistent throughout the novel. This form of implicit characterization makes the characters come alive through their use of language and enables the readers to form a mental (and acoustic) picture of a person, to recognize their idiosyncrasies, and, as they turn into familiar, identifiable figures, develop sympathy for the characters and interest in their further development.

On the whole, Ahern is rather ingenious in providing enough information in often very short notes to help the reader figure out how much time has passed and where in the chronology of Rosie's life we actually are, without making the novel sound artificial and constructed, but the text still presents a challenge to its readers. They are required to pause, thumb back a few pages to look up certain facts, remember specific details, and look for guidance and orientation in the introductory paraphernalia of the messages (e-mail headers: from – to, subject; for instant messages: "You have received an instant message from ..." plus name tags). With letters, it is necessary to check not only salutations ("Dear ...",) but also signatures (who is writing to whom) in order to identify the correspondents. It is up to the readers to assemble the various data offered to them, then draw their own conclusions, make their own judgements and thus contribute to the construction of the story and of its meaning. This, of course, requires a rather sophisticated reader, willing to co-operate and take the time to get used to the unwonted genre, even though the spoken, colloquial language combined with the short text passages makes the story easy enough to read, fast-paced and entertaining.

In this regard, it is interesting to take a look at the reactions of readers and reviewers. A short survey of comments by buyers of the novel on Amazon.co.uk provides some interesting insights. From out of a total of almost 700 entries (with 'officially' over 500 positive reviews), about one-fourth show an awareness of the novel's epistolary style. The majority of comments remark positively on the unusual form of presentation, in some cases admitting that it "took time getting used to" and was "off-putting at first", but well worth the effort, and calling it "refreshing", "innovative", "unique", "interesting", "fascinating", "unexpected", "captivatingly different", "amazing" etc. ("*Where Rainbows End.* Customer reviews", online).

A substantial number of readers, however, complain about the use of this format, most often finding it "boring" and "irritating", "frustrating" and "disappointing", and also criticize the "messiness" and the time gaps as unsettling the flow of reading and the structure of the narrative (using expressions such as "had to re-read", "reading for clues"), which disrupts the immersion into the story (failing to "draw you in") and makes it difficult or impossible to relate to the characters, identify with them, or even imagine what they look like.[10]

Another, certainly well-founded critique refers to the length of the novel, eliciting, e.g., comments on a "too drawn-out middle" and a "painfully stretched-out plot". Ahern's narratives do have a tendency to be extensive, but epistolary romances are, traditionally, "slow-motion affairs", a "dialogue *ritardando*", as Altman calls them (Altman 1982: 21). In *Rainbows*, such a retarding effect is a 'lost' letter, as the book might well have ended happily after less than the first half of the novel, when Alex declares his love for Rosie in a letter

---

[10] One buyer protested that "character development is almost impossible to portray through letters and e-mails", while another found that, conversely, the epistolary format "effectively allows the reader to grow up with the characters, learn about them from a personal level, and feel the heartbreaks and accomplishments that every person experiences [...]." ("*Where Rainbows End.* Customer reviews", online).

that he leaves behind in her kitchen, but that is intercepted by Rosie's jealous husband Greg.[11] In addition, there are complaints about the "unsatisfactory" conclusion for a "book of this genre", the rather quiet, unglamorous ending in a "magical silence". After such a protracted read, some readers obviously expect to be at least rewarded by the spectacular romantic declaration of love in front of a crowd that 'real' romance necessitates, with the hero going down on one knee and rose petals and champagne abounding, after which they live happily ever after (an ending that Ahern playfully refers to when Rosie tries to pass Greg's very 'simple' proposal off as 'romantic' and her friends remind her that she had always been the one to clamour for the 'real' thing; *Rainbows:* 149 ff.). Interestingly, judging by comments on the film version, however, the feedback is almost unanimously in favour of the book as the much better option, though the film version, which simplifies the plot quite considerably and cannot, of course, reproduce the epistolary form, receives a great deal of positive response, as well.[12]

The storyline is indeed rather twisted and 'drawn out'. Rosie and Alex start out as two Irish childhood sweethearts, who grow up together spending their time in school passing each other little scribbled notes across the classroom. They remain inseparable best friends, even as, like Hero and Leander, they are separated by the sea (the Atlantic ocean, in this case) and spend almost their whole lives failing to catch up with each other and secretly wondering about a "magical silent moment" (*Rainbows:* 74 f.) which they once shared and which almost made them aware of their true feelings (of more than friendship) for each other.

At times, it is the force of circumstance that could be held responsible for their 'star-crossed' relationship, like the series of misunderstandings and bad luck that keep Alex from flying in from Boston to accompany Rosie to her graduation ball. Rosie thus has to find a substitute partner at very short notice (Brian the Whine) and, on the night of the ball, drowns her frustration in alcohol and

---

[11] It makes one wonder whether Ahern is taking the delayed gratification of romance writing, the drawn out (often unfinished) quest of romance, to a new level (for a discussion of Derrida's concept of *différance* as applied to romance, see Parker 1979). Another text that humorously equals the deconstructionist 'endless deferral of meaning' to romance writing is David Lodge's academic romance *Small World* (1984), in which his fictional characters Morris Zapp and Angelica Papst elaborate on the similarities between romance writing, poststructuralist theories of meaning, strip tease and female orgasm (see esp. 322 ff.).

[12] This is particularly true of German reviewers ("*Für immer vielleicht: Roman.* Customer Reviews", online); the book was very well received in Germany and won the German CORINE Award in 2005 (Cecelia Ahern Homepage, online). The German translation appeared under the rather ambiguous title *Für immer vielleicht* (2005).

ends up getting pregnant, which in turn – as she refuses to have an abortion – keeps her from moving to the States to take up her studies in Boston and joining Alex. Sometimes the reason is people and relationships, as Rosie's and Alex's lives run parallel, but in a slightly nonsynchronous, temporally off-set manner. Whenever one of them is in a partnership, the other couple split up or vice versa: Alex, for instance, meets Sally during his medical studies at Harvard and gets married to her, but just when this first marriage is breaking up and the two separate, Rosie is courted by and falls in love with Greg and later marries him; when Rosie finally leaves Greg, her daughter Katie's father, Brian the Whine, who had deserted Rosie when he learnt of her pregnancy and 'escaped' to Spain, turns up wanting to meet his adolescent daughter and making up for missed parental duties. Consideration for her daughter Katie and Katie's desire to get acquainted with her father makes Rosie give up her plans to move to the States and join Alex for the second time, and he, in turn, starts a new relationship (with his teenage-love Bethany) in Boston. At times, it is also people who interfere, by obliterating letters (Greg pocketing Alex's epistolary declaration of love) or intercepting e-mails (Bethany suppressing Rosie's e-mails by controlling Alex's account). After years of exchanging news and varying emotions and confessions, a letter from Rosie's daughter Katie to her godfather Alex provides the final trigger for Alex and Rosie to admit their love for each other and, at the age of 50, come together at last: Katie happily relates how, through one of the 'magical silences' that her mother had told her about, she discovered her love for Toby, her long-time best friend from childhood and school and correspondent in numerous epistolary exchanges. This tells Alex that Rosie had experienced their long bygone encounter in the same way as he had and encourages him to take pen in hand once again.

As becomes evident in the "Epilogue", which finishes off the long succession of messages exchanged over the course of forty years, Rosie has kept and printed out all her messages, spread them over the floor of her room and has just spent a sleepless night rereading them – and by doing so she has been reliving her whole past life and the long process of self-discovery in a final review of these documents which represent the most important stages in her life – "her life in ink" (*Rainbows:* 555). Rosie is looking at them as at a mirror (an image often to be found in contemporary epistolary novels), a mirror that presents her with a reflection of her life bringing together the past and the present. Thus by reading the book, the reader has obviously been following Rosie's nocturnal perusal of these documents, before the final encounter with Alex in the early morning leads up to another 'magical silence', the mysterious moment of discovering one's true love in life, which finally closes off the novel.

There is a certain irony in the fact that a novel that celebrates volubility, wit and wordiness aims towards and is finished off with a 'magical silence', the wordless act of recognition or, since we are talking about Irish literature, an 'epiphany' that allows one to become aware of one's true feelings, and is after all a visual moment, as it enables one to 'see' the other person in a new light.

> It was like the world stopped turning in that instant. Like everyone around us had disappeared. Like everything at home was forgotten about. It was as if those few minutes on this world were created just for us and all we could do was look at each other. It was like he was seeing my face for the first time. He looked confused but kind of amused. Exactly how I felt. Because I was sitting on the grass with my best friend Alex, and that was my best friend Alex's face and nose and eyes and lips, but they seemed different. (*Rainbows:* 74f.)

Such a very quiet, subdued conclusion is well in keeping with the unsentimental tone of the novel achieved through the epistolary form, which makes the book less clichéd and stereotypical than its predecessor. If it was not for its rather unusual form of story-telling, *Rainbows* could well have been just another typical example of romantic and highly sentimental 'chick-lit', a 'rom-com' with its age-old tropes of undying love and friendship – two best friends who are kept apart by destiny and find out almost too late that it is love, not friendship, which they feel for each other. However, due to the epistolary format, *Rainbows* turns out to be a many-voiced chorus[13] (similar to Bakhtin's concept of the polyphonic novel; Bakhtin 1984/1929), a refreshing, original and up-to-date form of presenting a story that is somehow reminiscent of a radio-play.[14] Altman categorizes letters as epistolary dialogues and indeed talks about the closeness of epistolary discourse to radio communications, calling it "obsessed with its oral mode" (1982: 135).[15]

---

[13] Ahern's affinity to music suggests itself here, she was for some time a member of the Irish pop group *Shimma* ("Cecelia Ahern" 2012, online). Ahern even extends the circle of voices to add some more local colour by introducing the Relieved Divorced Dubliners' internet chat room, a virtual space that houses some most entertaining weird characters, and for good measure has a priest perform an online marriage ceremony there (*Rainbows:* 532–534).

[14] *Rainbows* as a radio play might, however, prove rather difficult to follow because of its very complex plot structure and the large number of characters. The novel might be well suited to adaptation for the stage, though, as was the case with Daniel Glattauer's e-mail-novel *Gut gegen Nordwind* (2006), which was very successfully performed on Austrian stages: in 2007 in Linz, in Vienna in 2009 (at the Wiener Kammerspiele), and in Graz (at the Schauspielhaus) in 2009/10 (for a discussion of the performances, see Wastl 2010: 82–85).

[15] She also mentions the epistolary cliché that letter writers remark on feeling as if they are speaking to their correspondent or can hear them speak and continues that in "writing to the moment" the epistolary utterance is given "the spontaneity of the oral one" (Altman 1982: 136).

Due to the impression of immediacy and spontaneity of these communications, with no obvious narratorial control or interference, the book takes on a dramatic rather than a novelistic character.[16] This lack of narratorial guidance, on the one hand, leads to the disruptions typical of the traditional epistolary novel, on the other hand, the rather 'dramatic' form of presentation also has its rewards for the readers. It not only assigns the reader an active role and challenges his/her intellect, but also results in discrepant awareness: the readers know more than the individual writers (who are not even aware of 'communicating' with an extratextual reader), they are informed of the secret and most intimate fears and hopes of the main correspondents as sometimes only confessed to their confidantes, which enables them to see the whole picture that the individual writers are unaware of, which, of course, also raises certain expectations in the readers, especially in sentimental fiction. Thus the readers are aware of Rosie's and Alex's feelings for each other, of how narrowly they sometimes miss confessing these feelings to each other, and they can see the happy ending coming. "After all, soulmates always end up together", as Rosie's wise older sister and confidante Stephanie knows (*Rainbows:* 37).

In terms of narrative transmission, *Rainbows* is a multi-perspectival narrative, with the various first-person narratives of the epistolary communication complementing each other. The additive presentation of events from multiple points-of-view makes it easier for the author to overcome the limitations of epistolary writing, the lack of authorial mediation and guidance for the reader and the resulting disconnected and non-linear arrangement of the story elements. It not only allows for a more differentiated perception (making up for the dearth of authorial support and direction) but it also shifts the attention of the reader from the action to the characters and their inner world. The first-person narrative favouring the experiencing self over the narrating self, a characteristic of epistolary presentation, additionally enhances the effect of immediacy and confidentiality. The 'epistolary urge' to pour out one's heart leaves no time for reflection on the narrative process, which adds to the impression of 'truthfulness' of the professed feelings and anxieties.

In accordance with the conventions of romance, the character constellation with its underlying pattern of binary oppositions features 'good' and 'bad' characters. The two protagonists and prospective lovers, Rosie and Alex, are surrounded by a group of minor characters: helpers in the guise of confidants,

---

[16] Mark Kinkead-Weekes in his "Introduction" to Samuel Richardson's *Pamela* also gives Richardson credit for inventing not merely the idea of writing in letters, but "the dramatic novel" (1962: v).

friends and supporters (family members), and antagonists both female and male (the respective partners, Alex's wives Sally and Bethany, as well as the 'false hero' Greg, Rosie's husband). They provide the obstacles to be overcome and the tests to be passed for the main characters on their way to a happy ending.

The focus is definitely on Rosie, and to a lesser extent on Alex, as the two main characters, and later on Katie as a younger version of Rosie (her relationship with her best friend Toby mirrors the relationship that Alex and Rosie had as children), and it is for these characters that the confessional function – an important element in epistolary novels – is most prominent (cf. Altman 1982, chap. 2). Rosie's sister Stephanie and Alex's brother Phil, who even calls these intimate online communications "the virtual confessional box" (*Rainbows*: 391), are the close and active confidants (Altman 1982: 51) for the two protagonists, who are told their most intimate thoughts and who are appealed to whenever council, guidance or consolation is needed, and it is to them that they confide their worries and cares, opening up their innermost feelings. The fact that the readers learn more about Rosie and Alex than about any other characters and can partake of their deepest emotions makes them identify and empathise with these two more readily than with the other characters in the novels.

The letters and other epistolary communications fulfil all the formal criteria of 'real-life' correspondence, with a personalized salutation or address and a signature. They are always addressed to a particular person and have a communicative, rather than an introspective, function (as, e.g., in a diary). Their focus is on the everyday life and experiences of the characters, often expressed in highly emotional, mostly informal colloquial language.

In terms of formatting, some (but not all) editions use an additional form of semiotic coding in order to facilitate orientation. Icons in the margin specify the type of medium involved: a pen for hand-written notes, an envelope for letters, a pencil for postcards and memos, the @-icon for e-mails, a laptop icon for online chats, cell phone icons for mobile calls, a calculator icon for invoices or bills, plus occasionally scissors for newspaper cuttings and articles, and a special symbol for horoscopes.

Ahern further differentiates her use of epistolary forms in terms of which medium is appropriate for what type of communication. There is an interesting distinction between more personal and more formal or informal messages. While most of the informal every-day communication is carried out via electronic media, hand-written letters are used for very private and intimate exchanges (such as highly personal messages between Rosie and Alex, e.g., Alex's love letter, letters of condolence or congratulations, birthday greetings, thank-you letters, Alex asking Rosie to be his best 'man', and the like); printed letters or cards carry more formal messages (e.g., wedding invitations, birth announcements, obituaries, etc.). The choice of medium thus also sometimes becomes part of the characterisation, indicative not only of social and cultural practices, but also of personal attention and sensitivity, discretion, and tactfulness (or lack thereof). Additionally, as already stated, the medium is also an indicator of the degree of intimacy or the confessional nature of the transmitted message.[17]

Ahern additionally includes self-reflexive elements in her novel, playfully justifying the use of epistolary communication by referring not only to the confessional character of epistolary writing (e.g., *Rainbows:* 391), but also to the fact that letter writing is often associated with women.[18] When Rosie's father is very worried about his son Kevin, he takes his pen in hand and writes a long and intimate letter, which he ends with the apologetic remark: "So I thought I'd join the Dunne women in writing. It seems that's all they do. Keeps the phone bills down, I suppose" (*Rainbows:* 223). This unheard-of occurrence gives immediate rise to comments and speculations. First Kevin himself is so upset by this fact as to write an e-mail to his sister, wondering: "Dad writing a letter is weird in itself but what he was writing was even more bizarre" (*Rainbows:* 223). Moreover, the female members of the family are so surprised by this outburst of male epistolary activity that they assume that "[s]omething must be in the water over there in Ireland". Stephanie actually asks her mother: "Did you even know that Dad could lick a stamp?" (*Rainbows:* 224) Rosie's husband Greg also comments on her extensive e-mail and instant message correspondence with her best friend Ruby (and the resulting high phone bill) and asks why she does not prefer meeting up with her friend instead. Rosie's answer is again very telling with regard to the privacy of letter-writing: "Because no establishment allows us to sprawl across their couches in our pyjamas and smoke. It's far more comfortable at home" (*Rainbows:* 168). Another time, it is Rosie's new boss, her former teacher Ms Casey (Miss Big Nose Smelly Breath Casey, as the children used to call her), who asks: "Why would you set up an instant messaging service with me when I am in the next room?", to which Rosie replies: "It means I can multi-task. I can speak to people on the phone and also do business online" (*Rainbows:* 425). And this is certainly what Rosie and her friend Ruby very often do, especially when their work is boring, routine or an unsatisfactory means of earning a living.

As becomes evident from these short examples, the new media are not only congenial to Ahern's female characters, smart, extroverted women with an 'inbuilt' epistolary urge, who love expressing their thoughts and feelings and are

---

17 For a discussion of the differences between letter writing and e-mails and their use and social function, see Meier 2002.
18 A further such reference, in this case to the genre of romance, is the above-mentioned ironic comment on declarations of love and marriage proposals (*Rainbows:* 148–153).

experts in using the new means of communication while working or coping with everyday routines. The epistolary form is also very well suited to Ahern's topics and style of writing romantic fiction, assisting her in producing light-hearted, witty and fast-paced narratives while probing the depths of her characters' psyches. The epistolary form not only creates intimacy with and sympathy for her characters; the specificity of the first-person narrative style also allows Ahern to orchestrate her verbal profile of the Irish with the colourful idiosyncrasies of her various correspondents, thereby redeeming her stories from the sugary-sweet sentimentality of romance.

4 Conclusion

As can be seen from the discussion of her first two novels, Cecelia Ahern, while drawing to a certain extent upon the tradition of epistolary novels, finds new uses of letter writing in her fiction. Similar to the majority of epistolary novels in the seventeenth and eighteenth centuries, both her novels are love stories about women, focussing on heroines who are suffering from a disruption in their lives and have yet to learn to come to terms with their new situation[19] – the loss of a husband in *PS*, and an unwanted pregnancy in the case of Rosie Dunne, which overthrows all her plans to study, her dreams of a career as a hotel manager and a life with her 'soul mate'. In both cases, letters are a 'therapeutic' way of helping them cope with their situations. *PS* is a unidirectional epistolary novel in the widest sense, as the protagonist Holly is not the writer but the recipient of letters that have, however, a great impact on the development and resolution of the whole novel. Holly is a partner in a one-sided correspondence in that she reacts to her husband's letters in her imagination by dreaming up conversations with Gerry. In her second novel, *Rainbows*, Ahern uses a multi-perspectival epistolary form to create a wide spectrum of different voices and present various perspectives on the world that the female protagonist inhabits, thus giving the readers a wider knowledge than the characters and allowing them to judge Rosie's progress from the vantage point of discrepant awareness and dramatic irony. Writing helps Rosie go through a lengthy process

---

[19] On her homepage Ahern affirms her interest in characters who are going through a dark period in their lives: "The thread that links my work is in capturing that transitional period in people's lives. I'm drawn to writing about loss, to characters that have fallen and who feel powerless in their lives. I am fascinated and inspired by the human spirit, by the fact that no matter how hopeless we feel and how dark life can be, we do have the courage, strength and bravery to push through our challenging moments." (Cecelia Ahern homepage, online).

of learning to cope with the ups and downs of her life and finding her true self, which culminates in the epilogue of the novel, when she reviews her whole life in the print-outs of her life-long correspondence and is finally ready to meet her new partner. The process of writing, self-discovery and self-definition comes to an end and achieves closure in the 'magical silence' of recognition in her final encounter with her life-long best friend.

As a writer of female fiction, and in particular of romantic fiction, Ahern appreciates the possibility inherent in all epistolary writing of creating intimacy by allowing her characters to express their innermost thoughts and feelings and open up their hearts to a virtual reader, providing insight into their psyche and thereby appealing to the sentiments of her audience and fostering empathy with her characters. Epistolary writing gives them a voice and provides them with the possibility to speak for themselves, at the same time allowing the reader to witness their process of finding their feet, proving their staying power, finding satisfaction in their work and realising their potential.

Through the process of writing letters, Ahern's protagonists are entering into a phase of re-vision of their lives, of re-orientation and re-organisation of their future. Her females are, however, not underprivileged, marginalized characters, incapable of communicating their needs, but highly articulate, witty and eloquent women, well able to express their sentiments and sometimes carrying their hearts on their sleeves, who fully exploit the wide variety of new media. This not only adds to the humour of their discourse and gives a special quality to their writing, it also draws attention to one of the perils of letter writing, the 'urge to communicate'. The possibility of giving voice to thoughts and emotions that are impossible to express when facing an interlocutor has the drawback that expressions are not checked or interrupted by a partner and his/her reactions, which makes it very tempting to give way to imprudent, spontaneous expressions of feelings, while being unaware of the consequences, and which may be regretted afterwards. This is all the more problematic with instant messaging, where an impetuous character like Rosie, for example, does not always have the chance to cross out the things she spontaneously put down (as she sometimes does in her notes or letters), or where messages may be accessed by the wrong person.

In contrast to major tendencies in the contemporary epistolary novel, Ahern also allows males to enter the traditionally female-dominated area of epistolarity, both in *PS* and *Rainbows*, though with a different focus. In *PS* the terminally-ill husband does not open his heart to the reader, but uses the medium of letter writing to 'remain' connected to his wife in her memory for some more time and at the same time extend his loving care for her beyond his lifetime in order to guide her through the most difficult months of mourning and reorientation. In

Rainbows, the main male correspondent is Alex, the sympathetic supportive soul-mate and best friend who is as adept at – though not as addicted to – communicating and expressing his emotions as Rosie or most of the other females, which grants him a very positive image with a female audience (in contrast to some of the other males, in particular Rosie's husband Greg, who communicates mainly through instant messages and a few e-mails and is never privileged to solicit sympathy in the audience).

Ahern's use of epistolary writing does not show any spectacular innovations in terms of form or content, but her achievements are the skilful handling of both traditional and new media to counteract the structural and chronological ruptures characteristic of epistolary writing, and her nuanced and differentiated application of different media to create whole lives in writing. The epistolary style makes her story more difficult for the reader to follow, but also more challenging intellectually, and saves her rather clichéd romances from tearful sentimentality. In this regard, as in many others, *Rainbows* is by far the better novel than *PS*.

Ahern obviously finds the epistolary form congenial to her interest in language and her preference for portraying characters through the way they express themselves. Letters give her the opportunity to write multi-perspectival narratives featuring a wide range of Irish society. They allow her to paint linguistic portraits of Irishmen and -women, creating a verbal polyphony of voices that provides a background to frame her romantic stories of true and everlasting love. In particular, electronic forms of communication with their rapid exchange of information can be used as an alternative to dialogues, and function as excellent forms of indirect characterisation. Overall, they make for a fast, varied pace and create entertaining and lively 'comedies of manner' that also appeal to a young audience, which may be one of the reasons why her 'chick-lit' novels have even started "[o]utselling Austen" (Coughlan 2008).

Works Cited

Ahern, Cecelia. 2004. *PS, I Love You*. London: Harper Collins.
Ahern, Cecelia. 2004. *Where Rainbows End*. London: Harper Collins.
Ahern, Cecelia. 2005. *Für immer vielleicht*, Transl. Christine Strüh. Frankfurt/M.: Krüger.
Altman, Janet Gurkin. 1982. *Epistolarity. Approaches to a Form*. Columbus: Ohio State University Press.
Bakhtin, M.M. 1984/1929. *Problems of Dostoevsky's Poetics*. Ed. and trans. Caryl Emerson. Minneapolis: University of Minnesota Press.
Bower, Anne. 1997. *Epistolary Responses. The Letter in 20th-Century American Fiction and Criticism*. Tuscaloosa, AL: University of Alabama Press.

Campbell, Elizabeth. 1995. "Re-visions, Re-flections, Re-creations: Epistolarity in Novels by Contemporary Women". *Twentieth Century Literature* 41.3. 332–348.

"Cecelia Ahern." 2012. *Contemporary Authors Online*. Gale. Literature Resource Center. <go.galegroup.com/ps/i.do?p=LitRC&sw=w&u=43wien&v=2.1&id=GALE%7CH1000156538&it=r&asid=3333d87aa40644528af3e108264ec770> [accessed 29 Sept. 2016].

Cecelia Ahern Homepage (online). <https://www.cecelia-ahern.com> [accessed 12 Nov. 2017].

Coughlan, Claire. 2008, June 27. "She's outselling Austen, but who buys Cecelia's books?". Herald.ie. *Literature Resource Center*. <http://www.herald.ie/opinion/comment/shes-outselling-austen-but-who-buys-cecelias-books-1422056.html> [accessed 29 Sept. 2016].

Frye, Northrop. 1957/1966. *Anatomy of Criticism*. New York: Atheneum.

"Für immer vielleicht: Roman. Customer Reviews". Amazon.de. <https://www.amazon.de/Für-immer-vielleicht-Cecelia-Ahern/dp/3596161347/ref=sr_1_1?ie=UTF8&qid=1514669136&sr=8-1&keywords=ahern%2C+cecelia%2C+für+immer+vielleicht> [accessed 10 Nov. 2017].

Ging, Debbie. 2008. "The Celtic 'Chick-flick': How About You (2007) and PS I Love You (2007)". [Rev.]. *Estudios Irlandeses* 3. 242–244.

Glattauer, Daniel. 2006. *Gut gegen Nordwind*. Vienna: Deuticke.

Hall, Katie & Bogen Jones. 2013. *The Closeness That Separates Us*. Bloomington: Trafford.

El Hamamsy, Walid. 2010. "Epistolary Memory: Revisiting Traumas in Women's Writing". *Alif: Journal of Comparative Poetics* 30. 150–175.

Harrison, Berenice. 2004. "Cecelia Ahern. PS, I Love You. Review". *Irish Times*, July 3, 2004. 62.

Kany, Charles E. 1937. "The Beginnings of the Epistolary Novel in France, Italy, and Spain". *University of California Publication in Modern Philology* 21. Berkeley: Univ. of California Press. 1–158.

Kinkead-Weekes, Mark. 1962. "Introduction". In: Samuel Richardson. *Pamela*. In two volumes. London: Dent. v–xiii.

Lodge, David. 1984. *Small World. An Academic Romance*. London: Secker and Warburg.

Meier, Jörg. 2002. "Vom Brief zur E-Mail – Kontinuität und Wandel." In: Arne Ziegler & Christa Dürscheid (eds.). *Kommunikationsform E-Mail*. Tübingen: Stauffenberg. 57–75.

O'Keeffe, Alice. 2009. "Marian Keyes: The Brightest Star in the Sky". *The Bookseller*, July 31, 2009. 21. *Literature Resource Center*. <http://go.galegroup.com/ps/i.do?p=LitRC&sw=w&u=43wien&v=2.1&id=GALE%7CA206055109&it=r&asid=9995acfbdc36b982ebce6e90870b0fd2> [accessed 10 Nov. 2017].

Parker, Patricia. 1979. *Inescapable Romance. Studies in the Poetics of a Mode*. Princeton, N.J.: Princeton University Press.

"PS, I Love You by Cecelia Ahern. The Editor press review." *The Guardian*, 16 February 2004. <https://www.theguardian.com/theguardian/2004/feb/16/digestedread.theeditorpressreview7> [accessed 12 Dec. 2017].

Richardson, Samuel. 1965. *Selected letters*. Ed. by John J. Carroll. Oxford: Clarendon Press.

Wastl, Nora. 2010. "Geschickte Liebe – Daniel Glattauers Gut gegen Nordwind oder die Geburt des E-Mail-Romans". Unpubl. Master's Thesis, University of Graz.

"Where Rainbows End. Customer Reviews". Amazon.co.uk. <http://amazon.co.uk/s/ref=nb_sb_noss/260-6838189-3845335?url=search-alias%3Daps&field-keywords=ahern%2C+where+rainbows+end> [accessed 12 Nov. 2017].

Ames Hawkins
An Open Letter to Nick Bantock OR Letters and/as Ephemera(l)
Desire, Transposition and Transpoetic Possibility with/in Epistolary Form

Abstract: In Nick Bantock's epistolary novel *Griffin and Sabine* (1991), postcard artist Griffin Moss receives a mysterious and unexpected postcard from stamp designer Sabine Strohem, a woman who claims to be able to see whatever he draws as he draws it, though she lives thousands of miles away and they have never met. While the mystery of Sabine's existence and cliffhanger endings (Griffin is reported missing), offer elements of a compelling narrative, it is arguable that the best-selling status and literary import of this work has to do with the visual reproduction and tactile presentation of the correspondence. The entire narrative is presented through nineteen pieces of mail – fifteen postcards and four letters that include removable pieces of paper stuffed inside attached envelopes. This experimental essay, written in the form of a letter, explores how the materiality of mail, reproduced as ephemera in literary projects such as *The Griffin and Sabine Trilogy*, impacts the telling of an epistolary story, opening for Hawkins, as reader-writer, queer possibility. Through a rhetorical and phenomenological examination that focuses on the work of the letter, the wonder, curiosity, excitement, and most importantly the desire contained in Bantock's book series is remade here through language – both in terms of content and the form of the piece.

Dear Nick,

How does it feel to you to think back more than twenty-five years, to the time just prior to the publication of *Griffin and Sabine: An Extraordinary Correspondence* (1991)? Can you recall what it was like to be the sole person in possession of the single copy you had created and were carrying around, waiting to show it to someone? I love the story you tell in your book *The Artful Dodger* (Bantock 2000) that reveals the origin of the project. I love this story more than the narrative that unfolds between Griffin, a struggling postcard artist in London, England, and Sabine, a stamp designer on Katie, one of a number of small islands forming a chain (imagined by you) in the South Pacific. Or, perhaps it's more accurate to say that I have come to better appreciate the story of Griffin and Sabine, which I promise to get to in a moment, now that I know more about its genesis.

Of course, you know the story of how you created these books, but I have always found that people like to hear about themselves. Or, at least like to hear about what others find fascinating about them. It could be you don't care at all. But, I am going to assume you're like most artists and authors and would want to know how I've reacted to your work, what I find gorgeous, amazing, beautiful, and perhaps even problematic, what I find worthy of exploring in terms of literary value and artistic influence. What you, dear Nick, have brought to me as a creative-critical scholar and transgenre writer and artist are, by extension, a host of possibilities regarding queer form, ephemera, and desire – magical openings I see that you have also brought to the world.

I love your admission—and do hope it's true—that the idea for this book, (which it seems important to note eventually turned into a series of seven books—two trilogies written a decade apart and then a final volume written twenty-five years after the first volume), emanated from a single moment in a post office when you took note of someone else's letter, wishing that the letter could be yours. A pin-prick of longing and a brief exchange with a woman in line at the post office became the catalyst for a project that pulled together all sorts of ideas you had in your mind, the answer to your own self-posed inquiry: "What would make the perfect mail?" (Bantock 1991: 55). Your interest in the work of the letter, an introspective exploration of the aspects of yourself as artist, and exploration of Gestalt therapy through the artistic presentation of two conflicting aspects of your personality, became the foundation of what was to become your answer (Bantock 1991: 55–56). You were interested in exploring two sides of yourself, as I understand it, and placed those 'sides' in conversations as Griffin and Sabine (Bantock 1991: 56). Each of them isolated, each an artist, each longing for something other, though she, with the gift of vision and the ability to literally see what Nick is drawing thousands of miles away, appears more settled in the world.

You started creating, and quickly realized, "If I included postcards in this fictitious exchange of mail, then I could sew together the threads of all those ideas and images that had preoccupied my adult years" (Bantock 1991: 55–56).

Here is where I become enthralled:

> It was beginning to fit together nicely, but there was still something missing from the mix, and it had to do with the jealousy I'd experienced in the post office around the envelope itself. One of the key pleasures of receiving a letter is the act of holding and entering the envelope—a sort of cross between Christmas and sex. What better way, I thought, of reproducing that physical sensation of expectation than providing the book's reader with the chance to open the envelope themselves? (Bantock 1991: 56)

This is what I wanted to discuss, this notion you've come to regarding the material experience of holding an envelope, removing its contents, engaging with the document, unmaking and remaking the meaning intended for you, and only you. In comparing the receiving, opening, and reading of a letter to both a culturally shared experience of Christmas and an intimately private moment of sex, what you say, without quite saying it, is that your intention for the book was to incite in the reader through and by and for and with/in shared desire.

I wrote this letter not wanting to give you an analysis or critique of your book. (A few others [Meyer 2010; Simon 2002; Krell 1995] have done so.) I want to tell you about my encounters with these texts, and with writing—both to another, and to myself. I want to tell you what the form of the book, of the letter and the repeated engagement with them has done and can do to and for a queer body; how books and letters with a reader can queerly move. I wonder whether you care about what scholars have said about your work. Even if the answer is no, I feel compelled to write.

Because I want to tell you how the act of reading ephemera does *something* more. More than what? More than the usual, the predictable; an investigation beyond an assumed impact, or narrative framing regarding what happens when a reader reads. It is the most ordinary of acts, the reading of a letter. But as Kathleen Stewart strives to explain, "ordinary is a shifting assemblage of practices and practical knowledges, a scene of both liveliness and exhaustion, as dream of escape or the simple life" (2007: 1). In the ordinary, there is always the possibility of a *something*, a to-be-will-might-happen(ing), in and of itself mundane, yet through the notion of movement, energetic transmission, the ordinary is always laden with possibility, alchemical potentials, imagination, and dreams. The ordinary act of writing this letter, the affective intention of engaging you as an imagined reader opening a space for transmaterialized magic, a becoming: an unfolding event of desire.

Desire. Desire in all the ways explored by throngs of theorists: Freud, Lacan, Derrida, Barthes, Žižek, as well as Lorde, Cixous, and hooks, just to name a few. The power of your books, I assert, stems from the fact that you desired, you wanted for us—your readers—that momentary pleasure, perhaps even the possibility of bliss!

In *The Pleasure of the Text*, Roland Barthes works to articulate the relationship—and difference—between pleasure and bliss. Pleasure, he explains, is comfortable and comforting. It's connected with and to the familiar and culturally synchronous experiences of reading. Bliss, he writes, occurs in a text that "imposes a state of loss," "discomforts," and "unsettles the reader's historical cultural, psychological assumptions, the consistency of his tastes, values, memories, brings to a crisis his relationship with language" (Barthes 1975: 10).

Pleasure reassures; bliss challenges. Pleasure soothes; bliss contests. Bliss, the fleeting moment of pain experienced when entering naked into water too hot for flesh; pleasure, the sensation felt once the body has comfortably been submerged in its entirety into a bath.

It would be a safe assumption, given the popularity of your books, that these texts achieved their fame and fortune because they incite pleasure. Pleasure itself tends to skew toward the universally acceptable, the verification of a normative desire. I wondered: Could it be that in these texts, as you seemed to want for your readers, there was room for rupture, capacity to slash, fracture, rip, tear, crack? Do these books also offer the opening, orifice, cavity, hole, epistolary slit that makes accessible the possibility of bliss?

Like Audrey Niffenegger (Do you know her?), who reviewed *The Pharaoh's Gate: Griffin and Sabine's Missing Correspondence* (2016), the seventh and final installment in the series, I can also remember when *Griffin and Sabine* made its publishing debut. The thing is, unlike Audrey, who describes feeling as though she had just been waiting for a book like this, buying it on the spot despite having little money, I was not captivated enough to make the purchase.

But, I so wanted to be.

I wanted to want these books. So much so that I can, like others (Niffenegger 2016; El-Mothar 2016), recall opening *Griffin and Sabine* the first time. It was a thrilling experience. The subject of the book was someone else's mail! And not just uniformly presented black text on a white page, the way most epistolary literature is published, but reproductions of the 'actual' postcards and envelopes, each one uniquely designed, with cancelled stamps. Envelopes glued right inside the book into which letters were placed so that each reader was able to engage in the physical experience of reading the letter, each of which is written by a character who comes to life through syntax, voice, symbols, style, and quite literally, their individual hand.

I skimmed the postcards, giving cursory glances to the art, but you were right. It was the inclusion of an actual envelope, stuffed with removable letter that captured my imagination. (I have to tell you, I believe this really is one of the main reasons these books did so well.) Sliding that first letter (the fifth piece of mail in *Griffin and Sabine* following two postcard exchanges) from its envelope, I felt the thrill and kink of voyeurism tempered by gentle romanticism. As an avid writer of letters, I should have been deeply captivated. But, I was not.

I think back and decide it was likely because I immediately noted the relationship unfolding was between a man and a woman, and at the time I had no interest in reading a heterosexual love story. I was struggling with my own sexuality and—a most important point here—with my own understanding of how social constructions of gender impacted how I thought about myself. Most of the letters I was writing then were thinly veiled, unrequited love letters to other women. The last thing I wanted at the time was to read some story that I assumed would end in, or at least existed within the possibility of a Disney-esque, heteronormative happily-ever-after.

But, I also remember thinking that I was being a little too narrow to refuse to read the book just because the main characters were presumably heterosexual. What actually repelled me was that when I finally did read some of the narrative, say the third or fourth visit to a bookstore, I recall rolling my eyes at the narrative construct of Sabine as a foundling, Nick as an orphan. *Oh come on!* I thought. *Why the need for such tropes? How incredibly uninteresting.*

Most relevantly, I was turned off by the tactile experience. Letter writing and reading are, for me, sacred events. The feeling of the slick, thick-weighted paper made too clear the mechanisms of publishing, keeping me from entering the world of Griffin and Sabine. The making of this book, I decided, was some kind of gimmick. A gimmick I so wanted to engage with, but at the time concluded just didn't work.

Which was, I now know, a criticism much too harsh. I now realize that it wasn't a particularly sophisticated critique that kept me from reading and buying the books. It was that I wanted them to be even more than they could deliver.

Here's what's interesting: Not reading them then is what prompted me to want to read, study, and write about them now. Because my own creative-critical practice includes exploration of the rhetorical work of the letter—the love letter more specifically—I wanted to think about the purpose and power of the inserted letters, to consider the rhetorical work of ephemera. I wanted to rethink why it was I didn't want to read them then, and consider their form in the context of their incredible popularity. I wanted to consider the queer possibilities in the transgenre form.

And, I am so very glad I decided to commit to engage with these texts, because here's what I discovered. In the literary world, ephemera usually refers to the bits of published texts that have little relevance. Their ephemeral quality comes from a lack of heft, or connection to a legitimizing source such as a publishing house. Beyond the initial curiosity of seeing how you handle the handwriting of Griffin, Sabine, and a whole cast of other characters over the course of the series, because of the limitations placed upon you by constraints of production, I simply don't find the inclusion of the ephemera to be important or interesting.

The four pieces of paper that a reader pulls from the four envelopes glued inside *Griffin and Sabine* don't add significantly to the narrative experience of reading this particular story. Sure, they offer more information than is on a postcard, but having the letters take the form of ephemera doesn't really matter much. The entire story could have been told in postcards, and it seems the only reason for the inclusion of the letters really was because you, Nick, wanted to share that experience with readers. You wanted to bring to them this possibility of inciting their desire.

It is a damn noble intention, one I applaud. Have you seen the recent collaborative project by J.J. Abrams and Doug Dorst called *S.* (2013)? This too reveals a passion—near obsession—with ephemera. I read this book with a friend in 2015, the story of which we included on our podcast, *Masters of Text*. We were both initially excited by the inserts in the Abrahms/Dorst book. How fun it would be, we thought, to engage with these material objects! The ephemera in *S.*, having been produced using technology thirty years following *Griffin and Sabine*, have a more authentic, 'real' quality. If I were only critiquing the letters in your series on tactile experience, then these ephemera ought to have been more effective in its narrative impact. The thing is though, there were so many inserts to deal with—postcards, letters, a map sketched on a napkin, newspaper clippings, memorial card, photographs—none of which had a particular place to be (such as an envelope), and we soon became overwhelmed and overworked by them. Few of them—besides a couple of the letters written between the main characters—seemed necessary to the movement of the plot.

Much of our discontent with the ephemera may be because of what Sunka Simon tells us about the *Inserata*, advertisements-as-letters appearing in the pages of books in Germany more than one hundred years ago (2002). Simon describes the Inserata "as disruptive. The insert interrupts for its message, thereby reinserting that narrative into the material world" (2002: 98). While we can't really know how the reader in the eighteenth century in Germany experienced these inserts, I feel a similar disruption in having to read the letters and inserts in both *S.* and all of the books in the *Griffin and Sabine* series. I want to pull them from the envelope, but when I do, each time I suddenly feel the thrill of removal, I am quickly dissatisfied once the action has ended. In removing the letter from the envelope, I am supposed to become more engaged in the story, but in reality I feel the sensation of disconnection from the book. Which makes me better understand that the letters as material ephemera aren't relevant to me. What matters is the way the letters require of the reader an ephemeral act.

This means that it isn't the letters as objects of desire that we ought to explore, but the fleeting momentary action—the kairotic event of letter-reading—that opens a space of possibility for a queer reading of these texts.

Nick, here's what I think: your books exploit a human desire to remove *inserata*, to pull from an envelope a secret sentiment intended for someone other than themselves. And despite the fact that such an action interrupts and disrupts, your visual style, symbolic imagery, text, and prose make the reading experience accessible; make it pleasurable, as indicated by the millions of copies sold around the world.

Did you ever consider the possibility and impact that disruption might have? Have you ever thought about whether your books moved individuals to a state of bliss?

For me, the moment we move from the physicality of ephemera to the performativity of the ephemeral act, we acknowledge and enable queer readings to occur. But, what does it mean to read a text queerly? What does it mean to write a queer piece of scholarship about a love story that most would understand and recognize as decidedly heterosexual? What does it mean if I, as a queer scholar, engage with these texts in a performative fashion? Is it queer to invite someone to remove a sheet of paper from a book?

The physical ephemera of the letters in these books invite the reader to participate in the performative act of removing a letter from the envelope, which isn't, in and of itself, particularly queer. But the ephemerality of the movement—fleeting, transitory, transient, ephemeral—opens a space of queer possibility. Mostly because queerness is never available in the concrete, or directly accessible via mainstream motivations or assumptions. As José Esteban Muñoz explains in his essay, "Evidence as Ephemera: Introductory Notes to Queer Acts":

> Queerness is often transmitted covertly. This has everything to do with the fact that leaving too much of a trace has often meant that the queer subject has left herself open for attack. Instead of being clearly available as visible evidence, queerness has instead existed as innuendo, gossip, fleeting moments, and performances that are meant to be interacted with by those within its epistemological sphere—while evaporating at the touch of those who would eliminate queer possibility. (1996: 6)

The instances may not be clear, they may not have been intended. And I am not saying there is a queer way to remove from an envelope a letter. But because I have come to experience your books with and in and through a queer body, because you've presented us with the disruption of decoding a codex with an ephemeral act, I know they can be read as queer.

I don't know you at all, Nick. But given what I've read about you, your own art, your creative processes, I feel OK in believing—or at least hoping with confidence—that you would never be interested in eliminating queer possibility accessed with/in/through the reading performance[?] of your books.

Which brings me back: to Desire.

In *Assuming a Body: Transgender and Rhetorics of Materiality*, Gayle Salamon (2010) conducts a valuable, deep reading of the queer potential in Maurice Merleau-Ponty's seminal work, *Phenomenology of Perception*. Salamon (2010) notes that while Merleau-Ponty makes clear the connection between desire and sexuality, sexuality and the body, the body and desire, he doesn't specifically place limits on the desire as being connected only in and to the body itself. Ok, that sounds a bit jargony, even to me. So, let me try this again: Merleau-Ponty maintains an important ambiguity in his description of sexuality and desire, refusing it seems, to make concrete connections between sexuality and particular body parts.

What does this mean? It means, as Salamon explains that "the most important aspect of sexuality is not any particular part—not even the behavior of that part" (2010: 51). Neither is it limited to a body part at all and can be any part of the body or even a part of the "body auxiliary that is not organically attached to the body" (Salamon 2010: 51).

It means it isn't exactly the letter, or content of the letter that we need to consider, but our desire. What *matters*, is that *something* that we anticipate in the tiniest of seemingly insignificant movements it requires to pull the letter from the envelope, engage a piece of paper with our fingers, move our eyes across the page. What matters most is our collective momentary flash of connection with and within letter-experienced-as-event that opens what Merleau-Ponty identifies as *transposition*. "Transposition," Salamon writes, "describes the process by which the desire that houses itself in my body *becomes* my body itself—not held proximately by thought, but felt and experienced (as opposed to only referred to), through and as the body" (2010: 52).

What this means for me? In reading *Griffin and Sabine*, any of the other books in the series, *S.*, or any other future or past literary project including letters as ephemera, it no longer matters who the letter is for, or whether I am interested in a story between one man (Griffin) and one woman (Sabine) who live thousands of miles apart. It no longer matters whether I am interested in their relationship, her connection to him by some sort of art-specific clairvoyance, his disbelief, or their journey. It means that this isn't about tab A fitting into slot B; it means it isn't about sexual acts as we typically understand. I don't need to want to know what happens, because in removing the letter from the envelope I am able to consider my own desire for epistolarity, see it in relationship with my own sexuality—whatever that may mean to or for me.

For me, this means this experience underscores my own assertion that my sexuality is best described as writer, my gender as butch dandy, connected to, but not exactly what we might currently understand as trans.

Does this mean all readings of *Griffin and Sabine* are queer? No. I don't need the books to be queer, and I would never argue we need to see them as such. I am saying that I note in these texts an opening for transposition that isn't phallocentric. I am saying that there's an opening for queerness. I am saying that I see in your work an aperture for the queer moment, movement, magic. I see the possibility, horizon, and futurity of queer (cf. Muñoz 2009: 1).

I want to believe that you would be interested in and open to my analysis of this work. I want to believe that you're invested in your own claim that you've left the endings open to interpretation because, Nick, as you've written, "Tying things up with a ribbon would be meaningless, especially as I believe that it's best if each individual comes to terms with his or her own interpretation of the elliptical aspect of the ending" (Bantock 2000: 63).

But it isn't just the ending that we need to explore. Rather, instead, from a queer perspective, it's the openings. The ways that we enter and see ourselves inside the characters that invite ever-changing possibilities.

Which brings me to my final point. For me, the success of these books, their wide-ranging popularity is due to the fact that you created the project driven wholly by your own desire to offer an audience Christmas-like pleasure and an orgasmic-esque bliss. However, if all we had been doing was removing a letter here or there from an envelope, I highly doubt global popularity could ensue.

What we also needed was the narrative you created, one that, as I admit above, I initially disregarded because of an assumption about the heteronormativity of the plot. Because this project is less about a carefully crafted story, and more as a way for you to manifest an internal dialogue with yourself, it was a perfect match for the rhetorical affordance of the way the love letter allowed you to write not only to someone else, but to an imagined, desired, could-be-me.

Through these characters, who represent conflicting, or at least struggling elements of your artist-self, we can see not only the power of *transposition* at work in your books, but also trans poetics. In "Trans Poetics Manifesto", Joy Ladin explains that trans poetics are "techniques that enable poetic language to reflect the kinds of complex, unstable contradictory relationship between body and soul, social self and psyche, that those who see ourselves as transgender experience as acute, definitive, life-changing" (2013: 306).

Now, Nick, rest assured, I wouldn't argue that your project reveals any kind of transgender crisis on your part, or that your prose is particularly poetic. However, as someone who has identified as such over the years, and worked with Ladin's ideas in other works, I do believe that in these books trans poetics are revealed via your artistic desire to explore two sides of yourself, in the ways you may have thought about what it would mean to represent your thinking with and through the character of a woman, in the presentation of the self as possible phantom, as well as your choosing of a name connected with a mythological creature half lion, half eagle. And, the form of the letter, whether you knew it or not, happens to be a particularly valuable and effective form for this sort of interrogation. Rhetorically speaking, letters foreground the work of dialogue, establish a spatial relationship with reading and writing, and draw attention to the reader/writer relationship, thereby opening a space of endless possibility for the expression of self.

The epistolary form increases a sense of intimacy between characters. In the body of a letter, a writer is able to offer not only that which everyone might be able to see, but also the thoughts and feelings that would reveal a secret, or perhaps even sacred, version of themselves. Through letters, from our hands to theirs, theirs to ours, we present the words as ourselves, we accept their words as them. We have at our disposal a means by which we may find ways of becoming a different self. Written first by us, read by another—or in this case millions and millions of others—we are/can/have/become recognized in the exchange as legitimate, as a possible latent, or future self.

When we read letters from Griffin, there is the never-always potential to read him as not-you, Nick. When we read letters from Sabine, she is ever-sometimes possibly Nick-as-female, too. We, as readers, are invited into a series of possible imaginings: both that we are reading someone else's secret correspondence, and that somehow we're connected to another (who really is some kind of version of ourselves) through this mysterious shared sight, too.

In the displacement of the desire from the story to the act of reading the letters, I am offered the opportunity to insert myself into the story not as a character, but as writer, not only as reader, but artist as well. As connected not to Griffin, or Sabine, or any of the many other characters there, but to their creator, Nick. To you.

When, at the end of *Griffin and Sabine*, Griffin writes a postcard which is never mailed, and decides, "This whole affair has gotten too intense. Too real. Sabine, you don't exist. I invented you", the actual project is revealed (1991: 34). We don't yet know it, but this promise of possible union really amounts to a longing as climax. Each book in turn, ends leaving us always on the precipice, the edge, the just-before-climax of finally knowing whether Griffin and Sabine are real, whether they ever got together, whether they lived happily-ever-after.

The books end as letters, with closings that resist closure. The end of any letter is merely the place where the reader may then pick up a pen and paper, and write back; begin.

This letter is coming to an end, Nick, and in the same way Griffin's epistles include a variety of questions, I ask this in the same self-conscious, rhetorical way Sabine tends to inquire: Do I imagine you reading this letter, dear Nick? I do. I've read all the letters between Griffin and Sabine more than a few times. As well as many of your books and interviews. When all is said and done, the experience makes quite clear that I don't know you, Nick. I don't know Griffin. And, I don't know Sabine. I don't know any of you. What I do know is that the you I've created is not the one who will read the letter. This is the you that is my version of you. Transpoetically transposed, this you is, in other words, me.

And I see myself there in the space between Griffin and Sabine. A space that isn't ever, but always requires bridging and crossing. I feel myself in the transposition offered as I remove a letter from an envelope. I see myself in the trans poetics of Griffin in/as/are/both/and Sabine have (have they?) finding-found-eachother potential-never-knowing-happiness bliss.

And though I'm exhausted by the way the two of them fail to ever connect, not in any clear way even in the seventh (and I am assuming last in the series) book, twenty-five years after that fateful trip to the post office sometime in 1990, I am strangely reassured.

I find myself returning again and again to the final statement in Griffin's final letter in *The Golden Mean*:

> I'd never experienced real desire till you arrived—for which I think and damn you alternately. We must find a way to be together, or I will combust. I doubt that I will ever be/able to express to you how much I love you. (Bantock 1993: 24)

It seems to me that, while it's totally an overstatement, the essence in this moment is true. I am very able to use this as a way to close/not-close desire for letters, for ourselves, for meaning, for love. For writing this letter (to me) to you.

With deep appreciation,
Ames

Works Cited

Abrams, J. J., & Dorst, D. (2013). *S*. London: Mulholland Books.
Bantock, Nick. 1991. *Griffin and Sabine. An Extraordinary Correspondence.* San Francisco: Chronicle Books.
Bantock, Nick. 1992. *Sabine's Notebook. In Which the Extraordinary Correspondence of Griffin and Sabine Continues.* San Francisco: Chronicle Books.
Bantock, Nick. 1993. *The Golden Mean. In Which the Extraordinary Correspondence of Griffin and Sabine Concludes.* San Francisco: Chronicle Books.
Bantock, Nick. 2000. *The Artful Dodger. Images and Reflections.* San Francisco: Chronicle Books.
Bantock, Nick. 2001. *The Gryphon. In Which the Extraordinary Correspondence of Griffin and Sabine is Rediscovered.* San Francisco: Chronicle Books.
Bantock, Nick. 2002. *Alexandria. In Which the Extraordinary Correspondence of Griffin and Sabine Unfolds.* San Francisco: Chronicle Books.

Bantock, Nick. 2003. *The Morning Star. In Which the Extraordinary Correspondence of Griffin and Sabine is Illuminated.* San Francisco: Chronicle Books.

Bantock, Nick. 2016. *The Pharaoh's Gate. Griffin and Sabine's Lost Correspondence.* San Francisco: Chronicle Books.

Barthes, Roland. 1975. *The Pleasure of the Text.* New York: Hill and Wang.

El-Mothar, Amal. March 27, 2016. "Reading Between Worlds with Griffin and Sabine". *NPR Book Reviews.* <http://www.npr.org/2016/03/27/471343987/reading-between-worlds-with-griffin-and-sabine> [accessed 18 June 2017].

Krell, David Farrell. 1995. *Lunar Voices. Of Tragedy, Poetry, Fiction, and Thought.* Chicago: The University of Chicago Press.

Ladin, Joy. 2013. "Trans Poetics Manifesto". In: TC Tolbert & Tim Trace Petersen (eds.). *Troubling the Line. Trans and Genderqueer Poetry and Poetics.* New York: Nightboat Books. 306–308.

Muñoz, José Esteban. 2009. *Cruising Utopia. The Then and There of Queer Futurity.* New York: New York University Press.

Muñoz, José Esteban. 1996. "Evidence as Ephemera: Introductory Notes to Queer Acts". *Women & Performance: A Journal of Feminist Theory* 8.2: 5–16.

Meyer, Therese-M. 2010. "Illuminating the occult: Y.B. Yeats in Nick Bantock's *Griffin and Sabine* Series". *Journal of the Fantastic in the Arts* 21: 5–25.

Niffenegger, Audre. March 11, 2016. "Griffin and Sabine's Magical Return". *The Washington Post.* <https://www.washingtonpost.com/entertainment/books/griffin-and-sabines-magical-return/2016/03/10/41c37d8e-dfaa-11e5-8d98-4b3d9215ade1_story.html?utm_term=.a7737bb53625.> [accessed 18 June 2017].

Salamon, Gayle. 2010. *Assuming a Body. Transgender and Rhetorics of Materiality.* New York: Columbia University Press.

Simon, Sunka. 2002. *Mail-Orders. The Fiction of Letters in Postmodern Culture.* New York: State University of New York Press.

Stewart, Kathleen. 2007. *Ordinary Affects.* Durham: Duke University Press.

Toni Bowers
The Epistolary Revenant

Teaching Against Linearity

Abstract: In an undergraduate course on Epistolary Fiction before 1800, why include contemporary works on an already crowded syllabus? This essay describes the pedagogical benefits of teaching epistolary forms from the twentieth- and twenty-first-centuries in a course focused on earlier ages. Recent epistolary works give students an accessible site from which to begin thinking about a genre that they may not have recognized or approached as such before, and allows them to perceive its long, vibrant history. Students are challenged to think historically and materially, to question the stable coherence of narrative forms and values, and to practice the close listening to past voices that builds empathetic connections across time and difference. Beginning with contemporary epistolary fiction helps students develop the strategies and confidence they need to approach texts like Behn's *Love-Letters* and Richardson's *Clarissa*, and to conceive of literary history in new ways.

1 Introduction: Seeing the Past through the Present

I regularly teach an undergraduate course in Epistolary Fiction. The course introduces the genre as a case study in how careful attention to 'merely' formal considerations can lead to many kinds of learning. To help English majors fulfill a departmental requirement in "Literature before 1800", it places emphasis on texts from the late seventeenth and the eighteenth century, but despite this relatively narrow historical focus, the reading list includes epistolary works from many times and places. It not only goes 'back' (in the reductive language of traditional, teleological literary histories) to Ovid's *Heroides*, but also 'forward' considerably past 1800, to Stoker's *Dracula*, Sayers's *The Documents in the Case*, and even epistolary works from the late twentieth and the early twenty-first century. These very recent works, and their place on a syllabus devoted to "Literature Before 1800", are the focus of this essay. Why teach contemporary works under a 'before 1800' rubric? I want to suggest that including these works, and in fact beginning the semester with them, is a productive choice for a number of reasons, one that I recommend to other instructors.

2 Reimagining Literary History, Building Empathy

Twenty-first century works give students a relatively comfortable site from which to begin thinking about the contours and affordances of a genre that many of them have never heard of before – epistolary fiction – where meaning emerges from the idea of textual exchange itself. What precisely is 'epistolary' about epistolary fiction, they learn to ask. What difference does it make to one's experience of reading a text, or to its possible interpretations, that it is written in an epistolary form? Starting with recent texts makes it easier for students to think such questions through. It also thickens the historical picture from the start, preventing students from imagining that one specific kind of epistolary fiction – tales that unfold in a series of fictitious personal letters – defines the form. Instead, they learn to understand epistolary fiction as a complex set of possible methodological and material strategies that signifies variously at various times and places. Starting with recent texts also pre-empts student tendencies to consider epistolary fiction as a temporally finite phenomenon, a charming old fad that, like wearing powdered wigs and dancing the minuet, was confined largely to the eighteenth century. Instead, they learn that epistolary fiction has an unbroken and still vibrant literary history, and has even enjoyed a resurgence in recent years in texts that include personal-letter correspondence alongside other exchange forms. In other words, they begin to think historically and materially.

Historical-material thinking, as I am using that phrase here, is a skill that contemporary undergraduates often need to be taught directly. As any college instructor reading this essay is likely to know already, undergraduates are not always enthusiastic about the prospect of detailed learning about the past. Many tend to understand history as a record of events that are by definition over and done with, and so largely irrelevant to the present except insofar as they can be boiled down to lessons and precedents; and they are viscerally drawn to the artistic productions of their own time. Even the best-prepared undergraduates at the Ivy League University where I teach, furthermore, seldom bring much historical knowledge to their studies. Few have practiced listening closely, over an extended period of time, to voices from the past, or have learned to build empathetic connections across time.

Teaching epistolary fiction offers unique pay-offs when it comes to helping students develop into historical-material thinkers. In particular, encounters with the form help students to appreciate the ongoing presences of many different pasts in their own contemporary experience – cultural pasts, linguistic pasts, past structures of thinking or belief or valuation, representational pasts, past ways of imagining and desiring. They practice making connections from an intellectual stance alert to differences rather than presumptive of similarities. They develop abilities to consider phenomena that initially appeared foreign and opaque as pleasurable and productive features of their own contemporary worlds.

These are crucial skills and attitudes now, when fascism is becoming mainstream and when time itself can seem to be accelerating. Student attention spans are supposedly (and notoriously) shortening; archival work is being denigrated as elitist even from within the profession of literary study; and beleaguered humanities departments, even when they survive, tend to skew curricula more and more toward study of the current moment. At this juncture it is important to teach (i.e., to model for students, to instruct them in, to give them practice developing) habits of careful attention to literary voices that do not imagine readers like them or focus on worlds they recognize – indeed, that predate them so markedly that the differences on display cannot even be readily defined in terms already familiar and comfortable. Students who encounter epistolary fiction develop new appreciations for the sheer *otherness* of others, and they rise to the challenge of adjusting themselves to difference, rather than trying to reorganize it into compatibility with their default expectations and preferences. The study of epistolary fiction has proven to be important for my students, in other words, not primarily because it keeps alive attention to the form *per se*, as an exercise in antiquarianism or connoisseurship, but because it helps them to develop their powers of empathy and self-correction, to increase their store of information and experience, and to grow into the intellectual and moral maturity required to function effectively in the world.

The same goals are addressed by humanistic study writ large, of course. The humanistic disciplines offer some of the richest locations in any university for the kind of empathetic learning I am describing – though certainly not the only location, just as the university itself is not the only place to gain a 'higher' education. I am not suggesting that there is something *uniquely* efficacious about studying epistolary fiction, only that such study epitomizes and helps to develop in students what is most valuably derived from education: habits of careful observation and informed questioning, attention to and respect for what is unfamiliar, and the lifelong teachable attitude required of those who enjoy social, cultural, and economic privilege. To make a case for the benefits offered by sustained attention to this form of writing is not to denigrate other forms, only to shine a light on one useful and often neglected resource. As part of that project, I am suggesting that teaching epistolary fiction "before 1800" can best be achieved by introducing students to the form through recent texts rather than through texts situated in the historical context of the course.

In all its manifestations over time, one of the hallmarks of epistolary fiction is its power to help readers hear many voices sounding simultaneously. Rich polyphony is apparent to student readers even in single-level epistolary fictions (where all the entries come from one person) to a greater extent than in the apparent self-sufficiency (i.e., triumphant liberal individualism) of the "soloists" whom novel studies routinely privilege: the omniscient narrator and the first-person teller of his or her "own," supposedly unique, tale. As students readily discover, even in the most stripped-down epistolary framework there are shading presences – readers within or on the edges of the fiction who stand, in the fiction's world, between the epistolary speaker(s) and ourselves, as well as real-life readers who have come before us, leaving particular kinds of felt impositions on our experience. Even when they remain silent, fictional readers are virtually inseparable from epistolary fiction because of the form's organizing pretext: that we are reading communiques not written primarily for us, but for character-readers within the story; we are reading other people's mail. Real-life readers who have come before are present in epistolary fiction's peculiar penchant for collaborative production and revision, and its long-standing tendency to accrue, even sometimes to incorporate, readerly comment, revision, and expansion.[1] Reading epistolary fiction makes it necessary for students to train their ears, as it were, to hear layers of voices sounding within any given utterance.

Including comparative attention to past and present-day epistolary fictions, even within an historically focused course, allows students to perceive the lingering echoes of never-quite-silenced voices not only in specific texts but also across literary history writ large, and to recognize in the process that their own presents are always infused with never-finished pasts. In this way, the form exercises a peculiar power to rearrange literary history's supposed teleological structure. Like comingling tracks in a well-mixed recorded song, layers of voices contain, echo, and respond to one another across time and textual place, constituting a challenge to literary-historical models based on sequence, hierarchy, and discrete individualism. Studying contemporary epistolary fiction in the frame of a course devoted to a far-removed past opens windows onto these processes, by countering default progress narratives that imagine literary history to be a competitive, irresistibly progressive process that creates winners and losers, texts and writers with innate staying power and others without. Such assumptions are still routinely bequeathed on our students by traditional literary

---

[1] For a famous instance, though only one of many: Samuel Richardson constantly rewrote not only drafts but also already-published work in response to readers' suggestions, complaints, and misunderstandings.

history. Considering contemporary epistolary fictions as part of a course focused on the past gives them a window on how potently the past inhabits the present. Epistolary form *per se*, they come to see, enacts a peculiar set of continuities, ruptures, repetitions, and hauntings that make the categories 'present' and 'past' inadequate.

Technological changes have continuously made new sets of tools and new structural conceits available to epistolary writers. In recent years that process has accelerated, and today epistolary fictions unfold not only in letters but in e-mails, text messages, and tweets – and, if one's definition of epistolarity is as expansive as my own, in journalistic writing (dispatches from "your correspondent", letters to the editor, advice and gossip columns), intimate writing ("Dear Diary"), and other forms. Epistolary writing consistently incorporates new platforms and colonizes the narrative territories they make available.

All this makes it possible to select, for inclusion on the course reading list, from a number of excellent epistolary fictions published very recently. And it makes it impossible to pretend that one is introducing students to a form that had a long-ago hey-day and has now been moribund for decades or even centuries. But these happy developments come with dangers of their own. There is so much excellent new epistolary fiction now available, and this new fiction incorporates so many new formal options, that instructors must guard against giving students the impression that post-modernity invented epistolarity. Focused as they are on the present, most students need little encouragement to assume that current epistolary works are derived wholly from and for the current moment; they need to be explicitly taught that recent works did not pioneer awareness of the materiality and vulnerable contingency of language. This danger can be circumvented if contemporary epistolary fictions are taught *alongside* examples from the past – another reason for mixing up the historical locations we teach from even when curricula seem to militate against that practice.

It is important, in short, for students to understand that the very possibility of current epistolary writing is predicated on, and continues to enact, the form's long history. They see this most clearly when current and past epistolary fictions are mingled. The imbrication of past and present voices in a single course, even if that course focuses on a specific location in the past, helps students avoid historical fallacies (e. g., the notion that the present is the apex of progress). As a corollary, furthermore, combining present and past epistolary writing does much to foster students' development of sophisticated critical reading skills. By giving students an interpretive platform from which to rethink what 'history' can mean *besides* a march from the primitive to the advanced, we encourage them to think in newly sophisticated ways. Structuring an historically focused course without limiting attention to works from a single historical period challenges students to reimagine literary history and their own places within it as readers and writers.

3 New Epistolary Fiction: Comeau, Bantock

The contemporary epistolary titles that I include on the Epistolary Fiction course reading list vary from year to year. Recently the course has successfully included Joey Comeau's *Overqualified* (2009) and Nick Bantock's *Griffin and Sabine: An Extraordinary Correspondence* (1991), titles that function on the reading list as illuminating pre-emptive supplements to the earlier epistolary fictions on which student reading will focus. I will briefly describe each of these comparatively new novels here, and discuss their functions within the course.

Comeau's *Overqualified* purports to be a collection of job-seeking query letters from a young Canadian, Joey Comeau, to a series of corporations, personnel departments, and other impersonal hiring entities. The book starts out as a highly appealing, snarky satire on the genre of job letters per se. It gradually morphs – still entertainingly and with a light touch – into a subtle critique of alienated labor under capitalism and a sophisticated, moving depiction of the central character's intimate experiences of grief and disillusion, and his tentative reach for authenticity and purpose despite paralyzing loss.

This masterful little book comes as a revelation to students. They read it at the hectic start of the semester, when settling down with a 400-page eighteenth-century novel might be daunting, even logistically impossible. Less than 100 pages long, *Overqualified* is accessible and welcoming, enjoyable for student readers and peculiarly relevant to the immediate concerns of third- and final-year undergraduates. The letter-writer is applying for jobs in a soulless economy, and that basic premise immediately draws students in. They express surprised pleasure at being assigned a course text that wittily and insightfully dramatizes the exact undertaking that many of them are struggling with as they read (and that the rest are dreading).

What I find most valuable about including *Overqualified* on the syllabus is precisely this strong connection with student readers, a connection that is part of their historical education. For *Overqualified* offers a twenty-first century version of the visceral, almost too-personal experience with which epistolary fiction has enthralled audiences for centuries. That experience can be difficult to recapture when students are asked to engage with 300-year-old texts immediately, before they have become skilled readers of epistolary fiction. Epistolary form demands that readers enter fictional worlds in a peculiarly intimate fashion: in the transgressive act of reading someone else's correspondence, readers are asked to use evidence to apprehend that other person in a level of detail that they have seldom encountered so directly in fiction. The kind of insistent, immediate grip that *Overqualified* makes on student readers helps them experience this peculiar aspect of the form. After reading Comeau, they do not need to be informed about the somewhat disturbing quality of the intimacies produced by epistolary fiction, or explicitly shown the interestedness, fundamental contingency, and partiality of epistolary narrators' efforts at self-representation: they have discovered these phenomena for themselves. They feel what it is to be at once voyeurs and participants, aliens and doppelgangers, invaders and allies – the defining experiences of epistolary fiction's readers for many centuries now.

Joey's shifting voice starts out with a glibness that only poorly masks immense anxiety about the prospect of finding employment. Over the course of the narrative his voice – the only voice we hear – becomes increasingly more desperate, angry, and unguarded. The shift challenges student readers, who have been enjoying Joey's arch tone and superior attitude, to think again about their desire to identify with him and about their expectations regarding their own future places in the corporate world. As Joey's letters become more and more self-revelatory, in fact, any pretense that he is really writing for corporate consideration falls away, and students must further adapt as readers. Joey emerges not as the confident job seeker with whom they imagined themselves to have much in common, but as an elusive, even secretive character – perhaps, indeed, more a pretext than a 'character' at all. Even as he seems to be revealing more and more of himself, in fact, Joey becomes more and more unknown. His failure to live up to the expectations of readers trained on realist novels destabilizes empathetic readers' assumptions about what it means to be a person.

As it gradually accrues from a number of small, seemingly disparate parts – epistolary style – *Overqualified* comes to exceed many student readers' expectations. It rebukes and diminishes students' default habits as readers (identifying with the speaking subject[s], gathering facts in order to assess and judge). Self-representation – the undertaking Joey is at once preoccupied with and afraid of – is revealed to be irreducibly unstable, dependent on material pressures and interests in specific moments. Not merely the representations, but even the self supposedly being represented, comes to seem partial and contingent, a series of negotiations of ongoing pasts rather than a stable entity moving through sequential time toward a distinct, supplanting future. Joey emerges gradually (and never fully), through specific sets of circumstances that exert pressure at the moment of writing and also reach far beyond that moment. Each of his many efforts at self-representation is subject to immediate revision, until 'Joey Comeau' becomes a compilation of effects (necessarily short-term, never definitive) rather than a coherent, reliable, stably existent entity.

In his purported collection of job-application letters, Joey deliberately provokes his ostensible readers, the H.R. representatives and machine-readers his letters address. He goads those in-the-fiction readers to recognize his lack of self-critique, indeed his lack of self, in ways that at first amuse student readers but before long unsettle them. The critique of capitalist systems is also a critique of students' complicity *in* those systems, even if so far that complicity is largely a matter of desire for inclusion. In these ways and others, Joey exercises a ruthlessness not available to 'objective' third-person narrators and seldom at work even in first-person fictions. Joey's letters exhibit a cold, permanent deferral of any intrinsic significance in Joey himself or in the contexts he thinks he desires. The epistolary form brings student readers into intimate confrontation with some harsh truths.

In these ways, *Overqualified* gives students a taste of epistolary fiction's peculiar power simultaneously to rivet, move, and destabilize readers, to challenge the temporal assumptions that drive the third- and first-person narratives that student readers are accustomed to interpreting, and to produce intense (if not always comfortable) pleasure. Students see, in a compressed space, how productively a literary form can exceed its own presuppositions and how organically humor, satire, and moral nuance can be built from epistolary materials. They learn that there are almost unlimited points of view available even within a single voice, and they learn to question the stable coherence of any perspective. Students become equipped, in short, to read the rest of the works on the reading list.

These valuable results depend most fundamentally on the contemporaneity of Comeau's book, and that is something that will not last forever. Every year, I am concerned that *Overqualified* may not continue to be immediately relevant for students when its informal locutions and popular-culture references (e.g., to specific computer games) become dated. To be sure that *Overqualified* is serving the functions for which I use it – contemporaneity, accessibility, material near-transparency, destabilizing readerly effects – I always ask students about their experience of the text. So far, they assure me that references to now-dated technology do not diminish their experience, and that they have no trouble connecting with the book's language as their own. If that changes, or if the diversity of the students in the room (not the same thing as the diversity among their complexions) thickens to the point where they do not start from default identification with Joey, I will likely look for another book with which to start students on the road to reading epistolary fiction.

After *Overqualified*, the reading list takes a small step back chronologically, to the end of the twentieth century and a work that students may already know, though they seem not to have before considered it an example of the genre of epistolary fiction. Nick Bantock's *Griffin and Sabine: An Extraordinary Correspondence* (1991), the first book in Bantock's *Griffin and Sabine* trilogy, is something of a novelty item – a gift book that spent years on the *New York Times* bestseller list – and not the kind of epistolary fiction that usually shows up on college reading lists.[2] I have found it an invaluable resource, however, and I continue to use it successfully even more than 25 years after its first publication. This is possible because *Griffin and Sabine* trades less on contemporaneity than on timeless fantasy. For that reason, paradoxically enough, it stands reliably alongside (and in contrast with) *Overqualified* (which, as I have suggested, may end up aging faster). Together, these two titles represent contemporary epistolary fiction in my 'before 1800' course.

Griffin and Sabine purports to be the unique material archive of actual epistolary objects that comprise a strange correspondence between two far-flung artists.[3] Lavishly and beautifully illustrated – it is an art book as well as a storybook – the novel takes the form of a bound collection of postcards and letters, folded and in envelopes, designed to seem authentically hand-written. To follow the plot, which becomes more and more mysterious and uncertain as it unfolds, readers have to read what look like real pieces of mail; they have to examine the fronts and backs of postcards, open envelopes and remove physical letters from inside. It is necessary, too, to pay close attention to material details like postage design, postmarks, return addresses, handwriting, smudges, doodles, changes in ink, and so on.

It would be difficult to overstate the semester-long benefits of this tactile reading experience for undergraduates embarking on the study of epistolary fiction. As the digitalization of all things proceeds, people in their late teens and early twenties may soon be unable to remember actually having written a physical letter, stamped it, and put it in the mail. (Even now, students often tell me that it has been years since they have received a personal letter in an envelope.) *Griffin and Sabine* allows students to experience this pleasure while making unmistakable the material aspects of epistolary fiction, its central problem – com-

---

[2] See Ames Hawkins' "An Open Letter to Nick Bantock OR Letters and/as Ephemera(l): Desire, Transposition and Transpoetic Possibility with/in Epistolary Form" in this volume.

[3] The correspondence continues over the course of two more short books in what comprises a trilogy, and Vols II and III change the meaning of Vol I. Instructors ought to be familiar with the entire trilogy, but I require the students to read only Vol I. I have found that not much is gained by asking students to do the extra purchasing – and this is a book that must be read in its original format. Every time I teach the course, however, a few students buy the other volumes on their own and read them with enthusiasm, and some write papers on the other volumes or on the whole trilogy.

munication, with all its built-in impossibilities – and the peculiar slyness of the form's truth claims. It reveals how important seemingly extraneous and adventitious details can be, and challenges students to read differently – more scrupulously, with greater alertness to a wider range of cues both linguistic and material – than they are used to doing.

Together, *Overqualified* and *Griffin and Sabine* develop in students strategies for reading epistolary fiction, and give them the confidence they will need when the reading list turns to less accommodating texts. Students find considerable satisfaction, for example, in discovering that they can read Ovid's *Heroides* using strategies that they have learned from reading Comeau and Bantock. In the context established by the more modern works, Ovid (or Montesquieu, or Richardson) addresses student readers not as an isolated Great Writer from an isolated past, but as an artist working in a multivalent tradition in which they already have a foothold.

As reference points, Comeau and Bantock also set an early brake on the student tendency, when confronted with modern editions of centuries-old epistolary fictions, to over-focus on the *text* – the arrangement of words on the page – as if it were detachable from the *work*, or as if any edition or reprinting or format were equivalent to any other. Bantock's hyper-material novel, in particular, helps students to think otherwise.

The early grounding in materiality that Bantock, especially, provides is also important because students will read much of the course's subsequent material in modern editions from publishing houses like Oxford and Penguin – streamlined, virtually identical commodities designed precisely to eliminate, as much as possible, any material peculiarity. Now of course, the material uniformity of standardized teaching editions has much to recommend it. Students appreciate the accessible annotations, the "Note on the Text" pages, and editors' Introductions, e.g.; and it is not too much to say that the availability of cheap, reliable primary texts makes a course like "Epistolary Fiction" possible. But material uniformity also presents a potential problem: whether students are reading the racy first volume of Behn's *Love-Letters* or Richardson's stately *Clarissa* or Stoker's *Dracula*, the reading experiences can feel identical, and that can make it more difficult for students to imagine early letter-fictions as historically and materially specific correspondence sets. Having read *Griffin and Sabine* helps students to remember the materiality of letters and to think critically, often for the first time, about what is gained and lost in the production of the modern teaching editions they often take for granted as transparent representations of literary works. Weeks into the course, I have heard students refer to Bantock retrospectively in order to remind each other to think in material terms – even when a given epistolary fiction seems as far as possible from *Griffin and Sabine*'s stuck-on envelopes and colorful, apparently hand-written postcards.

Both *Griffin and Sabine* and *Overqualified* also challenge students to think about the specific material requirements built into the transmission of physical letters at a given time and place – the necessary lapses in time between composition and receipt of letters, the spatial distances that must be bridged for letters' delivery, available means of moving mail from one place to another, and the possible interpretive repercussions of such matters of fact both within and outside of the fictional world. These are historical-material questions. Epistolary transmission is complicated and problematic even in Comeau's and Bantock's stories, and its difficulties are thematized there; but logistical problems often become positively disruptive in works produced in earlier centuries, when communications and physical movement were far more difficult and time-consuming than they are now. From *Overqualified* and *Griffin and Sabine*, students carry forward the realization that time, financial and material resources, weather and natural phenomena, and privacy concerns must be taken into account in order to read epistolary fiction.

In short, students find it easier, after Comeau and Bantock, to understand much earlier epistolary fictions as collections of discursive objects, objects with physical vulnerabilities, potentially without neat temporal sequentiality, even without necessary internal coherence. They perceive that the 'text' has been artificially and instrumentally arranged to *seem* coherent, changeless, and infinitely reproducible. Pluralizing identity on many levels (not just the personal or individual), *Overqualified* and *Griffin and Sabine* gesture, in different ways, toward representational and communicative phenomena that exceed the capacities of collation, homogenization, and reproduction, and expose the interests of those undertakings.

A further new idea to which *Overqualified* and *Griffin and Sabine* accustom student readers is the notion that no stable, permanent 'meaning' exists in works of literature: meaning is always dependent, to a significant extent, on changing formats and contexts (of writing, of reading) that students have often been trained not to see. As a genre, epistolary fiction reveals this fact by remaining at once very specifically fixed and strangely *un*fixed in time. *Clarissa*'s letters are datelined minutely, to specific days of the week and hours of the day; yet when readers have attempted to create timelines of the novel's action – including its central action, letter-writing – the exactitude implodes, casting doubt on the possibility of the text's very existence. When students encounter so complicated an epistolary work as *Clarissa* with interpretive tools provided by *Overqualified* and *Griffin and Sabine*, they can approach this paradox not as a failure of verisimilitude, but as its redefinition. They learn to reimagine all the writing they encounter, even those titles that most look like closed, coherent, changeless texts, as *processes*. This insight has the potential to alter the way students approach their studies and to influence the ways they learn.

Both *Overqualified* and *Griffin and Sabine* have proven to have staying power on my syllabi over several years now. Each remains powerfully instructive for my students. The point of starting with these two recent works is not, however, ultimately about the works themselves (despite the considerable time I have devoted to discussing them here), but about their usefulness in teaching students to approach other works on the semester's reading list – the earlier works of epistolary fiction that students find harder to read and to think about critically, and which it is my job to foreground. These two recent texts allow students to develop reading stances and strategies that will be required for adequate apprehension of epistolary fiction, stances and strategies that would prove much more difficult for students to develop were they starting out with more temporally distant works. (Having tried more linear-sequential formats, I feel confident insisting on this point.) Comeau's *Overqualified* and Bantock's *Griffin and Sabine* allow students to gain practice asking questions about form *per se* and its relation to meaning. These works offer spaces where students can gain critical perspective on themselves as readers, on received genre hierarchies, on the processes of literary history, and on specific practices of literary dissemination and the interests behind them.

For these reasons, I find that students benefit from reading recent epistolary fictions even in the context of a course that defines itself according to its focus on seventeenth- and eighteenth-century writing. Our own present, that supposedly singular phenomenon with which we are all obsessed, can seem to students to be a singular phenomenon that achieves unique quiddity in contrast with a monolithic other – the past – which, they tend to believe, is finished and over. In this course, students confront the present differently, and counterintuitively, with important results for how they think about the past. The present becomes a weirdly retrospective and repetitive starting place for learning about a literary form that makes visible some perhaps surprising facts: that what we call 'the past' is many pasts, only ever discernable in fragments and shadows; that the past is not synonymous with 'history,' a set of linear narratives constructed against, and in an effort to recuperate, discontinuity and multiplicity; that the past cannot be relegated to the simple perfect, and that literary history, which like every other history is always provisional, interested, and partial, may be best understood as going on in the present perfect progressive tense, the location of the always-ongoing past. There are many overlapping pasts and many competing versions of (literary) history, and they continue to make their cacophonous claims on every present.

Such paradoxes have proven easiest for my students to perceive when they appear first in *Overqualified* and *Griffin and Sabine*, but they do not originate or finish there. From those starting places, students carry into the rest of the semester a kind of pre-emptive echo: voices from the past continue to thicken the contemporary voices they heard with surprise and pleasure at the start of the semester, voices they continue to hear within other, earlier voices. These realizations can challenge and refine student understandings of central categories like 'past' and 'present,' 'new' and 'old,' 'modern' and 'historical.' They suggest new kinds of connections among texts, persons, and material phenomena, connections in excess of the sequential links of cause-and-effect and new-superseding-old that seem so natural when one begins from the assumptions of inevitable progress and forward development.

I close with two final observations. First, when students begin to hear past voices in the writing of their own generation and echoes of the present in writing from the past, they also learn to think differently about how they apprehend contemporaneity and their immediate contemporaries, including other students in class. They take steps toward recognizing built-in, indissoluble differences even in what they have been taught to think of as a society of peers.

Second, at least during a good semester another, perhaps surprising, pay-off can result: "mixing up" chronology (so to speak) actually helps students organize literary history – something they explicitly desire – and do so for themselves. They take steps toward constructing their own big pictures without falling into either a sequential parade of master-texts or a random assemblage of phenomena. They have a framework on which they can imagine literary history not as a linear phenomenon but as a circular one, or perhaps a phenomenon built on irregular narrative models like those famously pictured in Laurence Sterne's *Tristram Shandy* (Fig 1, 2, 3).

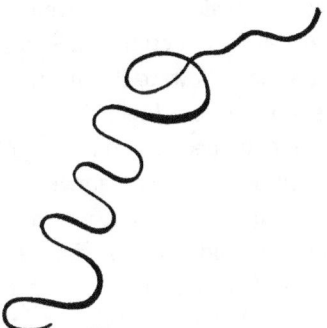

Figure 1: Laurence Sterne, *Tristram Shandy* (Norton, 1980, Vol. VI, Ch. XL, p. 333).

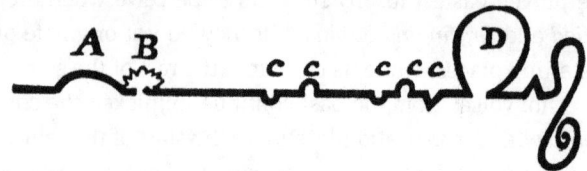

Figures 2: Laurence Sterne, *Tristram Shandy* (Norton, 1980, Vol. VI, Ch. XL, p. 333).

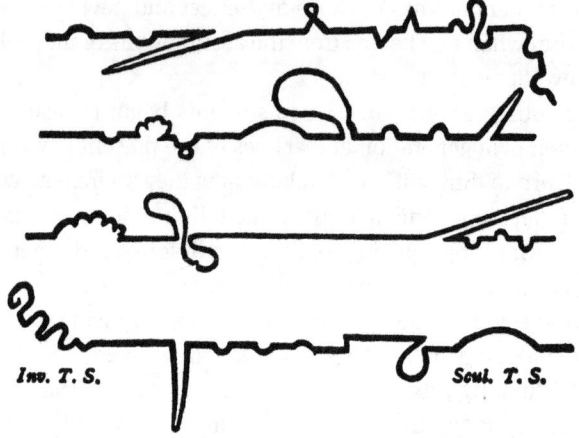

Figure 3: Laurence Sterne, *Tristram Shandy* (Norton, 1980, Vol. IX, Ch. IV, p. 426).

4 Conclusion

Epistolary fiction is a genre particularly well-suited to making alternative pasts and a variety of literary-historical narratives available to undergraduates. It allows them to understand history *tout court* not as a march toward the always indubitably better that leaves the comparatively simplistic and less-polished behind, and not as a debate in which various forms and speakers compete until a few triumph over the others at last, but as something more like a song: a harmonizing on many levels that never fully rejects dissonance, a constant resounding with difference. These are grand ambitions, and I do not claim that the introduction of these two titles achieves them all in full, not even in the small context of this particular undergraduate course. Rather, I am demonstrating that in a modest, local way, even a course that focuses on a rather unfashionable subject can resist its own temporal parameters and give breathing room, as it were, for students to imagine literary history as a more capacious, more tangible, less tame place.

Starting a course focused on literature before 1800 with a pair of contemporary texts hardly solves every problem faced by instructors teaching within curricula organized in implication with liberal teleologies. But the course described above, and especially its refusal to present epistolary fiction as a past-perfect phenomenon despite the implications of the specific curriculum in which I teach, illustrates how modest adjustments in reading-list structure can pay comparatively large dividends. Structured this way, Epistolary Fiction has become a course where, when everything works, I can remain responsive to both students' instructional needs and the institutional pressures they labor under, without losing sight of their need to experience pleasure in learning. Effective alternatives to teleological teaching are not uniquely available in epistolary fiction. But confrontations with epistolary form can make the need for such alternatives, their value, and some possible strategies for constructing them, visible to students. Including the twentieth and twenty-first centuries under a 'before 1800' course rubric can help students themselves to construct new practices of empathetic, materially alert, historical thinking.

Works Cited

Bantock, Nick. 1991. *Griffin and Sabine. An Extraordinary Correspondence.* San Francisco: Chronicle Books.

Bantock, Nick. 1992. *Sabine's Notebook. In Which the Extraordinary Correspondence of Griffin and Sabine Continues.* San Francisco: Chronicle Books.

Bantock, Nick. 1993. *The Golden Mean. In Which the Extraordinary Correspondence of Griffin and Sabine Concludes.* San Francisco: Chronicle Books.

Behn, Aphra. 1993/ 1684–87. *Love-letters between a nobleman and his sister.* In: Janet Todd (ed.). *The Works of Aphra Behn.* Vol. 2. Columbus: Ohio State University Press.

Comeau, Joey. 2009. *Overqualified.* Toronto: ECW Press.

Ovid. 1986/ approx. 5 BCE–8CE. *Heroides and Amores.* Loeb Classical Library 41, Ovid Vol. I. Translated by Grant Showerman. Revised by G. P. Goold. Cambridge: Harvard University Press.

Richardson, Samuel. 2011/ 1747–48. *Clarissa, or, The History of a Young Lady: An Abridged Edition.* Ed. Toni Bowers & John Richetti. Peterborough, Ont. and Buffalo, NY: Broadview, 2011.

Sterne, Laurence. 1980/1759–67. *The Life and Opinions of Tristram Shandy, Gentleman.* A Norton Critical Edition. Ed. Howard Anderson. New York and London: Norton.

Stoker, Bram. 2011/ 1897. *Dracula. Oxford World's Classics.* Ed. Roger Luckhurst. Oxford and New York: Oxford University Press.

Part IV: **Literature and Electronic Correspondence**

Thomas O. Beebee
E-Mail Epistlemologies

Abstract: On the basis of four case studies of early e-mail fiction, this essay explores the question of how closely related this fictional form is to the epistolary novel. Do the two forms share a similar epistemology? How does e-mail form help fiction answer (or evade) the three simple questions: "Who are you?", "Who is s/he?", and "Who am I?". The four case studies reveal significantly different approaches to these fundamental questions. Paula Danziger and Ann Martin's juvenile novel, *Snail Mail No More* (2000), adheres most strongly to the received humanistic dimension of letter fiction, showing the transition from "snail mail" to e-mail and messaging with minimal disruption. Paige Baty's *E-mail trouble: love and addiction @the matrix* (1999) projects a sincere and complex sender of messages who finds no correspondent due in part to the distancing effect of media. Matt Beaumont's office satire, *e* (2000), follows the Adornian line that shows how capitalist production processes, in which e-mail plays a central role, reduce the self to a caricature. This point is taken one step further in the detective fiction *The Daughters of Freya* (2005), which is delivered as a series of partly personalized e-mail messages to its readers, who are thus functionalized as cogs in an overall system of surveillance.

1 Introduction

The familiar letter has been at the heart of a series of humanisms in Europe, from the love story of Abelard and Héloise and its echoes in Jean-Jacques Rousseau, Alexander Pope, and others, to the rediscovery of Cicero's letters by Coluccio Salutati in Florence, to the *Lettres portugaises* that helped open an era of erotic sentimentalism in the seventeenth century, to the inversion of European perspectives in the novels written in the "Persian Letters" mode (more accurately, in the "Turkish Spy" mode). The letter has also played a role in delivering the post-colonial subject, in works as diverse as American Alice Walker's *The Color Purple*, Sengalese Mariama Bâ's *Une si longue lettre*, Taiwanese Li Ang's *Unsent Love Letter*, and the Angolan author José Eduardo Agualusa's *Nação Crioula*. In each of these cases, letters – real or fictional – have played a central role both in redefining subjectivity and intersubjectivity, and in expanding cultural relativism and historicism.

Paradoxically, while the relay mechanisms for mail delivery have become ever faster, and as privacy has become more of an assumed and prosecutable right, the letter's central role in projecting subjectivity, individuality, and humanism has shrunk concomitantly. The epistolary novel had become a rarity by about 1850, for example – though this volume shows that there has been a renewal of interest in the form in the last quarter of the twentieth century. Despite their basic formal resemblances in being composed of correspondence and thus reminding readers of complex, polyphonic conversations, it is not clear whether revivals of the form, such as A. S. Byatt's *Possession*, have anything in common with e-mail narratives such as S. Paige Baty's *e-mail trouble*, Matt Beaumont's *e*, or *The Daughters of Freya* that I will discuss in this paper. (The Anglophone focus of this volume precludes a discussion of Daniel Glattauer's 2006 *Gut gegen Nordwind*, perhaps the most successful e-mail novel to date in terms of sales.) As indicated by its subtitle, "A Romance", Byatt's novel is about the recovery of nineteenth-century letters that reveal a hidden dimension of a great author – his adulterous love affair, initiated and ripened through correspondence with a reclusive literary genius. Those in pursuit of these letters are not poets, but academicians and antiquarians. Their fascination with the epistolary exchange derives from their ability to watch the actors in the drama voyeuristically, from the outside and from a point far removed from them in history. They are Benjaminian collectors rather than participants. Correspondence becomes a stuffed museum piece, its romanticization equaling its capitalization both cultural and financial. Byatt's narrative, a pastiche in which Richardsonian or Rousseauvian subjectivities are framed by the satiric caricature of the "campus novel", thus exhibits the nostalgic quality that Fredric Jameson has identified with the post-modern:

> This approach to the present by way of the art language of the simulacrum, or of the pastiche of the stereotyped past, endows present reality and the openness of present history with the spell and distance of a glossy mirage. Yet this mesmerizing new aesthetic mode itself emerged as an elaborated symptom of the waning of our historicity, of our lived possibility of experiencing history in some active way. It cannot therefore be said to produce this strange occultation of the present by its own formal power, but rather merely to demonstrate, through these inner contradictions, the enormity of a situation in which we seem increasingly incapable of fashioning representations of our own current experience. (1991: 21)

What is the object of this nostalgia (whose very presence, if Jameson is correct, would be the humanistic dwarf driving the chess-playing automaton of postmodernity), and what is its exact relation to the form of the letter? Furthermore, does e-mail help or hinder us in "fashioning representations of our own current experience", which is certainly one of the hallowed roles of the letter as a document of humanism?

In Jürgen Habermas's view, the letter was a breakthrough technology of Enlightenment and a fundamental component of the public sphere (*Öffentlichkeit*). The publication of the private through letters, including especially the letter-novel, had crucial political, including gender-political, import. Elizabeth Cook has applied Habermas's idea to epistolary fiction, noting that "[j]ust as the social contract produced citizens of political republics [...] the literary contract of the epistolary novel invented and regulated the post-patriarchal private subject as a citizen of the Republic of Letters" (1996: 16). The Republic of Letters was, of course, historically conditioned and bounded. According to Habermas, advanced stages of capitalism replace the public sphere with a pseudo-public sphere, in which the literary-social contract of the letter no longer can function politically. Hence, Theodor Adorno's pronouncement that "In a social configuration in which each individual is reduced to the level of a function [...] the 'I' in the letter is always something of a mirage" (Adorno 1974: 586).

Has the replacement of correspondence by e-mail and messaging driven the final nail in the coffin of "letterature"? Scholars debate whether the novel form is dead, but the fact that no one writes letters any more hardly seems worth arguing about. Most readers of this chapter will have perused at some point the "Collected Letters [or Correspondence] of Their Favorite Authors". Can anyone imagine a volume with the title "Collected E-mails of..."? Why not? According to Sunka Simon, traditional methods of composing and sending correspondence are now

> activities associated with the unprofitable time-management and lackluster image of artists or endearing but overly sentimental romantics clinging to a simpler, more 'natural' age – a feminized image. [...] The artist of today is the tech-wizard whose e-mail and web-sites not only feature multiple frames and attachments but also images, movies, and sound. (2002: 213)

Letter-writing, by its retrograde technologies and slowness compared to newer technologies, becomes simply the latest form of Ludditism.

What, then, in contradistinction to the various historical instrumentalizations, is the epistemology, or more accurately the phenomenology, of e-mail? How does it help answer (or evade) the three simple questions: "Who are you?", "Who is s/he?", and "Who am I?" In the numerous studies devoted to the psychology and phenomenology of Internet use and computer-mediated communication, the use of electronic mail systems as a technology of the self is minimized in comparison to other aspects. Sherry Turkle's *Life on the Screen* devotes about 10 pages to e-mail, versus more than 40 to MUDs (i.e. Multi-User Dungeon, a type of role-playing game that takes place in real time in a virtual world), even though many more people use e-mail than MUDs. Katherine Hayles's *My Mother Was a Computer* does not even contain a separate index entry for electronic mail, even though it is one of the major umbilical cords of our daily life connecting us to the phallic Motherboard of our "ramified dreams" (Baty 1999: 19). Where there is a discussion of e-mail, it is most often embedded in a discussion of other digitized technologies of the self, such as bulletin boards, as in the following passage by Turkle:

> The formats of MUDs, electronic mail, computer conferences, or bulletin boards force one to recognize a highly differentiated (and not always likable) virtual persona, because that persona leaves an electronic trace. In other words, the presence of a record that you can scroll through again and again may alert you to how persistent are your foibles or defensive reactions. One New York City writer told me ruefully, "I would see myself on the screen and say, 'There I go again.' I could see my neuroses in black and white. It was a wake-up call." (1995: 205–06)

Complementary to this discussion of the e-message as a mirror stage of the self is that of observing oneself through the eye of the Other, which involves the recognition, among other things, that one's e-mail has both direct and indirect, carbon-copied and blind-carbon-copied, intended and unintended addressees – for example, the fellow Enron exec you intended to send the e-mail to vs. the government prosecutor and jury members reading the same incriminating e-mail afterwards. Nothing is ever really deleted. These ideas of trace and archive rather than experience as the locus of persona coincide, I think, with Katherine Hayles's definition of the post-human: "From the get-go, the posthuman subject is an amalgam, a collection of heterogeneous components, a material-informational entity whose boundaries undergo continuous construction and reconstruction" (1997: 243). Our postal selves have always been 'post'-something, yet the acceleration and pervasiveness of digital technology seem to increasingly lay bare the postness of constructions of the self. E-mail, then, whether as subjectivity or as phenomenology, disappears in two directions: On the one hand, it becomes hard to distinguish from bulletin boards, chat, blogs, text messaging, and other verbal media of the Internet, which are frequently interlinked with each other. In the formulation of Mark Nunes, "the interpellation of the electronic address [in an e-mail] not only arrives in the hailing of a subject heading, but it passes on and through my personal addresses to an undefined network of others" (2006: 94); on the other hand, there may well be a reason why the term e-mail has stuck, rather than some more arcane term such as blog, and that the difference between e-mail and instant messaging is clear to most users. This persistence of the idea that we are getting mail may hint at e-mail as an adaptation of traditional forms of correspondence.

Can e-mail replace the letter as a form of mutual dialogic self-fashioning, or does it possess the inner contradictions that always remind us of our incapacity for such? Is the e-mail novel always a nostalgic, post-modern pastiche of the epistolary novel? Do the material conditions for the creation, transmission, reception, and archiving of e-mail affect the content in ways analogous to what we find in the epistolary novel? I will explore these questions in four different e-mail novels, starting with Paige Baty's *E-mail trouble*.

2 Paige Baty and the Trouble with E-Mail

Baty, trained in political theory and author of a book on Marilyn Monroe, wrote a melancholy, self-reflexive narrative that provides a resoundingly negative answer to the questions of the post-human self. *E-mail trouble* appeared posthumously after the author's death from a heroin overdose in a University of Texas Press series called "Constructs", which "examines the ways in which the things we make change both our world and how we understand it. Authors in the series explore the constructive nature of the human artifact and the imagination and reflection that bring it into being" (Baty 1999: n. pag.). Am I the only one to experience ambiguity in the referent for "it"? In any case, the "thing made" that changed Baty was e-mail. The genre of the book is indefinable, though 'confession' perhaps comes closest. But it is also a self-help book, like *Courage to Change* or *One Day at a Time*, and even includes direct references to the Twelve Steps. The first sentences of the text read as though recorded at a meeting: "Hi. I'm Paige and I'm an addict" (Baty 1999: 3). Paige's addiction – in her semi-fictionalized account – is to e-mail correspondence, up to 30 messages a day:

> These are the confessions of an e-mail addict. I am writing after I've kicked, gotten clean, given up on virtual strangers and electronic connections. But addiction has to figure somewhere in this account of love, memory, belonging, and the Internet. I was desperately seeking something or someone and I thought I could find it in virtual time and space. As it turned out, this was not the case. [...] Did any of this *happen* at all? What's happening when there is no there there? Somebody else do a phenomenology of that. I'm just trying to tell a story. (Baty 1999: 36)

Computers are, as in the Baty quote I gave previously, the phallic Motherboard. Baty takes the idea of the "phallic mother" from Julia Kristeva's *Revolution in Poetic Language:* "At its base, isn't there a belief, ultimately maintained, that the mother is phallic, that the ego – never precisely identified – will never separate from her, and that no symbol is strong enough to sever this dependence? In this symbiosis with the supposedly phallic mother, what can the subject do but occupy her place, thus navigating the path from fetishism to auto-eroticism?" (Kristeva 1986: 115) Auto-eroticism is certainly at stake in Baty's e-mail addiction. William Gibson coined the term "cyberspace" for this u-topia, this no-place. Cyberspace has no dimensionality and hence gives only the illusion of space, but is by no means the first such utopia or heterotopia to do so. What about the nation-state, for example? Represented on maps, it seems to exist as a space when in fact it is a non-dimensional network of affective ties and power relationships.

Baty's writing reminds us, through a large collection of puns, how much the metalanguage of cyberspace seeks authenticity. One of the many subtitles she gives her book is a "computer geek tragedy" (1999: 1). She reproduces the entire dictionary entry for "matrix" as an ironic echo of the shelter she was unable to find in cyberspace, and the inadequacy of cyberspace as a prosthesis for her own fleshly womb that is troubled both by the absence of human companionship (she is unable to find true companionship in Amherst, Massachusetts) and by her medical condition of endometriosis. The punning resonances of "mail routes" vs. "male roots", and other combinations of these, remind her that cyberspace is a male matrix where reproduction is enforced, but conception impossible. She "circles in on her account" (1999: 12), both a computer account and also a retelling, that is full of "hard-driven memories" (1999: 26–27). People without prosthetic cyberselves are "people of no account" (1999: 71). If Jesus needed fishers of men, "on the Internet people become fissures of men. Cast your nets upon the waters. Cast your nets upon the daughters" (1999: 39). Delphi, an e-mail system, becomes the Delphic oracle. Paige orbits in sigh-ber-space. Spam is an anagram for maps (1999: 67). Her computer I.D. becomes her Freudian id: "The pseudonym is the externalized id. It is an I.D. made up of projection. [...] It was a lack of content that got to me. I was not content" (1999: 67).

The fatal attraction of e-mail for Baty was that it replaced depth with breadth, a false dimension of non-dimensional cyberspace:

> Now there was a new system of extension, and that would allow access without intrusion. All I needed to do was to give them my address, which I did, and they could write to me. It seemed like a good idea at the time. I had no idea what I was in for. Like the flesh-eating virus, these correspondences consumed my body and my life. I had less privacy in my life than at any time I have ever known. People could contact me at two in the morning. I was awash in correspondence, yet I was alone. (1999: 96)

Here, of course, the reader intervenes to offer the option of simply turning off the computer at two in the morning; but, to follow the addiction motif, this is a bit like saying "if you can't stop drinking, then never take a first drink".

The core plot is a trip to New Orleans, a reunion of people who had never met before except through e-mail. A central character in this novel is ominously yclept The Good Man, with whom Baty moves from e-mail to telephone, letters, a photograph, and so forth. The e-mail lovers' discourse is a series of back and forths, where language is marked by the hierarchical depth of unoriginality (the more pointy brackets, the less original and more recycled it is). When Paige arrives with her sister in New Orleans, she finds that the Good Man will barely talk to her or look her in the eye. The males do all the talking and the women are silent. E-mail has been a trap, the false dream of correspondence on a level playing field.

Formally, the text is marked by the insertion of e-mails in boldface and a typically monofont computer typeface that punctuate Baty's post-mortem of her addiction. Letters by Albert Camus, from Louisa May Alcott's *Little Women*, and quotations from Norman O. Brown are given in italics. The earliest e-mail dates from January 1995, the latest from August 1996. The New Orleans trip seems to have taken place in May 1995. The August e-mails cluster around a virus attack that apparently destroys the archive. On page 4, the author tells us that the "e-mail inserts are edited or invented by the receiver" (1999: 4). One such edit is the very last e-mail, dated 16 August 1996, and addressed to Williams-faculty@williams.edu and williams-staff@williams.edu, concerning an update to physical inventory that will soon be undertaken. "Do not be alarmed if you see someone looking at your computer" (1999: 158), it says reassuringly. A final line, separated by a space from the rest of the message, reports that "We couldn't find you" (1999: 158). This last line could not have been part of the original message, both because the former was preparatory in nature, and because it was addressed generally to faculty and staff at Williams.

After reproducing a letter from Albert Camus, Baty zeroes in on the difference she finds between e-mail and correspondence: "Letters often signify disappointment. E-mail seems at first to take care of that mess, but it can never take the place of any true correspondence. [...] Real letters mean really being there for the person to whom you are writing" (1999: 94). There is no true co-respondent in e-mail correspondence. This statement turns out to be a premonition of the disappointment of Paige's meeting with The Good Man. It affirms the fissure that marks the post-human, but remains mysterious, since letters always signify precisely the absence of the writer.

3 Matt Beaumont's *e*

The blurb for Matt Beaumont's e-mail novel *e* promises as much by proclaiming that in this work "The epistolary novel enters the Information Age" (2000: n. pag.). In contradistinction to Baty's psychologization of technology, his satire of office life seems intent on upholding the Adornian collapse of subjectivity into structures of appellation. The e-mails of which the novel is composed circulate entirely within the office environment of an advertising agency, where the central professional concern is to get the Coca-Cola account. The office personae emerge quickly, not only from the specific content of the e-mails, but also from their structure of delivery and exchange. One reviewer on amazon.com has said of this novel that "Having worked in an office full of gossip and passive-aggressive agendas, every single character in *e* was easy for me to picture" (pma 2004). 'e' stands for 'easy'. In fact, those who have seen the film *Office Space* or the television series *Office* will readily recognize several of the basic character types: the god-like CEO who writes only to hire or fire or complain and is so incapable of using e-mail that he always manages to carbon-copy the person he is insulting at the moment; two ditzy sluts, one male and one female, who of course find each other; the artsy-fartsy ex-hippie who ends every e-mail with a smiley-face emoticon; the nerd who uses blanket e-mails to advertise sales from his absurd collections of useless objects; the totalitarian manager whose every e-mail is full of directives such as which color bin to use to recycle various materials; the exec who finds a way to mention his rank and position in every e-mail he sends, etc.

As in many epistolary novels, the most interesting and cogent action is not reported, but actually carried out within the e-mails themselves. In addition, the meaning of each e-mail involves not only the text, but also sender, receiver, subject line, cc line, bcc line, date, and time, as well as frequently the visible quality of the text: font size, emoticons, graphics, etc. The protagonist is corporate; there is no individual character whose destiny the reader is to be concerned with. Most of the e-mails are sent on the intra-office system, are extremely short, and rarely if ever refer to extra-office matters, such as spouses, children, or hobbies. An interesting symptom for the way the resulting digital panopticon is constructed, and a difference from the epistolary novel, is that several e-mails are written more or less in the presence of the recipient. For example, the office Nazi, Susi Judge-Davis, writes the following to the female slut, Lorraine Pallister, while watching the male slut disappear under her desk: "What is Liam doing under your desk? Did you not read my earlier note re fraternization? Consider this a friendly warning" (2000: 164). Obviously, the sender is within shouting or signaling distance of the receiver, but actual contact is deferred by means of the e-mail system. Another character, the creative genius of the office, shields himself off completely from the outside world through e-mail. This deferral applies as well to the subject and object of desire in the novel.

Beaumont's is a popular novel, and of course (having spawned sequels like *e Squared* [2010] and *The e. before Christmas* [2000]), this is obviously not the first time that satire has worked by reducing characters to caricatures. New is that e-mail allows the characters to do it as a form of self-portraiture, which may be seen as an inversion of the humanistic self-portrait. These characters are as disappointed at entering the network as are Baty's. They just have not reached a level of self-awareness about the source of their discontent yet.

4 The Serial E-Mail Mystery: *The Daughters of Freya*

My third example, *The Daughters of Freya*, does not come in book form, but as a series of 116 e-mails to the reader's, in this case my, Yahoo! inbox. The positioning of the reader in this case is quite different. Unlike in *e*, where the readers might come away with a sense of plenitude of their own life experiences compared to the sterility of the office environment, *The Daughters of Freya* goes out of the way to enrich its characters with family conflicts, etc., while collapsing the reader into the structure of e-mail exchange and data-mining. For example, the second e-mail of the novel includes a number of details related to State College and to Penn State, where I am located:

> Hi Jane,
>
> It's hard to believe that it's been more than thirty years since we used to perch on the Wall on College Avenue, smoking a joint after one of Dr. B's lectures on Law and Ethics and giggling at the parade of absurdity that was Penn State circa 1972. Remember those all-nighters at the Collegian when you, Tom and I would be trying to put the paper to bed, arguing over every word as if a misplaced comma would prolong the war? (Betcherman 2005: message 2)

The details quoted above are not entered in order to provoke my interest, but to show me my complete lack of privacy within the epistolary web. Secondly, in Adornian fashion they collapse the distinction between art and advertisement, since the technology for personalizing my e-mails clearly derives from that for creating "smart ads", and lays bare the fact that e-mail, messages, cookies, and everything else in the Internet all comes under the heading of data-mining. A blogger who reviewed this novel unfavorably seems to remark on this overlap between fiction and surveillance:

> Imagine an author stands in the corner of your bedroom. Every night the author watches as you go to bed. He doesn't care if you're tired, busy, worked a 20 hour day or reading another book; he just waits to see if you pick up his. If you don't, he picks up his clipboard and puts a red cross by your name. If I have not picked up his book over a two week period the author storms up to me, wherever I am, waving the book, and red-faced, spits out that he is taking the book away from me. If I want to read it, I have to come back and ask. (Dena 2005)

The effect of the electronic snoopery is to interpellate the reader; the subject of the novel is an exchange of e-mails and, sure enough, the reader receives many of them: three a day in my in-box, thus collapsing the distinction between literature and a day at the office. This idea of being networked even figures into the advertising for the novel in an e-mail I received on 14 December 2008:

The Daughters of Freya
A Mystery by Michael Betcherman
and David Diamond

An email from a desperate friend sends journalist Samantha Dempsey to California to investigate a cult that believes sex is the solution to the world's problems. She soon finds out there is more to the cult than meets the eye.

What makes it so much fun is the urprising way it puts you smack in the lives of the characters.
- Marietta Dunn,
Philadelphia Inquirer
Opening your email will never be the same again!

As Sunka Simon (2002: 213) points out, then, the artist here has become a technologist with the capacity to hone in on each reader's IP address and adduce datapoints that construct a personalized world for him. The *frisson* is even greater than in the traditional epistolary novel, both because the opening e-mails can be altered to situate each reader, and also because the e-mails are received in their raw digital state. There is practically a one-to-one correspondence between the material of which the novel is composed and the material of its narrative unfolding – unlike letters, which must make the transition from handwritten or occasionally typewritten format to print. Secondly, the e-mail format of the novel allows for the use of hyperlinks to provide additional documentation. Given that all these documents, from web versions of the paper the protagonist publishes in, to photographs of her and the editor supposedly taken at a restaurant they had lunch at, to airplane itineraries and credit-card records, originated in digital format anyway, together they give a Baudrillardian "effect of the hyperreal." According to the authors, "several readers have commented that when the book ended they felt as if their friends had stopped writing them. And others have said that they found themselves wondering throughout the day how the characters were getting along, and had to remind themselves that they were fictional" (Visser 2005). The authors hope to move to the next level, the text-message novel, which will only become commercially feasible with unlimited service for a monthly fee and message lengths of 2000 or more characters. The *ketai shousetsu* or cellphone novel, which like *Daughters* is received as separate text message "chapters" on a reader's cellphone, reached extraordinary levels of popularity in Japan in the first decade of the twenty-first century, with the most popular examples being (re)issued as print books(!) and spawning movie adaptations. There seems to be little appetite for such a form in Europe or North America.

Such a set-up represents even further integration of the reader into the text, since it resembles the very real experiences of receiving wrong text messages. Unlike wrong numbers, where the perception of error generally curtails the message, errant texts always arrive at their destinations. I have, for example, a set of 15 or so such messages from a single number on my cell phone. I foolishly deleted a few early ones before realizing that I was receiving from a real person, for free, and at about the rate of three per day, what I had paid some authors to generate for me as a fiction, with messages such as the following, all from a single individual:

1. Morning babe, love you. Have a great day at the lake. Thinkin of you. [A nice bucolic beginning and a clear statement of a classic love relation]
2. G'night babe
3. Okay asshat... at least say hi or stfu ;p [The first of many similar phatic messages]
4. No word for awhile. You okay? [As a sign of tenderness (or lack of other things to do), "You" is spelled out rather than the normal "U." Note the ambiguity of "no word"; we do not live by bread alone]
5. Gonna go out for a bit. Left ya messages all over the place. Its about 130pm Sunday [Similarly, "go out" is ambiguous; work or play?]
6. I'm back babe. Had kitchen flood – bad dishwasher. How is Civ? Be SURE to download Fall from Heaven II from gameflood.com for civ [Similar suspense as to the identity of CIV. How is Civilization? Indeed, how is it, and how IS it?]
7. In the shop... pretty bad reception but seem to beable [sic] to txt. LoL Have ½ bar of dignal [sic]. Love ya [Notice the incessant self-reference; there is apparently nothing else to text about other than texting; communication is about communication (Luhmann).]
8. Heh... re-read yer txt to me. Real nice Tolson. Way to make me feel loved. [Sounds ironic, but can I be sure it is?]
9. when you say things like that to me... especially in response to what I said to you in my txt... makes me think why do I bother trying sometimes. :(
10. I love you. Wish you would see that in my text instead of criticizing me for what time I sent it baby. Kinda bummed about that.
11. –hugs you- On road to Vegas. Thinkin about you and hope you are doing better.
12. You okay? Nothing from you today. [Here I start to feel guilty for not messaging myself and warning that I am getting these messages instead of her boyfriend. I had already indicated, back around message #2, that this was the wrong number.]

13. Hey handsome! Miss ya... haven't heard from you so I hope you are doing okay. – hugs -
14. Hey... if you don't message me back... or even on your own... that kinda blows. Sends me quite a message all in itself.
15. Look... this is funny shit to me cuz you made a point to be sure I messaged you daily. I frickin did... you chose to ignore me the whole time. So...
16. It seems to me it is I that needs to take the hint and as you so lovingly put it... not bother. jesus [For some reason I received this message twice. My guilt – see #12 above was activated again, and I messaged this person – as I had once long before – that she had the wrong victim.]

After three weeks of this, I finally sent an explanatory message that I was not the intended receiver, and got this in response:

17. My apologies. It appears Vorizon's [sic] txt messaging mixed up my boyfriend's no. with yours... Tob – short for Tolson [see #8 above; I have changed the name]. I have contacted Verizon on this issue as [The message cut off there. This was the last message in my private fiction]

True, this text-message fiction was not strong neither on plot nor on language, but notice that what counts for the happy recipients of *The Daughters of Freya*, as it did for Paige Baty, and perhaps for the fanbase of *ketai shousetsu*, was not content, but becoming integrated into the system.

Hence, while in Beaumont's novel the reader's own feeling of plenitude is reinforced by each appellation of the e-mail system that speaks the characters, *The Daughters of Freya* removes this level of comfort, since it places its reader in the position of being the recipient of each and every e-mail, and asks her to readjust her daily routines to the rhythms of the two or three daily e-mails of the novel's continuation. One senses that the theme of the novel was chosen to resonate with this theme of connectivity: a number of characters are working at deprogramming a young woman who has joined the latest Marin County cult, the Daughters of Freya, whose mission is ostensibly to save the world through sex. Eventually, the protagonist reporter unmasks the cult as a prostitution ring for wealthy clientele associated with Silicon Valley firms. The coercion and masking that drive the Daughters conspiracy allegorize those of electronic surveillance in general. Concomitantly, the deceptiveness and hyperreality of e-mail drives the plot of the novel. Whereas *e* flattens its characters until they have no existence outside their functions, *The Daughters of Freya* provides a depth that is fictional. A cult runaway identifies herself as "Fred"; above all, Tom of 1972, who supposedly had hung out on the wall in State College, begins corresponding with the reporter heroine of the novel, but turns out to be an impersonator linked with the cult who kidnaps the protagonist in the story's thrilling conclusion. As part of the family side-plot, the protagonist unmasks an online friend of her mother's as someone who has manufactured his place of residence, and has plagiarized a novel that the protagonist easily locates online.

If one were to consider my two novels as inhabiting the opposing limits of the e-mail narrative, we seem to have a zero-sum game at work: either the characters become completely functionalized, as in *e*, or the reader does, as in *The Daughters of Freya*. In each case, the humanist dimensionality and individuation of the other party (reader and characters, respectively) is larger or smaller. And in both cases, of course, what is writ large is the Adornian Whole, the untrue. If we move to the less easily classifiable text by Baty, on the other hand, we find both a fully developed if neurotic main character, and a reader equipped for resistance through the devices of postmodern autobiography.

5 The Joys of E-Mail

Let me end with a text that embraces e-mail joyfully and sees none of the problems that wiser adults find in it. Paula Danziger and Ann Martin's self-help juvenile novel, *Snail Mail No More*, describes itself as conversation by other means: "Now that they live in different cities, thirteen-year-old Tara and Elizabeth use e-mail to talk about everything that is occurring in their lives and to try to maintain their closeness as they face big changes" (2000: n. pag.). The story of Elizabeth and Tara is told entirely through letters, e-mails, and instant messages. Elizabeth faces the challenge of an alcoholic father, while Tara adjusts to having a new baby sister and learns to moderate her somewhat wild behavior. The difference in temperament between the two keeps their exchange interesting, but also provides the third challenge, as Elizabeth's sharp rebuke to Tara when the latter experiments with alcohol threatens to break their relationship (as shown by the spacing of dates in the e-mails that are sent). 'Luckily', Elizabeth's alcoholic father kills himself in a car crash, and Tara flies in for the funeral, restoring their friendship.

The novel takes every opportunity to establish e-mail as merely a faster form of letter, which thus improves relationships by allowing communication to keep pace with changes in situation or mood. For example, the text starts out with actual, mailed letters, authenticated by cursive signatures, which are eventually replaced by the simple typed sign-off. Unlike Baty, who must seek partners on the Internet whom she has never met in person, the girls commence their e-mail correspondence sitting side by side on the computer. As soon as they send and read an e-mail, they are able to commence its oral post-mortem. When Elizabeth flies back home, Tara remarks, "I was sooooooo used to e-mailing you and then being able to talk with you in person right away" (2000: 42). The redundancy is perhaps as strange as anything in Paige Baty. Why compose the e-mail and then talk about it? But this redundancy is perhaps the crucial sign of a healthy attitude towards e-mail. As a juvenile self-help novel, it would seem that *Snail Mail No More* also tries to provide models for the proper use of e-mail and instant messaging, as ways of extending and maintaining relationships rather than creating them. Given the generic imperative of adolescent literature to show a self in development, the less sanguine, deconstructive scenarios of the previous texts yield to a vision of e-mail as enhanced conversation.

6 Conclusion

According to some scholars of media, despite chosen terminology that would encourage us to think of e-mail as mail, and in spite of narratives like *Snail Nail No More*, in fact e-mail represents a radical departure from any form of writing hitherto known: "The vast majority of people who communicate via email do this without wasting a thought on how their posting arrives at the recipient. No one takes responsibility any more for the perception [Wahrnehmung] of what he has written. That was unthinkable in the case of traditional letters"] ("TOFU" 2002).[1]

The word *Wahrnehmung* (perception) evokes epistemology in a curious way: a letter- (or e-mail-) writer should perceive telepathically the perception of their letter. Some would dispute this claim in either or both directions – that letter-writers inevitably took responsibility for their writing, and that composers of e-mails never do. E-mail systems and the postal service both do more than merely convey a message as though it were a physical object. In mediating the message they become part of it, and they also draw both sender and receiver into their networks. The epistolary fiction that has become canonical – by Samuel Richardson, Choderlos de Laclos, and others – made this mediation part and parcel of the plot. The earliest generation of e-mail fiction made this self-reflexive *Wahrnehmung* seem inevitable as a defense mechanism to preserve the self as something greater than a relay point in a communications system.

---

[1] The original quote reads: "Der weitaus größte Teil der Leute, die sich mittels E-mail austauschen, tut das, ohne einen Gedanken darauf zu verschwenden, wie die Post beim Empfänger ankommt. Die Verantwortung für die Wahrnehmung dessen, was man geschrieben hat, wird nicht mehr übernommen. Beim traditionellen Brief war das unvorstellbar".

Works Cited

Adorno, Theodor. 1974. "Benjamin der Briefschreiber". In: *Schriften 11: Noten zur Literatur*. Frankfurt am Main: Suhrkamp. 585–586.
Baty, S. Paige. 1999. *E-mail trouble. love and addiction @the matrix*. Austin: U of Texas P.
Beaumont, Matt. 2000. *e. A Novel*. New York: HarperCollins.
Betcherman, Michael and David Diamond. 2005. *The Daughters of Freya*. <https://www.amazon.com/Daughters-Freya-Michael-Betcherman-ebook/dp/B00BF3EHY6.> [accessed 28 August 2006].
Byatt, A. S. 1990. *Possession. A Romance*. New York: Random House.
Cook, Elizabeth. 1996. *Epistolary Bodies*. Stanford: Stanford UP.
Danziger, Paula & Ann M. Martin. 2000. *Snail Mail No More*. New York: Scholastic.
Dena, Christy. 2005. "The Stranger in Your Bedroom". WRT: Writer Response Theory. <http://wrt.ucr.edu/wordpress/2005/08/25/the-stranger-in-your-bedroom/> [accessed 15 March 2006].
Hayles, N. Katherine. 2005. *My Mother Was a Computer. Digital Subjects and Literary Texts*. Chicago: U of Chicago P.
Hayles, N. Katherine. 1997. "The Posthuman Body: Inscription and Incorporation in Galatea 2.2 and Snow Crash". *Configurations* 5.2: 241–266.
Jameson, Fredric. 1991. *Postmodernism; Or, the Logic of Late Capitalism*. Durham, NC: Duke UP.
Kristeva, Julia. 1986. "Revolution in Poetic Language". In: Toril Moi (ed.). *The Kristeva Reader*. New York: Columbia UP. 891–936.
Nunes, Mark. 2006. *The Cyberspaces of Everyday Life*. Minneapolis: U of Minnesota P.
Pma. 2004. "Just What the Doctor Ordered". <https://www.amazon.ca/Novel-Matt-Beaumont/dp/0452281881> [accessed 26 September 2017]
Schumacher, Julie. 2014. *Dear Committee Members*. New York: Anchor Books.
Simon, Sunka. 2002. *Mail-Orders. The Fiction of Letters in Postmodern Culture*. Albany: SUNY P.
"TOFU". 2002. *Institut für Text und Kritik*. <http://www.textkritik.de/schriftundcharakter/sundc008tofu.htm.> [accessed 05 June 2017].
Turkle, Sherry. 1995. *Life on the Screen. Identity in the Age of the Internet*. New York: Simon & Schuster.
Visser, Gerrit. 2005. "Author Interview about an "e-pistolary" novel – an e-mail mystery". <http://www.smartmobs.com/archive/2005/10/29/author_interview.html.> [accessed 12 December 2005].

Silvia Schultermandl
Stuplimity and Quick Media Epistolarity in Lauren Myracle's *Internet Girls* Series

Abstract: This chapter analyzes the aesthetics of quick media epistolary novels with the help of Lauren Myracle's *Internet Girls* series and argues that through the adoption of a quick media format which mimics real-life conversations between three teenage girls, quick media epistolary novels generate both boredom and astonishment as aesthetic effects. The constant online presence, which is highly familiar to Myracle's teenage readers as well as their parents, materializes through the novels' fast-paced conversations, the representation of exaggerated outpours of feelings over minor events, and the linguistic appropriation of teenage slang and netspeak. These stylistic properties of Myracle's novels invite readers' curiosity in the protagonists' lives yet frustrate them with formulaic plotlines and predictable cliffhangers. Considering this instant-messaging as an aesthetic feature of quick media epistolary novels raises issues about the kinds of aesthetic effects such texts can have on readers. This chapter shows that this simultaneous experience of boredom and astonishment functions as a social commentary on quick media usage, especially on the discrepancy between 'using' online media to communicate and constantly 'being' online and available.

1 Introduction

Digital media facilitate various new literary expressions and storytelling practices (cf. Zuern 2003; McNeill and Zuern 2015; Hayles 2008; McPherson et al. 2013; Schreibman et al. 2013). In particular, Web 2.0 technologies offer easy access and limitless possibilities to construct and consume online lives and stories. As Laurie McNeill contends, "millions of people have taken up digital technologies to tell their stories, in public, to potentially millions of readers" (2014: 145). They do so by means of quick media technologies, "cheap, easily accessible, and omnipresent tools of communication which allow us to connect to each other spontaneously and effortlessly" (Friedman and Schultermandl 2016: 4). The stories people tell online—Sidonie Smith and Julia Watson call them "everyday" autobiographies (1996: 3)—appear in the form of various quick media formats, and invite questions about how online media have shaped storytelling genres and practices precisely because creating online lives has become effortless.

https://doi.org/10.1515/9783110584813-013

The ubiquity of new media technologies also shapes the form of epistolary novels. Novels written in e-mail format abound, and collections of blogs and tweets eventually also get published as books.[1] Quick media, in particular, have shaped new cross-over genres such as auto/tweetographies or novels that adopt the layout of social networking sites (cf. McNeill 2014; Schultermandl 2016). To the same degree that epistolary novels initially mimicked practices of eighteenth-century epistolary correspondence, contemporary epistolary novels mimic quick media usage and thus offer valuable insights into digital communicative practices. This is also the case with Lauren Myracle's *Internet Girls* series.

Lauren Myracle's *Internet Girls* series represents quick media conversations through innovative literary form. The novels are entirely composed of instant messages, and the books' format, layout, and stylistic properties reproduce the interfaces and practices typical of quick media conversations. The four quick media epistolary novels in Myracle's series capture the lives and quick media usage of three teenage girls in Atlanta: Angela Silver (SnowAngel), Zoe Barrett (zoegirl), and Madigan Kinnick (mad maddie). In the first installment, *ttyl* (2004), they are high school sophomores, in *ttfn* (2007) and *l8r, g8r* (2008) they finish up high school and prepare for college, and in the final installment, *yolo* (2014), they are college freshmen. Myracle's young adult novels – although mere conversations about seemingly trivial and banal events in the lives of three white, upper-middle class teenagers – are interesting for a discussion of quick media usage in contemporary fiction because they not only depict quick media usage but because they capture the characteristics of online lives: the feeling of constant availability, the experience of connectivity as a reassuring yet burdensome quality of late-capitalist society, as well as the dependence on mediated relationships to complement or even replace embodied relationships.

In this chapter, I analyze the aesthetics of quick media epistolary novels with the help of Myracle's *Internet Girls* series and argue that through the adoption of a quick media format which mimics real-life conversations between three teenage girls, quick media epistolary novels generate both boredom and astonishment as aesthetic effects. I argue that the constant online presence, which is so familiar to Myracle's teenage readers as well as their parents, materializes through the novels' fast-paced conversations, the representation of exaggerated outpours of feelings over minor events, and the linguistic appropriation of teenage slang and netspeak. These stylistic properties of Myracle's novels invite read-

---

[1] See Gerd Bayer's "The Right Sort of Form for 'The Right Sort': David Mitchell's Tweet-Story" in this volume.

ers' curiosity in the protagonists' lives yet frustrate them with formulaic plotlines and predictable cliffhangers. Considering this instant-messaging as an aesthetic feature of quick media epistolary novels raises issues about the kinds of aesthetic effects such texts can have on readers. My chapter shows that this simultaneous experience of boredom and astonishment functions as a social commentary on quick media usage, especially on the discrepancy between 'using' online media to communicate and constantly 'being' online and available.

2 Quick Media and the Stuplime

Myracle's novels in the *Internet Girls* series hold a particular ground in the tradition of young adult literature, namely the sub-genre of "chick lit jr.", a genre which "reflect[s] current language (including slang) and methods of communication that were not present or popular as recently as five years ago" (Johnson 2006: 143). It mimics the conversational style of the Millennials, and by representing their quick media conversations, also offers insight into the kinds of topics that motivate their exchange. Personal conversations at all hours of the day capture the nature of the three girls' friendship, as the following example from the first novel's opening chapter demonstrates:

> SnowAngel: hey, mads! 1st day of 10th grade down the tube—wh-hoo!
> mad maddie: hiyas, angela, wh-hoo to u 2.
> SnowAngel: did u get the daisy i put in your locker?
> mad maddie: I did
> mad maddie: what's the story?
> SnowAngel: i just know that the end of summer always throws u into a funk, so I wanted to do something to defunkify u. (*ttyl:* 1)

For non-teenage readers, this everyday chit-chat through which the protagonists affirm their close bonds in habitual, even ritualistic ways, lacks literary finesse, and the confrontation of teenage conversations certainly invites critiques of the nature and extent of quick media usage. Still, reading seemingly unmodulated representations of teenage conversations makes for a particular aesthetic experience worth theorizing.

In her groundbreaking study *Ugly Feelings*, Sianne Ngai argues that boredom and fatigue qualify as aesthetic responses in their own right. In literary texts, so Ngai proposes, boredom or fatigue can be prompted through texts that overwhelm readers by deliberately 'underwhelming' them with aesthetic form that seems unpolished or lacking finesse. Ngai terms the aesthetic response such texts generate "stuplimity", a portmanteau term connecting the sublime with stupidity (2005: 271). The 'stuplime', which revisits Kant's classical aesthetic category of the mathematical sublime, "reveals the limits of our ability to comprehend a vastly extended form as a totality" in an aesthetic form in which "astonishment is paradoxically united with boredom" (2005: 271). Stuplimity as an aesthetic response harbors valuable social criticism. Ngai proposes that in the case of modernist avant-garde literature, the repetitions and variations characteristic of Gertrude Stein's *oeuvre* have to be considered in connection with the technocratization of modern Western societies, cubist art, and existentialist philosophy. Following Ngai's observation, I argue that for a better understanding of Myracle's quick media epistolarity, the connection to increasing digitalization, late-capitalist exhaustion, and other contemporary social and cultural phenomena need to be taken into consideration. This acknowledges the "gentle, yet brutal, revolution" (Fischer 2006: 8) brought on first by the Internet and more recently by Web 2.0 technologies, which can be employed for various purposes ranging from the formation of online kinship to digital surveillance. It also exemplifies the overwhelming breadth of digital technologies and the rate of their continuous development.

Several contemporary authors of American literature have responded to this ambivalent role of the cyberspace, which enables new forms of interpersonal connections but simultaneously endangers personal privacy. Novels such as Jonathan Franzen's *Purity* (2015) and Dave Egger's *The Circle* (2013) fabricate complex fictional worlds through plotlines that connect across history and geography in an attempt to elucidate the overwhelming intricacy of the Web. Their narratives attempt to show what a fully connected world looks like, and what dangers this connectivity might yield for individuals, for society, for a nation. These novels approach the overwhelming dimension of the Web 2.0 through intersecting plotlines and key motifs that span different spatial and temporal locales and non-descript minor figures who yield unsuspected, and often malignant, potential. True to their metamodernist re-appropriation of early-twentieth-century modernism's experiments with narrative form (cf. James and Seshagiri 2014: 93; Burn 2016), these novels are insightful and mesmerizing, but they do not appropriate the complexity of the Web's overwhelming scale.

In contrast, quick media epistolary novels capture the sense of online availability by adopting the stylistic properties of online conversations. While the worlds they sketch are accessible, and may even seem trite, they perfectly express the feeling of being constantly online. Novels such as *Purity* and *The Circle* are overwhelming because their plotlines unearth hidden connections and give rise to a general suspicion towards the integrity of the right to privacy in the face of online connectivity. In contrast, the novels in Myracle's *Internet Girls* series inundate readers with everyday conversations exchanged with the promise of constant full disclosure – an issue about quick media usage many critical minds deplore.

Hence what characterizes the stuplimity of Myracle's novels is the lack of defamiliarization of her literary-discursive representation. Like Stein, whose literary style is central to Ngai's argument about stuplimity, Myracle opts for representational strategies which seek to unearth a linguistic essence of meaning production through literary texts: for Stein, this lies in the realm of "thick or grammatically moody language" (Ngai 2005: 250) full of repetitions, unidiomatic syntax, and neologisms, for Myracle, in the realm of everyday, colloquial registers which mimic the netspeak of instant messaging linguistically and typographically. As already indicated by their titles, the novels feature Internet slang and other idiosyncrasies of the blog sphere, including emoticons and secondary text, which indicates tension and exhilaration as, for instance, in Angela's euphoria that the boy she has a crush on is in her French class: "cuz – drumroll, please – ROB TYLER is in my french class!!! *breathes deeply, with hand to throbbing bosom" (*ttyl:* 6). This literary style simultaneously produces boredom and excitement in readers.

Emphasizing the stuplime foregrounds the aesthetic dimensions of quick media epistolary novels, including literature's property of what Jacques Rancière terms the "distribution of the sensible" (2004: 4). This understanding of aesthetics as an aesthetic-political project through which to enter into a dialogue with the world is indebted to Enlightenment philosopher Alexander Gottlieb Baumgarten's understanding of aesthetics as "a science of sensitive knowing" or "a science of how things are to be known by means of the senses" (qtd. in Weinstein and Looby 2012: 5). Myracle's novels, however 'unliterary' they may seem, are great material to investigate the sensitive knowing which allows readers to aesthetically experience what Hervé Fischer (2006: 9) has identified as the "digital shock". While their intended audience is teenage girls, any reader familiar with contemporary American culture will also recognize contemporary patterns of teenage life, popular culture, and quick media behavior, especially in a US context. My discussion of the stuplime aesthetics of quick media epistolary novels builds on recent scholarship which conjoins aesthetic and political interest in American literature. To consider the aesthetic experience of Myracle's novels allows me to attend to their "active work" within their embeddedness in "a wider cultural network" (Gaskill 2012: 384). This form of aesthetic criticism attends to the political fabric of the text in the sense of Eric Auerbach's assertion that "formal features of a text, matters of style, can be indices to large intellectual and cultural matters" (Strier 2002: 211). Literary style is therefore to be understood as "an active response to cultural and intellectual problems" and as a marker of "a distinctive space for imagining writing and its critics: that of the shifting interface between felt experience and intelligent discourse" (Gaskill 2012: 376).

The above-cited passage from *ttyl* is representative of the literary style of Myracle's work and exemplifies the aesthetic experience of both boredom and exhaustion: nothing spectacular happens, and the chatty tone of the teenagers is at times difficult to bear, certainly for non-teenage readers. In addition, the fast-paced exchange in the quick media formats which the protagonists employ to communicate with each other is exhausting and boring at the same time. This stuplime effect is also achieved through the extended form of the series and its hallmark characteristic of repetition and variation (cf. Kelleter 2012): Every novel in Myracle's tetralogy follows the same formula: all three girls experience a problem individually, and at the same time their friendship is strained by external influences such as Angela's parents' decision to move from Atlanta to the California Bay Area, a fellow student at school whose defamatory rumors put the "winsome threesome" (*ttyl:* 2) to the test, or the spatial distance and interference of different time zones in their conversations across states when they finally enter college.

Because they are so similar to real-life teenage quick media behavior, Myracle's novels intervene as conversation starters between teenagers and their parents about sexuality and safety: Internet trolling, compromising photos that go viral, and the reliance on quick media technologies as safety net in harmful situations are issues on which the series expounds. The conversational nature of the quick media epistolary style lends itself to casual and verbally graphic descriptions of sexual temptations, taboos, and desires young teenage girls might face. The books' content is far from innocent, a fact which has made Myracle's *Internet Girls* series not only highly successful but also particularly subject to public critique and sanctions. As America's most banned author (cf. Flood 2015) whose novels topped the 2011 and 2009 lists of banned and challenged books issued by the American Library Association (cf. *ALA*), Myracle has more impact on the contemporary literary scene than her literary craft would let suspect. Taking the stuplimity of Myracle's novels as a point of departure, this chapter asks: how are the genre conventions of epistolarity affected by the quick media format and how does this particular literary form affect readers' sense of recognition? Furthermore, what kinds of social criticism does Myracle's literary form enable? And despite doing so, which cultural norms does it affirm?

3 Quick Media Epistolarity and Recognition

The novels in Myracle's *Internet Girls* series consist exclusively of instant messages – and in the original edition also reproduce the interface of an instant-message chatroom, complete with scroll-bars, send and cancel buttons, and a cursor-arrow on every page. The literary rendition of these quick media conversations makes for a particular kind of epistolarity, one that mimics the features of informal, oral discourse and the linguistic properties of netspeak (including the use of emoticons, capitalization for emphasis, and dramatic secondary text). One such feature of quick media epistolarity is the orality of instant message conversations. Another one is the use of typography to express the protagonists' identities. While the three protagonists encounter similar problems, the novels insist on typecasting three different feminine clichés: Angela is romantic, concerned about her looks and appearance, and seems in need of constant external validation for her thoughts and feelings; Maddie is tomboyish, vulgar and street-smart (to the extent that this is possible for a suburban middle-class teenager); and Zoe is pious, insecure and proper. These character traits are also amplified by the nicknames and specific fonts in which their instant messages appear in the novel: Angela (SnowAngel) uses a curly font which caters to the cliché of girliness with which she is associated; her font also picks up the fuchsia, chartreuse, purple, and deepsky-blue color of the respective volume covers; Maddie (mad maddie) writes in a bold, black font implying more assertiveness and a level of aggression, which corresponds to her behavior among her friends; and Zoe (zoegirl) writes in a very ordinary unspectacular font, almost as if she did not customize her writing in order to call less attention to herself.

To the same degree that the online nature of the conversations shapes the stylistic properties of their literary representation, it also influences the generic properties of epistolary fiction as such. The orality of these chat logs also precludes lengthy narratives and therefore lacks the narrative arc of prose letters. Concomitant with orality is the quick exchange of messages. The rapid succession of messages resembles dramatic dialogue more than the prose narratives of conventional letters. This entails that each protagonist is "heroine" and "confidante" at the same time, sometimes even within one chat log (Altman 1982: 54). Similarly, the switch from "active" to "passive confidante" (Altman 1982: 54) occurs frequently in all four novels and signals an important development in the heroines' life. For instance, when Maddie feels betrayed because Angela broke a secret she promised to keep, Maddie retreats from the group by turning on an offensive auto-reply message:

> zoegirl: maddie, r u there?
> Auto response from mad maddie: shove it up your ass
> zoegirl: maddie, i need to talk to you, please?
> zoegirl: it's about mr. h.
> zoegirl: he wants to go hot-tubbing with me. and i don't know what to do.
> zoegirl: maddie?
> zoegirl: ok, well, i really could have used your advice, but i guess u don't care! (*ttyl:* 196)

As a passive confidante who receives the message but refuses to reply, Maddie temporarily interrupts the community-building, making in turn the foundations of that community (in her case mutual truth) apparent.

The novel's discursive representation of the modes and habits of quick media communication among teenagers mimics the conversation style of its intended teenage audience. Kerry Mallan, for instance, argues that "online communities produce a range of discursive practices and expectations, which attempt to constitute young people in particular ways" (2008: 66). How quickly these modes of communication change can be seen in the fact that in the second edition of the series, the signature chat room interface – which is less in use among Millennials these days – disappeared from the layout. Instead, the updated editions are also available in ebook format. Myracle's novels tap into the – often bemoaned – phenomenon that the Millennials generally spend less time reading fiction and more time reading each other's messages. While *ttyl* was first only published in print, the 10th anniversary edition released in 2014 specifically markets ebook readers or, as the book ad on Myracle's homepage specifies, the "iPhone generation" (n. pag.). Reading an ebook consisting of texts on one's smartphone connects the act of fictional reading to the ritual of constantly checking one's messages and is comparable to the particularities of reality TV, which also "shamelessly mixes the generic attributes of fact and fiction" (Kavka 2012: 179). These particularities of discursive representation and the fact that the novels exist in ebook format and can be read on one's smartphone, raise interesting issues about the relevance of quick media epistolarity and its impact on readers' aesthetic experience.

Quick media epistolarity also replicates the tedium of excessive online presence. As the opening passage from *ttyl* quoted earlier indicates, Myracle's protagonists are prone to hyperbolic expressions of minor details. While the representation of everyday conversations without much further defamiliarization may lack a discernible degree of literary style, it is precisely the mimetic appeal of the novels' discourse that allows Myracle to entice readers. As this example shows, quick media epistolary novels embrace this implied immediacy in order to allow the reader to recognize the protagonists' tweeting, texting, or instant messaging as part of the same cultural practices they themselves witness or perhaps even adopt.

In *Uses of Literature*, Rita Felski defines recognition, enchantment, knowledge, and shock as potential aesthetic effects literary texts may have on readers. For Felski, recognition is a key variable in readers' ability to establish a connection between the fictional world of the text and the world of the reader. Felski suggests that "[w]hen we recognize something, we literally 'know it again'; we make sense of what is unfamiliar by fitting it into an existing scheme, linking it to what we already know" (2008: 25). This leads Felski to conclude that "any flash of recognition arises from an interplay between texts and the fluctuating beliefs, hopes, and fears of readers" (2008: 46). While Ngai's stuplimity highlights the stylistic properties of the literary text, Felski's notion of recognition privileges readers' ability to be affected by the text. By describing recognition as a 'use' of literature, Felski not only participates in current debates about the distinction between literary and cultural studies (cf. Bérubé 2005), the singular properties of literary theory (cf. Bruns 2011; Paulson 2001), or the status of critical theory at the 'end of critique' (cf. Anker and Felski 2017), she also theorizes the complex relationship between text and audience. Through recognition, the reader can relate to the cultural context in which Myracle's novels are embedded.

Myracle's novels provide readers with many instances of potential recognition, especially in terms of recognizing the ways in which quick media can potentially make teenagers' lives even more complicated. Here, the conversational style of Myracle's quick media epistolarity intensifies the aesthetic illusion of reading the three girls' conversations and immediate thoughts. For instance, on one occasion in *l8r, g8r*, Angela's monologue sent to Zoe transitions from one topic to the next in an uninterrupted expression of random thoughts. Prefaced with a greeting and a declaration of intent – "i'm just leaving you a message" (*l8r, g8r:* 143) – Angela records her thoughts merely in the attempt to share them with somebody:

> SnowAngel: can u believe it's only a little over a month until we graduate?!
> SnowAngel: omg, that means we have GOT to figure out our senior quotes. when are we supposed to turn them in? the end of april?
> SnowAngel: aside from that, get this: i saw glendy last night. the girl is internet-obsessed. she made me look at her facebook profile with her, where she now has—yes, it's true—4,987 friends. ridiculous! (*l8r, g8r:* 143)

This discursive representation implies that Myracle's protagonists are "transcribing uncensored streams of consciousness" (Perry 1980: 128), a fact which has gained epistolary fiction the status of being the lesser fiction. Such assumptions have since been critiqued and revised (cf. Bray 2003), and critics have emphasized the aesthetic complexity and social relevance of epistolary form. Quick media epistolary fiction, however, as the above example shows, gives rise to the feeling that the protagonists compose and send text messages in an attempt to communicate feelings and receive responses instantaneously. This does, in fact, evoke the aesthetic illusion of reading a protagonist's immediate, unfiltered and unpolished thoughts. As is true for epistolary novels in general, quick media epistolary novels mimic the act of reading letters in the sense that what the recipient of a letter in the fictional world reads is also what the novel's audience reads. On the one hand, this facilitates identification of the external reader with the internal reader (cf. Altman 1982: 88). On the other hand, the external reader, reading in fact all and not only those letters addressed to him or her, has a fuller understanding of the story which unfolds through the exchange of letters and creates a discrepancy of awareness between reader and protagonist. Quick media epistolarity shares these features with conventional epistolarity, but in line with Janet Altman's credo that "the medium chosen by an artist may in fact dictate, rather than be dictated, by his [sic] message" (Altman 1982: 8), it allows readers to recognize their own quick media usage in the quick media epistolarity they experience aesthetically.

Recognition is therefore also a means of making readers bond with the characters and empathize with their teenage malaise. From a reader-response perspective, this accounts for readers' participation in actualizing the fictional text by drawing from their prior knowledge. In a broader, political context, Myracle's novels also invite readers to critically examine these familiar practices of online communication.

4 Stuplime Aesthetics and Online Connectivity

While readers' aesthetic experience of Myracle's novels builds on stuplimity, it also invites them to critically engage with online communication habits altogether. Quick media usage itself is a subliminal topic which threads through the individual novels in the series as they depict erratic and excessive communicative behavior which constantly negotiates the boundaries between the protagonists' online and offline lives. In *ttfn*, for instance, when Angela temporarily lives in California and grapples with the changes in her friendship to Zoe and Maddie, a brief monologue addresses the frustration over separation and the disruption of their online habits:

SnowAngel: r u there, zo?
SnowAngel: ohhhhh, it's, what, after midnight there? so yr probably in bed, while here i am, not even in the same TIME ZONE as u anymore!
SnowAngel: i hate this so much, zo. (*ttfn:* 77)

Unlike the example of Maddie's auto-reply message, which signals lack of interest, this passage foregrounds lack of availability at a particular moment in time. In turn, Zoe replies upon waking up in the morning and continues the conversation when Angela is still asleep. In both cases, the heroine assumes that the conversational confidante would respond promptly in order to solve a 'problem' which demands immediate attention. After all, online media technologies create infrastructure which enables incessant online presence and therefore also facilitate a lifestyle of constant online availability.

This phenomenon of the Web 2.0 caused a noticeable collapse of the boundaries between offline and online lives (cf. Fischer 2006). The effects on everyday lives have been noted within many fields of study, and the general consensus is that quick media technologies are sources of empowerment and vulnerability at the same time: notions of a democratic (easily accessible and affordable) usage coalesce with issues of user security and big data mining on the one hand and new social division along the infamous 'digital divide' (cf. Youngs 2004) between internet-savvy users and those who lack the resources to participate in this form of online communication culture on the other. Quick media are convenient and exhausting. In *24/7: Late-Capitalism and the End of Sleep*, Jonathan Crary theorizes constant online availability and connects it to late-capitalist exhaustion. Crary argues that "many institutions in the developed world have been running 24/7 for decades now", which has the effect that "the modeling of one's personal and social identity, has been reorganized to conform to the uninterrupted operation of markets, information networks, and other systems" (2014: 9). Crary's observation intimates a complex social phenomenon: because online media potentially allow uninterrupted online presence, they also demand actual availability with no regards to the life circumstances a person might be in (including work, school, or even sleep). Examples where the protagonists text during class, if only to explain that they are actually not able to text more fully, abound in Myracle's novels. In turn, giving explanations why they are not able to spend time texting, also acknowledges the imperative to do so in the first place and underwrites the 24/7 social expectation surrounding online communication.

Myracle's novels address these assumptions about online availability also through the stuplime aesthetics of instant-messaging and the absence of offline lives from the novels diegesis. Because the discursive representation exclusively features text messages, the novel privileges quick media usage above lived experiences. It is true that in the temporal references above every new chat the novels demarcate particular times when the protagonists do not chat, but even then they are constantly online, as the few references to intermittent absences due to a lack of Wi-Fi access or a dead battery imply. That they are even online when they are asleep or when they intentionally ignore messages by sending auto-replies also affirms that their online and offline lives are completely merged. Moreover, the quick media conversational format exposes readers constantly to online lives and, in turn, locks them in a fictional world which seems to consist of a 24/7 online connectivity. It is part of the stuplime aesthetic experience to never get a break from the online messaging universe Myracle's novels fabricate, disallowing the reader to enjoy a release from the exhausting sequence of exchanges. In Hannah Arendt's philosophy in *The Human Condition*, a natural cycle of exhaustion and regeneration defines the quality of life in pre-capitalist economics and conditions of labor (cf. 1985: 134); in the late-capitalist context Myracle's novels address and their readers probably experience themselves, this overwhelming online presence generated through quick media epistolarity replicates this pressure of constant availability.

Myracle's novels assert that being online is the new normal. This emphasis on normalcy is also connected to the particular normality the novels depict by presenting three white, heterosexual, able-bodied, cis-gendered, upper-middle-class protagonists. Instead of being affected by questions of gender or ethnic diversity, the protagonists' identity quests primarily tackle the assumption that online availability constitutes the major quality of a fulfilling social life. In the novels' plot lines, the importance of being online becomes tangible in conversations that question online presence. Like situations of intentional and circumstantial unavailability, these moments create suspense. In a conversation about Zoe's temporary withdrawal from the habit of texting several times a day, Maddie and Angela debate their degrees of dependency on quick media technologies:

> mad maddie: I'm just acknowledging the fact that sometimes, when crappy things happen, it's tempting to disappear for a while.
> SnowAngel: *narrows eyes*
> mad maddie: and again, I'm not saying we're going to LET Zoe disappear. but don't you ever feel like you're constantly "on"? like you're chained to your phone/tablet/laptop/whatever? like you cldn't escape even if you wanted to?
> SnowAngel: as in, do I obsessively check for texts, emails, tweets, snapchats, and FB posts?
> SnowAngel: NO
> mad maddie: I do. sometimes I want to smash the internet with a rock. Then I remember that y'all live in there, so I don't. (*yolo:* 75)

This conversation addresses compulsive online presence and the demand to stay in touch in order to affirm the integrity of their interpersonal relationships. Their online lives are therefore entirely determined by potential online availability. The fact that all their epiphanies and conflict resolutions occur while being online ultimately underscores the benefits of quick media.

5 Quick Media Epistolary Novels and the Ways We Read Now

Quick media epistolary novels like Myracle's *Internet Girls* series arrive on the literary scene at a time when the field of literary studies undergoes important shifts. Several programmatic projects in the form of special journal issues and edited collections theorize the relevance of form and aesthetics in analyses of literature's meaning-making potential. While interpretation and critique were dominant angles that shaped the study of American literature since the cultural turn, current projects pay more attention to the structures which enable texts "to do what they do" (Culler 2010: 910). This question is in no small part occasioned by the emergence of new media literacy and the virtualization of the literary text through new media technologies, which allow texts to morph constantly, even at the reader's own desire, and the words on the digital page to become fluid, even ephemeral, compared to their analogous format. At a time when literary critique seems to have "run out of steam" (Latour 2004: 225) and when the emerging field of digital literary studies invites scholars "to attend with some care to the precise ways in which literature and technology constitute one another" (McPherson et al. 2013: 616), the representation of online lives in quick media epistolary novels demands close attention to literary aesthetics. This enables an appreciation of the stuplime as a particular aesthetic experience which is connected to late-capitalist exhaustion. But more so than that, it also provides occasions to reflect on the more general question what a literary text can do (and in the specific context of aesthetic experience, what it does to and with us), a question which offers cues about the pleasure of literary reading and literature's singular status within the humanities.

Works Cited

ALA. <http://www.ala.org/bbooks/frequentlychallengedbooks/top10#>
Altman, Janet Gurkin. 1982. *Epistolarity. Approaches to a Form*. Columbus: Ohio State University Press.
Anker, Elizabeth S. & Rita Felski (eds.). 2017. *Critique and Postcritique*. Durham: Duke University Press.
Arendt, Hannah. 1958. *The Human Condition*. Chicago: Chicago University Press.
Bérubé, Michael (ed.). 2005. *The Aesthetics of Cultural Studies*. London: Blackwell.
Bray, Joe. 2003. *The Epistolary Novel. Representations of Consciousness*. New York: Routledge.
Bruns, Cristina Vischer. 2011. *Why Literature? The Value of Literary Reading and What it Means for Teaching*. New York: Continuum.
Burn, Stephen J. 2016. "Second-generation Postmoderns". In: Brian McHale & Len Platt (eds.). *The Cambridge History of Postmodern Literature*. Cambridge: Cambridge University Press. 450–464.
Culler, Jonathan. 2010. "Introduction: Critical Paradigms". *Special Topic: Literary Criticism for the Twenty-First Century PMLA* 125.4: 905–915.
Crary, Jonathan. 2014. *24/7: Late-Capitalism and the Ends of Sleep*. London: Verso.
Felski, Rita. 2008. *Uses of Literature*. Malden, MA: Blackwell Publishing.
Fischer, Hervé. 2006. *Digital Shock. Confronting the New Reality*. Montreal: McGill.
Flood, Alison. 2015. "Author Lauren Myracle calls on overprotective parents to stop banning books". *The Guardian* September 25. <https://www.theguardian.com/books/2015/sep/25/author-lauren-myracle-calls-on-overprotective-parents-to-stop-banning-books> [accessed 10 September 2017].
Friedman, May & Silvia Schultermandl. 2016. "Introduction". In: May Friedman & Silvia Schultermandl (eds.). *Click and Kin: Transnational Identity and Quick Media*. Toronto: University of Toronto Press. 3–24.
Gaskill, Nicholas. 2012. "What Difference Can Pragmatism Make for Literary Study?" *American Literary History* 24.2: 374–389.
Hayles, N. Katherine. 2008. *Electronic Literature. New Horizons for the Literary*. Notre Dame, IN: University of Notre Dame Press.
James, David & Urmila Seshagiri. 2014. "Metamodernism: Narratives of Continuity and Revolution". *PMLA* 129.1: 87–100.
Johnson, Joanna Webb. 2006. "Chick Lit. Jr.: More Than Glitz and Glamour for Teens and Tweens". In: Suzanne Ferriss & Mallory Young (eds.). *Chick Lit. The New Woman's Fiction*. London: Routledge. 141–157.
Kavka, Misha. 2012. *Realty TV*. Edinburgh: Edinburg University Press.
Kelleter, Frank (ed.). 2012. *Populäre Serialität. Narration – Evolution – Distinktion*. Bielefeld: transcript.
Latour, Bruno. 2004. "Why Has Critique Run out of Steam? From Matters of Fact to Matters of Concern". *Critical Inquiry* 30: 225–248.
Mallan, Kerry. 2008. "Space, Power and Knowledge: The Regulatory Fictions of Online Communities". *International Research in Children's Literature* 1.1: 66–81.

McNeill, Laurie. 2014. "Life Bytes: Six-Word Memoirs and the Exigencies of Auto/tweetographies". In: Anna Poletti and Julie Rak (eds.). *Identity Technologies: Constructing the Self Online.* Madison: University of Wisconsin Press. 144–164.
McNeill, Laurie & John David Zuern (eds.). 2015. *Online Lives 2.0. Special issue of Biography* 38.2: v–323.
McPherson, Tara, Jagoda, Patrick & Wendy H.K. Chun. 2013. "Preface: New Media and American Literature". *New Media and American Literature special issue American Literature* 85.4: 615–628.
Myracle, Lauren. 2004. *ttyl.* New York: Amulet.
Myracle, Lauren. 2006. *ttfn.* New York: Amulet.
Myracle, Lauren. 2007. *l8r, g8r.* New York: Amulet.
Myracle, Lauren. 2014. *yolo.* New York: Amulet.
Myracle, Lauren. Book ad for the 10th anniversary edition of ttyl. <http://www.laurenmyracle.com/site/ttyl.html> [accessed 10 September 2017].
Ngai, Sianne. 2005. *Ugly Feelings.* Cambridge: Harvard University Press.
Paulson, William. 2001. *Literary Culture in a World Transformed. A Future for the Humanities.* Ithaca: Cornell University Press.
Perry, Ruth. 1980. *Women, Letters, and the Novel.* New York: AMS Press.
Rancière, Jacques. 2004. *The Politics of Aesthetics.* London: Continuum.
Schreibman, Susan, Raymond George Siemens & John Unsworth (eds.). 2013. *A Companion to Digital Literary Studies.* Malden, MA: Blackwell.
Schultermandl, Silvia. 2016. "Of Literary Letters and IMs: American Epistolary Fiction as Regulative Fictions". In: May Friedman & Silvia Schultermandl (eds.). *Click and Kin. Transnational Identity and Quick Media.* Toronto: University of Toronto Press. 118–136.
Smith, Sidonie & Julia Watson (eds.). 1996. *Getting a Life. Everyday Use of Autobiography.* Minneapolis: University of Minnesota Press.
Strier, Richard. 2002. "How Formalism Became a Dirty Word, and Why We Can't Do without It". In: Mark David Rasmussen (ed.). *Renaissance Literature and Its Formal Engagements.* New York: Palgrave Macmillan. 207–215.
Weinstein, Cindy & Christopher Looby. 2012. "Introduction". In: Cindy Weinstein & Christopher Looby (eds.). *American Literature's Aesthetic Dimensions.* New York: Columbia University Press. 1–36.
Youngs, Gillian. 2004. "Cyberspace: The New Feminist Frontier?" In: Karen Ross & Carolyn M. Byerly (eds.). *Women and Media. International Perspectives.* Malden, MA: Blackwell Publishing. 185–209.
Zuern, John David (ed.). 2003. *Online Lives. Special Issue of Biography* 26.1. v–242.

Silke Jandl
In the Age of Vlogging

Functions of the Letter in YouTubers' Fiction and Non-Fiction

Abstract: In the face of instant messaging services letters might seem to be a thing of the past. Yet, there is a noticeable trend towards letters and other forms of materiality in the artistic output of digital influencers. The fact that YouTubers and other social media stars are quite successfully publishing books is an indicator that there is a demand for the creation and consumption of physical objects. Letters, too, are inherently physical objects, and even invoking their materiality appears to be suggestive enough to make use of their continued cultural capital. As the several different uses and functions of letters in YouTubers' fiction and non-fiction publications between 2015 and 2017 show, letters, whether represented as material pieces of communication or in a purely metaphorical way, remain a valuable asset in the contemporary media landscape.

1 Introduction

In an age in which we have instant communication at our fingertips the art of letter writing and sending letters via the so-called 'snail mail' seem somewhat out of place and out of time. Ever since the emergence of e-mail as a household technology, the death of the (literary) letter has been declared, and instant messaging seems to have eliminated the need for letter writing once and for all. However, letters have not gone away, although their prime role as tools enabling communication has transformed significantly.

An area in which letters might not necessarily be expected to play a role at all is the YouTuber book genre. YouTubers are, after all, famously digital in their professional lives. However, looking through the works of young, successful YouTubers who have started to venture into the book market with their various publications since 2014, it becomes clear, that letters and epistolarity continue to serve multiple purposes, even in the writings of twenty-first-century social media (micro)celebrities.

In the following, several different uses and functions of letters in YouTubers' fiction and non-fiction publications between 2015 and 2017 will be examined. Questions raised include: why is the letter still used in publications that are otherwise so dependent on the digital and how are letters or the epistolary mode used in these publications? Approaching answers to these questions should furthermore help to illuminate whether letters represent a kind of cultural capital that is purposefully utilized for these books, and more generally establish the position of letters at the intersection of social media and the book market.

2 Fiction: Darcy's Letter in the *LBD*

The Lizzie Bennet Diaries (*LBD*) was a highly successful web series from 2012 to 2013, and in fact the first ever literary adaptation produced specifically for YouTube. In the process of adapting the plot of Jane Austen's *Pride and Prejudice* for the vlog[1] form and for a twenty-first-century audience the original story has undergone significant transformation: Lizzie Bennet becomes an independent and ambitious career woman, similarly Charlotte does not marry Mr. Collins, but rather works for him, Lydia is much more self-aware and manages to not end up in Wickham's trap etc. All the characters are rather well versed in all things technological: Lizzie and Charlotte study mass communication at university, Darcy is the CEO of Pemberley Digital, and Lydia repeatedly proves her proficiency in the use of social media. Their lives are consequently highly dependent on all sorts of technologies that have become quite natural to Millennials. Yet, significantly, one of the key plot points, Darcy's explanatory letter after professing his love for Lizzie, remains a physical letter in this modern adaptation.

The *LBD* was not merely a straight-forward adaptation, rather it was a transmedia storytelling experiment that told its story over the course of a year and on several Internet platforms besides YouTube – including, for example, Twitter, Tumblr, and Pinterest. The book releases of *The Secret Diary of Lizzie Bennet* (Su and Rorick 2014), and later of *The Epic Adventures of Lydia Bennet* (Rorick and Kiley 2015), are examples not only of further transmedial expansions, but also of the continued interest in the exploration of these characters, and their voices. As a transmedial expansion *The Secret Diary* does offer a few expansions on Lizzie's thoughts, the perhaps biggest expansion, however, is the inclusion of Darcy's full letter, the contents of which were only partially revealed in the web series.

Before delving deeper into the significance of Darcy's letter for this adaptation, and how it was handled, it is necessary to look at the assumptions and medial/narratological feasibilities underlying the two different media outlets in

---

[1] Vlogs are video blogs, primarily focusing on personal experiences or opinions that are usually delivered by one person to the camera and subsequently made public on YouTube or another video platform.

which the letter makes an appearance. In the YouTube narrative, Lizzie and Charlotte create the web series for an engaged online audience, and its content is constructed to be shown to as large an audience as possible. The book on the other hand is significantly called the 'secret' diary, and is presented as a reproduction of a homodiegetic diary that the character Lizzie is supposed to have kept while the videos were being uploaded. While the videos were clearly presented as being produced and marketed by the characters – Lizzie and Charlotte for the main channel, Lydia for the side-channel and the respective characters for their various social media accounts – the marketing of the book is no longer homodiegetic. While the book is clearly a further transmedial expansion of the *LBD* franchise, it is the only expansion that is not suggested to be published by any of the fictional characters.[2]

It is, in fact, the letter that turns out to be the most important element to illustrate why the publication of *The Secret Diary of Lizzie Bennet* by a homodiegetic character is incompatible with the character set-up. The transmedial expansion of the book is based on the promise that it will reveal even more details than the vlog did, yet in the vlog Lizzie makes it very clear that some parts of the letter contain information that she not only adamantly refuses to share with her audience, but that she also keeps from her best friend Charlotte as well as, initially, from her family. Elsewhere I outlined how some aspects that are only revealed in the letter are actually fed into the on-camera conversation in order to give the audience crucial information, a step that seemed necessary, since Lizzie's character growth to a large extent depends on her steadfast refusal to share large parts of the letter's contents to her audience (see Jandl 2014: 50).

In the web series, as well as in Austen's original, it is interesting to note that Darcy's letter is never actually sent. In both versions the letters are hand-delivered, which in both narrative universes underlines the delicacy of the content within, as well as the trust Darcy has that Elizabeth will not share the sensitive information that he entrusts her with in that letter. *The Secret Diary*, unlike the vlog, does present the letter in full, although with an interesting disruption. The book promises to 'tell-all' and to be the authentic diary made public, although clearly not in an intradiegetic universe. However, the letter that Darcy gives Lizzie in the video is ridiculed for its clearly outdated materiality: it is wax sealed and hand-written. Yet the letter that is included in the book, is computer typed rather than cursive. Even though it is, therefore, clearly not a reproduction of the

---

[2] This, of course, excludes the social media accounts that were devoted to behind the scenes material, social media accounts by writers, producers and actors etc., i.e. those outlets that might well be connected to the franchise and benefit the web series' promotion, but are not in any way connected to the homodiegetic world of the overall narrative.

original, the writers have still made an aesthetic decision that suggests that the letter has been included in the diary physically, complete with folded looking paper backgrounds and decorative washi tape securing the letter to the diary.

This decision raises a few questions that readers might not otherwise have asked: Did Lizzie keep a hand-written diary? Did she keep a digital diary? And if it was the latter, did she then print her diary entries and bind them in a book? The inclusion of something that is made to look like it is taped to the page suggests a physical diary, however, the rest of the book is typed. Another question that is then raised is why did Lizzie decide to type up the letter? One reason might be to circumvent the problem of the letter having been double sided, and thus of finding a solution that would not hide one half of the letter or result in loose pages in the diary. Another explanation might be that typing up the letter would allow Lizzie to exercise editorial power over what goes into the diary, which however, leads to further questions: Was Lizzie's diary not as secret as it is advertised to be? Are there still details in the letter that are not revealed even in the book? What did she do with/where does she keep the original letter?

A question that should be examined more closely is: why is it so important to preserve the illusion of materiality when it comes to letters. There has clearly been made a choice that sets the letter apart in *The Secret Diary of Lizzie Bennet*. This question, however, is not only relevant for the *Pride and Prejudice* adaptation, rather there is a broader tendency in products that come out of the digital sphere, that mainly, primarily, or almost exclusively exist in the virtual space, to foreground materiality, and the suggestion of materiality is more pronounced than in purely analogue texts. YouTubers seem particularly intent on the depiction of materiality in their books; thus, for example, Miranda Sings' *Selp-Helf* is a book that consists entirely of photographic reproductions of physical collages compiled into a book (Ballinger 2015), and Alfie Deyes' two first books ask their readers – or perhaps rather consumers – to physically interact with the pages of the books (Deyes 2015). A further example is an experiment like the limited edition of *The Amazing Book Is Not On Fire* where the YouTube authors Howell and Lester, with their publisher, go even further in their use of materiality, as it contains snippets of the audio book invisibly embedded in the front cover and is fully functional when headphones are plugged in. Thus, examining the suggested materiality of letters in YouTubers' non-fiction will provide a few hints as to the relationship between the physical and the virtual sphere of communication in letter-form.

3 YouTubers' Non-Fiction and Transmedial Expansions

The majority of the books YouTubers have published so far can be seen as adaptations of the YouTube content around which the writers have built an audience. However, given that there are several other media through which YouTubers also expand their personality brands (i.e. various social media platforms, live shows, television cameos, radio shows, podcasts, movies, documentaries etc.), it is perhaps better suited to look at the books as a further transmedial expansion to the personality brand that has been carefully created and curated over several years and over several media.

Although there are numerous approaches to transmediality, the focus will be on one of the best known that has been extensively theorized by Henry Jenkins. To summarize briefly, he says transmediality is "a process where integral elements of a fiction get dispersed systematically across multiple delivery channels for the purpose of creating a unified and coordinated entertainment experience" (Jenkins 2007). Jenkins mostly discusses fictional material, but his approach has been fruitfully applied to non-fiction.

While Jenkins envisions that all the media that form a whole together are ideally equal, and that those media provide medium-specific content, he is aware that there is very often a core medium or core story from which transmedial expansions emerge. The originating medium/story/personality is in this case of course comprised by the eclectic accumulation of YouTube videos by one creator over time, which forms the basis of the personality brand that has emerged as the principal point of interest for most subscribers.

What follows is a brief discussion of what can be considered a subsection of transmediality, and which I call 'autobiographical expansion'. This form of expansion is primarily interested in the multiplicity of ways many of which are concentrated on various social media sites to form a complex and coherent online persona. Autobiographical expansion furthermore encompasses the need to cultivate and regularly update this persona, as well as the incessant demand of the respective persona's following to be provided with ever more autobiographical input. The centrality of autobiographical expansion is demonstrated in the way that YouTubers' books are advertised. YouTubers and publishers have taken pains to market the books as more intimate, revealing more information, and presenting the YouTuber in an even more authentic light[3] than they are al-

---

[3] The promotional texts on the Simon and Schuster website (see http://www.simonandschuster.

ready perceived to be in their online content. When YouTubers go on to write their autobiographies, advice books, and other kinds of books, they often reiterate scenes they have already captured or discussed online but promise more contextualization and further insights into their personal lives in the books. One strategy for autobiographical expansion seems to be to write letters, or to have others write letters for them.

3.1 Letters from Family: Adding Authenticity

Eminent YouTubers have produced significantly more non-fiction than fiction, most of which focuses to a great extent on personal stories and advice. In these non-fiction publications, letters have taken on many different functions. Used most often in strongly autobiographical publications, it is surprising to note – given the tradition of autobiographical documentation – that personal letters are not included to prove historical accuracy.[4] Indeed, the letters included in these publications have typically been produced for the expressed purpose of being published for larger audiences in these books, rather than for individual recipients.

Two YouTubers have included letters or e-mails from family members into their autobiographical book publications. In both cases proof of authenticity seems to be the primary function of the letters, be it by presenting corroborating stories in parental voices in one case, or the proof of a sister's involvement and voice in the form of e-mails in the other.

---

com/), the publisher of virtually all American YouTubers' books, exemplifies the marketability of autobiographical expansion. Here is a selection of specific examples [my emphases]: On Graceffa's *In Real Life:* "A **confessional**, uplifting memoir from the beloved YouTube personality."; on Shane Dawson's *I Hate Myselfie:* "In *I Hate Myselfie*, Shane steps away from his larger-than-life Internet persona **and takes us deep ino the experiences** of an eccentric and introverted kid, who by observing the strange world around him developed a talent that would inspire millions of fans."; and on Dawson's 2nd book: "In this new collection of original personal essays, Shane **goes even deeper, sharing never-before-revealed stories** from his life [...]"; on Oakley "[...] Tyler Oakley brings you *Binge*, his *New York Times* bestselling collection of witty, **personal**, and hilarious essays."; on Franta: "In this **intimate** memoir of life beyond the camera, YouTube star Connor Franta shares the lessons he has learned on his journey from small-town boy to Internet sensation—so far."; on Franta's 2nd book "Now, two years later, Connor is ready to **bring to light a side of himself he's rarely shown on or off camera.**" And finally, on Justine Ezarik's (iJustine) *I, Justine:* "A one-woman media phenomenon and a leading YouTube influencer **takes readers behind the camera, and deep inside her world.**"

4 The only exception is Riordan Lee's inclusion of acceptance letters in *Caspar Lee*.

Connor Franta: "Letters from my Parents"

Connor Franta's first book *A Work in Progress: A Memoir* devotes one chapter to letters from his parents. These letters have been written to Franta upon his request and were always intended to become an element of added authenticity in his memoir. In a book that the then 22-year-old Franta wrote about himself and his life, his parents' letters are in effect the only other voices present in the book. Their contributions are meant not only to provide some further anecdotes but also to make Franta's history and character more complex.

The parental letters in Franta's book are also a form of autobiographical expansion, as outlined above. Importantly, Franta points out that "if you are to know a little more about me, this part of the book is a necessary step. So this is what my uncensored parents thought of me as a child. The floor is yours, Mom and Dad" (Franta 2015: 31). He, thus, sees it as inevitable to present different perspectives on his childhood, which his parents presumably remember more accurately than he can himself. Thus, opening the floor to his parents, as a gesture, is in itself more authentic than the content of said letters may be. Although the letters clearly represent voices different from Franta's, readers should bear in mind that they are carefully curated, rather than spontaneously authentic. Despite the assurances that the letters are 'uncensored' (Franta 2015: 31), they are not actually hand-written, but typed, which makes editorial work easy to hide as well as quite possible, if not probable.

Aesthetically, the two parental letters again are printed in the book in a way that makes them look like physical letters. Even more interesting than the visual background of crinkled paper and the slightly slanted positioning of the letters, is perhaps the choice of fonts. The type-faces in these two letters are highly important, as they, too, bank on the cultural capital of letters by suggesting materiality and by visually distinguishing the two letters from one another. Although rarely considered in the analysis of fiction, fonts do convey meaning:

> There is more to type that just being an invisible transmitter of words. The different shapes and styles of the typefaces themselves stimulate responses independently of the words they spell out, and before we even read them.
> Type triggers our imaginations, evokes our emotions, prompts memories and links to all of our senses. (Hyndman 2016: 26)

Especially in an era of visual abundance in new and traditional media, fonts are a further visual tool of meaning-making. In Franta's parents' letters the choice of fonts is clearly gendered, the mother's being slanted and cursive, suggesting neat handwriting and feminity. The father's typewriter font, on the other hand, suggests technological prowess, old-fashioned, perhaps, but classic and efficient.

The two letters, although written for the memoir and consequently for a large and diverse readership, are nevertheless addressed to Connor directly and, as characteristic for letters, consistently refer to him as 'you' in their letters. However, they do not contribute much new information to the narration of Franta's life, rather these letters read like sentimental accounts of loving parents who know that what they write is going to be made public. Nevertheless, they seem to achieve the intended effect of lending a form of authenticity to the autobiographical expansion that the book as a whole is, providing more voices that testify to the personality brand that Franta has created for his audience online. Thus, the mother's assertion that "you liked the limelight even then", and that "Speaking your mind and expressing your thoughts came easy", as well as referring to his art and computer classes as his "turning point" (Franta 2015: 32) are essential to corroborate the personality traits Franta is trying to show throughout the book, as well as reiterating the traits many readers expect and are familiar with from having observed the writer online for years. Similarly, his father's exclamation that "[...] we share a passion for the water, we love anything to do with videos and photography, we both like to lead by example and we were both 'chubby' as children (those genes you also got from me!)" (Franta 2015: 34) further reinforces the image that the videos and the book construct, while also presenting Franta's career as inevitable, and his talents as inherent. Furthermore, these epistolary voices stand for the family relationship often referenced in Franta's content, signalling the frequently invoked virtue of harmonic family life via a proud father's insistence on comparing himself to his son.

Caspar Lee: Sisterly E-Mails

In his book *Caspar Lee*, a South African YouTuber of the same name, has played with including different voices from relatives to a much more extreme extent than Franta has. The bulk of the book was actually written by the YouTuber's mother Emily Riordan Lee, and the text is continuously intersected by printed 'scribbles' from the YouTuber. In many ways Lee's book can be seen as an extensive exercise in meta-reference.

Apart from Lee's own written intersections, the book also includes a few e-mails from Lee's sister, Theodora, who has evidently been asked to look over certain chapters. Her comments are then included alongside a chapter, pointing to exaggerations, corroborating stories or adding quantifiers. Overall, the inclusion of these e-mails puts the writing process and the conflict of contradicting memories centre stage. Moreover, the sister's e-mails represent an alternative perspective, strengthen the perception of family bonds that the book tries hard to represent, and exemplify the modern way of communication, which is especially pertinent in a family as widely spread as the one that is the focus of the book: Lee living in London, his mother and sister in South Africa.

Even though this example does not include an actual letter, nor the depiction or simulation of the materiality of hand written or typed letters, the book nevertheless attempts to give the e-mails materiality and authenticity by representing not merely the copy-pasted content of the e-mail, but also insists on visually including the typical Apple frame around it, pointing to the physicality of the Mac-Computer on which the e-mail was evidently received. This simultaneously reinforces the YouTube brand, which in most successful YouTubers is, perhaps disproportionately, linked with Apple products.

Theodora's e-mails in the book are both addressed to Emily Riordan Lee, who evidently sent chapters that concerned her daughter to her to be reviewed. The e-mails, included at the end of two chapters are, thus, direct responses to the content of said chapters, with some minor additional information from the third perspective. The main purpose of these e-mails, however, is to solidify the notion of the close relationship between the siblings. Observing the interactions between a YouTuber and their various family members, partners and friends is one of the most popular types of content personality vloggers can make, and can propel the family member in question to some 'Internet fame' of their own.[5] Thus, those who are intent on accumulating or maintaining an online following are mutually interested in regularly displaying performances of their relationship in public. Given that the e-mails are presented with the Apple frame, and besides also include the subject line and the time stamp,[6] they are clearly meant to be seen as the real and original correspondence; however, it is impossible to determine whether or not the e-mails are indeed authentic. Nevertheless, the e-mails function as sibling-relationship affirmations. In response to a story in which the older sister played a trick on her brother, Theodora, for example, states, "Caspar and I were, and still are, very best friends [...]", and Caspar, in

---

5 Early YouTuber Charlie McDonnell's mother, for example, has garnered an online following because of her son's success; Joe Sugg, little brother of YouTube sensation Zoella, has also been able to carve out a career on YouTube because of his sister's success. Similarly, Theodora, Caspar Lee's sister, has enjoyed some fame online since she appeared in various of her brother's videos. Relationships between YouTubers are not only relatively common, they also boost the viewer numbers of both YouTubers involved to such an extent that the authenticity of the relationship is often challenged.

6 As mentioned above, the book is in many ways an exercise in metareference; the time stamps that are displayed with the e-mails are a further instance of metareference, as they point towards the time line of writing and editing the book, while also showcasing the manner in which it was written.

scribbles, responds to the e-mail, rather than the story: "Of course, I love you as a sister, Theo [...]," and "But, OK, you were a pretty good sister otherwise and I have been very nice about you in other parts of the book" (Riordan Lee 2016: 55). Even though Lee addresses his sister directly, the performativity of the familial bonds is unmistakably for the benefit of the book's readers.

3.2 'Dear Me' Letters

Writing letters to oneself is a common exercise in schools, creative writing classes, and advice literature; it is most commonly used as a tool to assess the current personal situation, to reflect on the past, and to visualize the future. Many YouTubers have taken inspiration from these exercises and posted videos in the form of open letters to their past or future selves.[7] In fact, 'writing' video-letters to an older or younger self has been a common practice, more or less since the onset of YouTube. In the YouTube and YouTuber book context, however, a communicative feature is added that is not usually part of 'dear me' exercises. The letters are not private self-reflections, rather they are public self-characterisations with thinly disguised elements of advice for recipients. This advice is typically tailored to the audiences' needs because experienced YouTubers are aware of who their viewers are and what they are worried about. Whether these letters are addressed to past, present or future selves, they typically revolve around the same themes; themes that teenagers often struggle with, i.e. the topics on which YouTubers are most often asked to give advice. As will be shown below, two young YouTubers, Jenn McAllister and Connor Franta, have both decided to use 'dear me' letters as integral parts of their autobiographical books.

Connor Franta's first book already promised to provide more and deeper insights into Franta's life. Indeed it dealt extensively with Franta's struggles coming to terms with his homosexuality and detailed his rural upbringing, school

---

[7] See for example the following examples of YouTubers' video letters to themselves:
https://www.youtube.com/watch?v=Gr7vsEUK610 (lukeisnotsexy)
https://www.youtube.com/watch?v=iJ6lzWBrFOA (jennxpenn)
https://www.youtube.com/watch?v=mLKnS4Cp1KA (the gabby show)
https://www.youtube.com/watch?v=_6wnxpNKeek (charlieissocoollike)
https://www.youtube.com/watch?v=HokiTQwctnQ;https://www.youtube.com/watch?v=uPcb1Q2nzgk (dodie)
https://www.youtube.com/watch?v=zU_g21F6W0M (Dan Howell)
https://www.youtube.com/watch?v=QRIfb03IT90 (Hannah Hart)
https://www.youtube.com/watch?v=3lZse-OB5o8 (LDShadowLady)
https://www.youtube.com/watch?v=exSYcNrDnDM (Hannah Witton)

and college experiences. Franta contrasts it to his second book, *Note to Self*, in the following manner:

> If my first book *A Work in Progress*, was a reflection of my exterior life so far, then this follow-up is a reflection of my interior life right now, and all the things that concern me – not so much a continuation of my story but more of a deepening. I'm here to spew my madness on the page and, perhaps, make a little sense of it along the way. Writing is my therapy. Sorting it out has, in the end, proven cathartic. (Franta 2017: 4)

The craving for ever more depth, ever more intimacy and authenticity is clearly evident in this quote, as is the marketability of the promise of these elements, as further made clear by the publisher's official description of *Note to Self*:

> Now, two years later, Connor is ready to bring to light a side of himself he's rarely shown on or off camera. In this diary-like look at his life since *A Work in Progress*, Connor talks about his battles with clinical depression, social anxiety, self-love, and acceptance; his desire to maintain an authentic self in a world that values shares and likes over true connections; his struggles with love and loss; and his renewed efforts to be in the moment—with others and himself. (simonandschuster.com)

One of the selling points is that Franta, again, includes two letters addressed to his past and future self in the book. The letter to 'Past Me' is, as many of the video letters referenced above, a way to solidify his current status by reflecting on how he got to where he is.

Simultaneously, this letter serves as a more or less disguised piece of advice to readers, in a similar vein to most YouTuber's advice literature, i.e. a mixture of reflection on their personal past with what they, at the time of writing, perceive as the lessons learned from them. This tendency can be seen implicitly in the introduction to his letter: "What follows is an open letter to all of those versions of my past self, from the age of twelve onward. If I'd actually received this note in real life, maybe it would've made things a lot easier..." (Franta 2017: 28).

Implicitly and explicitly it acknowledges teenage struggles as both universal and deeply intimate and encourages allowing those feelings. It also promotes the belief that the pain, struggling and suffering will ultimately shape the character of the person going through them. Looking back at his own life and reflecting on his current privileged position, Franta operates from a standpoint that his younger readers try to reach themselves, and thus, it seems as if he is implicitly trying to make them feel better about their situation while promising that their suffering will ultimately lead to something better. While, overall a positive message that is effectively aimed at younger readers rather than literally at Franta's past self, the letter is also not quite as revealing as the introduction and the marketing of the book would have readers expect.

At one point the letter hints at self-harming or even suicidal thoughts that Franta seems to have had at a teenage period in his life, yet the letter refuses to go into detail. On the one hand, Franta, thus, denies the full and authentic access to his mind that the book promises, while it also exemplifies his caution when it comes to the controversial topic of suicide. There is a larger debate going on as to whether or not suicide should be discussed with teenagers at all,[8] and Franta chooses to remain as vague as possible about this aspect in the letter. Presumably, many of his readers may not recognize at all that he is in fact hinting at self-harm or suicidal thoughts when he says

> [...] you'll experience intense self-loathing behind closed doors, bringing you within inches of doing something you know you'd regret. But these struggles don't need to be validated in text. You know how far south things have gone, and only you can feel the feelings you feel. Only you can fully understand what those experiences did to you. No one else. (Franta 2017: 29)

While this passage is kept deliberately vague, Franta does what a lot of teenagers seem to crave from YouTube stars in general, and from their books in particular: validation of their struggles and feelings without judgement or belittlement from the adults in their lives. Because of its vagueness the letter is relatable, a value that has only recently become common place in our culture and that has been embraced particularly by social media stars.

The sense of vagueness is much less pronounced in Jenn McAllister's video letter to her younger self, in which she reflects on the past two years in her life. The video mentions all the milestones from those two years, which regular viewers will be largely familiar with, in a reflective way. McAllister's "Letter to my younger self" was posted onto YouTube on January 3rd 2015, 8 months before her book was sold in stores. It is in this example that the deep interconnectivity between YouTube as a medium and the transmedial expansion in book form is easy to see. Given the delay in publishing a book, and the near-instantaneity of YouTube videos, it is likely that both letters were in fact written in very close temporal proximity. Moreover, McAllister has chosen to end her video letter and the letter in her book in very similar words: "Keep Creating, keep inspiring & keep dreaming" ("Letter to my younger self"); and "Keep being yourself. Keep Creating. Keep Inspiring. Keep Dreaming" (McAllister 2015: 235). Both letters are full of practical advice, of life-affirming encouragement, and a general positive out-

---

8 The controversy around the Netflix series "13 Reasons Why" based on the YA novel of the same name in which a teenage girl presents thirteen reasons for her suicide is a recent example of this debate.

look. Thus, both letters represent what McAllister wants her transmedial content to be, personal, encouraging and positive.

In the book, the letter to her 30-year-old self stands in for a conclusion. Rather than summing up the events of her life so far, or retrospectively reflecting on them, this letter is a manifesto of what McAllister plans to achieve professionally as well as personally, and it reflects her current set of values alongside her ambitions. Writing the letter in lieu of a conclusion, the then 19 year-old YouTuber showcases an awareness of her young age, and after a book filled with teenage anecdotes decides to look into the future rather than to provide another reading of her past.

Franta's second letter to himself, like McAllisters', functions as the final chapter of his book, and is also addressed to his future self. Similarly, Franta does not look too far into the future but rather he vaguely imagines his future self some ten years from 2017. He too reflects on his present, and focuses on professional and personal goals. In contrast to McAllister, Franta puts a stronger focus on personal and character developments than goals such as professional projects, living arrangement, travelling or relationships, and rather hopes for personal growth and insight. Generally, this letter is, again, not really aimed at Franta's future self, but rather a statement of his views as to what makes a good life, and the values this implies. It is thus, also, another character reference, showing that he is a good and happy person by presenting what he is striving for in the coming years. Both letters to the not-too-distant-future selves are effective conclusions for the books, as they pre-empt the frequent criticism of writing autobiographical books at a very young age, while also neatly tying together core values and motivations.

3.3 Letters as Metaphor: Anna Akana's *So Much I Want to Tell You: Letters to My Little Sister*

Anna Akana's subtitle *Letters to My Little Sister* seems to promise a collection of letters addressed to her younger sister Kristina, who, as fans will know, committed suicide aged 13 – Anna Akana was 17 at the time. While Akana engages with the suicide and her sister in the book, it is notable that she does not include actual letters at any point. Rather, she sees the entire book – which combines anecdotes from her own life since the suicide with pieces of advice – as letters to her sister,

> This book isn't just inspired by her, it's *for* her. I want to tell her what I've learned these past ten years. I want to tell her about all the mistakes I've made – and the hard-won lessons

> that came out of them. [...] This book is filled with the advice I that I would give her if she were still here, the advice I want to reach out and give to young, lost, teen girls who need it. (original emphasis; Akana 2017: xviii)

This makes clear that Akana sees the letters of her subtitle rather metaphorically. The subtitle, and especially the explicit reference to her sister achieves a few things: it suggests that Akana's account is authentic and honest, as she would presumably be in writing actual letters to her dead sister; also, letters are associated with intimacy, especially when addressed to a family member; and lastly, writing to a deceased younger sibling suggests a certain degree of vulnerability, a quality that readers love to see in their idols. Choosing the medium of letters in the title consequently enhances the suggestions of honesty, intimacy and vulnerability, as these traits are connected to epistolarity. Akana's choice to invoke letters in the subtitle of her book is furthermore indicative of the separation that Akana feels between herself and her younger sister. Letters usually imply a distance (geographical, temporal, relational etc.) that the writer seeks to bridge, thus, letters, i.e. the written word, are an attempt to fulfil the sentiment expressed in the title of Akana's book "so much I want to tell you". Her desire to talk to her sister looms large in this title and the book in general.

Despite a representational lack of letters in her book, she references a physical letter she wrote to her sister after the suicide, along with some of its contents, but does not represent it in full. This points towards Akana's insistence that the book is like all of her work for her sister in one way or another; all her screenplays, for example, are prefaced with the words "Dear Kristina". Moreover, the reference to the letter is there to exemplify her way of dealing with grief, her attempts to reconcile with the idea of death, and reveals some of her core beliefs. Relating her ongoing feelings of guilt, Akana goes on to tell her readers about the letter:

> I wrote her a letter. I said I was sorry, that I loved her, that I hoped she was okay wherever she was. I asked her to visit me in a dream to say goodbye, because I wanted so badly to see her one last time. I burned the letter, because it seemed like the only way to mail it to the afterworld. And then I cried. (Akana 2017: xvi)

Writing a letter was an attempt to simulate a way of communication and to bridge the distance between the living and the dead. Even though there is little expectation of any form of response, it is interesting that she would choose to write such a letter and to 'mail' it. The act of communicating, even if the communication must necessarily remain one-sided, and sending off the sentiments expressed in writing showcase the therapeutic value in simulating all aspects of letter-writing.

Furthermore, the invocation of the epistolary in the subtitle, introduction and conclusion serve as structuring devices. The fact that Akana's sister committed suicide in 2007 is the starting point of the book's narrative and allows Akana to disregard – or perhaps protect from public scrutiny – memories and lesson's from before that time. She discloses many personal stories, almost all of which date from after the loss of her sister, which allows her, in a way, to keep childhood and teenage memories connected to her sister – and also the rest of her family – private. While she, at one point, goes into some detail about her early school days, she is careful to keep the stories concise and to remain consistent with the overall point she is trying to make in the chapter, as she does, for example, in a chapter detailing her business skills by offering stories about her selling candy and art in school (Akana 2017: 81–83). Unlike other YouTubers' memoirs and autobiographical books, she does not try to evoke the image of a happy childhood, as for the most part her childhood is off limits. This, of course complies with the intention of the whole book being for her sister, who would not need reminders of memories she participated in.

4 Conclusion

In the face of instant messaging services via which anybody can instantly send texts, images and video, letters might seem to be a thing of the past. It is surprising then that there is a noticeable trend towards letters and other forms of materiality in the artistic output of digital influencers. The fact that YouTubers and other social media stars are quite successfully publishing books – one of the most traditional media, whose death has been falsely predicted and declared time and again – is an indicator that there is a demand for the creation and consumption of physical objects. Letters, too, are inherently physical, and even invoking their materiality appears to be suggestive enough to reap the fruits of its continued cultural capital. Indeed, as the variegated examples of different uses of epistolarity in YouTubers' book publications show, letters continue to be an effective and versatile tool in contemporary fiction as well as non-fiction.

In the *LBD* adaptation, Darcy's letter embodies the romantic notion of pre-digital times. It also provides modern viewers with a strong intertextual link harking back to the original version of Austen's *Pride and Prejudice* story and arguably a certain nostalgia for the Regency era. As an object, the letter in the adaptation serves most strongly to reinforce Darcy's characterisation: by choosing to make the letter handwritten – in cursive, no less – and have it wax sealed, he is unambiguously old-fashioned, traditional and marked as coming from a rich family. Simultaneously, producing a handwritten letter exemplifies the trust Darcy places in Lizzie, while also hinting at a potential distrust in the security of digital means of communication. Handwritten letters are, after all, unhackable and thus, the delicate contents may just be safer in analogous form, which implies an acute awareness of Darcy's position as a target for hackers.

In YouTubers' non-fiction, i.e. autobiographies, letters are used to aid in characterisation as well. Thus, letters and e-mails from family members are used to provide a different voice to add more layers of complexity to the respective YouTuber's character. Primarily, however, these letters are a form of written performance, showcasing the family dynamics and strengthening the image of the family that has been presented in online videos prior to the book publications. Letters have long been used in autobiographies as a form of proof of historical accuracy; in YouTubers' publications, however, they are included to demonstrate relational accuracy, i.e. to prove that the family relationships are indeed as they have been portrayed elsewhere.

When YouTubers write letters to themselves, rather than incorporating letters from family members, they do more than provide self-assessment and self-characterization. These letters are, in fact, tools to give advice in an understated way. Based on personal anecdotes, these letters are a way to circumvent platitudes and a potentially condescending tone in doling out advice. In analysing these 'dear me' letters as tools for communicating advice to readers, they are highly indicative of the purpose and motivation behind YouTubers' non-fiction books, which is, besides financial gain, their desire to help recipients by providing personal stories imbued with nuggets of advice.

Lastly, Akana's example of evoking letters in her book is an effective example of the usage of letters' enduring cultural capital. Especially values and promises associated with letters, such as sincerity, intimacy, and vulnerability are conveyed in her book. Additionally, her metaphoric use of the epistolary provides an interesting insight into the YouTuber/viewer relationship and opens the floor to thinking about all autobiographical YouTuber books as open letters to their most devoted viewers. In a way most of the YouTuber books can be argued to be a variation of a letter, the well-meaning YouTuber explaining and teaching the reader while also relating – one-sidedly, but quite knowledgeable about their readers – personal stories. Thus, letters, whether represented as material pieces of communication or in a more metaphorical way, remain a valuable asset in the contemporary media landscape.

Works Cited

Akana, Anna. 2017. *So Much I Want to Tell You. Letter to My Little Sister*. New York: Ballantine Books.
Austen, Jane. 2001/1813. *Pride and Prejudice*. In: Donald Gray (ed.). London, New York: Norton Critical Edition (3rd edition).
Ballinger, Coleen. 2015. *Selp-Helf by Miranda Sings*. New York: Gallery Books.
Bennet, Lizzie. Nov. 5th, 2012. YouTube. "Yeah, I Know – Ep: 61". *The Lizzie Bennet Diaries*. https://www.youtube.com/watch?v=rlZ86QA9Qro [accessed July 31 2017].
Bennet, Lizzie. Nov 8th, 2012. YouTube. "Letter Analysis – Ep: 62 ". *The Lizzie Bennet Diaries*. http://www.youtube.com/watch?v=QTS60Gll1HQ [accessed July 31 2017].
Deyes, Alfie. 2014. *The Pointless Book. Started by Alfie Deyes, Finished by You*. London: Blink Publishing.
Franta, Connor. 2015. *A Work in Progress. A Memoir*. New York: Keywords Press.
Franta, Connor. 2017. *Note to Self*. New York: Keywords Press.
Howell, Daniel & Phil Lester. 2015. *The Amazing Book is Not on Fire. The World of Dan and Phil*. London: Ebury Books.
Hyndman, Sarah. 2016. *Why Fonts Matter*. London: Virgin Books.
Jandl, Silke. 2014. "'The Lizzie Bennet Diaries'. An Analysis of the Online Modernized Adaptation of Jane Austen's *Pride and Prejudice*". Unpubl. Master Thesis, University of Graz.
Jenkins, Henry. 2006. *Convergence Culture. Where Old and New Media Collide*. New York and London: New York University Press.
Jenkins, Henry. 2007. "Transmedia Storytelling 101". Confessions of an ACA Fan: The Official Weblog of Henry Jenkins. March 22, 2007. <http://henryjenkins.org/2007/03/transmedia_storytelling_101.html.> [accessed 31 July 2017].
Jenkins, Henry. 2011. "Transmedia Storytelling 202: Further Reflections". Confessions of an ACA Fan: The Official Weblog of Henry Jenkins. August 1, 2011. <http://henryjenkins.org/2011/08/defining_transmedia_further_re.html.> [accessed 31 July 2017].
Keywords Press. <http://www.thekeywordspress.com/.> [accessed 31 July 2017].
McAllister, Jenn. 2015. *Really Professional Internet Person*. New York: Scholastic.
McAllister, Jenn. "A letter to my younger self". <https://www.youtube.com/watch?v=iJ6lzWBrFOA> [accessed 31 July 2017].
Riordan Lee, Emily & Caspar Lee. 2016. *Caspar Lee*. London: Penguin Random House.
Rorick, Kate & Rachel Kiley. 2015. *The Epic Adventures of Lydia Bennet (A Novel)*. New York: Touchstone.
Simon&Schuster. http://www.simonandschuster.com/books/Note-to-Self/Connor-Franta/9781501158018. [accessed 19 August 2017].
Su, Bernie & Kate Rorick. 2014. *The Secret Diary of Lizzie Bennet*. New York: Touchstone.

Elizabeth Kovach
E-pistolary Novels and Networks
Registering Formal Shifts between Henry Fielding's *Shamela* (1741) and Gary Shteyngart's *Super Sad True Love Story* (2010)

Abstract: The popularity of the first epistolary novels in Britain coincided with infrastructural conditions that allowed letter writing to become a common means of social connection. The epistolary novel of the eighteenth century offered a vicarious lens into the intimacies of, albeit fictional, relationships and social networks sustained by penny post. Such an intimate form of networking represented an activity that moved against the grain of compartmentalized life within an increasingly industrial economy and disciplinary society. Today, however, networking does not perform the insurgent function that it once did, as networked forms dominate virtually all sectors of sociopolitical life. Henry Fielding's *Shamela* and Gary Shteyngart's *Super Sad True Love Story* serve as case studies for registering what this transformation has meant for the meaning and potential of the contemporary e-pistolary novel. This paper proposes reading epistolary and e-mail novels as indices of infrastructural, technological, social, economic, and political forms. Such novels serve as reference points for registering diachronic shifts in historical contexts as well as for the meaning and significance of the e-pistolary genre.

1 Introduction: Registering Diachronic Shifts from the Epistolary to the E-mail Novel

As depictions of networked communication, epistolary and e-mail novels are also implicitly about infrastructural, technological, economic, social, and political forms.[1] All of these forms are inextricably linked: infrastructures and technologies make certain forms of communication possible, economy and politics drive infrastructural and technological developments, and social connection is in turn shaped by all of these structures and influences. Novels that simulate let-

---

[1] Some ideas and sources presented in this paper were first developed and cited in an analysis of *Super Sad True Love Story* in *Novel Ontologies After 9/11: The Politics of Being in Contemporary Theory and U.S.-American Narrative Fiction* (Kovach 2016).

https://doi.org/10.1515/9783110584813-015

ter and e-mail exchanges, from the earliest specimens of eighteenth-century Britain to the latest works of contemporary fiction, can thus be used as reference points for registering major historical shifts tied not simply to communications networks but also to the infrastructural and technological, economic, social and political environments within which these networks are embedded.

Henry Fielding's *Shamela* and Gary Shteyngart's *Super Sad True Love Story* will serve as cases for registering such shifts. Both works satirize their respective epistolary and e-mail novel forms as well as the networked structures and ways of life that were developing at the time of their writing. Although a comparison of these novels demonstrates the persistence of certain characteristics of the genre of the epistolary novel over centuries, it also sheds light on drastically different kinds of networked life. The epistolary novel of Fielding's time depicts a nascent phase of networking culture in which human connection through letter writing fulfilled a liberating, even "insurgent," function against changes brought on by urbanization, the rise of capitalism, and apparatuses of disciplinary control that increasingly compartmentalized life into a series of stages and alternating roles (cf. Kovach 2016: 156). Networking was thus a force that moved against the grain.

In the twenty-first century, however, what was once an insurgent activity has become a globally expansive norm. The advancement from telegraphic and telephonic to digital communications networks has, in the words of Mark Nunes, "transformed industry and the economy *as a whole* into a system predicated on networking" (2014: 356). What is more, discourses about the democratic potential of social networking have, most recently in the wake of the 2016 U.S.-American presidential election, been countered by discourses about the demonstrated use of social networks to act as channels of manipulation and control.[2]

The e-mail novel by Shteyngart depicts a dystopian world in which the dangers surrounding these trends and transformations are carried to extremes. In this novel, networks are apparatuses of political control that negatively taint the means and meaning of social connection. For Shteyngart, networking culture in full fruition is not conducive to the sense of liberation and openness that early letter writing seems to have allowed. Consequently, in their commentaries on the pitfalls and promises of networked communication and the ways of life that this

---

[2] Consider, for instance, the controversy surrounding the data–mining company Cambridge Analytica, hired to both sway the Brexit vote and the election of Donald Trump by profiling thousands of Facebook users (cf. Funk 2016).

enables, *Shamela* and *Super Sad True Love Story* also estimate the expressive potential of the e-pistolary novel in radically different ways.[3]

The identification of major shifts in the meanings and functions of networks that these two novels bring to light will be delineated in three stages: First, I will elaborate on my interpretation of form as both a compositional and contextual category of analysis. Second, I will contrast the ways in which *Shamela* and *Super Sad True Love Story* stand in relation to networked and other formal structures and lifestyles of their times. Third, I will compare what the novels respectively convey about their own expressive potentials, arguing that, while *Shamela* was composed at a nascent and optimistic phase in the life of the genre of the novel, *Super Sad True Love Story* is a novel that performs the exhaustion of its form. The optimism of Fielding's eighteenth-century epistolary novel and the pessimism of Shtyengart's twenty-first-century e-mail novel, I argue, is directly related to the dominant forms that structured life at the times in which they were written. To conclude, I will reflect on the major historical shifts that this comparison of novels reveals and suggest a further avenue of research.

2 Conceptualizing Form as a Compositional and Contextual Category

Epistolary and e-mail novels have similar structures, as both are composed as simulations of written or digitally transferred exchanges between characters. Even though *Super Sad True Love Story* reflects digital technologies that were unimaginable in eighteenth-century England, its composition follows a basic structure established centuries earlier. The novel is comprised of e-mail messages between the two main as well as various additional characters and one protagonist's diary entries, much in the way that *Shamela* is composed of letters exchanged between the female protagonist and various other recurring characters. Yet the meanings of these dialogic structures are more than exchanges in written communication.

The networked exchanges that such novels simulate can be read as indices of sociopolitical circumstances that condition communications networks and vice versa. My contention is that the networked forms of e-pistolary novels must be interpreted in terms of the networks and other formal structures that

---

[3] When I refer to both novels in conjunction, I use the term 'e-pistolary' to denote both the traditional epistolary form that simulates letter exchanges and the contemporary e-mail novel that simulates digital correspondence.

give shape to the sociopolitical contexts from which these narratives emerged and upon which they comment. This perspective is inspired by an argument presented by Caroline Levine in *Forms: Whole, Rhythm, Hierarchy, Network* (2015). Levine champions an approach to literary analysis in which form "will mean all shapes and configurations, all patterns of repetition and difference" (Levine 2015: 3). The adoption of such an expansive understanding of form results in

> immediate methodological consequences. The traditionally troubling gap between the form of the literary text and its content and context dissolves. Formalist analysis turns out to be as valuable to understanding sociopolitical institutions as it is to reading literature. (Levine 2015: 2)

The idea is that the "shapes", "configurations", and "patterns" that structure a poem, story, or novel can likely also be identified on a contextual level: "A rhythm can impose its powerful order on laboring bodies as well as odes. Binary oppositions can structure gendered workspaces as well as creation myths" (Levine 2015: 7). In other words, a literary work's structure should not be interpreted as merely a compositional choice but also as a "shape" or "pattern" that is formed and must be understood in relation to the structures of nonliterary contexts and circumstances.

The forms of epistolary and e-mail novels, according to this framework, are to be read in relation to other forms that shaped society, economy, and politics at the time of their composition. *Shamela* was written at a time in which letter writing was a novel behavior facilitated by new postal infrastructures. The forms dominating family life, work, leisure, and politics, however, were much more hierarchical and contained than those of the network. The epistolary novel's form thus contrasted with forms that shaped and impacted the way lives were predominantly lived. *Super Sad True Love Story*, in contrast, was written at a time and place in which networks dominated in virtually all sectors of society, economy, and politics. Reading these novels as forms that either contrast with or echo the forms that shape social, economic, and political life offers a perspective that elucidates the changing cultural roles and expressive potentials of e-pistolary novels over time.

Thus while the general form of the e-pistolary novel has in many ways persisted over its centuries-long history, its significance has continuously shifted. As Levine emphasizes, "while [a given form's] meanings and values may change, the pattern or shape can remain surprisingly stable across contexts" (Levine 2015: 7). This is certainly the case when one considers the forms of *Shamela* and *Super Sad True Love Story*, whose structural differences are, at face value, not particularly striking. One must look beyond the isolated forms of these novels to recognize the shifts in "meanings and values" that they represent. In the following section I shall therefore contrast the narrative and contextual forms of these novels.

3 Formal Shifts from *Shamela* to *Super Sad True Love Story*

Shamela is Fielding's famous response to Samuel Richardson's *Pamela*, which was published one year prior in 1740. *Pamela* is the story of a servant girl whose letter exchanges reveal how she resolutely resists the advances of her master. Pamela's virtue is rewarded, as her master eventually proposes marriage, enabling Pamela's entry into the upper class. *Shamela* is a bawdy parody of Richardson's sentimental tale. Fielding, in criticism of both the style and messages of Richardson's wildly popular novel, tells the 'real' story of Pamela, whose actual name in Fielding's world is Shamela, a scheming prostitute who calculates her betrothal to and seduction of her master from the very start through to their wedding night: "I behaved with as much Bashfulness as the purest Virgin in the World could have done. The most difficult Task for me was to blush; however, by holding my Breath, and squeezing my Cheeks with my Handkerchief, I did pretty well" (*Shamela*: 34). For every moment of virtuous behavior described by Pamela in Richardson's novel, Fielding provides a cynical counterpart in which the heroine's purity and innocence are undercut as mere posturing.

Nonetheless, both novels are meant to simulate the visceral experience of reading through real people's private letters. Apart from their opposing tones of sincerity and cynicism, both novels present exchanges whose content is intimate and confessional (although it is important to note that in *Shamela* every bawdy detail is always also a satirical meta-comment on the story of *Pamela*). While *Pamela* is meant to reach the reader as a sincere account and *Shamela* upturns this sincerity to expose it as a 'sham,' both novels aim for exposure and revelation in their own ways.

The effect of this exposure and revelation, in tandem with the sensation of the 'novel' literary form, was what readers of the time craved. In his discussion of the historical conditions that primed *Pamela* for sensational popularity, Ian Watt (2000: 443–444) emphasizes the "rise of economic individualism, the increase in the division of labor, and the development of the conjugal family" as a convergence of developments that characterized urbanized life in eighteenth-century England. These developments resulted in new experiences of social isolation and the compartmentalization of life into alternating roles and distinctly framed spaces.

The dominant form of social organization was that of the enclosure – or, perhaps more accurately, a series of enclosures through which people passed, each of which was characterized by clear hierarchies and prescribed roles. Watt elaborates upon the "city dweller's experience" by stressing

> the fact that he belongs to many social groups – work, worship, home, leisure – but no single person knows him in all his roles, and nor does he know anyone else in all theirs. The daily round, in fact, does not provide any permanent and dependable network of social ties, and since there is at the same time no other over-riding sense of community or common standards there arises a great need for a kind of emotional security and understanding which only the shared intimacies of personal relationship can supply. (Watt 2000: 449)

In Watt's description, the "social groups" to which one belonged and the "roles" demanded of a single person in eighteenth-century London were distinguished through the spatial compartmentalization of "work, worship, home, leisure". The formal structures underlying experience are described as a series of distinct spaces that do not flow into one another.

This formal arrangement led to a sense of fragmentation and transience and, as Watt phrases it, "[t]he daily round [...] does not provide any permanent and dependable network of social ties," which in turn gave rise to "a great need" for "emotional security" and "shared intimacies" (Watt 2000: 449). Letter writing thus became a way of sustaining personal, emotional ties, upholding and enforcing social networks, and thereby working against the disciplined ways of life that urban, industrial, capitalistic developments of the time demanded. The epistolary novel, in its simulation of networking activity, emotional confession, or, in the case of *Shamela*, the revelation of 'true' motives and calculating thoughts, was the cultural expression of what many people had begun to desire. The networked forms of epistolary novels, as well as the networking activities and infrastructures that they indirectly called forth simulated, collided, and contrasted with the forms that dominated the way readers' lives were increasingly organized.

Watt's description of the lifestyle that made the epistolary novel so appealing coincides strikingly with Michel Foucault's notion of 'disciplinary society' described in *Discipline and Punish* (1975). Gilles Deleuze, in his 1992 "Postscript on the Societies of Control" (1992), to which I will return in my discussion of *Super Sad True Love Story*, summarizes Foucault's notion of disciplinary society as follows:

> Foucault located the *disciplinary societies* in the eighteenth and nineteenth centuries [...]. They initiate the organization of vast spaces of enclosure. The individual never ceases passing from one closed environment to another, each having its own laws: first, the family; then the school ("you are no longer in your family"); then the barracks ("you are no longer at school"); then the factory; from time to time the hospital; possibly the prison, the preeminent instance of the enclosed environment. (1992: 3)

The eighteenth-century life characterized by Watt in terms of "groups" and "roles" is indeed what Foucault identified as life within disciplinary society. What I find worth emphasizing is the spatial form of the "enclosure" that both Watt (implicitly) and Foucault (explicitly) identify as the definitive trait of this society. The epistolary novel, not only in its promotion of networked narrative form but also in its depiction of people engaged in social networking, moved against the grain of disciplinary society in its early stages.

The form of the network was perhaps fundamentally appealing because it contrasted with the forms of enclosure that imposed disciplinary structure upon an industrializing society. While *Pamela* offered readers a sentimental world in which emotional confession and connection is sustained by penny post, *Shamela* – in addition to its systematic parody of *Pamela* – presents a female protagonist who exposes herself as everything other than what was socially expected and demanded of a young servant girl. In this way, the character of Shamela ruptures a social frame. Shamela's self-exposure through letter writing is enabled by a networked form of communication. The expression of her personality and identity, not to mention her mode of communication, flow outside of enclosures on narrative, social, and even infrastructural levels.

In 2010, the year of *Super Sad True Love Story*'s publication, the long era of discipline had given way to a different societal dominant. The genre of the epistolary novel had also broadened to include the sub-genre of the e-mail novel. This transformation entails, and is indeed promoted by, a new ascendancy in form structuring sociopolitical life. The behaviors of networking depicted in Shteyngart's novel, namely, do not move against but rather with the grain of a society, an economy, and political order largely predicated on networked structures.

In the world of this novel, set primarily in a New York City of the near future, each individual uses a smartphone known as an "äppärät" (cf., e.g., *Super Sad*: 39). In a parody of contemporary 'first-world' life, all characters in the novel are obsessed with and dependent on these communications devices, which are in active use at all times. The devices allow characters to meet the demands of the market and completely blend work with leisure time so that no distinction can be made between the two. When the novel's protagonist, Lenny, meets his friend Noah in a bar after having been in Italy for the past year, Lenny learns that Noah "would be airing our reunion live on his Global Teens stream, 'The Noah Weinberg Show!'" (*Super Sad:* 79). Their meeting is constantly interrupted by Noah's addresses to his phone, which records and broadcasts their interaction to a live audience, upon whom Noah is dependent for advertising revenue.

This confluence of work and leisure illustrates a key component of what Manuel Castells identifies as "network society," a society that is "made of networks in all the key dimensions of social organization and social practice" (2010: xviii). In network society, "the penetration of all time/spaces by wireless communication devices blur[s] different practices in a simultaneous time frame through the massive habit of multi-tasking" (Castells 2010: xli). This results in what Castells calls "timeless time," which is "the kind of time that occurs when [...] there is a systematic perturbation in the sequential order of the social practices performed in this context" (Castells 2010: xli; cf. Kovach 2016: 157). Such blurring of 'kinds' of time, not to mention spaces designated for different activities, immediately contrasts with the compartmentalization of time and space so central to disciplinary society.

Advances in networking technologies not only foster social networking but they also allow life to take on networked forms in which what were once alternating roles, spaces, and phases enter a continuous flow. This is a development that Deleuze also identifies, though he uses the term "society of control" to describe the sociocultural system that replaced disciplinary society and in which "the man of control is undulatory, in orbit, in a continuous network" (1992: 6). These metaphors of movement and connectivity describe a complete turn away from those of fragmentation and compartmentalization that Deleuze employs to describe disciplinary society. In the world of *Super Sad True Love Story*, Lenny and his friends certainly embody the "undulatory" mode that Deleuze describes. They are constantly engaged in digital networking activities, and not out of their own volition but rather as subjects of a society, economy, and labor market that demands that they engage in ceaseless activities of networked connection.

Shteyngart's novel is, as its title indicates, also a love story of sorts. Lenny meets and falls in love with a young Korean-American, Eunice. Their relationship is never one of true connection: Lenny is old fashioned, reads books, and seeks social connection in a traditional sense, while Eunice is fully immersed in digital worlds and interactions. At one point in their relationship, Eunice admits, "I never really learned how to read texts, [...] [j]ust to scan them for info" (*Super Sad:* 277), and she feels most in her element when browsing online retail sites (*Super Sad:* 308; cf. Kovach 2016: 154). Lenny, on the other hand, represents a minority that actually reads and owns books, which in the novel's world people have come to refer to as "bound, printed, nonstreaming media artifact[s]" (*Super

Sad: 90). He tells his books, "'No one but me still cares about you. But I'm going to keep you with me forever. And one day I'll make you important again.' I thought about that terrible calumny of the new generation: that books smell" (*Super Sad:* 52). Lenny's articulate prose contrasts starkly with Eunice's e-mail messages (e.g.: "What's up, twat? Missing your 'tard? Wanna dump a little supar on me? JBF" [*Super Sad:* 28]), and the alternation between the two writing styles dramatizes a transformation in communication brought on by the digital technologies the characters use. Lenny and Eunice live together for a brief period, always in a state of awkward disconnection, before their relationship comes to its 'super sad' end. As contradictory as it may seem, in this world of digital interaction, social connectivity is not at all conducive to senses of intimacy or even community. In fact, it fosters the fragmentation and isolation that private correspondence via epistolary networks in the eighteenth century strove to combat.

These glimpses into some details and the general tone of *Super Sad True Love Story* demonstrate how the novel satirizes a society predicated on networking. As a novel comprised of Lenny and Eunice's e-mail exchanges (though diary entries are also included), its networked narrative structure echoes rather than collides with what many have identified as the dominant form that structures sociopolitical life in the early twenty-first century. In the world of the novel, networks are by no means sources of insurgent, liberating behaviors that undermine the demands and structures of the status quo. Rather, they are vehicles through which political control is exerted.

This novel is not only a satire but also a dystopian rendering of network society. It corroborates what new-media and communications scholars Alexander Galloway and Eugene Thacker refer to in their book *The Exploit: A Theory of Networks* as follows: "the liberation rhetoric of distributed networks [...] is a foil for the real workings of power today" (2007: 16). As Galloway and Thacker explain, in "the high modern period, [...] the network form rose to power precisely as a corrective to the bloated union of hierarchy, decentralization, and bureaucracy" (2007: 15). This "union" had only just begun to take shape when Richardson and Fielding wrote their epistolary novels. In the twenty-first century, after "the network form" had performed its subversive function against the structures of enclosure that characterized disciplinary society, the "corrective" functions of networks are countered by the functions of control that they have also come to embody.

In *Super Sad True Love Story*, the U.S. government takes on the form of a totalitarian regime. People's 'äppäräti' are monitored, there are security checkpoints throughout the city, and scanning devices on street corners screen people's monetary health. The government ultimately performs what in the story is referred to as "The Rupture," a deadly orchestrated attack on the poor and those critical of the government (cf. *Super Sad:* 233). This is followed by a period of reconstruction in which people's 'äppärati' are shut down and reactivated in order to make sure that all networked communication is under the watch and control of the government. In the short period during which people's personal communications devices are momentarily switched off, some resort to suicide. Two people in Lenny's building

> wrote suicide notes about how they couldn't see a future without their äppärati. One wrote, quite eloquently about how he 'reached out to life,' but found there only 'walls and thoughts and faces,' which weren't enough. He needed to be ranked, to know his place in the world. (*Super Sad:* 270)

Without the networked structures to which Lenny's former neighbor was accustomed, life no longer seemed worth living. In this world of dystopian exaggeration, the form of the network, in the realms of communication, infrastructure, economy, and government, is void of subversive potential and functions as a dangerous, ubiquitous structure of dependency and control.

The novel's message about its own subversive potential is equally bleak. By contrasting the characters of Lenny and Eunice, Shteyngart puts two expressive modes on display. Lenny, a lover of classic literature, writes with a sentimental, confessional style that is in line with the kind of expression found in Richardson's *Pamela*. Eunice, on the other hand, communicates with a sparse shorthand prose that is purely functional – composed on the go on a handheld device – and is the antithesis of sentimental expression. Eunice repeatedly makes fun of and feels alienated by Lenny's desire for and display of emotional connection and intimacy. In this way, *Super Sad True Love Story* in many ways displays the dueling voices of sincerity and cynicism that *Pamela* and *Shamela* represent individually.

This indicates what I contend is an advanced stage in the life of the e-pistolary novel. In its advanced life, this novel unites the tones of sincerity and cynicism that, at the beginning of the genre's life, were represented by separate works. In this way, it reflexively comments upon the historical roots of its own mode of expression. As I will suggest in the next section, Shteyngart's novel is also pessimistic about its own potentials, and this pessimism is a direct result of its inability to formally conflict with the dominant structures of its time.

4 A Twenty-first-century E-pistolary Novel of Exhaustion

Richardson and Fielding were indeed inventors of the epistolary novel as a literary form in the English-speaking world, and their clashing modes of expression worked together to shape the genre. As Michael McKeon states in "Generic Transformation and Social Change: Rethinking the Rise of the Novel," the contrast between "naïve empiricism" and parody that *Pamela* and *Shamela* constituted indicates a vacillation between and instability amongst two different "epistemologies" of the time:

> I would argue that they [these epistemologies] attain stability not in themselves but in each other, in their dialectical relationship, as two competing versions of how to tell the truth in narrative, which, in their competition, constitute one part of the origins of the novel. The paradigmatic case is *Pamela* (1740) vs. *Shamela* (1741), since it is then that the conflict emerges into public consciousness and is institutionalized as a battle over whether it is Richardson or Fielding that is creating the 'new species of writing.' My argument is that it is, rather, the conjunction of the two. (2000/1985: 389)

McKeon stresses that the "dialectical relationship" between *Pamela* and *Shamela* has to do with competing versions and visions of what a novel can and should be. Fielding wrote *Shamela* as a rebuttal to the sentimental style and messages of Richardson's novel. He thereby put the satirical potential of the novel on display and promoted it as a way of undercutting pretensions and arriving at the truth by jabbing and undermining the "naïve empiricism" that *Pamela* epitomized.

I would add that *Shamela* undermines the culture that *Pamela* reflects. It parodies a mode of networking – letter writing – that, in the world created by Richardson, performs the work of upholding, even deepening and strengthening, a set of behavioral norms and expected roles. The characters of Richardson's novel develop their senses of self and reinforce their sentiments and morals through the practice of writing to one another. By parodying this vision of early networking culture, Fielding offers an alternative world in which letter writing is used to expose the unvarnished truth. For both writers, the novel is a vehicle through which they offer visions of the meaning and potential of social networking in a nascent phase of disciplinary society.

Both visions are optimistic in the sense that they are contributions to and constituting elements of a new formation. The immense popularity that they garnered attests to the fact that their experiments in literary expression struck a nerve. They supply rival versions not only of what social networking via letter writing can achieve but also about how the novel can put these potentials and limitations on display. According to McKeon, one of the two visions did not outweigh the other. It is the dialectical synthesis of the two that defines the early contributions of the epistolary novel.

Super Sad True Love Story contains this dialectic as well, with its dueling voices of sentiment and cynicism represented by Lenny and Eunice. However, its overall message about the expressive potential of the e-mail novel is pessimistic. In his persistent lamentations about the insignificance and unpopularity of literature, not to mention books in general, Lenny is the figure through which the novel functions as an autoreferential commentary on its own cultural impotence. While Fielding employed satire to exhibit the expressive potentials of the epistolary novel, the satirical bent of *Super Sad True Love Story* is channeled through a dystopian vision regarding not merely U.S.-America's sociopolitical future but also the e-pistolary novel's cultural significance.

At the end of the novel, the reader learns that the e-mail exchanges between Lenny and Eunice have been published within the world of the novel. Their e-mail accounts were hacked and their contents released to the public. Directly addressing the reader, Lenny describes his astonishment over the book's success:

> [I]t never occurred to me that any text would ever find a new generation of readers. I had no idea that some unknown individual or group of individuals would breach my privacy and Eunice's to pillage our GlobalTeens accounts and put together the text you see on your screen. (*Super Sad:* 327)

One reviewer comments on the archaism of Lenny's voice, stating that his portions of the text are "a tribute to literature as it once was" (*Super Sad:* 327), while Eunice's fully un-poetic messaging is praised as "interesting" and "alive" (*Super Sad:* 327; cf. Kovach 2016: 165). Linguistic mastery and precise composition are not of interest or value in this future world. As Shteyngart himself stated in an interview about the novel, the story is "about the collapse of the United States" as well as "the death of literature. [...] It's something I'm very worried about, obviously. Where things are trending" (Brown and Celayo 2009: 29; cf. Kovach 2016: 165). Shteyngart renders a world in which precisely such a depiction has little cultural value. Lenny fears and laments the prospect of literature's demise in the face of a digitally networked society whose means of communication work antithetically to a certain kind of literary expression.

Interestingly enough, the endangered kind of literary expression that Lenny's prose represents is similar to that of a character in Richardson's novels. Shteyngart thus continues the traditions of both Richardson and Fielding in the sense that he promotes both nostalgia for sentiment and sincerity while he also engages in an unrelenting satire of twenty-first-century control society.

Sincerity and satire are juxtaposed throughout the novel. *Super Sad True Love Story* unites in one work what Richardson and Fielding contributed in dialogue.

This indicates an advanced stage in the life of the e-pistolary novel. What were once individual, 'novel' experiments in the eighteenth century persist in Shteyngart's novel as well-worn and entangled traditions in the twenty-first. Yet while *Pamela* and *Shamela* were written in the spirit of breaking new paths, *Super Sad True Love Story*'s juxtaposition of sincere and satirical voices stages an impasse. Lenny's nostalgia for an earlier form of sentimental expression and the sense of interpersonal connection that it fostered is framed as a futile indulgence. However, Eunice's shallow mode of expression and existence is equally unappealing. Neither path leads to fresh territory, and so the novel oscillates between the two.

After the U.S. government stages the "Rupture" in the novel, Lenny moves to Italy. In a final scene, after he has told new friends about his experience in New York City at the time of the totalitarian takeover, he ends his narrative by describing what he had come to desire most: "silence, black and complete" (*Super Sad:* 331). In this moment, he "realized what was happening to me. I had begun to grieve. For all of us" (*Super Sad:* 331). This story about the demise of U.S.-American democracy and the waning importance of literature within contemporary culture ends in grief and with silence. In its imagination and satirizing of the dangers of living within a networked society of control, the novel points to the need for new methods and modes of literary expression but does not embody such a form itself.

In its oscillation between two exhausted modes of e-pistolary writing, *Super Sad True Love Story* is a tale of loss that merely declares the need for something other than itself without positively imagining it. *Shamela*'s satire, in contrast, is paradoxically a sincere effort to steer the direction of the epistolary novel's development. *Super Sad True Love Story* continues the tradition of the satirical e-pistolary novel but with a tenor of exhaustion. Its satire is performed in vain; its reason for being is to stage impasse and not move beyond it.

While Fielding's satire was charged with utopian intentions, Shteyngart's narrative exemplifies what has been identified as typical twenty-first-century dystopia. In a recent review essay on contemporary dystopian fiction for *The New Yorker*, Jill Lepore discovers a widespread pessimism:

> Dystopia used to be a fiction of resistance; it's become a fiction of submission, the fiction of an untrusting, lonely, and sullen twenty-first century, the fiction of fake news and infowars, the fiction of helplessness and hopelessness. It cannot imagine a better future, and it doesn't ask anyone to bother to make one. (Lepore 2017: n. pag.)

What I would add to Lepore's diagnosis is that failure to "imagine a better future" goes hand in hand with failures to find 'novel' forms of expression that would allow for such imagining to take place.

Perhaps this moment of impasse can, at least in part, be understood in terms of form. A novel like Shteyngart's simulates networked communication and, as such, reiterates the form dominant in and demanded within virtually all sectors of life. In their discussion of the network as a ubiquitous form in the twenty-first century, Galloway and Thacker claim that

> This is why contemporary political dynamics are decidedly different from those in previous decades: there exists today a fearful new symmetry of networks fighting networks. [...] To be effective, future political movements must discover a new exploit: A wholly new topology of resistance must be invented that is as asymmetrical in relationship to networks as the network was in relationship to power centers. Resistance *is* asymmetry. (2007: 15, emphasis in original)

Galloway and Thacker's conception of "resistance" as "asymmetry" can be usefully translated into the discussion at hand. As argued earlier, the appeal of the first epistolary novels was that they fostered networking activities that moved against the grain of the series of enclosures that defined life within an increasingly disciplinary regime. The appeal was born out of a formal "asymmetry." Now that the network form dominates, however, a contemporary e-mail novel like *Super Sad True Love Story* does not move against the grain. Rather, symmetry characterizes the positioning of this narrative within its sociopolitical environment. A lack of friction underlies its situation of impasse.

5 Conclusion: E-pistolary Novels in Relation to Sociopolitical Formal Contexts

Forms are used to define eras. Foucault's seminal description of disciplinary society focuses on the organizing structure of the enclosure and compartmentalization, while definitions of network and control society stress the ubiquity of networks and continuous flows. From the phone line to online communication, from the factory to the digital economy, from the panopticon to data surveillance, from the age of empire to global and finance capitalism, from warfronts to continuous drone strikes – shifts in structural paradigms can be measured in all realms of social and political life. The e-pistolary novel offers a unique case study for measuring such shifts, as it is a genre that from its beginning has simulated networked exchanges that are directly shaped by the infrastructural, technological, social, and political structures in which they occur.

To register formal shifts from *Shamela* to *Super Sad True Love Story*, I have defined 'form' in an open manner. Forms have been understood as structures and patterns that can be identified across texts and their contexts. The networked forms of the e-pistolary novels I have examined – which are both thematically portrayed and structurally simulated – have been read in relation to the forms shaping the sociopolitical environments within which they were created and upon which they comment.

By determining that *Shamela* formally collided with the dominant structures of its environment while *Super Sad True Love Story* stands in symmetry with the contexts that it aims to critique, I have arrived at several conclusions. Firstly, approaching form as both a compositional and contextual category offers a productive way with which to analyze literary form. Secondly, formal (a)symmetries between a given literary text and its context can be helpful in considering not just the expressive but also the political potentials of the text. Lastly, over its centuries long history, the epistolary novel has not undergone dramatic change in terms of its basic structure. Despite the fact that many contemporary e-pistolary novels simulate digital communications rather than letter writing, now a fully arcane activity, the basic dialogic structure of messaged communication persists. An appreciation of the drastic shifts that have taken place in terms of the genre's function and significance must thus be undertaken by considering form as both meaningful content and a contextual category.

This study has been an attempt in this direction via its focus on form, though there are certainly many other possible paths for research. One would be to investigate a larger corpus of contemporary e-pistolary novels to consider which exhibit degrees of exhaustion similar to *Super Sad True Love Story* and which, if any, are expressions of optimism and innovation. The question would then be whether exhaustion and innovation can be linked to a work's degree of formal (a)symmetry in relation to its contextual environment. Such a project could surely begin with a perusal of the primary texts presented throughout this volume. Exhausted or energized, the e-pistolary novel of the past and present offers a unique lens through which to consider not simply literary conventions and commentaries related to social networking and exchange but also the forms of infrastructure and technology, society, economy, and politics implicitly inscribed within these novels.

Works Cited

Brown, Sara & Armando Celayo. 2009. "I am the World, I'll Eat the World: A Conversation with Gary Shteyngart". In: *World Literature Today* 83.2: 29–32.
Castells, Manuel. 2010/1996. *The Rise of Network Society. The Information Age: Economy, Society and Culture Vol. I.* Cambridge/Oxford: Blackwell.
Deleuze, Gilles. 1992. "Postscript on Societies of Control". In: *October* 59: 3–7.
Fielding, Henry. 1999/1741. *Shamela*. In: Judith Hawley (ed.). Joseph Andrews *and* Shamela. New York: Penguin Books.
Foucault, Michel. 1995/1975. *Discipline and Punish. Birth of the Prison*. Trans. Alan Sheridan. New York: Random House.
Funk, McKenzie. 2016. "The Secret Agenda of a Facebook Quiz". 19 November 2016. <https://www.nytimes.com/2016/11/20/opinion/the-secret-agenda-of-a-facebook-quiz.html?_r=0> [accessed 19 June 2017].
Galloway, Alex & Eugene Thacker. 2007. *The Exploit. A Theory of Networks*. Minneapolis/London: University of Minnesota Press.
Kovach, Elizabeth. 2016. *Novel Ontologies After 9/11: The Politics of Being in Contemporary Theory and U.S.-American Narrative Fiction*. Trier: WVT.
Lepore, Jill. 2017. "A Golden Age for Dystopian Fiction: What to Make of Our New Literature of Radical Pessimism". 5 & 12 June 2017. <http://www.newyorker.com/magazine/2017/06/05/a-golden-age-for-dystopian-fiction> [accessed 19 June 2017].
Levine, Caroline. 2015. *Forms: Whole, Rhythm, Hierarchy, Network*. Princeton/Oxford: Princeton University Press.
McKeon, Michael. 2000/1985. "Generic Transformation and Social Change: Rethinking the Rise of the Novel". In: Michael McKeon (ed.). *Theory of the Novel. A Historical Approach*. Baltimore/London: Johns Hopkins University Press. 382–399.
Nunes, Mark. 2014. "Networking". In: Marie-Laure Ryan, Lori Emerson & Benjamin J. Robertson (eds.). *The Johns Hopkins Guide to Digital Media*. Baltimore: Johns Hopkins University Press. 355–358.
Richardson, Samuel. 1985/1740. *Pamela. Or, Virtue Rewarded*. London: Penguin Classics.
Shteyngart, Gary. 2011/2010. *Super Sad True Love Story*. New York: Random House.
Watt, Ian. 2000/1957. "From *The Rise of the Novel:* Studies in Defoe, Richardson, and Fielding". In: Michael McKeon (ed.). *Theory of the Novel. A Historical Approach*. Baltimore/London: Johns Hopkins University Press. 441–466.

Gerd Bayer
The Right Sort of Form for "The Right Sort"
David Mitchell's Tweet-Story

Abstract: David Mitchell's Twitter-Short-Story "The Right Sort" was published in dozens of tweets between July 14 and July 18, 2014. Later worked into a central episode of his (short) novel *Slade House* (2015), this short-paced experimental take on the epistolary form in a social-network age calls into question what 'letter' means in the digital age. Mitchell frequently elides the limitation of the social message service by employing a form of cross-post enjambement; yet he also demonstrates a commitment to restrict himself to the character limit as provided by the system, committing himself to a paratactical style that evokes another variant of the letter, the telegraph system. By engaging in this type of restricted writing, itself reminiscent of early post-war formal experiments in the style of OULIPO, Mitchell also puts stress on the format of the letter, which increasingly takes on spectral qualities, in full accordance with the short story's ghostly theme.

1 Introduction

Twenty-first century forms of communication increasingly rely on technologies based on virtuality and the Internet, with short text messages, electronic mail and social network postings all allowing users to share information with individuals or groups. Epistolary literature, while looking back on its own history of pen-and-paper letter writing, nevertheless has caught up with these changes, and various writers have played with the opportunities opened up by these newer forms of exchanging information. While Luddites are always quick to bemoan the end of civilization with the appearance of any new technology, a more restraint view of what virtual communication allows writers (and their fictional characters) to achieve will notice that aspects such as ease of access and speed of delivery are accompanied by dependence on technology (signal and battery power) and new forms of restriction that require stylistic accommodation, as in the case of the character limits imposed by Twitter.

    Concepción Torres Begines traces the history of Twitter literature – which she terms in Spanish "Twitteratura" and "Tuiteratura" – to a moment in 2008, when Matt Richtel wrote what he termed a "Twiller", that is a thriller written

https://doi.org/10.1515/9783110584813-016

on Twitter. Also discussing the tradition of the official #TwitterFictionFestival, Begines includes writers like Neil Gaiman, Jennifer Egan and Margaret Atwood in her discussion of Twitter literature (2016: 382), amongst whose key features alongside expectable parameters like brevity and hypertextuality she also lists synchronicity and virality (2016: 385–386). The latter two aspects of a literary text published through Twitter relate to its specific temporality: the moment of writing is almost identical to the moment of reception; and the speed with which reception can multiply clearly exceeds that encountered by conventional forms of print publication. However, it is obvious that both these aspects derive less from the particular constraints of Twitter and more from the technical nature of Internet and social media communication. Seen this way, both twitterature and twillers would be kinds of hyperfiction; and both can be seen as extensions of the tradition of epistolary writing.

2 Mitchell's temporalities

Given that Twitter fiction relies on a rather unique sense of temporality, it is not surprising that David Mitchell felt drawn to this format. Almost all of Mitchell's novels are marked by an intensive engagement with the form of narrative fiction, in particular with the relationship between subgenres of fiction defined by their length. Both Mitchell's greatest success, *Cloud Atlas*, and the two books that frame "The Right Sort", *The Bone Clocks* and *Slade House*, are examples of what have been called composite novels (cf. Dunn & Morris 1995). Alternatively, they could be seen as experiments or variants of the short story cycle (cf. Bayer 2018: 245–259). Mitchell's approach to fiction is clearly invested in testing out how the small-scale temporality of individual short narratives relates to our understanding of history and chronology, with generous asides that address ethical discourses related to colonialism, racism and the status of humanity in both pre- and post-industrial societies. Readers of Mitchell's fiction are invited to reflect how this two-fold chronological temporality affects their approach to culture and history as always already existing within a time-fold of presence and return (cf. Bayer 2015); for Mitchell, any eschatological reflection should be accompanied by the admittance that apocalyptic catastrophes have accompanied humanity for quite some time, in particular if one is willing to eschew a Eurocentric worldview and engage with the realities of cultures and biographies outside the mainstream. While this aspect of Mitchell's formal experimentation signals towards the small, with his works habitually consisting of shorter parts packed together to create a type of whole (cf. Childs & Green 2011), Mitchell's literary output can also be viewed in its entirety as creating a type of über-novel that

Sarah Dillon has aptly compared to a "house of fiction" (Dillon 2011). As characters from individual novels make cameo appearances in other texts, Mitchell's oeuvre becomes meaningful as the unique texts are placed into some form of communication, where elements from one text explain aspects of another. In this sense, each of Mitchell's publications exists simultaneously at a level that is below that of the actual physical entity of the book – for instance by consisting of only loosely connected short stories, as in *Ghostwritten*, Mitchell's first published novel – and at a level that transcends the covers of any individual publication.

In the light of this aspect of Mitchell's strategies of textual creation, it was only a logical next step for him to turn to one of the smallest possible scales as a means to reach beyond the confines of a recently published novel. With *The Bone Clocks* just finished, Mitchell published "The Right Sort" in 191 individual Tweets between July 14 and July 18 of 2014. Over the four day period, posts were fairly evenly distributed (clocking in at 38, 36, 40, 40, and 37 per day). When dividing the total number of signs used (24.554) by the number of Tweets, the average comes out as 128.55, showing that Mitchell mostly got pretty close to the maximum of 140 characters. Only nine posts (including the very last one) break up in mid-sentence and use three leader dots (…) to carry the reader over into the next post; one of them, markedly, keeps the reader in mid-sentence suspense between the final post of one day (July 17, ending with "No time, now. I'm running …") and the first Tweet of the following day (July 18, beginning with "… low, fast, hard"). A few times the narrative is in the middle of some sort of free indirect discourse, where the protagonist's thoughts are rendered in rather disconnected short junks that then carry over into the next post, with the overall syntactic pattern already tending towards paratactical disconnectedness, making the interruption forced on the discourse by the technological medium (Twitter's character limit) less of an intrusion on the actual narrating. For instance, as Nathan panics during the attack by a dog, two posts read: "and I'd scream if I could but I can't my chest's too full of panic I can't blast out it's choking me it's choking me because it's not Jonah" and "Christ it did Christ there's Jonah's head flipping side to side Christ from its fangs dangling by a flap of skin Christ closer closer closer". Both Tweets are free of any form of punctuation or conventional syntax, and hence the character-constraints imposed by Twitter hardly disrupt the 'flow' of language at this point in the narrative. While at moments like these, the outer constraints work seamlessly with the publication format, the same is also true at moments where the end of a Tweet coincides with the end of a sentence. The overwhelming majority of posts in fact consists of complete sentences that end nicely with a full stop just before hitting the character boundary. These posts may still feel truncated; yet they work nicely with the overall atmosphere of the short story, its breathlessness and the sense of disorientation as experienced by its main characters. In other words, the media environment suits the sujet; or one should probably reverse this and notice that Mitchell had chosen his topic well for the environment through which he was going to release it.

In the absence of any archival material that documents this work's genesis one has to resort to pure speculation when thinking about how Mitchell may have composed this short story. He may well have been in the kind of inspired flow that allowed him to type directly into his Twitter account; or he may have labored over the text prior to posting, with enough time to partition the narrative into small segments of just the right size. Given that the rules imposed by Twitter are famously inflexible and that so many of the posts fit the constraints so nicely, one is tempted to assume Mitchell must have taken the painful second route; yet one underestimates the gifts of writers at one's own peril. Given that the version of "The Right Sort" that opens *Slade House* shows signs of major reworking, it is at least clear that Mitchell did not commit to Twitter a piece of prose that he was already perfectly happy with. Indeed, the subsequent alterations and emendations imply that Mitchell was not really taking the format all too seriously, seeing his Twitter experiment as just that, probably with the added bonus of creating some sort of hyper-attention for his past and future publications. The Twitter feed that created his short story, seen this way, primarily served as a feeding tube into the Mitchell empire of selling stories (and books) to readers.

While one need not necessarily agree with the assessment that "Twitter promotes an increasingly sophisticated type of literary performance art" (Al Sharaqi & Abbasi 2016: 17), it is easy to see how, in a literary landscape largely driven by commercial directives and the need to compete with colleagues over the short-term attention span of a social-media driven marketing sphere, Twitter is seen as an attractive outlet by writers not just for its "casual immediacy" (Al Sharaqi & Abbasi 2016: 18) – a feature whose abysmal depths are excessively explored by Donald Trump – but also as a challenge against which they are willing to test their talents.

3 Epistolary resonances

The short bursts of texts make Mitchell's Twitter story resonate clearly with the epistolary form and its eighteenth-century encoding as a novelistic practice that allows authors to involve their readers by creating a fiction of intimacy and insight. Dating back to early examples such as *The Portuguese Letters*, which was a pan-European success in the late seventeenth century, or Aphra Behn's sensationalist roman-a-clef *Love-Letters between a Nobleman and His Sister*, which appeared in three volumes between 1684 and 1687, the epistolary form came into its own with Samuel Richardson's *Pamela: or, Virtue Rewarded* (1740) and J.W. von Goethe's *Die Leiden des jungen Werther* (1774). Published at a time when Enlightenment interest in personal and social betterment could align with a Romanticist fascination with individuality and moral torments, epistolary writing allowed readers to become involved with the most intimate feelings of a text's protagonist, gaining direct access to somebody else's consciousness (cf. Bray 2003). While the generic context may thus have evoked notions of reliability or what later critics may have described as an instance of a reality effect, even the early modern age had already grown partly suspicious when it came to the supposed reliability of epistolary forms (cf. Beebee 1999). Many texts even employed what is now described in scholarly parlance as epistolarity (cf. Schneider 2005) with the clear intent of signaling to their readers the built-in potential within any form of mediated communication to create falsehoods, deception and outright lies (cf. Bayer 2009). One aspect to which letters have attested as long as they have been used within literary culture is therefore the physical absence of a speaker and the impersonal relationship that also attains to the author-text-reader engagement (cf. Wright 1989).

Historically, epistolarity was clearly defined by the textual establishment of a form of epistolary 'you', a form of narratee to whom a particular letter is addressed. The relationship between the person writing the letter and his or her reader was usually one of close friendship or even of intimacy, allowing for the very kind of insight that the epistolary novel promised its readers; and frequently also delivered. As late as 1818, Mary Shelley's *Frankenstein* framed the embedded narrative of the ambitious scientist Victor and his creature with an equally ambitious scientist who writes letters to his sister, allowing readers to enter the diegetic world of Shelley's tale through a character whose professional background combined with the privacy of the epistolary conversation to create an atmosphere of trust and reliability. Walton's letters, supposedly including the first person accounts both of Victor and of his creature, thus extend the eighteenth-century epistolary novel into the early days of science fiction, the genre to which Mitchell's *Slade House*, the novel which would eventually come to include Mitchell's Twitter story, clearly owes a major debt.

While these generic parallels may well provide grounds for comparisons – with Tweets taking over as the form of communication that twenty-first century society has come to rely on and (sometimes) even trust in – there are also some substantial innovative elements in Mitchell's use of epistolarity. One crucial way in which "The Right Sort" departs from the prehistory of its genre is by its lack of addressee. Unlike the form of intimacy that historical epistolary writing established between writer and recipient, Mitchell's Tweets are not addressed to anybody in particular but rather constitute forms of what in an earlier social-media age may have been called posts or even blogposts. Here is a writer who makes his latest thoughts and feelings known by posting them through his personal account, allowing those interested in following his postings to take note of what he is doing. Given that Mitchell was already a well established, even major figure within contemporary British literature, one can safely assume that his Twitter posts – and hence also his short story – were addressed to his readers. This, however, substantially changes the diegetic balance of earlier epistolary writing in that it marks a clear and metaleptic break with the diegetic realities. Whereas earlier epistolary novels made epistolarity a feature of the textual world, with letters being sent back and forth between characters who exist within the (extra- or intra-) diegetic spheres of the particular textual creation, in Mitchell's case the narrative per se does not include any sort of epistolarity. To put this bluntly, none of the characters that Mitchell invents for "The Right Sort" have any clue that they are part of a Twitter story; and they furthermore do not make use of the medium to which they owe their existence (while, admittedly, the final section of *Slade House* makes extensive use of cell phone text messaging). In other words, if this story in fact belongs with epistolary writing, then only through its form of dissemination and distribution, which may or may not belong to the actual literary sphere.

This distinction becomes even more pronounced when looking at the future fate of "The Right Sort". When re-published as the opening episode of *Slade House*, there are no traces whatsoever that would signal to readers that what they are now reading as part of a printed book (or its ebook version) used to be an experiment in epistolary writing that relied entirely on a very different media environment. Given that the setting of the novel's first episode clearly predates the days of Twitter, the characters would have to understand their status of being-told through Twitter anachronistically. The element of epistolarity in Mitchell's text exists purely on the level of erstwhile transmission and as such does not affect the diegesis in the same way that historical epistolary forms affected the characters that actively made use of them. Unlike a lover in an early romance anxiously expecting a reply to a tender missive, nobody within the textual world of Mitchell's story is waiting for the next Tweet – it is rather the readers who are on tenterhooks, waiting for the next time Mitchell hits the submit button.

By keeping readers tied to this frame of expectancy, Mitchell not so much employs an epistolary mode but rather returns to the Victorian format of serialized publication. In the same way in which Charles Dickens's readers were waiting for a new installment to appear in print in order to learn more about the fate of Dickens's characters, those following the slow trickle of Tweets through which Mitchell released "The Right Sort" were hoping to see more text appear on their screens rather sooner than later; with the big difference that there was not a firmly established and reliable schedule of publication such as the one that Victorian readers would have enjoyed through the publication scheme of the weekly or monthly magazines that serialized long novels.

This shift in release structure also changes the way in which these two textual traditions employ tension. While both textual formats see themselves structured by a limit in terms of word count, Mitchell's Twitter story in addition has the ability to create suspense through the simple act of not posting further Tweets. This suspense exists strictly speaking not within the diegetic realm and as such is maybe no longer a form of cliffhanger because, after all, the hanging is now no longer being done by a character within the narrative but by the readers expecting the next posting. The individual Tweets simply do not provide enough space to create textual tension through plot devices in the same way that a longish section of a serialized novel can do. The fluctuating rhythm of building up suspense as found in serialized narrative is now replaced by a staccato of segmentation.

4 After the Twitter fiction

However, this particular form of epistolary suspense only applies to the singular event of the short story's original release through Twitter. Only then did readers not know how many more Tweets to expect on a particular day; or for how many days Mitchell would be able (or willing) to sustain his posting. Even a Mitchell reader busy at work during the day (or living in a different time zone) would be able to read all Tweets of a single day more or less uninterruptedly. And given that the very existence of this short story became well known to a larger audience mostly after *The Guardian* had reported about it post factum, one may wonder how significant the short story's existence as a Twitter story was in the first place, at least as far as its narrative reception is concerned. The occasion may well have been more of a news item, living off of the (supposed) sensation that an established writer had used this particular publication form; and here, of course, a big portion of the interest must have stemmed from the fact that Mitchell made his literary work available to anyone interested without any charge. When all these observations are put together, it becomes somewhat questionable whether "The Right Sort" really is a Twitter story; at least if the word Twitter is seen as creating any sort of formal descriptor and not merely a word that names the place of publication.

Leaving aside the concerns about the generic status of Mitchell's short story, its level of commitment to the legacy of epistolary writing, and the precise level at which readerly anxiety is triggered through the sliced-up nature of the individual Tweets, one can still find traces of an engagement with textuality that acknowledge, or at least toy with the idea, that Mitchell reflected on the right sort of form for "The Right Sort". The story tells of a pianist and single mother who takes her socially awkward (and possibly slightly autistic) son to a little soiree at a rather uncanny location. Located in a small side alley, called Slade Alley, sits the urban mansion of Lord and Lady Briggs, who otherwise reside in the country. The entrance to their house is hidden away behind high walls that run along both sides of the alley; and as readers (of the full novel *Slade House*) find out later, this small iron door is a gateway into another time-space reality, where superhuman forces of evil trap unsuspecting yet highly gifted humans in order to feed off their souls in an attempt to extend their quasi-eternal life span. Readers of early Mitchell might be surprised to find such a high dosage of the thriller (which already featured in individual episodes of, for instance, *Cloud Atlas*), of the high-flying fantastic (which provided the central narrative device for *Ghostwritten*) and of socially subversive sci-fi fiction in the tradition of E.M. Forster's dystopian *The Machine Stops*; yet on many counts this short story works simply as a sequel to *The Bone Clocks*, which already pitted the forces of good against a cohort of devilish demons.

While Mitchell clearly must be enjoying himself when strolling through these diverse generic fields, his text nevertheless includes at least short gestures of ironic detachment, as when he has Nathan, the main focalizer in this narrative, reflect about his secret drug abuse, courtesy of stolen pills from his mother's purse: "The pill's just kicking in now. Valium breaks down the world into bite-sized sentences. Like this one. All lined up. Munch-munch". Nathan here comments on how his own substance abuse works to reduce what to him is an overwhelmingly complex reality into smaller units, what he tellingly calls "bite-sized sentences". The text goes on to note, in blatant parataxis and with a witty gesture towards the story's format of publication as individual Tweets: "Like this one. All lined up". While Nathan cannot really know that the author who invented him also decided to choose Twitter as the means of publication, the wording seems to imply that despite this being a severe case of metalepsis, Nathan is perfectly aware of the fact that what he is thinking in a form of interior monologue is simultaneously pressed by 'his' author into the character-limit of a Twitter post. Mitchell in fact conjoins metalepsis and metafiction when he invents pre-Twitter characters who speak and think in precisely the language and style that subsequently will not only define the everyday casual communication patterns of their readers but furthermore determine the very framework through which the narrative is related.

If one reverses the direction of this allusion, Mitchell almost suggests that communication on Twitter is like entering a secret universe, one where everything looks stunningly beautiful – just like the garden Nathan and his mother enter on the other side of the steel door – yet where, upon entrance, a door is shut invisibly, "like a butler closed it", making those newly arrived feel like "trespasser[s]". While Nathan's mother seems oblivious to the potentially threatening nature of this new world (maybe because she is not only significantly older but also a much more committed abuser of her psychoactive drug of choice), Nathan responds differently, in particular once he encounters Jonah, the Lady's son, whom he immediately sizes up for potential conflict and for the kind of teenage-boy rivalry he knows only too well from being a low-status pupil at his school. It is in this context that Mitchell's clearly outlined markers of social class come into play, creating some obvious counter-movements to the format he chose for publication. While social contact in "The Right Sort" is throughout heavily overwritten with each person's belonging to a particular economic group, such old-world reliance on habitus and class is supposedly evaded once people socialize virtually, as done in the social-media environment of platforms like Twitter, which hold the unspoken allure of being both democratic and egalitarian in the face of an elitist world of actual physical and social encounters. Similar to the characters in Mitchell's short story, users of these platforms leave their old (or one could add, real) world behind to confront each other in a more egalitarian and thus less competitive environment. Yet the manner in which Mitchell confronts Nathan with a nightmarish and potentially deadly experience belies this positive effect. It is upon entering the garden that Nathan notes "Here, I'm the pleb", labeling himself with a time-tested British term of class snobbery. The escape from an environment that he has frequently experienced as alienating and isolating falters, and Mitchell's text cleverly associates the systemic failure with the media environment on which it puns so metafictionally.

If the first parallelism is already taking a twisted turn, Mitchell's conclusion makes it even more difficult to assign a clear message to his short story as far as its relationship to its chosen medium, Twitter, is concerned. After Nathan and Jonah start their running game, Nathan encounters a terrifying dog that badly scares him. While the version of the short story that made it into the novel would prepare readers for this traumatic experience by an earlier short scene in which Nathan responds with a mix of fear and panic to the sudden appearance of a dog, the original short story does not quite explain why teenage Nathan falls into such a nightmare scenario. It is only at the very end of the story that

Nathan tries to rationalize his experience and comes up with a brain chemistry solution: it was "bad Valium" that causes him to perceive what he calls "mind-puke" and thus turns into an abject vision of his own fears. While Nathan can talk himself out of having faced a huge mastiff, he is not so sure whether his nausea and panic could not have been noticed by people around him. The final Tweet not only has Nathan reassure himself "Thank God nobody saw"; it also has an ending that is far from reassuring: "Could Jonah have seen? I hope not. Probably not. Probably ...". This closing section is not only a textbook example of a thriller narrative that raises the option, even after a happy conclusion, that whatever causes terror is still lurking somewhere outside; it also stands as another moment where Mitchell returns to some elements of Twitter, albeit in a rather muted manner.

When Nathan worries whether people witnessed his panic, he quietly admits that some form of reality exists only through physical presence. The short story here evokes the power of affects as they become visible and noticeable in a person at particular moments such as emotional duress. As he is held in the throngs of panic, Nathan is bodily distressed. It is the corporeality of this form of affect that establishes elaborate differences between forms of communication that are face to face and those that are highly mediated. Epistolary fiction has always accounted for its disembodied status by drawing on forms of syntax, on emotionally loaded punctuation (primarily question and exclamation marks but also forms of ellipses that signal a mind that cannot finish sentences) or simply on short letters. The body of the writer was thus evoked as it went through horror or delight, and it was through the medium of the letter that this physicality was allowed to emanate. Twitter does not quite allow for this range of expressions. The limits on characters and the telegram-inspired style of writing make of it a medium that is largely devoid of emotionality (which may explain the frequent recourse to emoticons) and that only rarely allows for nuance or detail. Nathan's concern about bodily witnesses to his fear can thus be read as a gesture Mitchell includes in his Twitter story to remind readers of the distance that such a highly regulated form of communication places between speaker and listener. Read this way, the short story's conclusion allows for another moment where Mitchell turns against the medium he employed to promote his latest literary output.

5 Conclusion

Taken together, these various gestures combine to form an image of Twitter literature about which David Mitchell seems to have rather mixed feelings. If an earlier historical moment has decried religion as 'opium for the people'. Mitchell seems to takes this metaphor even further by presenting social media communication as "bad Valium": as a form of auto-medication that can easily turn sour and that furthermore creates an excessive distance between people and their environment, in effect screening them off of each other. Lest such a reading should appear overly moralistic, it is worth remembering that the two novels published before and after "The Right Sort" are driven by an ethically charged and highly allegorized battle between good and evil. The ethical field within the present short story therefore should also be exposed to this test; and even though there is very little that connects this story on the diegetic level to the phenomenon of Twitter fiction, Mitchell nevertheless appears to take a rather skeptical view of what virtual spaces and un-real realities have to offer.

Yet this skepticism exists almost entirely outside the diegetic sphere in which his characters subsist. It takes rather critical (or academic) readers to relate the text back to its original medium and to connect text-intrinsic discussions to the medium the author selected for initial publication. When read simply as a short-paced thriller story that largely relies on interior focalization, "The Right Sort" works quite well even when consumed through the truncated format of 140-character units. While Mitchell's experiment may not have demonstrated how Twitter as a medium of communication relates to the reality of his characters, it forcefully shows that the technology can have an impact on how authors relate to their readers, and thus on how literature engages with virtual and highly restricted forms of social contact. That Mitchell should take an at least implicitly critical glance at the risks involved in disembodied human contact puts his text well within the fold of epistolary literature, which from its very beginnings has been accompanied by an underlying drone of skepticism and distrust. Just like eighteenth-century readers both enjoyed the intimacy of reading other people's private letters and simultaneously knew that letters always bring with them the potential of deception, so Mitchell's text embraces his medium and at the same time attempts to identify its risks.

Works Cited

Al Sharaqi, Laila & Irum Abbasi. 2016. "Twitter Fiction: A New Creative Literary Landscape". *Advances in Language and Literary Studies* 7.4: 16–19.
Bayer, Gerd. 2009. "Deceptive Narratives: On Truth and the Epistolary Voice". *LiLi: Zeitschrift für Literaturwissenschaft und Linguistik* 39.154: 173–187.
Bayer, Gerd. 2015. "Perpetual Apocalypses: David Mitchell's *Cloud Atlas* and the Absence of Time". *Critique: Studies in Contemporary Fiction* 56.4: 345–354.

Bayer, Gerd. 2018. "The Short Narrative Form in David Mitchell's *The Bone Clocks*". In: Florian Kläger & Patrick Gill (eds.). *Constructing Coherence in the British Short Story Cycle*. New York: Routledge. 245–259.

Beebee, Thomas O. 1999. *Epistolary Fiction in Europe, 1500–1850*. Cambridge: Cambridge University Press.

Begines, Concepción Torres. 2016. "Literatura en Twitter: A propósito del *Twitter Fiction Festival*". *Castilla: Estudios de Literature* 7: 382–404.

Bray, Joe. 2003. *The Epistolary Novel. Representations of Consciousness*. New York: Routledge.

Childs, Peter & James Green. 2011. "The Novels in Nine Parts". In: Sarah Dillon (ed.). *David Mitchell. Critical Essays*. Canterbury: Gylphi. 25–47.

Dillon, Sarah. 2011. "Introducing David Mitchell's Universe: A Twenty-First Century House of Fiction". In: Sarah Dillon (ed.). *David Mitchell. Critical Essays*. Canterbury: Gylphi. 3–23.

Dunn, Maggie & Ann Morris. 1995. *The Composite Novel. The Short Story Cycle in Transition*. New York: Twayne.

Mitchell, David. 2014. *The Bone Clocks*. London: Sceptre.

Mitchell, David. 2014. "The Right Sort". Twitter. 14–18 July.

Mitchell, David. 2015. *Slade House*. London: Sceptre.

O'Donnell, Patrick. 2015. *A Temporary Future. The Fiction of David Mitchell*. New York: Bloomsbury.

O'Dwyer, Erin. 2016. "Of Letters, Love, and Lack: A Lacanian Analysis of Ian McEwan's Epistolary Novel *Atonement*". *Critique: Studies in Contemporary Fiction* 57.2: 178–190.

Schneider, Gary. 2005. *The Culture of Epistolarity. Vernacular Letters and Letter Writing in Early Modern England, 1500–1700*. Newark: University of Delaware Press.

Wright, Susan. 1989. "Private Language Made Public: The Language of Letters as Literature". *Poetics* 18: 549–578.

Contributors

Gerd Bayer is Professor and Akademischer Direktor in the English department at the University of Erlangen-Nürnberg (Germany), having previously taught at the University of Toronto, Case Western Reserve University and the University of Wisconsin-Whitewater. He is the author of a book on John Fowles and of *Novel Horizons: The Genre Making of Restoration Fiction* (Manchester University Press), as well as the (co-)editor of seven essay collections, most recently of *Early Modern Constructions of Europe* (Routledge) and *Holocaust Cinema in the Twenty-First Century* (Columbia University Press). He has published essays on postmodern and postcolonial literature and film, early modern narrative fiction, Holocaust Studies and heavy metal.

Thomas Beebee is Edwin Erle Sparks Professor of German and Comparative Literature at the Pennsylvania State University – University Park. His specializations include epistolarity, eighteenth-century literature, translation (theory, practice, and literary mimesis), mental maps in literature, law and literature, bibliotrauma and bibliomachia, and Brazilian-German cultural entanglements. His most recent books are *Conjunctions and Disjunctions of German Law and Literature* (Continuum, 2011), *Transmesis: Inside Translation's Black Box* (Palgrave-MacMillan, 2012), and the edited volume *German Literature as World Literature* (Bloomsbury, 2014). Beebee is editor-in-chief of the journal *Comparative Literature Studies*, and general editor of the Bloomsbury series, *Literatures as World Literature*.

Toni Bowers is Professor of English and Gender Studies at the University of Pennsylvania. She has written or edited four books and fifty scholarly articles and reviews, and is currently at work on two editions and a new monograph. Bowers teaches undergraduate and graduate courses, advises doctoral research, and contributes to curricular and academic governance. She is active in the global eighteenth-century scholarly community, having delivered talks in Britain, Canada, Finland, France, and elsewhere. She has served as a visiting professor at King's College London and at the University of Edinburgh. In 2018, she will teach as the visiting McLean Distinguished Professor at Colorado College. She has received a number of national and international scholarly grants and awards.

Kym Brindle is Senior Lecturer in Contemporary Literature at Edge Hill University, Lancashire, England. She has a PhD from Lancaster University for an Arts Council funded study of Neo-Victorian fiction. She has published essays on literary theory, historical fiction, Neo-Victorian and the Gothic, and the mid-twentieth-century women writer, Barbara Pym. Her book *Epistolary Encounters in Neo-Victorian Fiction. Diaries and Letters* was published by Palgrave MacMillan in 2014. She is currently researching and writing about the letter writing strategies of Intermodernist women writers.

Maximilian Feldner holds a PhD in English and American Studies from the Karl-Franzens-University Graz (2017). In his dissertation, *Narrating the Diaspora – Transmigration and Socio-Cultural Imaginaries in 21st-Century Nigerian Literature*, which was awarded the 2017 Award of Excellence by the Austrian ministry of science, he focused on Nigerian diaspora literature. Having studied English and American Studies in Graz, Limerick, and New York, he is a lecturer at the English department of the University of Graz. His research interests lie in the fields of English-language narrative fiction of the twentieth and the twenty-first centuries, film and popular culture.

Wolfgang Hallet is Professor of Teaching English as a Foreign Language at Justus Liebig University Giessen and was a founding member of the Executive Board of the International Graduate Centre for the Study of Culture until 2017. He is co-editor of two series of handbooks on teaching literature and culture, of the *Giessen Contributions to Foreign Language Research* (Tübingen: Narr), the *Giessen Contributions to the Study of Culture* (Trier: WVT) and of the international book series *Concepts for the Study of Culture* (CSC; Berlin & New York: de Gruyter). In literary studies, he has published on contemporary novels and narratology, the spatial turn in literary studies and spatial semiotics in literature, the contextualization of literary texts, and on intermedial methodology. A large number of publications concerns multimodality in literature and the multimodal novel.

Ames Hawkins is a writer, educator, and art activist. The Associate Provost for Faculty Research and Development at Columbia College Chicago, Ames currently teaches courses in the First Semester Experience, Cultural Studies, and Literature. A multimodal composer who uses writing and art to explore the interstices of alphabetic text, image, and sound, Ames theorizes the power and pleasure of queer(ing) form. Ames's creative-critical scholarship appears in a number of edited volumes, as well as across a range of academic and literary publications – both print and online – such as *enculturation, The Rumpus, Palaver, Computers and Composition Online, Slag Glass City, The Feminist Wire, Interdisciplinary Humanities*, and *Water~-Stone Review*. Ames's current project, *These are Love(d) Letters*, is a transgenre book that uses a finite set of textual artifacts, (the twenty love letters written by her father to her mother over a six-week period), as a framework for a complex visual and textual exploration of the infinite implications regarding the rhetorical, cultural, theoretical and literary work of the love letter. Her online portfolio can be found at http://www.ameshawkins.com.

Silke Jandl received her BA and MA in English and American Studies from the University of Graz, Austria. As part of her alma mater's Joint Master's Degree Programme, she studied at the University of Roehampton, London, for one semester. During the 2013/14 academic year, she served as a Teaching Assistant at the University of Minnesota. She is currently working towards her PhD on inter- and transmedia(l) connections between YouTube videos and YouTubers' books at the University of Graz, and serves as a board member for the young scholar's network AYA (Austria's Young Americanists). She has presented her research at various international conferences and has also assumed a part-time position at the Centre for Intermediality Studies in Graz where she teaches classes at the American Studies department.

Lisa Kazianka is a PhD candidate in children's literature at the Faculty of Education, University of Cambridge, where she has also completed her MPhil. She has previously worked as an adjunct lecturer and writing instructor. Her PhD project, funded by the UK Arts and Humanities Research Council and Churchill College, is a study of contemporary adaptations of the Arthurian legend for young readers, using a masculinity studies/gender studies approach. Her other research interests include identity and young adult fiction, and non-fiction for children.

Elizabeth Kovach is a postdoctoral researcher and Coordinator of the International PhD Programme "Literary and Cultural Studies" at the Justus Liebig University Giessen. Her doctoral dissertation, entitled *Novel Ontologies after 9/11: The Politics of Being in Contemporary Theory and U.S.-American Fiction* won the Dr.-Herbert-Stolzenberg prize for Excellent Dissertation Project in the Study of Culture and was published in 2016 by WVT Trier. Her postdoctoral research focuses on the ethics and aesthetics of work in U.S.-American fiction from industrial to post-Fordist economies. Other research interests include theories of the novel, genre theory, contemporary U.S.-American fiction, film theory, and political philosophy.

Maria Löschnigg is Associate Professor of English Literature at the University of Graz, Austria. Her publications include *The Contemporary Canadian Short Story in English. Continuity and Change* (2014), *Migration and Fiction: Narratives of Migration in Contemporary Canadian Literature* (co-edited with Martin Löschnigg, 2009), and the first history of Canadian Literature in German, *Kurze Geschichte der kanadischen Literatur* (with Martin Löschnigg, 2001). She has published articles on Canadian authors such as Mavis Gallant, Di Brandt and Alice Munro and on subjects such as the Canadian short story cycle and the Chinese-Canadian short story, on African literature, modern drama, Jane Austen and ecocriticism. In her most recent work she has been focussing on epistolary forms (letters, emails etc.) in contemporary literature in English.

Ingrid Pfandl-Buchegger, Mag. Dr. phil., studied English, French and General and Applied Linguistics at the University of Graz, Austria. She is currently employed as a senior lecturer at the Department of English Studies (University of Graz), where she teaches English literature, pronunciation and language teaching methodology. She is the director of the project FauvoT, a joint inter-departmental project (in co-operation with the Technical University of Graz) in the field of FLT at the University of Graz. Her current research explores aspects of foreign language learning (in particular the teaching of pronunciation and aspects of foreign-accented speech), representations of space in literature, aspects of gender, and intermediality studies (literature and dance). In collaboration with a colleague from the University of Music and the Dramatic Arts in Graz, Austria, Gudrun Rottensteiner (Dept. of Early Music and Performance Studies) she has published on the semiotics of dance, the performing body, narrative across media, and metareferentiality in dance.

Rebekka Schuh holds a PhD in English and American Studies from the University of Graz, Austria, and has recently completed her doctoral dissertation "Stories in Letters – Letters in Stories: Epistolary Liminalities in the Anglophone Canadian Short Story" funded by the university's 'Research Management and Service'. Her publications include a journal article about the epistolary mode in Alice Munro's stories and a book chapter about epistolary motifs as border motifs in Austin Clarke's short fiction. In both her teaching and her research, she has focused on North American literature, with special emphasis on the Canadian short story, narratology and the work of Alice Munro.

Silvia Schultermandl is an assistant professor of American Studies at the University of Graz, where she teaches courses in American literature/culture studies. Silvia is the author of a monograph on the representation of mother-daughter conflicts in Asian American literature and the (co)editor of five collections of essays which explore various themes in transnational studies, American literature and culture, as well as family and kinship studies. Since 2009, she has served as series editor for *Contributions to Transnational Feminism* (currently finishing volume 6). She is currently at work on a monograph on the aesthetics of transnationalism in American literature from the revolution to 9/11 and is developing the *Palgrave Series in Kinship, Representation, and Difference.*

Index

Abbasi, Irum 280
Abrams, J. J. & Doug Dorst
– *S. Ship of Theseus. By V.M. Straka* 138f., 141, 186
Adichie, Chimamanda Ngozi
– *Americanah* 91, 99f., 105
– "The Thing Around Your Neck" 8, 91f., 97–99, 105
Adorno, Theodor 213
Agualusa, José Eduardo
– *Nação Crioula* 211
Ahern, Cecilia 9, 170–178
– *Für immer vielleicht* 170
– *Love, Rosie* 160
– *PS, I Love You* 2, 9, 159–161
– *Where Rainbows End* 2, 9, 159f.
Akana, Anna
– *So Much I Want to Tell You*
  – *Letters to My Little Sister* 255–258
Al Sharaqi, Laila 280
Alcott, Louisa May
– *Little Women* 217
Alexis, André
– "My Anabasis" 39
Altman, Janet Gurkin 4f., 24, 73, 76f., 85, 87, 91, 98, 105, 110, 114, 120, 153–155, 169, 172, 174, 233, 236
Amis, Martin
– *Yellow Dog* 30
Ang, Li
– *Unsent Love Letter* 211
Anker, Elizabeth S. 235
Arendt, Hannah 238
Asquith, Mark 118
Assman, Aleida 47, 49
Atta, Sefi 98, 102, 104
– "News from Home" 91f., 96f., 105
– "Yahoo Yahoo" 8, 91f.
Atwood, Margaret 278
– *Alias Grace* 32
Auerbach, Eric 231
Austen, Jane 20, 160, 178
– *Pride and Prejudice* 257

Bâ, Mariama
– *Une si longue lettre* 211
Bakhtin, Mikhail 26, 172
Ballinger, Coleen 246
Bantock, Nick
– *Griffin and Sabine* 9, 138, 141 190
– *The Artful Dodger* 181
– *The Golden Mean* 191
– *The Pharaoh's Gate*
  – *Griffin and Sabine's Missing Correspondence* 184
Barnes, Julian 8
– "Evermore" 3, 65–66
Barthes, Roland 183
Bateman, John 28
Baty, Paige 214
– *E-Mail trouble. Love and addiction @the matrix* 10, 211f., 215
Baumgarten, Alexander Gottlieb 231
Bayer, Gerd 17f., 51, 55, 278, 281
Beaumont, Matt
– *e* 2, 10, 211f., 217f., 222
– *e Squared* 2, 218
– *The e. before Christmas* 218
Beebee, Thomas 5, 15, 17, 47, 144, 281
Behn, Aphra 159
– *Love-Letters Between a Nobleman and His Sister* 193, 202, 281
Bellow, Saul
– *Herzog* 6, 21
Betcherman, Michael & David Diamond
– *The Daughters of Freya* 10, 211f., 219, 222f.
Birdsell, Sandra
– "The Bird Dance" 36
Bowen, Elizabeth
– "The Demon Lover" 64
Bower, Anne 5, 49, 117, 146
Bower, Rachel 6, 36, 47f., 59, 69
Bowers, Toni 1, 15f., 29
Brandtzæg, Siv Gøril 6
Bray, Joe 1, 5, 15, 19–22, 57f., 110, 154, 236, 281

Index

Bray, Rosemary 111, 120
Brindle, Kym 5f.
Brockmole, Jessica 67, 69
– *Letters from Skye* 2, 67
– "Something Worth Landing For" 66f.
Brown, Norman O. 217
Brown, Sara 272
Bruns, Cristina Vischer 235
Burford, Bill 110, 114
Burn, Stephen 230
Byatt, Antonia
– *Possession* 24, 31, 212

Cadden, Mike 143–145, 154f.
Campbell, Elizabeth 144, 148, 155, 162
Camus, Albert 217
Castells, Manuel 268
Cather, Willa 80
Celayo, Armando 272
Chbosky, Stephen
– *The Perks of Being a Wallflower* 9, 18, 154–156
Childs, Peter 278
Cicero, Marcus Tullius
– *Letters by Coluccio Salutati* 211
Cisneros, Sandra
– "Little Miracles, Kept Promises" 37
Cixous, Hélène 183
Clarke, Austin 37
– "Waiting for the Postman to Knock" 39f.
Cleary, Beverly
– *Dear Mr Henshaw* 144
Coady, Lynn
– *The Antagonist* 2
Coats, Karen 143f., 146, 149, 151
Cole, Teju
– *Every Day is for the Thief* 92
Coleridge, Samuel
– "Ancient Mariner" 63
Cook Heckendorn, Elizabeth 5, 213
Cortázar, Julio 37
Coughlan, Claire 178
Coupland, Douglas
– *The Gum Thief* 2
Cox, Ailsa 83
Crane, Dede
– "What Sort of Mother" 39

Crary, Jonathan 237
Culler, Jonathan 239

Dalley, Hamish 104
Danielewski, Mark Z.
– *House of Leaves* 136
The Whalestoe Letters 136, 137
Danziger, Paula & Ann Martin
– *Snail No More* 10, 211, 223
Davey, Frank 65
Dawson, Shane
– *I Hate Myselfie* 248
Deleuze, Gilles 37f., 266
Derrida, Jacques 170, 183
Deyes, Alfie
– *The Pointless Book* 246
Dickens, Charles 282
Dillon, Sarah 279
Donoghue, Emma 37
Dreiser, Theodore
– *Hoosier Holiday* 108
Drucker, Johanna 116f.
Duncan, Isla 84
Dunn, Maggie 278
Dunn, Mark
– *Ella Minnow Pea* 36
Duyfhuizen, Bernard 110

Eastman, George 109
Egan, Jennifer 278
Egger, Dave
– *The Circle* 230
Einhaus, Ann-Marie 47f., 50, 59–69
El Hamamsy, Walid 161
El-Mothar, Amal 184
Ezarik, Justine 248

Favret, Mary 5
Feldner, Maximilian 93
Felski, Rita 235
Ferguson, Will
– *419* 30, 101
Fielding, Henry 269, 271
– *Shamela* 10, 265
Fischer, Hervé 230f., 237
Flood, Alison 232

Forster, E. M.
- *The Machine Stops* 284
Foucault, Michel 151–153, 266f., 274
Frangipane, Nicholas 88
Franta, Connor 248
- *A Work in Progress. A Memoir* 249
- *Note to Self* 253
Franzen, Jonathan
- *Purity* 230
Freud, Sigmund 183, 216
Friedman, May 227
Fröhlich, Vincent 79
Funk, McKenzie 262

Gadpaille, Michelle 84
Gaiman, Neil 278
Galloway, Alexander 269, 274
Galsworthy, John
- "Told by the Schoolmaster" 61f.
Garcia, Antero 152
Gasco, Elyse
- "Mother Not a True Story" 39
Gaskill, Nicholas 231f.
Gaynor, Hazel
- "Hush" 64, 69
Genette, Gérard 35, 110
Gibbons, Alison 134, 138, 141
Gibson, William 216
Gifford, Daniel 108, 115
Gilroy, Amanda 5
Ging, Debbie 162f.
Glattauer, Daniel
- *Gut gegen Nordwind* 172, 212
Goethe von, Wolfgang 159
- *Die Leiden des jungen Werthers* 18, 164, 281
Goldsmith, Elizabeth 5
Gordimer, Nadine 37
Graceffa, Joey
- *In Real Life* 248
Graham, Rawle
- *Diary of an Amateur Photographer* 139
Green, James 278
Guattari, Félix 37f.
Guilleragues de, Gabriel
- *Letters of a Portuguese Nun* 211, 280
Gumbrecht, Hans-Ulrich 140

Habermas, Jürgen 213
Habermas, Tilmann 141
Habila, Helon
- *Measuring Time* 105
Haddon, Mark
- *The Curious Incident of the Dog in the Night-Time* 135
Hall, Katie & Bogen Jones
- *The Closeness that Separates Us* 160
Hallet, Wolfgang 27f., 139
Halliday, Michael 129f.
Hardy, Thomas 80, 82
Harris, Oliver 5
Harrison, Bernice 165
Hawkins, Ames & Ryan Trauman
- *Masters of Text* 186
Hayles, Katherine 213f., 227
Heble, Ajay 84f., 87
Heighton, Stephen
- "Noughts & Crosses: An Unsent Reply" 40
Henkin, David 110
Hornby, Nick
- *Juliet, Naked* 1, 3, 141
Howell, Daniel & Phil Lester
- *The Amazing Book Is Not On Fire* 246
Howells, Coral Ann 74
Hunter, Adrian 37f.
Hutcheon, Linda 112, 119
Hyndman, Sarah 249

Iser, Wolfgang 79

James, David 230
James, Henry
- "A Bundle of Letters" 37
- "The Point of View" 37
Jameson, Frederic 212
Jandl, Silke 245
Jenkins, Henry 247
Jepson, Edgar
- "Albert's Return" 60
Jhabvala Prawer, Ruth
- *Heat and Dust* 162
Johnson, Joanna 229
Jolley, Elizabeth
- *Miss Peabody's Inheritance* 162

– "Wednesdays and Fridays"   37
Joyce, James
– *Dubliners*   167

Kant, Immanuel   230
Kany, Charles E.   162
Kate, Rorick & Rachel Kiley
– *The Epic Adventures of Lydia Bennet*   244
Kauffman, Linda   15, 23
Kavka, Misha   234
Kellaway, Lucy
– *Who Moved My BlackBerry*   2
Kelleter, Frank   232
Kerouac, Jack
– *On the Road*   107, 108
Keyes, Marian   166
Kinkead-Weekes, Mark   173
Koepke, Wulf   24f., 51, 79, 94
Kovach, Elizabeth   261f., 268, 272
Krell, David Farrell   183
Kress, Gunter   126, 129
Kristeva, Julia   215
Kusche, Sabrina   141

Lacan, Jacques   183
Laclos de, Choderlos   159, 224
Ladin, Joy   189
Latour, Bruno   239
Lau, Doretta
– "God Damn, How Real is This?"   40f.
Lawrence, D. H.   84
Lee, Caspar   250f.
Leeuwen van, Theo   126, 129f.
Lepore, Jill   273f.
Lessing, Doris   37
Levine, Caroline   264
Llewellyn, David
– *Eleven*   2
Lodge, David
– *Small World*   170
Looby, Christopher   231
Lorde, Audre   183
Löschnigg, Maria   1, 25, 27f., 37, 40, 62, 64, 74f., 78

Mallan, Kerry   234

Marsden, John
– *Letters from the Inside*   144
Marsh, Richard
– "Scandalous"   60
Martens, Lorna   146
Matos, Angel Daniel   150
Matthews, Timothy   148
Maugham, W. Somerset   61
– *Ashenden, Or, The British Agent*   61
– "Giulia Lazzari"   51, 60f.
McAllister, Jenn   252, 254f.
McCallum, Robyn   147, 156
McDonnell, Charlie   251
McEwan, Ian
– *Enduring Love*   31f.
– *Nutshell*   31
McKeon, Michael   271f.
McNeill, Laurie   227f.
McPherson, Tara   227, 239
Meier, Jörg   175
Meikle, Jeffrey   107, 118
Merleau-Ponty, Maurice   187f.
Meyer, Therese-M.   183
Milne, Esther   109, 118
Mistry, Rohinton   37
– "Swimming Lessons"   35
– *Tales from Firozsha Baag*   35
Mitchell, David
– *Cloud Atlas*   278, 284
– *Ghostwritten*   279, 284
– *Slade House*   278, 280f., 284
– *The Bone Clocks*   278f., 284
– "The Right Sort"   11
Molloy, Sylvia
– *Certificate of Absence*   162
Montesquieu   159, 202
Moore, Lorrie   76
Morris, Ann   278
Mullan, John   24f., 29–31
Muñoz, José Esteban   187, 189
Munro, Alice   8, 37
– "A Wilderness Station"   39
– "Accident"   18
– "Before the Change"   18, 36
– "Carried Away"   69, 74f., 78–80, 84, 87
– "Hateship, Friendship, Courtship, Loveship, Marriage"   51, 74

– "How I Met My Husband" 74
– "Material" 39
– *Open Secrets* 74
– *Something I've Been Meaning to Tell You* 74
– "Tell me Yes or No" 74, 78, 80
– "The Jack Randa Hotel" 51, 74
Myracle, Lauren 230 f., 234
– *Internet Girls Series* 10, 144
– *l8r, g8r* 228, 235
– *ttfn* 228, 236 f.
– *yolo* 228, 238

Ngai, Sianne 229–231, 235
Niffenegger, Audrey 184
Nikolajeva, Maria 145, 148, 153, 156
Nischik, Reingard 37
Nunes, Mark 214, 262
Nünning, Ansgar 1 f., 24, 27, 35, 55
Nwaubani, Adaobi Tricia 102
– *I Do Not Come To You By Chance* 91 f., 102–104

Oakley, Tyler 248
Oates, Joyce Carol
– "Dear Husband," 37
– "Dear Joyce Carol," 37
Oguine, Ike
– *A Squatter's Tale* 98, 105
Omotoso, Yewande
– *Bom Boy* 106
Ondaatje, Michael
– *In the Skin of a Lion* 6, 48
Osachoff, Margaret Gail 86
Osundu, E. C.
– *Voice of America* 92
Ovid 202
– *Heroides* 164, 193, 202

Parker, Patricia 170
Paulson, William 235
Perry, Ruth 17, 19, 51, 145, 235
Pitcher, Annabel
– *Ketchup Clouds* 9, 143, 147
Pool, Gail
– *Other People's Mail* 37
Pope, Alexander 211

Primeau, Ronald 108
Proulx, Annie
– "Brokeback Mountain" 8, 117–118
– *Postcards* 8, 111–120

Rancière, James 231
Richardson, Brian 18, 33
Richardson, Samuel 6, 20, 159, 196, 202, 212, 224, 265
– *Clarissa* 193, 202 f.
– *Pamela* 164, 173, 265, 267, 281
Richmond, T. R.
– *What She Left* 2, 17, 20, 26, 36
Richtel, Matt 277
Riordan Lee, Emily & Caspar Lee
– *Caspar Lee* 248, 250
Robson, Jennifer
– "All for the Love of You" 69
Roth, Philip
– *The Human Stain* 30
Rousseau, Jean-Jacques 6, 159, 211
Rupp, Jan 1 f., 24, 27
Rushton, Rosie & Nina Schindler
– *PS. He's Mine!* 2
Ryan, Marie-Laure 27

Salamon, Gayle 187 f.
Saro-Wiwa, Ken 56 f., 59
– *Adaku and Other Stories* 56
– "Africa Kills Her Sun" 50, 57
Sayers, Dorothy L. & Robert Eustace
– *The Documents in the Case* 193
Schmidt-Supprian, Alheide 76 f., 87
Schneider, Gary 281
Schoemperlen, Diane
– *At a Loss for Words* 18
Schreibman, Susan 227
Schuh, Rebekka 24, 37, 67
Schultermandl, Silvia 227 f.
Semple, Maria
– *Where'd You Go, Bernadette* 2, 128
Senior, Olive 37
Seshagiri, Urmila 230
Shakespeare, William 31
– *Hamlet* 31
– "Sonnet 29" 31

Shelley, Mary
– *Frankenstein* 281
Showalter, Elaine 1, 6
Shriver, Lionel
– *We Need to Talk about Kevin* 36
Shteyngart, Gary 262, 272
– *Super Sad True Love Story* 10, 261–275
Siegert, Bernard 110
Simon, Sunka 183, 186, 213, 220
Sings, Miranda
– *Selp-Helf* 246
Skow, John 108
Slethaug, Gordon 108
Smith, Sidonie 227
Smith, Zadie
– *On Beauty* 29 f.
Stacilee, Ford 108
Stein, Gertrude 230 f.
Sterne, Laurence
– *Tristram Shandy* 205 f.
Stewart, Kathleen 183
Stewart, Susan 118
Stoker, Bram
– *Dracula* 5, 193, 202
Strier, Richard 231
Su, Bernie & Kate Rorick
– *The Secret Diary of Lizzie Bennet* 244 f., 257
Sugg, Joe 251
Swift, Graham 8, 55–57
– "Haematology" 50, 57 f.
– *Wish You Were Here* 32

Thacker, Eugene 269, 274
Thon, Jan-Noël 27
Torres Begines, Concepción 277
Trites, Roberta 144 f., 148 f.
Turkle, Sherry 213
Turner, Frederick 108

Unigwe, Chika
– *Night Dancer* 105

Vaule, Rosamond 109
Ventura, Héliane 85 f.
Verhoeven, W. M. 5
Visser, Gerrit 221

Walker, Alice
– *The Color Purple* 6, 211
Walter, Scott 47 f.
Wasserman, Emily 146
Wastl, Nora 172
Watson, Brad
Miss Jane 131–134
Watson, Julia 227
Watt, Ian 20, 265–267
Waugh, Alec
– "An Autumn Gathering" 60
Webster, Jean
– *Daddy-Long-Legs* 143
Weinstein, Cindy 231
Wells, A. W. 8, 62 f.
– "Chanson Triste" 62–64
Wolf, Werner 75, 77–79, 87 f.
Wright, Richard B.
– *Clara Callan* 2, 3, 18, 20
Wright, Susan 281

Youngs, Gillian 237

Žižek, Slavoj 183
Zuern, John David 227
Zusak, Markus
– *The Book Thief* 135, 137

www.ingramcontent.com/pod-product-compliance
Lightning Source LLC
Chambersburg PA
CBHW061934220426
43662CB00012B/1898